MI

OF

THEOBALD WOLFE TONE.

WRITTEN BY HIMSELF.

COMPRISING

A COMPLETE JOURNAL OF HIS NEGOTIATIONS TO PROCURE THE AID OF THE FRENCH FOR THE LIBERATION OF IRELAND.

WITH

SELECTIONS FROM HIS DIARY

WHILST AGENT TO THE IRISH CATHOLICS.

EDITED BY HIS SON,

WILLIAM THEOBALD WOLFE TONE.

Victrix causa Diis placuit, sed victa Catoni.

PHARSALIA, lib. i. v. 128.

IN TWO VOLUMES.

VOL. II.

LONDON:

HENRY COLBURN, 8, NEW BURLINGTON STREET.

1827.

MEMOIRS

OF

THEOBALD WOLFE TONE.

DIARY

CONTINUED.

July, 1796.

1. (Sings, with great courage,) " Oh, July the first in Oldbridge-town, there was a grievous battle." We made no great figure that day, that is the God's truth of it. Well, no matter ; what is past, is past. We must see and do better the next time ; besides, we pulled up a little the year after at Aughrim, and made a most gallant defence at Limerick. But I am writing a history of the wars in Ireland, instead of minding my business. Suffice it to say, (God forgive me for lying) that "we are undoubtedly the bravest nation in Europe." There are, however,

some brave men scattered here and there through the French army, but let that pass. "I hope to see a battle yet before I die:" huzza! generally!

2. Clarke has been confined to his room, and I believe to his bed, for these four days; he is cut down by continual labour in his bureau. This delays my affair a little. I saw his aid-de-camp to day, who told me by his orders, "that he hoped to see me the day after to-morrow; that he wished to consult me on an affair of great importance, on which he must also see another person besides, and that when we met, we should arrange certain matters," &c. This is a flourish to amuse the aid-de-camp, or perhaps he has translated Clarke into his own language; "else why do we wrap the gentleman in our rawer breath?" My friend Fleury is, however, a fine lad, and I have no doubt would fight like a tiger. Apropos! I desire my readers, (viz. P. P. Miss Mary, and my dearest love,) to take notice that I recant every word I have said heretofore in these memorandums, to the prejudice of General Clarke. *No. I lie! I lie!* "He is a tall, handsome, proper young man, with a face like a cherubim." I would blot out all the passages which reflect upon him, but upon second thoughts, I will keep them as a memento to prevent my forming hasty judgments of people. In fact it was Aherne, Sullivan, and even Madgett, (but particularly the two first,) that turned me against him, for I am myself, "magnanimous, artless, and credulous," as P. P. used to say; whereas they have been used, I will not say to intrigue, but at least to look at people intrigu-

ing here a long time, which is some excuse for them. However, I have now made him the only recompense in my power, by retracting on the same ground where I gave the offence, for my remarks to his disadvantage have not travelled beyond my memorandum-book. I think that is handsome.

3. I see to-day that the Channel fleet is preparing at Spithead, to the number of twenty-one sail of the line, (d—n and sink them!) with God knows how many Admirals; that the camps are not yet formed in Ireland, but that vast quantities of arms and ammunition are daily imported into that country, as also tents and camp equipage. I am glad of that, because I hope it will appear in the event, that it is for us the worthy John Bull is putting himself to all this expense and trouble. I see likewise that the British have taken three of our best frigates, being the entire of a flying squadron, sent to cruize in the chops of the Channel; that is d—d bad; but then again the French are defending themselves in St. Lucie, like devils incarnate; that is good. There is also news to-day of another victory on the Rhine, by Moreau, "but this gentleman will tell you the perpendiculars," which are not yet published; I hope it is true. *Vive la Republique!*

4. Called to-day on Clarke; he has not yet left his room, so that I did not see him, but I saw Fleury, his aid-de-camp, who brought me word as before, that the General expected to see a person, in order to arrange my business, and begged I would call the day after to-morrow. I wrote him a polite

and tender note, praying him to lose no time, and which I gave Fleury, and so we parted. Confound these delays! I am sick of them.

I want to change my domicile. I am lodged in the house of a little "*bossue*," (Anglicè, a hunchback,) and she hangs out certain allurements which (as I pique myself upon a choice morality) I determine to resist. To tell the God's truth, there is no great merit in my resistance, for she is as crooked as a ram's horn, (which is a famous illustration) and as ugly as sin besides: rot her, the dirty little faggot, she torments me! "I will not march through Coventry with her, that 's flat."—Moreover, I see to-day official news, (Buonaparte's letter,) that the King of Naples has concluded an armistice, withdrawing all his troops from Beaulieu's army, which will prejudice the latter gentleman considerably, particularly in the article of cavalry; he likewise withdraws his ships from Hotham, in the Mediterranean, which will tend somewhat to the edification of John Bull; and finally, he sends Prince Pignatelli to Paris, to negotiate a peace with the Directory. I like that dearly. The French always oblige the enemy to come to Paris to negotiate, which, besides the triumph, gives them prodigious advantages. I hope they may make as good and as haughty a peace with him, as they have done with the King of Sardinia. *Imprimis,* I hope they will take care to secure the fleet; that is what they want. I see likewise that his Holiness has at last been obliged to submit, and Buonaparte has granted him an armistice, and he also sends an

Ambassador to Paris to negotiate. There is a pretty batch of Italian Ambassadors just now here. Salicetti mentions in his letter to the Directory, that in the conditions granted provisionally to the Pope, he did not neglect to avail himself of the terror which the French arms have inspired through all Italy; I dare say not indeed; who doubts him? I am heartily glad that old Priest is at last laid under contribution in his turn. Many a long century he and his predecessors have been fleecing all Europe, but the day of retribution is come at last; and besides, I am strongly tempted to hope that this is but the beginning of his sorrows. Well, I must see if we cannot make something out of him touching our affair, as I hinted to Clarke already. It is also said, with confidence, that the French have taken possession quietly of Leghorn. I hope that is true for fifty reasons; among others, John Bull I know has generally a bale or two of broad cloth, and a few cases of hardware stored up there, and the Republic perhaps has occasion for them, and as he has passed sundry wise and humane laws touching French and Dutch property, I want to see how he will like a little confiscation in his turn. I do not see where he will victual and water his Mediterranean fleet now, unless it be in his kingdom of Corsica, which, by all accounts, is in a fair way to be speedily reduced to the circumference of Bastia and its environs. Sir Gilbert Elliot, the viceroy, has found the air of Corsica disagree with him, so he is gone to England for his *health!* It would not, to be sure, be decent for the King's representative to fall into the hands of republicans and rebels. What would I give that another of his sacred Majesty's representatives found himself suddenly attacked with the same complaint! Well, all in good time, we shall see. I hear nothing of Moreau's victory, mentioned in yesterday's memorandum, so I suppose it is *premature*.

5. " 'Twas a sad rainy night, but the morning is fine." I think it rains as much at Paris as in Ireland, and that kills me. I am devoured this day with the spleen, and I have not settled with Clarke yet, and every thing torments me. Time! Time! I never felt the *tædium vitæ* in my life till the last two or three months, but at present I do suffer dreadfully, that is the truth of it. Only think, there is not, at this moment, man, woman, or child in Paris that cares one farthing if I were hanged,—at least for my sake. I may say the Executive Directory are my "nearest connections," Charles De la Croix my "chosen of ten thousand," and General Clarke "the friend of my bosom;" certainly I respect them all, and wish them sincerely well on every account, but I would rather spend an hour talking nonsense with P. P. than a week with any one of them, saving at all times my business here. I do not speak of the loss of the society of my dearest love, and our little family, for that is not to be replaced. Well, if ever I find myself at Paris, Ambassador from Ireland, I will make amends for my former privations; "I will, by the God of war!" And I will have P. P. here too, and I will give him

choice Burgundy to drink, *ad libitum;* and Matty and Miss Mary and he and I, will go to the opera together, and we will be as happy as the day is long. "Visions of glory, spare my aching sight!" This is choice castle-building, but what better can I do just now to amuse myself? Trifling as these memorandums are, they are a great resource to me, for when I am writing them, I always fancy I am chatting with P. P. and my dearest love. I wish I had my commission though; I long to see myself in regimentals. (Sings) "Zounds, I'll soon be a brigadier!" That is choice.

Evening, 5 *o'clock.* It was not for nothing that I have been in the horrors all the forenoon. On the 26th May, I wrote to my wife, to Rowan, and Dr. Reynolds, respecting the immediate removal of my family to France; and to-day I see in an English paper given me by Sullivan, that the vessel which carried my letter, an American (the Argus, Capt. Fanning,) was carried into Plymouth on the 25th June last, and is detained. That is *pleasant!* This event throws my private affairs into unspeakable confusion, and I am too angry just now to see how to rectify them. I was this very morning counting that my dearest love would have my letter in about a fortnight. Was there ever any thing so distressing? These are the fruits of the American treaty; but it is hard my poor little family should suffer for it. See how their fifteen stripes are respected in England! I am infinitely embarrassed by this event; one thing consoles me; in all my letters, I have hardly mentioned one word of politics, or of my business here, and the little I have said is calculated to mislead; for at the time I wrote, appearances were as gloomy as possible. Well, this is the second time in my life I am indebted for a serious evil to master John Bull. He hunted me out of my own country first, and now he is preventing me from bringing my family to France; and does he think I will forget all that? No! that I won't, no more than his attempt to press me for a sailor on my passage out to America. Well, it does not signify cursing or swearing; I am in too great a fury to write any longer. God knows now when my family will get my letters, or whether they will ever get them.

6. Saw Clarke this morning; he is almost recovered; and tells me my business is delayed solely by the absence of General Hoche, who is coming up with all privacy to Paris to confer with the Directory; that on his arrival every thing will be settled; that I must be introduced to him, and communicate with him, and most probably return with him to the army, where my presence would be necessary. All this is very good. I shall be glad to be introduced to Hoche; it looks like serious business. Clarke also told me he wanted to have my commission expedited instantly by the Minister of War, but that Carnot had decided to wait for Hoche. I told him it was the same to me, and also begged to know when he expected Hoche. He replied, "Every day." I then took occasion to mention the state of

my finances, that in two or three days I should be run out, and relied upon him to prevent my falling into difficulties. He asked me, could I carry on the war some little time longer? I answered, I could not, for that I did not know a soul in Paris, but the Government. He seemed a little taken aback at this, by which I see that money is not their forte at present. Hang it for me! I am sure I wish there was not a guinea in the world. So here I am, with exactly two louis in my exchequer, negotiating with the French Government, and planning revolutions. I must say it is truly original. "*Crescit amor nummi, quantum ipsa pecunia crescit.*" That is not true as to me, for my passion increases as my funds diminish. I reckon I am the poorest Ambassador to-day in Paris, but that gives me no great concern. Huzza! *Vive la Republique!* "When Christmas comes about again, oh then I shall have money." To be sure I am writing most egregious nonsense, *mais c'est égal.* I told Clarke of the miscarriage of my letters, by way of precaution against certain unknown apprehensions which I felt. How lucky it was that I hardly mentioned a word of my business to any one. Well, Lazarus Hoche, I wish you were come with all my soul. Here I am "in perplexity and doubtful dilemma," waiting your arrival. Sad! Sad! I am gnawing my very soul with anxiety and expectation. And then I have a vision of poverty in the back-ground, which is truly alarming. "*O cives, cives, quærenda pecunia primum.*" I think I will stop, for the present, with this pathetic appeal to the citizen Directors. I had like to forget that, after leaving Clarke, I sat down in an outside room, and wrote him a note, desiring him to apply to Carnot for such assistance, in the premises, as he might think fit; adding, that any money advanced to me was to be considered as advanced on public account, and that I would call on him the day after to-morrow. In the mean time I will devour my discontents, "and in this harsh world draw my breath with pain." May be my friend Lazarus, "who is not dead, but sleepeth," may make his appearance by that time. It is, to be sure, most excessively ridiculous, "*vu les circonstances actuelles*," that I should be run out of money. Clarke told me Jourdan had recrossed the Rhine at Neuwied, and gained another victory; Moreau's victory is confirmed; he is now beyond Offembourg, and has cut off the communication between Wurmser and the Archduke Charles.

8. Called again on Clarke. He tells me my commission will be made out in two or three days. I returned him my acknowledgments. I am surprised at the *sang froid* with which I view this affair of my regiment; but it is my temper. I am sure if I were made an emperor it would not in the least degree elevate my spirits, though on some points I am susceptible enough. Is that in my favour, or not? No matter; "*Je suis, comme je suis,*" and that is enough about myself for the moment. Moreau has had what other nations would call another victory; but what we content ourselves with calling an *advantage.*

The French troops scaled the highest of the Black Mountains, and stormed a redoubt on the summit; the General, "whose name I know not, but whose person I reverence," being the first to leap into the fossé. Remember that, Mr. le Colonel! If a man will command French troops, he must be *rather* brave; and beside I shall have the honour of the sod to support. Well, I will do my best. Horne Tooke had good reason to say that the French Generals not only gave the *command,* but the *example,* to their soldiers. They are noble fellows, that is the truth of it. I see in the papers that Lady Elliot is ordered by her physicians to the baths of Lucca, the air of Corsica disagreeing with her also, as well as with her spouse. These removals bode ill for the kingdom of Corsica. I see also the poor Emperor has made an application to the Empress of Russia for assistance; and what assistance, in God's name, do you think she has given him? A declaration, addressed to the petty princes of Germany, calling on them, poor devils, to assist the head of the empire, and telling them it is a *shame for them not to support him better; and that she is quite surprised at them for her part, &c.* After all it is a more decent declaration than Brunswick's, but I do not believe it will have a prodigious effect on the army of the Rhine, or that of Sambre and Meuse. But to return to our own affairs. I reminded Clarke about the Pope, and told him that the Legate for Ireland was Cardinal Antonelli, and that if we could artfully get a line from him to Dr.

Troy, it might perhaps save us some trouble. Clarke promised to think of it. He also told me that my proclamation had been translated into French, to lay before the Directory. If they adopt it, it will be a decisive proof of the integrity of their principles as to Ireland; for I have worded every thing as strongly in our favour as I knew how, and have made no stipulations for any return as to France; but left every thing to the justice, honour, and gratitude of the Irish people. I am sure it is with regard to France herself the wisest course, and therefore I hope they may adopt my proclamation.

9. By dint of perseverance I am getting through the remainder of my cash. When I am near being run out, I am always more extravagant; and, like the "Old Batchelor," run into the danger to avoid the apprehension. Last night I was at the theatre *Vaudeville* where I was exceedingly amused by "Hazard, fils de son pere," a parody of "Oscar, fils d'Ossian." Laporte, who played Hazard, imitated Talma in Oscar incomparably. He beats Jack Bannister, for mimicry, all to nothing, and that is a bold word. But I am always alone at these theatres, and that kills me. To-day I scaled Mount Martre, by myself, and had a magnificent view of Paris under my feet, but it is terrible to have nobody to speak to, nor to communicate the million of observations which "rise and shine, evaporate and fall" in my mind. Money! money! money! I declare for my part I believe it is gone clear under the ground. I have this day six

crowns in silver, being "of dissipated wealth the small remains." Sad! sad! I hope Citizen Carnot may "bid his treasurer disburse six pounds to pay my debts:"—otherwise the consequences, I fear, will be truly alarming. In the evening lounged all alone, as usual, to the Champs Elysées, and drank coffee by myself. It is dismal, this solitude. For society, I might as well be in Arabia Deserta, not Arabia Felix. I am sure my country is much my debtor, if not for what I have done, at least for what I have suffered, on account of her liberty. Well, I do not grudge it to her, and if ever she is able she will reward me, and I think by that time I shall have deserved it at her hands. To-morrow I will go see Clarke, and hear what he has to say for himself. He assures me, (for I asked him a second time for greater certainty,) that my friends in Ireland know I am here. I am heartily glad of it. I was dreaming all last night of Plunkett and Peter Burrowes, and George Knox, and I believe it is that which has thrown me into the blue devils to-day. I remember Swift makes the remark as to dreams, that their complexion influences our temper the whole day after, and I believe he is right. Perhaps the marvellous state of my finances may a little contribute to plunge me into a state of tender melancholy, for Shenstone says, there is a close connection between the animal spirits and the breeches-pocket. Aristotle has many fine things on that subject.

11. Called on Clarke, who took down my name, and the day and place of my birth, in order to have

my commission filled up, which he expects to have done to-morrow. He was very civil, and mentioned that if it rested with him, the business would have been done long since. He then asked me that boring question, "Did I know one Duckett?" I answered I did not, nor did I desire to know him. He asked, why? I answered, I understood from Madgett, and others, that he was a blackguard. He seemed a little taken aback at this, and said, "Ay, but he is clever." I replied I knew nothing more about him; that it was disagreeable to me to speak ill of any body, especially of a person whom I knew merely by report, but in a business of such consequence as ours, I felt it my duty to speak without the least reserve. Clarke said, "Undoubtedly," and so the matter rested. I am to call the day after to-morrow, at which time I hope my eternal commission will be ready. Bought the "*Reglement pour le service de la Cavalerie*," and sat down to study it. I must get a sensible *sous officier* (non-commissioned officer,) to drill me a little before I join the regiment. I am tired now of tactics, so I think I will go walk a little to refresh me.

12. *Battle of Aughrim.* As I was sitting in my cabinet, studying my tactics, a person knocked at the door, who, on opening it, proved to be a dragoon of the third regiment. He brought me a note from Clarke, informing me that the person he mentioned was arrived, and desired to see me at one o'clock. I ran off directly to the Luxembourg, and was shown into Fleury's cabinet, where I remained

till three, when the door opened, and a very handsome well-made young fellow, in a brown coat and nankeen pantaloons, entered and said, "*Vous vous êtes le citoyen Smith?*" I thought he was a *chef de bureau*, and replied, "*Oui, citoyen, je m'appelle Smith.*" He said, "*Vous appelez, aussi, je crois, Wolfe Tone?*" I replied, "*Oui, citoyen, c'est mon veritable nom.*" "*Eh bien,*" replied he, "*je suis le General Hoche.*" At these words I mentioned that I had for a long time been desirous of the honour I now enjoyed, to find myself in his company. He then said he presumed I was the author of the memorandums which had been transmitted to him. I said I was. "Well," said he, "there are one or two points on which I want to consult you;" and he proceeded to ask me, in case of the landing being effected, might he rely on finding provisions, and particularly bread? I said it would be impossible to make any arrangements in Ireland, previous to the landing, because of the *surveillance* of the Government, but if that were once accomplished, there would be no want of provisions; that Ireland abounded in cattle, and, as for bread, I saw by the Gazette that there was not only no deficiency of corn, but that she was able to supply England, in a great degree, during the late alarming scarcity in that country; and I assured him, that if the French were once in Ireland, he might rely that, whoever wanted bread, *they* should not want it.—He seemed satisfied with this, and proceeded to ask me, might we count upon being able to form a provisory Government, either of the Catholic Committee, mentioned in my memorials, or of the chiefs of the Defenders? I thought I saw an opening here, to come at the number of troops intended for us, and replied, that would depend on the force which might be landed; if that force were but trifling, I could not pretend to say how they might act; but if it were considerable, I had no doubt of their co-operation. "Undoubtedly," replied he, "men will not sacrifice themselves, when they do not see a reasonable prospect of support; but, if I go, you may be sure I will go in sufficient force." He then asked, did I think ten thousand men would decide them? I answered, undoubtedly, but that early in the business the Minister had spoken to me of two thousand, and that I had replied that such a number could effect nothing. "No," replied he, "they would be overwhelmed before any one could join them." I was glad to hear him give this opinion, as it was precisely what I had stated to the Minister; and I repeated that, with the force he mentioned, I could have no doubt of support and co-operation sufficient to form a provisory Government. He then asked me what I thought of the Priests, or was it likely they would give us any trouble? I replied I certainly did not calculate on their assistance, but neither did I think they would be able to give us any effectual opposition; that their influence over the minds of the common people was exceedingly diminished of late, and I instanced the case of the Defenders, so often mentioned in my memorials, and in these memorandums. I explained all this, at some length, to him, and concluded by saying, that, in prudence, we should avoid as much as possible shocking their prejudices unnecessarily, and that, with common discretion, I thought we might secure their neutrality at least, if not their support. I mentioned this merely as my opinion, but added that, in the contrary event, I was satisfied it would be absolutely impossible for them to take the people out of our hands. We then came to the army. He asked me how I thought they would act? I replied, for the regulars I could not pretend to say, but that they were wretched bad troops; for the militia, I hoped and believed that when we were once organized, they would not only not oppose us, but come over to the cause of their country *en masse;* nevertheless, I desired him to calculate on their opposition, and make his arrangements accordingly; that it was the safe policy, and if it became necessary, was so much gained. He said he would, undoubtedly, make his arrangements so as to leave nothing to chance that could be guarded against; that he would come in force, and bring great quantities of arms, ammunition, stores, and artillery, and for his own reputation see that all the arrangements were made on a proper scale. I was very glad to hear him speak thus; it sets my mind at ease on divers points. He then said there was one important point remaining, on which he desired to be satisfied, and that was, what form of Government we should adopt in the event of our success? I was going to answer him with great earnestness, when General Clarke entered, to request we would come to dinner with Citizen Carnot. We accordingly adjourned the conversation to the apartment of the President, where we found Carnot and one or two more. Hoche, after some time, took me aside and repeated his question. I replied, "Most undoubtedly, a Republic." He asked again, "Are you sure?" I said, "as sure as I can be of any thing: I know nobody in Ireland who thinks of any other system, nor do I believe there is any body who dreams of monarchy." He then asked me, "Is there no danger of the Catholics setting up one of their chiefs for King?" I replied, "Not the smallest," and that there were no chiefs amongst them of that kind of eminence. This is the old business again, but I believe I satisfied Hoche; it looks well to see him so anxious on that topic, on which he pressed me more than on all the others. Carnot joined us here, with a pocket-map of Ireland in his hand, and the conversation became pretty general between Clarke, Hoche, and him, every one else having left the room. I said scarcely any thing, as I wished to listen. Hoche related to Carnot the substance of what had passed between him and me. When he mentioned his anxiety as to bread, Carnot laughed, and said, "There is plenty of beef in Ireland; if you cannot get bread, you must eat beef." I told him I hoped they would find enough of both; adding, that within the last twenty years Ireland had become a great corn country, so that, at present, it made a considerable article in her exports. They then proceeded to confer; but I found it difficult to follow them, as it was in fact a *suite* of former conversations, at which I had not assisted, and besides, they spoke with the rapidity of Frenchmen. I collected, however, if I am right, that there will be two landings; one (from Holland,) near Belfast, and the other (from Britany,) in Connaught; that there will be, as I suppose, in both embarkations, not less than ten, nor more than fifteen thousand men,—twelve thousand was mentioned; but I did not hear any time specified. Carnot said, "It will be, to be sure, a most brilliant operation." And well may he say so, if he succeeds. We then went to dinner, which was very well served, without being luxurious. We had two courses, and a dessert. There were present about sixteen or eighteen persons, including Madame Carnot, her sister, and sister-in-law; Carnot, his brother, Hoche, Truguet, the Minister of Marine, Clarke, two or three officers, and Legarde, the *Secretaire General.* I sate by Hoche. After coffee was served, we rose, and Carnot, Hoche, Truguet, Lacuée, and Clarke, retired to a cabinet and held a council on Irish affairs, which lasted from six to nine o'clock. In the mean time, I walked with Legarde in the gardens of the Luxembourg, where we listened to a symphony performed in the apartments of La Reveilliere Lepaux, who is lodged over Carnot. Legarde tells me that La Reveilliere has concerts continually, and that music is his great resource after the fatigues of his business, which are immense. At nine the council broke up, and I walked away with Clarke; he said every thing was now settled, and that he had himself much trouble to bring every thing to bear, but that at last he had succeeded. I wished him joy most sincerely, and fixing to call upon him to-morrow at twelve, we parted.—This was a grand day; I dined with the President of the Executive Directory of France, beyond all comparison the most illustrious station in Europe. I am very proud of it, because it has come fairly in the line of my duty, and I have made no unworthy sacrifices to obtain it. I like Carnot extremely, and Hoche, I think, yet better.

13. I cannot help this morning thinking of Gil Blas, when he was Secretary to the Duke of Lerma. Yesterday I dined with Carnot, and to-day I should be puzzled to raise a guinea! I am almost on my last louis, and my commission is not yet made out, though Clarke tells me it is done; but I will never believe him till I have it in my hand. I will push him to-day, that is positive. *Allons!* Saw Clarke; nothing new; my commission not yet come. I charged Clarke with great vigour, and he promised positively for the day after to-morrow, at farthest. So I must wait, and I am tired of waiting. Hoche called for a moment on Clarke, to say that he had no further questions to propose to me. So matters rest!

14. *Taking of the Bastile,* 1789. No business! Hoche yesterday praised Sir Sydney Smith, now prisoner in Paris, as a gallant officer: he said, "*Il a une rude reputation en Bretagne,*" and that there was hardly a cape or headland on the coast, which was not marked by some of his exploits. I like to hear one brave man praise another. Carnot said they would take care of him for some time, and that he

should certainly not be exchanged. I am glad of that too, for one or two reasons. Hoche also spoke of the ignorance of the Bretons; he says they know no more of the real state of the Revolution than the inhabitants of Tartary; that they always call the Government the Convention, and had a report, when he set off, that the Convention had ordered the Pope to the bar. I think there is no part of Ireland more ignorant, by his account. Carnot said he was satisfied that Babœuf's plot was the work of the Orleans faction. When I walked in the garden with Legarde, whom I found very conversable, we spoke of the astonishing successes of the armies, particularly of the Army of Italy. He assured me that, before the opening of the campaign, he trembled for the event; that the reluctance of the *jeunesse* to join their colours was almost insurmountable; that the Government was obliged to employ the most rigorous measures, even to tying them neck and heels, and transporting them in that manner, on carts, to the army; "and yet," said he, "you see how they fight, for all this." It is, to be sure, most astonishing. Hoche yesterday told Clarke, speaking of me, that he had got me by heart. Was that by way of compliment? "Ha! there may be two meanings in that!" either that he had studied my memorials diligently, which is good, or that he had fathomed me in one conversation, which is not quite so flattering: I fear he does "spy into the bottom of this Justice Shallow." No matter! no matter! Let me see and get the business done. If that is once effected, it is of very little consequence whether I have any talents or not. Huzza! I am in a good humour to-day.

16. Saw Clarke. He tells me the *arreté* of the Directory for my commission will be signed to-day, and that he will write to the Minister at War to send back the brevet to him, so that I shall have it by to-morrow at twelve o'clock. He tells me, also, that there is a change in the arrangement. The cavalry of the *ci-devant Legion de Police* has been formed into a regiment of dragoons, the twenty-first. The Colonel had given the Directory to understand there were supernumeraries of men and horses enough to form a second regiment, which was intended for me. It appeared, however, on inspection, that the contrary is the fact, for the twenty-first is even ten men short of its complement. In consequence, I am to serve in the infantry, with the rank of *Chef de Brigade,* which answers to that of Colonel; and Clarke tells me the pay and rank are the same, with less trouble. One must not look a gift horse in the mouth; so I said, of course, I was perfectly satisfied, and we parted the best friends in the world, and I am to return to-morrow at twelve for this weary brevet. Called on Madgett on my way home, to desire him to find me two louis d'or in two days at farthest, for I am just now run out, and I shall have my lodgings to pay for in three days from this, which is most fearful, for I dread my little *bossue* of a landlady more than the enemy a thousand times; but Madgett has promised to supply me, and so

> "Hang those who talk of fear;
> Our castle's strength will laugh a siege to scorn."

I forgot to mention in its place, that Hoche has a famous cut of a sabre down his forehead, eyebrow, and one side of his nose. He was pretty near the enemy when he got that, and, luckily, it does not at all disfigure him. He is but two-and-thirty, Jourdan five-and-thirty, Buonaparte twenty-nine, Moreau about thirty, and Pichegru, who is the oldest of all, about six-and-thirty. The French have no old generals in service; it is their policy to employ young men, and the event has shown they are right. Moreau and Jourdan continue to drive the Austrians before them, in all quarters. Every Gazette brings new victories, so that now we are beginning not to mind them.—In the evening, the opera: Tarare, (which I have seen twenty times.) It is brilliant, but the music by Salieri very inferior to that of Gluck.

17. Called, as usual, on Clarke. My eternal brevet not yet come from the War Office, but he gave orders to Fleury to write again to the Minister to have it sent directly. He tells me Hoche will leave town in two or three days, and that he will endeavour to give me a corner in his carriage, if possible. I answered, it would be highly flattering to me to have the honour of travelling with him; at the same time, I hoped he would give me a few days' notice, as I had no clothes but *habits bourgeois*, &c. He said he could not be sure to give me four-and-twenty hours' notice, and as to regimentals, I could get them made up at quarters. I replied, as to myself, I was ready at a moment, and the sooner the better. He then desired me to call every day at twelve, and we parted So, here I am, at single

anchor, ready to cut and run. As to money matters, I am extremely embarrassed; I have not a guinea. I think I must write to Carnot and demand a supply. I am sure I have reason to expect that much from the French Government; at the same time, God knows whether I shall get it or not, and, at any rate, it is very disagreeable to be obliged to make the application; but what can I do? This embarrassment is a drawback on the pleasure I should otherwise feel at the promising appearance of our business. Sat down and wrote two pages of a letter to my dearest life and love, informing her very obscurely of my success here, and of my having obtained the rank of *Chef de Brigade;* desiring her to sell off every thing, and embark in the first vessel for Havre de Grace. I will not finish my letter for a day or two, till I see how things turn out on one or two topics. I do not write to Rowan or Dr. Reynolds, because, as my last letters were intercepted and carried to England, I do not like to run any more risks. I forgot to mention in its place a trifling anecdote. The day I dined with Carnot, Hoche's aid-de-camp came up to me, and asked me how I liked my reception in France? I vented some compliments on the nation: "Yes," replied he, "but you have been well received, particularly." I answered, the French were ever remarked for their politeness and hospitality to strangers. He then struck at me directly: "Yes," said he, "but you are here on some private negotiation: you are accredited?" I looked up in his face with infinite good humour, and did not reply one word. He repeated his question, and I continued to smile on him with all possible stupidity; so he found he could make nothing of it, and, turning on his heel, left me. He was, I thought, a sad impudent fellow.

18. Rose early this morning and wrote a threatening letter to Citizen Carnot, telling him, "If he did not put five pounds in a *sartin* place, —— !!" It is written in French, and I have a copy. God forgive me for calling it French, for I believe, properly speaking, it is no language; however, he will understand that money is the drift of it, and that is the main point. Called at twelve on Clarke. At last he has got my brevet from the Minister at War. It is for the rank of *Chef de Brigade*, and bears date the 1st Messidor, (June 19th.) It remains now to be signed by Carnot and Legarde, which will be done to-day, and to-morrow, at nine, I am to pass muster. Clarke embraced me on giving me the brevet, and saluted me as a brother officer; so did Fleury, and my heart was so full, I could hardly reply to either of them. I am as proud as Punch. Who would have thought this, the day I left the Lough of Belfast? I would have thought it, and I did think it. That is manly and decided, as P. P. used to say. I now write myself *Chef de Brigade*, "in any bill, bond, quittance, or obligation—Armigero." Huzza! huzza!—Let me have done with my nonsense and huzzaing, and mind my business. Clarke asked me, would we consent, in Ireland, to let the French have a direct interference in our Government? adding,

that it might be necessary, as it was actually in Holland, where, if it were not for the continual superintendence of the French, they would suffer their throats to be cut again by the Stadtholder. I answered that, undoubtedly, the French must have a very great influence on the measures of our Government, in case we succeeded, but that I thought, if they were wise, they would not expect any direct interference; adding, that the most effectual way to have power with us, would be to appear not to desire it. I added that, for that reason, I hoped whoever was sent in the civil department, would be a very sensible, cool man, because a great deal would depend on his address. Clarke replied, "We intend to send nobody but you." That stunned me a little. What could he mean? Am I to begin by representing the French Republic in Ireland, instead of representing the Irish Republic in France? I must have this explained in to-morrow's conversation. Clarke then went on to say, they had no security for what form of government we might adopt, in case of success. I replied, I had no security to offer but my decided opinion, that we should establish a Republic. He objected, that we might establish an aristocratic Republic, like that of Genoa. I assured him the aristocracy of Ireland were not such favourites with the people, that we should spill our blood to establish their power. He then said, "Perhaps, after all, we might choose a King; that there was no security against that but speculation, and that the people of Ireland were in general very ignorant." I asked him, in God's name, whom should we choose, or where should we go to look for a King? He said, "Maybe the Duke of York?" I assured him, that he, or his aid-de-camp, Fleury, who was present, had full as good, and indeed a much better chance, than his Royal Highness; and I added, that we neither loved the English people in general, nor his Majesty's family in particular, so well as to choose one of them for our King, supposing, what was not the case, that the superstition of royalty yet hung about us. As to the ignorance of our peasantry, I admitted it was in general too true, thanks to our execrable Government, whose policy it was to keep them in a state of barbarism; but I could answer for the information of the Dissenters, who were thoroughly enlightened and sincere republicans, and who, I had no doubt, would direct the public sentiment in framing a government. He then asked, was there nobody among ourselves that had any chance, supposing the tide should set in favour of monarchy? I replied, "Not one." He asked, "Would the Duke of Leinster, for example?" I replied, "No: that every body loved and liked the Duke, because he was a good man, and always resided and spent his fortune in Ireland; but that he by no means possessed that kind of character, or talents, which might elevate him to such a station." He then asked me again, "Could I think of nobody?" I replied, "I could not; that Lord Moira was the only person I could recollect, who might have had the least chance, but that he had blown his reputation to pieces by accepting a command against France; and, after him, there was nobody." "Well," said Clarke, "maybe, after all, you will choose one of your own leaders; who knows but it may be *yourself?*" I replied, "we had no leaders of a rank or description likely to arrive at that degree of eminence; and, as to myself, I neither had the desire nor the talents to aspire so high." Well, that is enough of royalty for the present. We then, for the hundredth time, beat over the old ground about the priests, without, however, starting any fresh ideas; and I summed up all by telling him, that, as to religion, my belief was, we should content ourselves with pulling down the Establishment, without setting up any other; that we should have no state religion, but let every sect pay their own clergy voluntarily; and that, as to royalty and aristocracy, they were both odious in Ireland to that degree, that I apprehended much more a general massacre of the gentry, and a distribution of the entire of their property, than the establishment of any form of government that would perpetuate their influence; that I hoped this massacre would not happen, and that I, for one, would do all that lay in my power to prevent it, because I did not like to spill the blood, even of the guilty; at the same time, that the pride, cruelty, and oppression of the Irish aristocracy were so great, that I apprehended every excess from the just resentment of the people. The conversation ended here. Clarke gave me Hoche's address, and desired me to call on Fleury to-morrow, at nine, and that he would introduce me at the War Office, where I must pass review.—From Clarke I went to the Luxembourg, where I had an audience of Carnot. I told him I was come, in the first place, to return him my acknowledgments for the high honour conferred on me by the Directory, in giving me the rank of *Chef de Brigade* in the armies of the Republic; and I mentioned that, as General Clarke had told me that I should probably be ordered to join my regiment at a day's notice, and as my resources were entirely exhausted, I had taken the liberty to address a short memorial to him, requesting a supply. He asked me, "Had I spoken to Clarke?" I said, not explicitly on that subject. He then ran his eyes over my letter and desired me to give it to Clarke, and that he would report upon it to him, and see what was to be done. I then took my leave. Carnot's manner was very friendly, but I see no great certainty of the cash. I returned to Clarke, and wrote him a note enclosing my memorial, and requesting his good offices, &c.; adding, that if ever I reached my own country, and had it in my power to render any service to a friend of his, he might command me. That is a little stroke of intrigue.

19. I am writing these memorandums at four o'clock in the morning, for sometimes I cannot sleep. Called on Fleury at 9 o'clock, and walked with him to the War Office. When we arrived, found, like a couple of wise heads, that we had forgot my commission; so that business is postponed till to-morrow. He tells me the pay is thirty-five francs in cash, and six

hundred in mandats, per month, with three rations of meat, amounting to one and a half pounds, and three of bread, to four and a half, besides haricots, salt, and wood, to I know not what amount. But in God's name what shall I do with bread and meat? After all, I fear I must consult Madgett, and that is what I do not wish to do. Well, well! I will wait, at all events, till to-morrow, when I will see what impression I can make upon Clarke, concerning trade affairs. I am exceedingly embarrassed with my rations. Went muzzing with Madgett, in the evening: as we were walking through the Tuileries, who should we meet, full plump, but my old friend Stone of Hackney, walking with Helen Maria Williams, authoress of the Letters on France. I was fairly caught, for I have avoided Stone ever since my arrival, not that I know any thing to his prejudice, but that I guard the incognito. He made me promise to call on him to-morrow, and as he is already acquainted with almost the whole of my history, I will tell him that I am here memorializing the French Government for some compensation for what I have suffered in their cause, and that if I succeed, I mean to settle in France. That is the truth, but not the whole truth. Went on with Madgett, and drank punch; told him of my commission, having first sworn him to secrecy. What shall I do with my rations? To-morrow I will see Clarke, and learn what report he makes on my letter to Carnot.

20. Called at Clarke's, and saw Fleury, who gave

me my brevet, signed by Carnot, and so now I am, to all intents and purposes, *Chef de Brigade* in the service of the Republic. Fleury is to bring me to-morrow at nine to the *Commissaire Ordonnateur*, to pass review, and from thence to the Treasury to receive a month's pay, so *Vogue la galere!* Fleury also told me, by Clarke's orders, another thing not quite so agreeable, viz. that Carnot's answer to my memorial was that he thought a month's pay in advance, a handsome compensation: nevertheless, if I thought otherwise, he desired that I might signify to Clarke, what I deemed reasonable. I desired Fleury to tell Clarke, I would consider of it, and let him know the result to-morrow, or the day after. I do not think it at all a compensation. What is a month's pay? *3l. 2s. 6d.* sterling. It is absolutely nothing. I will put the thing to Carnot as a debt of honour, and let him pay it or not, as he pleases. As to my rations, I am quite at a loss to know how I shall manage with them. A Frenchman would soon settle it, but it is a different thing with a foreigner.

23. Called at Clarke's, on Fleury; coming out met General Hoche, who desired to see me to-morrow morning, at seven o'clock, in order to talk over our business, and settle about my leaving Paris. That looks like business. Went to the *Commissaire* and passed my review; from that to the Treasury, where the forms are terribly slow. I received for my month's pay, thirty-five francs in cash, six hundred in mandats, worth to-day twenty-four, and three

hundred in assignats, worth, I suppose, about sixpence. Dined very pleasantly with Stone and Helen Maria Williams. All our politics English. Stone was very hearty, but H. M. Williams is Miss Jane Bull, completely. I was quite genteel and agreeable. Wrote to Monroe, to know if I might, in case of necessity, draw on him for fifty pounds. Bed very early; thinking of my interview with Hoche.

23. Called on Hoche, at seven, and found him in bed, talking with two Generals whom I did not know. One is going to Italy, very much against the grain. General Sherlock called in. I collect from what was said, that he is to be of our expedition, and that he does not know it himself yet. After they were gone, Hoche asked me "When I would be ready to leave town?" I answered, I was at his command, but wished, if possible, to have four or five days to make some little arrangements. He said, by all means; that he proposed leaving town in seven days himself, and that, if he could, he would give me a seat in his carriage; but if not, he would settle that I should travel with General Cherin, his most particular friend, who was to have a command in the business, but to whom, as yet, he had not opened himself on the subject. I made my acknowledgments, and asked him, at the same time, whether my appearance at head-quarters might not give rise to some suspicions, from the circumstance of my being a foreigner? He replied, he would settle me in a village near Rennes, his head-quarters, where I should

be incognito, and, at the same time, within his reach. I asked him then, was he apprized of the Directory having honoured me with the rank of *Chef de Brigade?* He replied he was, and made me his compliment. I then observed to him, I presumed I might be of most service in some situation near his person; that I spoke French, as he might observe, very imperfectly; nevertheless, I could make myself understood, and as he did not speak English, I might be useful in his communications with the people of Ireland. He replied, "Leave all that to me; as soon as you join, and that your regiment is formed, I will apply for the rank of Adjutant General for you; that will place you at once in the Etat Major, and besides, you must be in a situation where you may have a command, if necessary." I returned him a thousand thanks; and he proceeded to ask me, "Did I think it was likely that the men of property, or any of them, wished for a revolution in Ireland?" I replied, "Most certainly not," and that he should reckon on all the opposition that class could give him; that, however, it was possible that when the business was once commenced, some of them might join us on speculation, but that it would be sorely against their real sentiments. He then asked me, "Do you know Arthur O'Connor?" I replied, I did, and that I entertained the highest opinion of his talents, principles, and patriotism. He asked me, "Did he not some time ago make an explosion in the Irish Parliament?" I replied, he made the ablest and honestest speech, to my mind, that ever was made in that House. "Well," said he, "will he join us?" I answered, I hoped, as he was "*foncierement Irlandais*," that he undoubtedly would. So it seems O'Connor's speech is well known here. If ever I meet him, as I hope I may, I will tell him what Hoche said, and the character that he bears in France. It must be highly gratifying to his feelings. Hoche then went on to say, "There is a Lord in your country; (I was a little surprised at this beginning, knowing as I do, what stuff our Irish peers are made of;) he is son to a Duke; is he not a patriot?" I immediately smoked my lover, Lord Edward Fitzgerald, and gave Hoche a very good account of him. He asked me then about the Duke. I replied that I hoped for his assistance, or at least neutrality, if the business were once commenced. He then mentioned Fitzgibbon, of all men in the world. I endeavoured to do him justice, as I had to the others he spoke of, and I believe I satisfied Hoche, that we will not meet with prodigious assistance from his Majesty's Lord High Chancellor of Ireland. He proceeded to ask me, "What quantity of arms would be necessary?" I replied, the more the better, as we should find soldiers for as many firelocks as France would send us. He then told me, he had demanded 80,000, but was sure of 50,000. That is a piece of good news. I answered, with 50,000 stand to begin with, we should soon have all the arms in the nation in our hands, adding, that I had the strongest hopes the militia, who composed the only real force in Ireland, would give us no opposition. We then spoke of the aristocracy of Ireland, and I assured him, as I had done Clarke, that what I apprehended was, not the aggrandizement but the massacre of that body, from the just indignation of the people, whom they have so long and so cruelly oppressed; adding that it was what I sincerely deprecated, but what I feared was too likely to happen. He said, certainly the spilling of blood was at all times to be avoided, as much as possible; that he did conceive, in such explosions as that which was likely to take place in Ireland, it was not to be supposed but that some individuals would be sacrificed; but the less the better, and it was much wiser to secure the persons of those I mentioned, or to suffer them to emigrate to England, as they would, no doubt, be ready to do, than to put them to death; in which I most sincerely agreed, for I am like Parson Adams, "I do not desire to have the blood even of the wicked upon me." Hoche mentioned, also, that great mischief had been done to the principles of liberty, and additional difficulties thrown in the way of the French Revolution, by the quantity of blood spilled: "For," added he, "when you guillotine a man, you get rid of an individual, it is true, but then you make all his friends and connexions enemies for ever to the Government:"—a sentence well worth considering. I am heartily glad to find Hoche of this humane temperament, because I hope I am humane myself, and trust we shall be able to prevent unnecessary bloodshed in Ireland, which I shall, most sincerely, exert my best endeavours to do. He then desired me to call on him every two or three days, at seven o'clock, at which time I might be sure to find him disengaged, adding, that he did not wish to mix me with the crowd; and after several expressions of civility and attention on his part, all which I set down to the credit of my country, we parted. I like Hoche more and more. He is one of the pleasantest fellows I ever conversed with, possessing a fine manly mind and a fine manly figure.—On my return, I found a very friendly answer from Monroe, inviting me to dinner for to-day, in order to settle about trade affairs.—I should have mentioned, that Hoche asked me whether the Defenders had ever sent any one to France, to make representations. I answered, I could not positively say, but I believed not, they being, for the most part, the peasantry of Ireland, and, of course, having neither means nor proper persons to send. At twelve, I went and saw Clarke. We were both a little out of humour, about my application for money; but our ill temper was pointed against the Directory, rather than against each other. He said he was sure they would give me nothing. I asked him then how was I to leave Paris, in five or six days, as General Hoche had that morning given me orders to hold myself in readiness to do? "Well," said he, "but you ask too much." "So far from it," returned I, "I ask nothing. I barely state, how much I have spent of my own money, and leave it to Carnot's honour to determine what he thinks reasonable."—"But I do not see," continued he, "how it is to be done, or on what fund." I answered, "I came by order of De la Croix, the Minister of Foreign Affairs, and of Adet, the Ambassador of the Republic, in America;" which last had offered me money for my expenses, an offer I had refused—some proof that I did not want to extort from them; that the natural way was, therefore, to give an order to De la Croix, to make me such compensation as the Directory might think fit. Clarke then "began to complain of the scarcity of silver, which I improved, by complaining of the scarcity of gold, and we both agreed that money never was so scarce as at present." At last, Clarke said he would speak again to Carnot, but I confess I see no great hopes, which is pleasant. I made many fine reflections in my own mind, during this spar, on the gratitude of nations, &c. However, after all, I am a *Chef de Brigade*, about to be an Adjutant General. By what I see, however, we are like to reap more glory than profit, in this business. Well, my own country will pay me, sometime or other, so *allons!* I then took Clarke up, on our conversation of the 18th, relative to a direct interference on the part of France. I said, if he meant, by that, to admit a representative of the Republic into any part of our Government, it was what France ought not to expect, nor we to grant. That what he said of Holland, did not apply to us. The French had conquered Holland, and had a right, if they pleased, to throw it into the sea, but it was not so with Ireland. We rather resembled the situation of America, in the last war. Clarke seemed satisfied with all this, and I proceeded to ask him, had they thought of a person to reside near the future Irish Government? He said General Hoche would be there. I replied, he would be moving about, but I meant a sort of Chargé d'Affaires, who should be stationary. Clarke replied, undoubtedly, a proper person would be sent. I said, I hoped the French Government would be very delicate in their choice, and send a man of great temper and discretion, as much would depend on his conduct. I then observed, that Clarke had often asked me what security Ireland would give that, if her independence was once established, she might not forget her obligations to France, and perhaps hereafter be found leagued with her enemies? To which I offered him, as the only security, our honour as gentlemen. Now I begged leave, in return, to ask him what security he had to give us, that if England offered to renounce every thing, provided France would sacrifice us, France would not accept the offer? He answered in my own words, "Our honour as gentlemen," and assured me, in the strongest manner, France would be, as I believe myself, incapable of such conduct. I asked him then, whether he thought, if our Government was once organized, we could borrow money in Spain or Holland? He said, "he doubted it very much; that Holland had no money, and Spain very little." If so, we must only make assignats, and then mandats, like our betters. It is now two o'clock, and I must go dress for dinner, at Monroe's. "Fine times, Mr. Rigmaroll." Nothing but Generals and Ambassadors.—Dinner at Monroe's: very pleasant. Mrs. Monroe, a pretty little woman, with very white teeth. After dinner, went with the Ambassador into his cabinet. He tells me he is just now poor, but offered to supply me to the amount of 50*l.* in sums of ten or fifteen, as I might want it; or else desired me to go to Skipwith, the Consul for the United States, and see if he would give me cash for my bill on Philadelphia, which he would guarantee, or for one to the same amount on himself, at a short date, which he would accept. He offered me, at the same time, ten louis, for my current expenses. All this is very handsome in Monroe. After thanking him, I told him I would avail myself of his permission to try Skipwith, but that I was not in any difficulties for some days to come, and consequently refused, with many acknowledgments, the money he offered me. He goes out of town to-night for two days; on the third I am to call on him, and in the mean time see the Consul, so called *a consulendo*, because I mean to consult him. Once for all, hang the money for me! I will make no more memorandums about it, that's flat. It degrades the dignity of my history. This is a long day's journal, nine pages, and it is now about six o'clock. I have run through a good deal of business to-day, besides writing these nine pages. I had like to forget that Hoche showed me my proclamation printed and signed by himself. It is the one intended for distribution, and I think it will be found to be an honest one.

25. Running about all this morning on trade

affairs. Saw Clarke; he tells me I am to travel with Hoche, and that we set off the 30th, in five days. Called at Monroe's; the Secretary tells me there is a person arrived this week, who has a letter for me. My heart is up in my mouth. Please God I will run off the minute I swallow my dinner. I am in a frenzy till I get my letter. I have not had one line since I left New York, now six months. How is my dearest life and soul, and our darling little babies? The little things! my life lies in those children. Well, I hope I shall hear news of them to-night. Poor little Will, and my Fantom, and my girl that I doat upon, and their darling mother. Oh that I had my letter! (Evening.) My lover gone out: left a note, that I would call to-morrow at eleven, and desiring him to leave the letter for me in case he should be obliged to go out before that time. I know nothing that agitates me so much, as an incident of this kind. I am projecting all possible kinds of accidents and misfortunes; it is terrible; I will not torment myself any longer, that 's flat. I will go walk in the Champs Elysées to dissipate my chagrin. Home; early bed!

26. Up at six, and called on Hoche at seven; he was gone out, so I had my walk for nothing. "I hope my early rising will do me no harm." I want to settle with him about our journey. Called at eleven on Colonel Fulton, and got my letter, which is from Hamilton Rowan; it is dated March 30th, nearly four months since, at which date all my family were well. He tells me also

that my brother Matthew arrived in America in December last; that gives me most unspeakable satisfaction, as he will be a protection for my wife and family during my absence, or in case of the worst happening to me in this contest wherein I am about to embark. My mind is now as much at ease as I can rationally expect it to be for some time to come. I look on this letter as a good omen before my departure. Met Aherne, for the first time God knows when. He tells me, that rascal Duckett is proclaiming to all the world that there is to be an invasion of Ireland, and that he has it from Clarke and General Hoche, with whom he is in confidence; is not this most dreadfully provoking? Here I have doomed myself to a rigorous solitude for six months, to avoid the possibility of alarm, and now a blackguard is sounding the trumpet! I will call on Clarke to-morrow, and abuse him for his indiscretion in opening himself, as I know he has done, and I believe Hoche also, to such a scoundrel. It is vexatious beyond all bearing. I am in a rage. Met my *compagnon de voyage*, D'Aucourt, with whom I lodged on my first arrival; he was very civil, and tells me he is applying for the rank of *Chef de Brigade*, to be sent out to the West Indies. Well, other people are *Chefs de Brigade*, as well as he; but he does not know that. I know not how it is, I have spent five dreary months in Paris, without forming one connection, male or female, that I care a farthing about, or that cares a farthing about me; yet I find myself low-spirited, now that I am about to quit it; that is curious enough, but I have often had occasion to remark the same sentiment. I am as dull to-night as a cat.

27. Clarke tells me this morning that the Directory have ordered me three months' pay. That is, "*tant de pris sur l'ennemi,*" but I am forced to borrow 50*l.* from Monroe, which grieves me sorely, for it is breaking in still more on the sacred funds of my little family; it is, however, unavoidable, as I cannot go down to quarters without some money in my pocket. Went to the Champ de Mars to see the *Fête de la Liberté*; very superb, but I am not now in a humour to relish *fêtes*. I want to be off, and my impatience is still growing greater, the nearer the time approaches. Paris is as bad to me now, as Havre was the first week of my arrival. Apropos! it is extremely attentive of Hoche to take me with him; I believe I am not sufficiently sensible of it. The fact is, I am surprised myself at the *sang froid* with which I regard the progress of my business here, so infinitely beyond my expectations. I had very little expectation of success the day I left Sandy Hook, and in fact I came merely to discharge a duty. Things have turned out miraculously, to be sure. Think of my being at a council of war with Carnot, Hoche, and Clarke; of my rank of *Chef de Brigade*; of my travelling now with Hoche, besides what yet may follow! It is absolutely like a romance. There is one thing I must say for myself. On reviewing my conduct in France, I do not see an indiscretion with which I

have to charge myself. I think in my conscience I have conducted myself very well. I have, to be sure, laboured very hard in this business.

There is another thing I wish to remark here. I owe unspeakable obligations, and such as I can never repay, to my masters of the General Committee; I have, in consequence, never lost sight of their honour or their interests here, as will appear from my memorials delivered to the Executive Directory, in which I have endeavoured to make them the basis of the National Legislature. If that succeeds, I shall have been instrumental in throwing a great game into their hands, and I hope and believe they will have talents and spirit to support it. At any rate, I have, I think, done my duty by them, and in part at least acquitted the debt of gratitude I owed them. I will never forget their behaviour to me in the hour of my persecution, and their heroic refusal to sacrifice me at the requisition of Grattan and the Whigs. If I contribute to seat them in the places of the aforesaid Whigs, it will be a proof that with parties, (I may say with nations,) as well as with individuals, honour and honesty will ever be found to be ultimately the true policy.

28. Called on Hoche early, and saw him for a minute. I travel with him, and we set off on the 31st. That is a day later than I hoped. I am to see him again the day after to-morrow. Saw Clarke. Nothing new there. I am to get my order for three months' pay to-morrow. Called at Skipwith's, the American Consul, who gave me 50*l.*, for which I

gave him a bill on Doctor Reynolds, in Philadelphia, for 55*l.* I would have given 65*l.*, rather than go without the money. I am now ready to march. I see the Orange-boys are playing the devil in Ireland: I have no doubt it is the work of the Government. Please God, if I get safe into that country, I will settle those gentlemen, and their instigators also, more especially.

30. Called on General Hoche. He tells me I am to travel with General Cherin, *Chef de l'Etat Major*, and that we set off about the 12th of next month. I had rather set off this morning. He desired me to call on Cherin, and present myself as the person of whom he had spoken, which I did accordingly; but Cherin was gone out. Called at the War-Office and got an order for three months' pay. I should have mentioned, that I gave yesterday to Skipwith a packet, directed to Holmes and Raines, Philadelphia, containing two letters, one for Hamilton Rowan, and the other for my dearest love, in which I repeat my orders for the removal of my family and property with all possible speed to France. Skipwith promised me to put them in a way of going with speed and security, so I am in hopes they will have better fortune than my last.

31. Received my pay, "and are all as drunk as so many swabbers." I insist upon it this is a very good quotation, from Rigdum Funnidos. The monotony of my life just now will appear from the stupidity of these memorandums, and especially from

the dulness of my jokes. I cannot express how much I long to be "*en route*."

AUGUST, 1796.

1. (Sings) "Oh, merry be the first, and merry be the last, and merry be the first of August." This is a sprightly beginning, however. I am plaguy musical this morning, but God knows the heart! Called on Clarke from mere idleness; did not see him; but, coming out, met General Hoche, who took me in his carriage to General Cherin, with whom I am to travel. On the way, I told Hoche that I hoped the glory was reserved for him to amputate the right hand of England for ever; and I mentioned the immense resources in all respects, especially in men and provisions, which Ireland furnished to that country, and of which I trusted we were now on the eve of depriving her. Hoche observed, that his only anxiety was about finding subsistence for the troops. I replied, as to that, I hoped there would be no difficulty; that it was Ireland which victualled the navy, the West Indies, and the foreign garrisons of England; and I reminded him of what I had before communicated, that, in the late scarcity, so far from difficulties at home, she exported vast quantities of corn to that country. I might have added, but it did not occur to me, that we are now on the eve of harvest, so, I am sure we shall find abundance of every thing. I went on to say, that my difficulty was not how to

subsist, but how to get there, for that I dreaded that eternal fleet. Hoche laid his hand on my arm and said, "*Ne craignez rien, nous y irons ; vous pouvez y compter ; ne craignez rien!*" I answered, that being so, I had not a doubt of our success. Hoche then asked me, "Who are these Orange-boys ?" I explained the term to him, adding, that as to them it was an affair of no consequence, which we would settle in three days after our arrival. "*Oh,*" said he, "*ce n'est rien.*" I then told him I hoped he would take care to have a sufficiency of cannoniers and artillery, with which we were quite unprovided. "You may depend upon it," said he, "that I will bring enough, and of the best, particularly the *artillerie legère.*"

He then asked me, had we many great plains in Ireland ? I said not ; that, in general, the face of the country was intersected with fences, and I described the nature of an Irish ditch and hedge to him. By this time we arrived at Cherin's, who was indisposed and in bed. I was introduced by Hoche, and I remember now he is one of the generals with whom I dined at Carnot's. After a short conversation, in which it was fixed that we set off from the 7th to the 10th, I took my leave, Hoche and Cherin desiring me to call on them in the mean time, without the ceremony of sending up my name, which is civil of them. So, now I have "*les petites entrées.*"

2, 3. Blank. My time drags just now most horribly.

4. Called on General Hoche. No news. He

tells me that it may be the 16th or 17th before we set off, which is desolation to me. "My soul's in arms, and eager for the fray." He tells me also, that when we get to Rennes, he and I will settle the proclamation. I mentioned to him, that as we should arrive in the middle of harvest, there could be no doubt about our finding subsistence. He answered, he had thought of that himself. Called on Cherin twice, and saw him for about a moment. I cooled my heels in his antechamber for above an hour; but that is only a petty mortification. I always find the subalterns greater men than the principals. One thing I must keep in mind. As I have begun by dancing attendance on others, if ever I arrive at any situation, I must remember the anxiety and vexation I suffered in my time, and not give myself airs. Called on Clarke. I am out of luck to-day. He was engaged and could not see me, so I left my name. Altogether, I am out of humour. I believe it is the delay of our departure which has vexed me. Cherin tells me we shall set off the 16th or 17th.

5. Blank. Terrible! terrible! I feel myself absolutely sick at these delays. Dined with Madgett and three other Irishmen in the Champs Elysées. Stupid as a horse. Every body is talking of our business. I hear of it from fifty different quarters. That is most terribly provoking.

8. Saw Hoche and Cherin together this morning. Both very civil, but no news. Hoche, I believe, sets off on the 11th.

10. Fêtes to celebrates the anniversary of the subversion of royalty in France. Foot-racing, horse-racing, and running at the ring in the Champ de Mars. The Directory, Ministers, and constituted authorities, assisted in grand costume, with the foreign ambassadors. It was a delicious evening. The prizes were all military, sabres, pistols, and carbines, of the manufactory of Versailles. This is exactly as it should be. The concourse of people was immense, and I was very glad to observe that every body seemed pleased and happy. When the Directory rose from their place to retire, the people forced the sentinels, and got into the centre, in order to see them. I was delighted to observe that circumstance, which I look upon as by no means trifling. After the exercises in the Champ de Mars were over, the people retired *en masse* to the Champs Elyseés, where there was a most magnificent illumination and fire-works. I never saw anything so brilliant in the way of *coup d'œil.* The Muscadins and elegant women of Paris made it a point to stay away, but nobody missed them. The French enjoy these kind of spectacles better than any people on earth, and, for my part, I never was more amused and gratified than in observing the spectators. Altogether, I spent a very pleasant, I may almost say a happy day.

13. Saw Cherin this morning: he tells me it may be ten days yet before we get off. Hell! hell! hell! How shall I get over these eternal delays? Hoche set off yesterday.

14. Put on my regimentals for the first time; as

pleased as a little boy in his first breeches; foolish enough, but not unpleasant. Walked about Paris to show myself; huzza! *Citoyen Wolfe Tone, Chef de Brigade* in the service of the Republic! Opera in the evening: Lays, incomparable in Panurge; Mme. Guenet a charming singer; Mme. Gardel and Nivelon, in the *pas russe,* inimitable; it is worth a voyage from Ireland to America, and from America to Paris, to see that single dance. I think now I have got on regimentals, I begin to write like a very pretty gentleman. There is a strong report, and I believe a true one, that Hammond, who was Ambassador from England to the United States, is now at Calais, with some proposals for peace on the part of the English Ministry. I do not at all apprehend that anything will come of it; it is a manœuvre of Pitt's, in order to prepare for meeting the new Parliament with a declaration that he has been ready, on his part, to make peace, but that the pride and haughtiness of the French Government would listen to no conditions but such as were dishonourable to England. John Bull is not at all beaten into his senses as yet. For my part I do not see how it is possible for France or England to make peace, preserving their respective Governments: I think one or other must go down; I do not speak of the nations, but merely of the Governments.

20. The gaps in my journal will demonstrate how time hangs on my hands. Called on General Cherin this morning; found him very courteous; he tells me we shall certainly set off in ten days, viz. the

30th. Well, ten days more; however, "'Tis but in vain for soldiers to complain." He tells me, also, that a valet de chambre has presented himself to be hired with him, who speaks English, and has lately been through England, Scotland, and Ireland; that he has not at all the appearance or manners of a domestic, and that he (Cherin) suspects that he may be an emissary, slipped at him as a spy. It is very probable. He promises to send him to me, on a message, in two or three days, in order that I may sift him as to his knowledge of England, &c. *A la bonne heure.*—I see in the papers, and hope it is true, that the French Admiral Richery has sailed from Cadiz, in company with a powerful Spanish squadron. If that be so, it will probably bring matters to a crisis between England and Spain. If they pick up the Brest squadron, and the Dutch fleet, now lying in the Texel, I think they must be an over-match for anything John Bull can produce against them.

23. Met Cherin to-day driving about in his cabriolet; he stopped me, and asked me was I ready to set off? I answered, "In five minutes, and that I only waited for his orders." He then desired me to call on him to-morrow at eleven, in order to settle about our departure; so, perhaps, we may set off before the 30th. The armies continue victorious in all quarters. The news, at least the *report* of to-day, is, that Richery and the Spaniards are before Lisbon, and that a French army is in full march across Spain, in order to enter Portugal; that would be a blow to

Master John Bull fifty times worse than the affair of Leghorn. Why the unhappy Portuguese did not make their peace at the same time with Spain, I cannot conceive, except, as was most probably the case, they durst not consult their own safety for fear of offending the English. What an execrable nation that is, and how cordially I hate them! If this affair of Portugal is true, there will not remain one port friendly to England from Hamburgh to Trieste, and probably much farther both ways. It is impossible she can stand this long. Well, if the visitation of Providence be sometimes slow, it is always sure! Oh that I were, this fine morning, at the head of my regiment on the Cave Hill! Well, all in good time.

24. Saw Cherin; our departure is fixed for the 1st of September. "The devil take Henry of Lancaster and thee;" "Patience is stale, and I am weary of it." He asked me to dine with him the day before we set off: saw the servant of whom he spoke to me; found nothing suspicious about him, yet, after all, he may be a rogue. It is seven days yet at least to our departure.

25. The report to-day is, that Spain has declared war against England, and that the declaration, to speak technically, contains sixty-three counts. I hope in God it is true!

SEPTEMBER 1796.

2. Here I am yet! To divert the spleen which is devouring me, I have been, for some days past

throwing memorandums of my life and opinions on paper,* from recollection. They are very ill done, and probably inaccurate in the dates, but they are better than nothing. I have already filled nearly two books as big as this. Saw Cherin to-day. He knows no more about our departure than I do, but promised me faithfully to write a pressing letter to Hoche on the subject.

5. Called on Cherin; he knows nothing farther than that Colonel Shee, a relation of Clarke's, is gone down to Rennes. He advised me to call on Clarke; came home in a rage, and wrote a letter to Clarke, supplicating an order for my immediate departure, which I gave to his aid-de-camp, Fleury.

8. This evening received a note from Cherin, informing me that he had received a letter from General Hoche, and desiring to see me in the morning, so at last I hope we are about to move. I never suffered so much *ennui* in all my life as since Hoche's departure, which is now almost a month. Scribbling now and again at my memoirs, which I have brought down to the beginning of 1792; stupid enough; but when my mind is agitated as it is at present, I can neither read, write, nor think. I hope in God I am at last going to act; it is high time, but it is no fault of mine that I did not begin long since. Well, better late than never!

9. Called on Cherin; he states, positively, that

* These "memorandums" form the first section of this work; namely, to page 91, vol. i.

we set off on the 13th, and desires me to call on him the 12th in the morning, to receive his definite orders.

12. Called on Cherin by appointment; he is gone to the country for two or three days. Hell! hell! hell!

15. At last I have brought Cherin to the point; he has received a courier last night from General Hoche, and tells me now I may set off with the first courier, or wait a few days for him; but I am tired of waiting. I wrote, therefore, by his direction, a note to the Minister at War, praying an order to depart, with the first courier, for Rennes, and he has promised to get it for me by to-morrow. Huzza!

16. Got my order and presented it to the directors of the post. There is a courier for to-morrow, with whom I secured my place; packed up my kit as gay as a lark.

17. Took leave of Madgett, Aherne, and Sullivan; wrote two letters of acknowledgment to Carnot and De la Croix, thanking them for their kindness, &c. At three o'clock in the afternoon left Paris. It is now exactly seven months and five days since I arrived there—a very important era in my life: whether it was for good or evil to my country and to myself, the event must determine; but I can safely say I have acted, all through, to the very best of my conscience and judgment, and I think I have not conducted myself ill. I certainly did not expect, on my arrival, to have succeeded as well as I have done; and I have been under some difficulties at times, having not a soul to advise or communicate with. I

have now done with Paris, at least for some time, and God knows whether I shall ever revisit it; but, at all events, I shall ever look back on the time I spent there with the greatest satisfaction. I believe there is no part of my conduct that I need wish to recal, at least with regard to business. As to pleasure or amusement, I had very little. I formed, and endeavoured to form, no connections. I visited and was visited by nobody, French or foreigner, and left Paris after seven months' residence, without being acquainted with a single family. That is singular enough. The Theatres formed my grand resource against the monotony of my situation; but, on the whole, I passed my time dull enough. Well, if ever I return, I will make myself amends. I am now like the Turkish spy, "who passed forty-five years at Paris, without being known or suspected." I dare say Mr. Pitt knew I was there, as close as I kept; if he did, it was by no fault or indiscretion of mine. It is singular enough, that having passed my time in a manner so monotonous, and not leaving behind me a single person whom, on the score of personal regard, I had reason to regret, I yet quit Paris with something like reluctance. But I made that remark before. *Allons!* I am now afloat again: let us see what will come of this voyage.

THE PERIOD OF GENERAL TONE'S ATTACHMENT TO THE ARMY OF THE WEST.

September 19. On the road — no adventures. Passed the second day through the country of the

Chouans: it is delicious; as well wooded as New Jersey, of which it often put me in mind. The second night, (for we travelled night and day,) "fear fell upon me." How if the *Chouans* were to stop the mail, as they have sometimes done? Looked at my sabre and pistols, and was consoled. Determined to die hard in case of a battle; for I knew there was no quarter with those brigands. Luckily, all quiet. Did not see a single Chouan: Huzza! Travelling a bad business. I hate it; never made a tour completely to my satisfaction but with P. P. He is, indeed, an agreeable companion in a post-chaise: I wish he were beside me in the mail instead of this beast of a courier. Well, we may meet yet!

20. At three this morning arrived at Rennes, having passed three nights agreeably without sleep. "A hundred and twenty miles in thirty-four hours is pretty smart riding, but nothing to the fatigue of recruiting." I do not think that quotation any great things myself, but let it pass. "Well, now I am in Ardenne; the more fool I; when I was at home, I was in a better place." Went to bed, and slept like a dragon till eleven. Rose and sent for my adjoint, Mac Sheehy, who has been here some days. He tells me all is going on, as he believes, prosperously. General Hoche is gone out fishing, and does not return till night. I am glad Hoche is a fisherman, because I am one myself. Wrote a note to let him know I am arrived, and gave it to Mac Sheehy to deliver. Dined alone, deliciously,

and drank a bottle of excellent claret, with divers patriotic and constitutional toasts. Thought of P. P. and my dearest love a thousand times. I am as pleased as Punch to find myself in quarters at last. "Good apartments, Jack." Went in the evening to the Comedie: *bitter bad!* The piece was, to my great surprise, Addison's Drummer, very tolerably translated, and I was glad to see the French enjoy it extremely, especially Mr. Vellum. I remember Vellum used to be P. P.'s "*grand cheval de bataille,*" and furnished him with divers inimitable quotations—"The gift is two-fold," and "A thundering dog." I delight to recall the nonsense that P. P. and I have vented together; and I would this night gladly give one-half of the contents of my purse, (which, indeed, to speak candidly, is no enormous sum,) for the pleasure of his company. "Ah! those were fine times, Mr. Rigmaroll!" Well, I do love the dog dearly, that is the truth of it. I am tired now, so I will go to bed, and try to recover the arrears of sleep which are due to me.

21. Called on General Hoche, and sate with him for about a quarter of an hour; very civil, but no news as yet. I am to be for some time Mr. Smith, an American. He asked me about Duckett, who is here, it seems. I said I neither knew, nor intended to know him, and mentioned his prating at Paris to all his acquaintance, about his influence with General Clarke, and with Hoche himself. So now, if Hoche puts any confidence in this fellow, at least it is not my fault. Hoche spoke obscurely as

if there were somebody here who knew and wished to see me; but I did not press him for an explanation, and he did not offer it. A few days may show more. Called on Colonel Shee, uncle to General Clarke, who is here. He tells me he was stopped on this side of Laval, at two o'clock in the day, by seven Chouans, who robbed him of every article of his property, except a box of papers relating to our business, which he was bringing to Hoche, and which escaped their search, as it were by miracle. It was most fortunate! This was but a few days since: so I have had a good escape. I doubt if I should be able, single-handed, to conquer seven Chouans, armed with firelocks, as he tells me his lovers were. They offered him no personal injury, and he has learned since that the favour was not intended for him, but for a Commissary, who was expected to pass with money to pay the troops. Dined at head-quarters, with the staff, Hoche, Hédouville, Mermet, &c. All very slovenly and soldier-like, but nobody minds a dirty plate or thing of that kind here. *A la guerre, comme à la guerre*, as the French say.

22. This being the first Vendemiaire, and, of course, the first day of the fifth year of the French Republic, *one, indivisible, and imperishable*, we had a grand review of the troops in the Champ de Mars, with horse racing, &c. and speeches from the constituted authorities. After the review, I met Hoche. He asked me, " Did you hear the cannonade?" I said I did. " Ay," said he, " you will soon hear

enough of that." I answered, "The sooner the better." In the evening at the Comedie, to see a new piece, written by Privat, one of Hoche's Aids-de-camp, on the termination of the war in La Vendée, in which he introduced some apposite and well-timed compliments to the General and the Republic. The characters were filled by the young men of the Etat Major, and it went off very well. The theatre was free for the ladies of the town, and, after the play, there was a grand ball at the *Hotel de Ville,* given by Hoche, for which I had a ticket; but, unluckily, I was not well; so instead of going to the ball, I came home and went to bed, which was a pity; for,

> "With my hat so well cock'd, and my hair so well curl'd,
> I look'd like a man of the very first world."

I believe that quotation is not correct; but no matter, it is as good as one of P. P's quotations, at any rate.

23. At work all the morning with Colonel Shee, making an analysis of the distribution of the troops actually in Ireland. The General called in, and sate with us half an hour. Dined as usual with the Etat Major. I am now, to all intents, one of the family, and I like it of all things. (Sings) "How merrily we live that soldiers be," &c. I have got rooms at head-quarters, and moved my kit accordingly. We are all lodged in the palace of the ci-devant Bishop of Rennes, a superb mansion, but not much the better of the Revolution. The chapel,

for example, is converted into a stable; and divers other changes, of a like nature, have taken place. I do not know but I sleep to-night in his Lordship's bed-chamber. Colonel Shee, in his turn, asked me to-day, did I know Duckett? I said to him, as I had said to Hoche, that I neither knew him, nor desired to know him; for that I believed him to be a blackguard. Shee answered, it was exactly his own notion; that Duckett had made two or three sets at him, but that he had always avoided him. He added, that Duckett had told several people that he was sent here by the committee of nine, who manage the affairs of the Catholics, as their Plenipotentiary. The impudence of this last stroke did, to be sure, astonish me. I answered, that Duckett was a scoundrel, and if he were to tell so outrageous a lie in my presence, I would knock him down on the spot. I also besought him to put Hoche on his guard, particularly as to this last story, offering, at the same time, to confront him before the General, and compel him to speak the truth. Shee answered, that was unnecessary, for that he was sure Hoche saw through him completely. But I am not yet satisfied; and I believe I will take an opportunity myself to set this matter on its right footing. D—n the impudence of the rascal! My brother Ambassador! Marry come up indeed! I'll Duckett him, the scoundrel, if I can catch him fairly in my grip.*

* I wonder my father did not record a laughable incident which occurred at one of these dinners, and which he often mentioned to my mother. The conversation was running on the

24. Walked with Colonel Shee in the garden. He tells me that Hoche has selected the elite of the Army of the Ocean, which consisted of 117,000 men, for our expedition ; that the arms and every thing were ready, and that we are waiting only on the marine. He also spoke as if in a fortnight or less we might put ourselves in motion; but I did not press him for specific information. The season is slipping away fast through our fingers. However, I believe they are doing their best.

25. Walked as usual in the garden with Col. Shee. I turned the discourse upon my own situation, and that which I had filled in Ireland. Shee told me that both the Executive Directory and General Hoche were perfectly satisfied as to who and what I was, through a channel which he was not at liberty to inform me of, but that I might be perfectly easy on the score of my credit. I answered that I was extremely glad they had satisfied themselves as to my veracity, and that I dreaded no investigation or scrutiny into my character or principles. I added

great Lord Chatham, and the funeral honours which he received at the national expense, which my father was explaining to General Hoche. Duckett thrust himself between them, and observed, that, to receive such a recompense had always been the highest object of his ambition. All stared at the modesty of the declaration. when Mr. Shee gravely observed, that he never saw any one who was more likely to be gratified in such a wish —(A pause ensued, and every eye was cast with wonder upon him)—" for," continued he, " wherever you die, the *parish* will surely have to bury you."—*Editor.*

that I was the better pleased at this, inasmuch as I did not know but I might appear to them in the same light with that scoundrel Duckett, who is here. He assured me again that they were perfectly assured that I had said nothing of myself but the strict truth. He added that he had spoken to Hoche about Duckett, and that Hoche said he would send him back to Paris instantly; but that he had desired the General to keep the fellow here until the last moment, and then despatch him. I was very glad to hear this, because I disliked exceedingly the idea of such a rascally adventurer thrusting himself into our business. However, he is now, I believe, sufficiently known, and of course can do no mischief. We then spoke in general of our expedition, which is delayed entirely by the marine. The General sets off to-morrow for Brest to hurry them; and as he has extraordinary powers, I am in hopes that he will work *Messieurs les Commissaires.* I collect from Shee's discourse, that we will have 1,000 cavalry ready to mount; but the Irish must find horses. I do not yet know the number of our infantry. At dinner, Privat, one of Hoche's aids-de-camp, and author of the piece that was played the other night, told me that Hoche and he were private soldiers in the *Gardes Françaises*, and were made corporals together on the same day. He also told me that Hoche's *coup de sabre* was received in a duel with a fellow-soldier.

26. The general set off this morning for Brest. I hope in God he may hurry those fellows. I dread

the equinoctial gales passing over and finding us unprepared. By Shee's discourse I fancy it is intended that we shall make a race for it. Happy go lucky in that case. I was in hopes the Spanish fleet would have joined us at Brest, but he tells me they are returned to Cadiz, after escorting Richery to some unknown latitude.—D—n their foolish souls, they will be beaten, and the French also, in detail; whereas, if they were instantly to join, their united fleets in the Channel would be stronger than any thing England could for some time oppose to them, and a week would be sufficient for our business. If they let this occasion escape them, as I fear they will, they need never expect to meet such another. I am in the horrors to-day. Well, let us see what Hoche's expedition will produce. He will be absent for five or six days. Brest is 180 miles from this. Time, time! At all events, for me the die is cast, and I am utterly desperate as to the event. Come what come may, I have done, and am doing my duty; and if I fall, I fall. I have not, on that score, the smallest burthen on my mind. A short time now must, I think, put me at least out of uncertainty; and I am sure that the worst that can befal, cannot be much more painful than the state of suspense and anxiety in which I have so long languished. Once again "courage!" Let us see what Hoche will say on his return.

27. The report is that Thomas Grenville is at Paris, with some proposition for peace. I do not mind it; it is a fetch of Pitt's, if it be at all true

that he is there. Besides, Colonel Shee has letters to-day from General Clarke, which make no mention of his arrival, but assure us that every thing is going on as fast as possible. As fast as possible is, however, too slow for my impatience. My life hangs terribly on my hands. After all, however, I had rather stagnate at Rennes than at Paris.

October, 1796.

1, 2. Blank! Blank!

3. The *Journal des Defenseurs de la Patrie*, published under the authority of the Directory, gives the lie, this day, to the arrival of Thomas Grenville. I did not much mind the report at the time, but am greatly pleased with the spirit of the contradiction, which is by an official note. The Directory seems fully bent on humbling the pride of England; and lay down as a principle, that the peace to which they will consent must be one which will ravish from her, her maritime preponderance, restore the liberty of the ocean, give a spring to the Spanish, Dutch, and French marine, and carry to the highest degree of prosperity the industry and commerce of these nations, whom England has regarded as rivals and enemies, when they would no longer submit to be dupes. If the Directory act up with firmness to these principles, and if Spain be not utterly besotted, I think it impossible but England must be reduced within her proper and natural limits; the first step to which, be it ever kept in mind, is the independence of Ireland.

5. I find great amusement in chatting with Colonel Shee, who is a very agreeable old man, and has served as a good officer of cavalry now thirty-six years. He told me last night, as I was sitting with him, that General Clarke had written to him that he might have full confidence in me; nevertheless, he does not tell me much, if indeed he knows much himself; that, however, gives me very little concern. I shall learn every thing time enough. I collect, however, that it is resolved, if possible, to turn in a gang of six or seven thousand desperadoes into England, who will live at free quarters, and commit all manner of devastation. If this takes effect, it will embarrass her extremely. She has never yet seen the smoke of an enemy's fire; and I always remember, that 5,000 ragged, half-starved Highlanders, forced their way to 100 miles distance of London, and might, perhaps, have achieved what remained, if the Pretender had not been a poltroon. It is, to be sure, a horrible mode of making war, but England showed the way, by disgorging so many hordes of emigrants into France, and the enormities which have been committed, in consequence, in this country, are such as to justify France in adopting any means of revenge; it is, in a word, but strict retaliation. I am curious to see how England will relish a war of Chouans in her own bowels. Colonel Shee and I were employed yesterday in digesting and arranging different routes from the several harbours, where we might land, to Dublin. I find him very reasonable. We agreed

that our first object was to get ashore any where, and, of course, the nearest port to Brest was the best, as we could make any shift when we were once landed, our army being composed of veterans who have been in service in La Vendée for years, and are steeled against every hardship; having been well used to dispense with clothes, shoes, or even bread, at times. Supposing, however, we had a port to choose, we agreed it should be Belfast, or at least, as near Belfast as possible; if not, Waterford, or that neighbourhood. The distance from Dublin is pretty nearly equal. We calculated, however, for, I believe, a dozen different landing-places round the coast. He tells me Hoche has a great magazine of clothing, which he took from the British at the time of his famous victory at Quiberon; that is literally "*tant de pris sur l'ennemi.*" We talked a good deal of my affairs. I observed that, supposing our expedition was, by any unforeseen accident, prevented, I was a little anxious as to what the Directory might determine with regard to me; that I had almost utterly ruined myself, partly in their service; that since I came to France I had subsisted entirely on my own means, having drawn nothing from the Republic but my pay, which he knew was not sufficient to pay my washerwoman; that, on my journey and during my stay in Rennes, I had not drawn even my pay; nor did I intend it, as it was to my own country I looked for indemnification, in case we ever got there; but I again observed, if our expedition did not take place, I could hardly suppose the Directory would suffer me to be utterly ruined, which must be the case if I were not retained in their service. Shee answered, he had not the shadow of doubt but, in that case, I would be employed, as he did not think the Directory capable of acting dishonourably by a man who had such strong claims on them; and he added, that he was satisfied General Clarke would take effectual measures in my behalf. This was a considerable relief to my mind, an account of my wife and our dear little babies. We then began to build *Chateaux en Irlande*, as magnificent as any in Spain. Shee told me he had some notion, in case we succeeded, of selling what property he had in France and settling in Ireland. I answered, I, for one, should be heartily glad of it; and indeed I spoke but the truth. I added, that we should have occasion for his talents, and especially for his long experience as a military man, in arranging our army; and, in that case, I hoped we should find for him a situation which might recompense him for the services he would have rendered, and the sacrifice of quitting his family, and exposing his health, (which is not very firm,) and his person, to the fatigues of a voyage and the perils of a winter campaign. As he seemed very much to relish this discourse, I took the opportunity to throw in a word or two on my own situation and expectations. I reminded him that hitherto I had drawn nothing either from France or Ireland; but, on the contrary, had sacrificed time, labour, person and property in the common cause of both countries; that I had no doubt, if we succeeded, of being amply recompensed; nevertheless, that the more attention was shown to me by the French Government, and by the General, on our arrival, the greater services it would be in my power to render to France, to Ireland, and to our friends embarked in the expedition. That I believed he knew my zeal and affection for the cause of the Republic, as well as my gratitude to the Directory; and I left him to consider whether, in framing our government in Ireland, it might not be desirable for France to have, in an efficient station, a man on whose principles and attachment she might safely count,—a circumstance which might be materially forwarded and most probably secured by the attention, on the part of the General, to which I alluded—an attention which both Catholics and Dissenters would consider as shown to themselves, much more than to me personally, as I could have no claim upon it other than as I stood in the capacity of their agent, and possessing, as I would venture to say I did possess, their confidence. Shee heard me with great attention, and said he saw clearly the advantages resulting from what I proposed; that every thing I said was perfectly reasonable, and he was satisfied the General would see it in the same light, and regulate his conduct accordingly. I desired him to think of all I had said, and that we would resume the subject once more before our departure.

7. I like old Colonel Shee more and more; his

conversation is my sole resource against the ennui which devours me. He was Secretary to the late Duke of Orleans, for whose memory he cherishes the sincerest regard. He has amused me these two days with an infinity of anecdotes relating to that unfortunate prince, who, I almost begin to believe, has been most grossly calumniated by all parties in the Revolution. The zeal and affection which Shee manifests for the honour of a man who can no longer serve or prejudice him, is, at least, a strong proof of the goodness of his own character. It is highly interesting to see the earnestness and warmth with which he labours to impress me with a good opinion of the Duke; and, indeed, from his reports, I am satisfied, not only of that prince's innocence as to the accusation on which he was guillotined, but as to his general character as a man of honour, courage, and probity. I think I see that he has been a victim of a double cabal—of the court, and of the jacobins. *Mais parlons d'autre chose.* General Hédouville showed the Colonel to-day a letter from Hoche, wherein he says he is moving heaven and earth to get things in readiness at Brest, and that he hopes in three weeks we may be getting aboard. The marine agents are scoundrels, and there is a scarcity of seamen, but orders have been this day expedited to all the military commanders along the coast, to make diligent search, to secure, and send on to Brest all seafaring persons, and there is a reward of six livres a-head to the soldiers for all they can find, which will sharpen them up to the business. It will be November before we arrive, if we are so fortunate as to arrive at all; of course we shall have, in that case, a winter campaign of it. No matter; we are better able to stand it than those who will be opposed to us. The country gentlemen of Ireland, with their warm feather-beds, their beef and claret, will make, I think, no great figure before our grenadiers, who have been seasoned these four years to all manner of hardships and privations in this execrable war of La Vendée, which Hoche has had the glory of terminating. "D——n it; we 're all militia captains, and who 's afraid of death?" I have written out about thirty Irish airs for the band of my regiment, if I am to have one, which I doubt a little, whereby I must *insense* Hoche on his return, because "when both house and lands are spent, then learning is most excellent." Good! good! —hold! I meant *abominable!* That is a vile quotation, to tell the God's truth of the matter.

8. I must change my apartment to-morrow to make room for General Debelle, brother-in-law to Hoche, who is just arrived. *A la bonne heure.* "They talk of further alterations, which causes many speculations." My quotations latterly are as pert and stupid as you please, but how can I quote when I am in this horrible suspense?

12. The General returned last night at eight o'clock, having been absent since the 26th of last month. Colonel Shee saw him this morning for a quarter of an hour; he tells me Hoche is bent on going, *coute qui coute*, and that every thing is ready

but seamen, whom he has given orders to be pressed all along the coast, as far as Bordeaux. Oh! that we were aboard. Oh! that we were aboard! or rather, indeed, that we were ashore, after being aboard. "I 'gin to be a-weary of the sun!" Shee told Hoche that we had prepared divers routes during his absence, and took that opportunity to speak of me, and I suppose he was pleased to say something handsome, but what it was, of course, I did not inquire. I see an article in a French paper that thirty persons have been arrested in Dublin for high treason. Who can they be? Are any of my friends of the number? for there are no names mentioned. I hope in God we shall be in Ireland time enough to liberate them, be they who they may. I think General Hoche will be pretty security for their appearance, and I fancy that even my own bail would not, in this case, be refused. Colonel Shee and I have been reading over the American Ordonnance, and making our observations on it. If we arrive safe, I will propose adopting it, with a few necessary alterations. It is excellent, for an army that must be made in a hurry, being clear and concise.

14. The General set off, unexpectedly, for Paris, this day at twelve o'clock. It seems, on his visit to Brest, he had reason to be discontented with the administration of the Marine; however, they promised him fair, and he returned to Rennes, leaving orders with a confidential person to let him know how they were going on. This person has written him word,

that since his departure all the preparations are slackened, and, in conseqnence, he is set off in a rage for Paris, and I trust will return in a few days with full powers to cashier a parcel of those scoundrelly agents of the Marine. I have written, by Colonel Shee's desire, a short address to the peasantry of Ireland, explaining to them the great benefits which the Revolution has procured to the peasantry of France. This he has translated into French, and gave the copy to the General to read on his way to Paris. I see by two English papers of the 13th and 14th of last month, that they are importing daily large quantities of arms, ammunition, and artillery into Ireland. I am glad of it, for divers reasons. It is also said they are going to restore the fortifications of Derry, and to mount one hundred pieces of artillery on the walls. This I take to be rhodomontade, for I cannot see to what end they should fortify Derry. I wish we were once in Ireland, and we would make short work with their fortifications. These eternal delays kill me; but then Hoche is a man of the greatest activity, and he is embarked, body and soul, in this business. I am sure he is as earnest to the full as I am myself, and that is a great comfort to me. I suppose he will be about a fortnight absent.

16. The General returned, unexpectedly, this morning at nine o'clock. It seems he met a courier on the road with despatches, which rendered his trip to Paris unnecessary. Colonel Shee tells me to-day, that it was intended, after landing us, to despatch

the fleet with three thousand men to the East Indies; but, in consequence of a mutiny at the Mauritius, that scheme is given up, and we are to keep both ships and men. I mentioned to him a report I had heard, that we were waiting for cannoniers from the army of the Sambre and Meuse, which I thought very odd if it were true; he assured me it was no such thing; we have already three companies of cannoniers, and, in short, every thing is ready except the seamen, to procure whom the most positive and pressing orders have been given by the Minister of Marine and Directory. He told me also that, perhaps, about the time of our landing, I should hear of some combustion in England, and that he hoped, before we had done, we might pay John Bull a visit. According to my laudable custom, I did not ask him to explain what this combustion was to be. It will, probably, explain itself time enough.

17. Our expedition, as well as the life of the General, has had a most providential escape. Last night, between nine and ten, as he was returning from the Comédie, with Generals Debelle and Hédouville, a ruffian, who was posted at a corner, fired a pistol at him, within five or six yards, which fortunately missed, and the villain instantly ran off, but was stopped by two of the aids-de-camp, who happened to come that way, before he had run one hundred yards. The pistol was likewise found where he had dropped it. On his being seized and examined, he confessed that he was hired by a per-

son, whom he described, to assassinate General Hoche, and was to have fifty louis for his reward. He threw himself on his knees before Hoche, who behaved incomparably well, and desired him to rise, as no man should kneel to him, and tell the whole truth; assuring him that he had not himself the least resentment against him. The fellow then repeated his story exactly, and the two aids-de-camp set out with a guard in quest of the other villain, whom they found in bed, and brought to head-quarters. A magistrate being sent for, the two were confronted, and the latter denying every thing, they were both, after a long examination, committed to prison. It seems the fellow who fired the shot is a workman employed in the arsenal, the other is lately from Paris, and says he is a horse-dealer: in order to induce the former to commit the murder, he told him that he was a Royalist, and that it was for the King's service to assassinate Hoche, which, together with the promise of the fifty louis, determined him. The name of the former is Moreau, and of the latter Teyssierd. Nothing could be better than the General's behaviour through all this affair. For my part, I do not see what the Royalists could promise themselves from his death; at the same time, it is beyond all doubt that this villain Teyssierd, has come down from Paris expressly to have him assassinated. I do not at all suspect the English of assassination; but certainly, at this moment, *they* are much more interested in Hoche's death than that miserable Louis XVIII. In short, I know not what to think of the motives of this abominable affair; a few days may probably explain it further.

18. In consequence of the affair of yesterday, a search was made in the lodgings of Teyssierd, and a case of pistols, two fusils, and three air-guns, were found,—the two last articles buried in the garden; there were also among his papers the directions of several persons in Paris and *London*. I should be sorry, much as I detest the English nation, to suspect them of such vile and horrible means of effectuating their purposes, as that of assassination; yet they have already done several things in this war as bad, at Quiberon, and elsewhere. I am very much afraid the English Cabinet is implicated in this infernal business, the more so as the General received notice a few days since, from the Minister of Justice at Paris, to be on his guard, as an attempt was intended to be made on his life by some English agents. Hoche is entirely too careless of his person, which, as he is circumstanced, though it may be very magnanimous, is not very wise. He was out till past ten o'clock last night.—Chatted a good deal to-day with Colonel Shee, who is my only companion here, and whose conversation I find extremely amusing and instructive. He tells me he expects we shall soon set off now; that the General has no confidence in the marine, but is determined, if we fall in with the English fleet, that fight they shall;—for, as the military will be at least two to one on board, he will give it out in general orders, that the first man,

officer or seaman, of whatever rank, that offers to flinch, shall be instantly shot on the quarter-deck. That is stout of Hoche, or as P. P. would say, "manly and decided." I had rather, however, that our valour was tried on *terra firma*, for I am of opinion with the Turks, "that God has given the sea to the infidels, and the land to the true believers." A sea-fight is our *pis aller*; nevertheless, if it must be, it must. Those d——d Spaniards! why are they not this moment in Brest water? They have mortally offended the English by escorting Richery out of Cadiz, and now they are temporizing with half measures, which is always miserable policy; whereas, if they joined us instantly, we could strike our blow in security, and the navy of England, (or I am utterly deceived,) would be no longer formidable either to France or Spain. I wish I was at the head of the Spanish Cabinet for one month.—Shee told me a good story to-day:—The English had lodged fifty louis to pay the printer here for a copy of the proclamation which they foresaw Hoche would publish, wheresoever he was bound. He got wind of this, and, by Shee's advice, prepared a proclamation for the Portuguese, and then began to search with great secrecy and diligence among the priests, for some one who understood Portuguese, in order to have it translated. (It was a pity Mr. Fitzsimons, of whose talents for the Portuguese I have already made honourable mention, was not here.) Having thus spread the report among these knaves, he sent off Shee privately to Angiers, where there is a printer on whom he has reliance, and caused the proclamation to be printed there, taking every possible precaution that not a copy should escape. It was very well imagined of Colonel Shee, and I have no doubt but those rascally priests will take care the story of the Portuguese proclamation shall find its way to England. All fair! All fair! We talked a little of my affairs, and Colonel Shee, after saying handsome things of my services, assured me he would take care, if we arrived safe in Ireland, to state very fully, when and where it might be necessary, of what important consequence my exertions in France had been, &c. He spoke with great friendship and regard, and I have no doubt his representations may be of material use to me. I do not think there is any thing wrong or like intrigue in all this. Have I not sacrificed every thing to the cause? and have I not rendered some service, and I may say essential service, to my country? I assured Colonel Shee, in return, that if ever I found myself in a situation which might enable me, he should see the sense I entertained of his kindness for me. There the matter rested, and there I will let it rest.

19. Since my arrival here, I have not had the least communication with the General; we have scarcely even spoken at meals when we met, and I began in consequence to grow a little uneasy at it; for as there are two Irishmen here (M'Sheehy and Duckett,) besides myself, and as the first is a blockhead and the last a scoundrel, I did not exactly

know whether the General might not lump us all off together, in forming his opinion. I therefore hinted remotely to Colonel Shee, yesterday, my uneasiness at the great reserve of the General towards me, and in consequence of what I said, which was indeed but very little, he spoke to him of it at dinner. The General assured him that he by no means confounded me with the two others; but observed, which is the fact, that if he was to mark me by any particular attention, it would be immediately observed and set people on making inquiries, which would be very inconvenient, as it was absolutely necessary that I should remain *incognito* as much as possible; he added, that, in time and place, I should see how he wished to treat me. This has satisfied me entirely. Colonel Shee also told me, that it was a long time a moot point whether our expedition should be undertaken or not, as the Minister of the Marine, Truguet, was very much wedded to a scheme he had for India; but that, at last, with considerable difficulty, General Clarke had managed it so that our affair had the precedence. If we yet get to Ireland, it will be worth fifty of Truguet's schemes. *At night.* I have mentioned above what the General said yesterday, with regard to me. To-day, after dinner, he took Colonel Shee aside and repeated his reasons for not being more attentive to me, which he begged of him to explain to me. Colonel Shee told him he had done so, and that I was perfectly easy on that score. The General then told him he had appointed me to the rank of Adjutant General, which will give me, as a military man, very great advantages; and he added, that one reason which kept him under restraint as to me, was the presence of that rascal Duckett, who had written him an impertinent letter, and whom he intended to cashier next morning. He added many other civilities, to which Colonel Shee made the proper acknowledgments on my part. Certainly, nothing can be handsomer than this conduct of the General. I am heartily glad, for divers reasons, that he is resolved to send Mr. Duckett to wander. Colonel Shee then told me that he expects he will set off in four or five days; that he had requested of the General that we might travel together, and that the General had given orders to his aid-de-camp, Poiton, to that effect. The General has likewise read my address to the peasantry of Ireland, which he entirely approves; so all, as to me at least, is going on as well as I could desire. Huzza! I am an Adjutant General! Well, to be sure, but it is droll! Shall I make a good officer? Why not? "It is a life I have desired; I will thrive." We read the King's speech, in which he announces a desire to make peace, but I do not mind this. Shee told me that, perhaps, at this very hour there was something going on in England which would embarrass them not a little, and that we might perchance hear of it in four or five days. This is, at least, the third time that he has spoken to me darkly on that subject; but I make it a rule never to press him for explanations. We talked over the plan of an address to the people at large, in Ireland, inciting them to establish their independence, to be published on our landing; and I sat down beside him, and wrote a few pages to begin. I think I will make it a flaming production; but I am tired now, it is late and so I will go to bed. I am a pretty fellow to be an Adjutant General! "Mr. Klinker—Floyd, I would say, hi, hi, hi,—I suppose you are too great a man to acknowledge your old acquaintance, ho, ho, ho." Well, that is a vile stupid quotation, to tell the truth of it, but a soldier is not obliged to quote like a pedant,

> "With their Novids, and Omars, and Blutracks, and stuff.
> By Gad, they don't signify this pinch of snuff."

"D—n Homo, with all my heart, I am sure I have the marks of him sticking on my a— yet." Oh Lord! Oh Lord! witty quotations for an Adjutant General.

20. This day received my orders to set out for Brest the day after to-morrow, being the 1st Brumaire. Huzza! Huzza! I am to travel in General Debelle's carriage, with Hoche's cousin, and Privat, his aid-de-camp. Settled all my affairs at Rennes instantly, and hove short. I am ready at a minute's warning. I have been hard at work to-day on my pamphlet, which is scurrilous enough. Colonel Shee translates it as I go on, for the inspection of the General, and I like it better in his French than in my own English. I think it will do tolerably well, when it is finished.

21. Last night I met the General in the Gallery alone. He immediately came up to me and asked me, had I occasion for any thing before my de-

parture? I thanked him, and replied, I had not. He then continued, "Because, if you have, I desire you will apply to me, as to your friend, without reserve." I again thanked him, and said, that if I was under any necessity, I would avail myself of his permission, but that at present I was not. He then said, "I am not a man to make professions, but I beg you will, on all occasions, look upon me as your friend, and treat me accordingly." I thanked him for the third time, and so we shook hands and parted. It was very civil of him, and I desired Colonel Shee to let him know again how sensible I was of his kindness.

22. Set out from Rennes, on my way to Brest, with Privat and Marie Hoche. Travelled very agreeably through a beautiful country, covered with wood, the very seat of *Chouannerie.* The farms beautiful; the towns, for the names whereof I refer to the map, mean, and the villages abominable. England far beyond France in that respect, but very inferior in all the other beauties of a landscape. Halted at Montauban. Our whole caravan amounts to eighteen officers, mostly of the Etat Major. Supped very pleasantly. A furious penury of beds. Privat and I, to show a good example, lay rough on a mattress on the floor. Lay awake half the night, laughing and making execrable puns. We were not *much* crowded, there being only *nine* of us in one small room. I like this life of all things. There is a gaiety and a carelessness about military men, which interests me infinitely. We mess to-

gether. I pay nothing, as the General gave orders to that effect to his cousin; and also, as Marie Hoche told me, to treat me with all possible attention and respect; all which is highly agreeable. Once again, I like all this mightily!

23. As yesterday. Halted at Broon, where we slept. Mess pleasant, as usual, and good accommodations at the Auberge. Two very fine lads of the name of Dalton, nephews of Colonel Shee, and sons of an Irish officer, are of our party, and are particularly civil and attentive to me: for which, if we reach our destination, I will be civil and attentive to them. I like them both, James and Alexander, very much. I wish they could speak English, which they do but very imperfectly.

24. Halted at Lamballe. I can see a very great difference in the behaviour of my companions since we set out. Whilst we were at Rennes, nobody was uncivil, but nobody was attentive to me; now the case is different. I am placed in the seat of honour, lodged single, and in the best chamber, whilst the rest are obliged to fag. I hope I need not say that I give myself no airs on all this; on the contrary, I endeavour to recommend myself as much as possible by a very modest and guarded behaviour, and have the pleasure to see that my discretion, in that respect, does not pass unnoticed. The alteration in the behaviour of my comrades is so striking, that I think it worth mentioning here, and I believe they like me as well as I like them. It is peculiarly incumbent on a foreigner, in the French service, to

be delicate on all points ; and I am, at least, sensible of what I ought to do, whether or not I am able to execute it. I like the French more and more ; their very foibles, of which they have plenty, amuse me, whilst the singularities of an Englishman are almost always offensive.

25, 26, 27, 28. As usual. Halted at St. Brieux, Guincamp, where we remained one day to repose. Belle Isle en terre and Morlaix. At Morlaix dined with General Harty, an Irishman, in the service of the Republic.

29. This morning before we set out, General Harty sent for me, and showed me an English paper that he had just borrowed, (the Morning Post,) of September 24th, in which was an article copied from the Northern Star of the 16th precedent. By this unfortunate article, I see that what I have long expected, with the greatest anxiety, is come to pass. My dear friends Russell and Sam. Neilson, were arrested for high treason on that day, together with Rowley Osborne, Haslett, and a person whom I do not know, of the name of Shanaghan. The persons who arrested them were the Marquis of Downshire, the Earl of Westmeath, and Lord Londonderry, together with that most shameless of all ——, John Pollock. It is impossible to conceive the effect this heavy misfortune has upon my mind. If we are not in Ireland time enough to extricate them, they are gone ; for the Government will move heaven, earth, and hell, to ensure their condemnation. Good God ! If Russell and Neilson fall, where

shall I find two such men to replace them? My poor friend Russell, with whom I have spent the happiest hours of my life, and whom I love with the affection of a brother! a man who would, I know, sacrifice his life for me or my family, if it were necessary; and Neilson, an honest, brave, and worthy fellow, a good Irishman, a good republican; both of them men who have rendered such essential service to their country. My heart smites me now for the levity with which I have spoken of my poor Russell in these memorandums, under the name of P. P. Well, that levity exists no longer; it is time now to think of other matters. I will not expend myself here in empty menaces, which as yet I have not the means to execute. God, I hope, has not so totally deserted me, but I may yet arrive in time to deliver my friends. If, to my unspeakable loss, I should arrive too late to rescue, at least I shall be able to revenge them, and, in that case, "woe to their persecutors!" I see that they have behaved in a manner worthy of themselves, and of the cause to which I fear they will fall victims. Neilson and Russell surrendered themselves voluntarily. Wm. Sampson acted with the greatest spirit, and, particularly, insulted Lord Westmeath two or three times, in the grossest manner. This most unfortunate of all events brings to my mind the death of my poor friend Sweetman, which I shall ever regret, and the arrestation of John Keogh. With regard to the latter, as I have seen the English papers pretty regularly ever since, and have found no further mention of that affair, I am in great hopes that he was immediately discharged, and that nothing disastrous ensued. If ever I return to Ireland, God only knows in what state I shall find the invaluable friends I left behind me, or how many of them may be in existence. I am in unspeakable distress at this moment, the more so, as I can do nothing for their relief. I will go to Hoche the moment I reach Brest, and acquaint him with this unfortunate event; but, as to him, that is unnecessary, for I am sure he is doing his very best to hurry things forward. Good God! If I am so unhappy as to arrive too late, what shall I do? I cannot bear to think of it. If they conduct themselves well, they may postpone their trials for a considerable time, and in that case, we may yet save them. It is but forty-five days since they were arrested. But if, to my unspeakable misfortune, that should not happen, my only consolation is the hope of revenge. Once again, I will not indulge in premature threatenings. If I arrive, and arrive too late, we shall see what is fit to be done.

30. After halting last night at Landerneau, arrived this day at one o'clock at Brest, having been just ten days on the road. Ran immediately to find the General, but he was gone out. Called on Colonel Shee, and informed him of the situation of our friends. He tells me if they manage to delay a little, he is in hopes we may arrive time enough to deliver them. God Almighty send! He tells me a relation of his, a general officer in the service of the Republic, who was sent by the Executive Directory

into Ireland, about four months since, is just arrived, and will probably be in Brest in about five or six days. He will of course bring us authentic intelligence of the state of the country.

NOVEMBER 1796.—(BREST.)

1, 2. I have been hard at work ever since my arrival, on an address to the Irish people, which is to be printed here and distributed on our landing. I have hardly time to eat; but I do not work with pleasure, from the reflection which recurs to me every instant, that the men whose approbation I should most covet, are, perhaps, at this moment on trial for their lives. Well, let me, if possible, not think of that longer. I have not yet seen the General. Colonel Shee tells me that General Quantin has been despatched from Flushing with 2,000 of the greatest reprobates in the French army, to land in England, and do as much mischief as possible, and that we have 3,000 of the same stamp, whom we are also to disgorge on the English coast. It is a horrible mode of making war, and such as nothing can possibly justify, but the manner in which England has persecuted the Republic. Much as I detest the inhumanity of punishing the inhabitants of a country for the crimes of their rulers, I cannot blame the French, when I recollect the treachery of England at Toulon, or the miseries which she has caused in that part of the Republic through which I have just passed, by her false assignats and counterfeit louis, but, especially by her most atrocious and unheard-of system of starving the whole French people,—a measure so abominable, and which produced such dreadful suffering and misery in France, as justifies any measures of retaliation, however terrible. The English Ambassador is arrived at Paris; Spain has, at length, declared war against England, and begun, it is said, by taking a man-of-war of 56 guns. D—n them! why are they not to-day in Brest waters? Corsica is evacuated by the British; so all goes on pretty well.

Evening. I have just read, in the Moniteur, the memorial given in by Lord Malmesbury, the English Plenipotentiary in Paris, the note of Charles de la Croix, and the reply of the Directory, which is admirable. I have not time to abstract them, but the negotiation is at an end for the present. I never thought any thing would come of it, for I did not believe Pitt serious; and, apparently, the Directory is of the same opinion, for it is on that principle they have framed their answer. My Lord Malmesbury may now go back, if he pleases. I am curious to know the result of Quantin's expedition, which, I presume, is the business of which Colonel Shee spoke to me indirectly two or three times. I had rather it had followed than preceded ours; for if they commit, as doubtless they will, great enormities, it may alienate people's minds against us, as they will make no distinction between one corps of French troops and another. The Spaniards are parading in the Mediterranean, to assist us in taking Corsica, after the English have evacuated it. This fashion of making war puts me in mind of the London Aldermen fox-hunting. I have worked this day like a horse, and I am as stupid to-night as a horse, and in wretched low spirits; every hour that passes is like an age to my impatience; I do not even sleep.

4. This morning, on the parade, I met Poiton, the General's first aid-de-camp, who whispered me that, by a vessel from Liverpool which was brought in yesterday, intelligence was received that the revolution was effected in Ireland; that the people were up in arms, and had seized the arsenal in Dublin and driven 10,000 English troops, being all that were in the country, back to England. I was not a little astonished at this piece of news, and ran off immediately to Mr. Shee, who confirmed it to me, adding, that they had found thirty thousand stand of arms in the arsenal; that the news was certain, and that the General had written off to the Directory last night for positive orders to sail, on the return of the courier, with what force was ready, without waiting for the remainder. He told me farther, that he expected every moment the captain of the prize, in order to examine him, in which he desired my assistance, as the General had written to Joyeuse, the Admiral, to have him sent up. All this I found very circumstantial; yet I felt I know not what presentiment, that it would turn out at least an exaggeration of the fact. On leaving Mr. Shee, I met the General himself, who embraced me after the manner of the French, kissing me on both cheeks, and wishing me joy of the

event. I returned shortly after to Colonel Shee, whom I acquainted with my doubts as to the extent of this report, and mentioned the anecdote of a Liverpool captain, who seeing the Dublin volunteers parade on this very day of the month, in the year 1779, with their cannon, and their Colonel, the Duke of Leinster at their head, immediately ran down to his ship in a fright, set sail for England, and, on his landing, swore before the Mayor of Liverpool, that all Ireland was up in arms, and that he had seen the Duke of Leinster proclaimed King, in College Green, which he himself certainly believed. Colonel Shee seemed a little taken back with this anecdote; however, he told me he had great hopes the present news was true, for that, to his knowledge, 15,000 stand of arms had been lately introduced into Ireland. I asked him was he sure of that, as I did not see where money could be got to purchase them, without communicating with so many people, as must infallibly lead to a discovery of the affair. He replied, they were purchased by one person, who was wealthy, whom he knew, and whom I knew, and that in time and place I should learn who he was. I said that satisfied me. In the meantime, I cannot form the least conjecture who this person is: 15,000 stand of arms would cost 30,000*l*, and I do not see amongst my acquaintance a man who is at once able and willing to advance such a sum. Well, no matter who it is. At last the author of our intelligence arrived, with two other seamen, taken on their way from Newfoundland, about the same time, eight or nine days ago. A council was immediately held, consisting of the General, the Admiral, Colonel Shee, and myself. Our informer said he was an American; that he sailed from Liverpool on a Wednesday; that, before his departure, news came by the packet that all Ireland was up for a Republic; that the Liberty Boys and the Weavers were up, and the Clearday Men, and that he had seen 10,000 English troops embark at Liverpool, three or four days before he left it, in order to quell the insurrection. This was the sum of his information; he added, that after they were taken by the French, they had fallen in with two fleets, one he judged might be of twenty sail, and in the other he counted twelve sail of line-of-battle ships, and that he heard there was a third fleet below again. I was not disappointed in finding the news turn out so different from what it was at first reported, supposing even what the fellow said to be true, which it certainly was not, for, in the first place, he set out with a lie, in saying he was an American, for he was a Scotchman, with a broad accent. He could not tell the day of the month that he sailed, nor the burthen of his vessel. The 10,000 troops he spoke of, turned out to be one regiment of Scotch, one regiment of Welch, and a regiment of Irish, who were embarked, as he said, in four large vessels and five or six brigs. Altogether, he lied and prevaricated so much that I do not pay the least attention to his story; so there is an end of the insurrection. I am, however, heartily glad of this event, for I hope it will produce positive orders from the Directory to sail immediately. Dined at head-quarters, in state, with the Admirals and several Captains of the fleet, and the staff of the army—a grand affair. This dinner is to manifest to the public that there is a perfect harmony between the land and sea service, which I am very sorry to see is far from being the case. Sate late at dinner, and after dinner retired to Colonel Shee's room with the General, the Admiral, General Debelle, and Colonel Shee. I did not come in till some time after the others, and on my entry found Hoche pressing Joyeuse, extremely, to be ready for the expedition, and Joyeuse starting every possible difficulty, particularly on the score of the transports. Hoche then said he would go with the men of war only, crowding as many men aboard as they could carry. Joyeuse then came down to five sail of the line and five frigates, the best sailors, who might, by dint of seamanship and quick sailing, escape from the English, who were, he said, in waiting for them off Cape Clear, and who had also *eclaireurs* off Ushant, as every morning the report was that two large ships and three frigates were seen there. Colonel Shee asked him how many men, for a short passage, he could stow on the ships he mentioned; he said 600 on each of the line-of-battle ships, and 300 on each of the frigates. That makes in all but 4,500 men. The General then said that his word was pledged to the Government and to his friends in Ireland; that the time was even elapsed for which he had engaged himself; that he would go in a single frigate, if the Admiral could give him no more, and he pressed him again and again in the strongest manner. Joyeuse still hung back, and I believe he was sorry, to judge by his manner, that he had spoken of even five ships of the line; at length he proposed (merely, as I think, to gain time,) to send out a vessel to reconnoitre, and bring positive intelligence of the state of the country; and another to learn the actual position of the English fleet; and, upon this proposal, the meeting broke up. I augur the worst possible event from any business in which the marine of France is concerned. Joyeuse wants to prevent our expedition, in order to get out to India, where there is more money to be made; and, in consequence, is throwing every difficulty in our way. Attempts are even made to set the soldiers and seamen by the ears, but the General is determined to shoot the very first who fight, upon the spot. There has been one duel already between Rapatelle,* an officer of the Etat Major, and a Lieutenant of the navy, in which the former was victorious, having wounded his adversary in two places. From all this I see, first, that if we arrive at all, which is at this moment very doubtful, we shall not arrive in force. No matter. With 5,000 men, our *Artillerie legere*, and

* The same who accompanied Moreau in 1813, and in whose arms he died. He was my father's Adjoint in this expedition.—*Editor.*

Hoche, I have no doubt of success. Would to Heaven we were, even with that force, on the Cave Hill, this fine morning! I would soon have my dear and unfortunate friends out of jeopardy. I see, likewise, that there is no mention whatsoever of the Spanish fleet. D—n them! They are now parading in the Mediterranean. To be sure, the folly of that is beyond all human endurance. The General told me last night, that, by this, there were five or six thousand French in England, playing "*le diable a quatre.*" I suppose he spoke of Quantin's expedition. This has been an eventful day. I have spent it with celebrated men, and who will make hereafter a figure in history, and yet, God knows, I am, at this moment, far from being satisfied. Hoche is behaving incomparably, but for the Admiral—Well, "what can't be cured, must be endured." Let us see what the the Directory will say to us.

5. At work at my pamphlet. I have no stomach to that business. I dine every day with the General, by his orders, which is the greater favour, as there are never more than five or six of us; himself, his brother-in-law, General Debelle, Marie Hoche, Col. Shee, Poiton, and myself.

6. Chatting with Col. Shee. I am in great hopes, from something he said, that we shall turn out Villaret Joyeuse, and get an admiral of our own choosing; perhaps, in that case, we may get out. I asked him whether, when the General said that his word was pledged to his friends in Ireland, he spoke really the fact, or said it merely to spur on the Ad-

miral. Mr. Shee assured me that Hoche had both seen and spoken with some of the leaders in Ireland.* So here are two plots running on at one and the same time, mine and theirs, whoever they are; no matter for that. I am not afraid of our jostling, for our object is, I see, precisely the same, and I am even the better pleased to have these invisible co-operators, as it divides the responsibility, and does not leave any thing resting on my single assertion. I asked Col. Shee, supposing we gave up the transports, how many men could we carry in the men-of-war? He said in twelve sail of the line, we could carry 6,000, and in ten frigates, we might have 2,500; so I see our armament is to be of that force. He added, however, that we must not give up the transports, as with them we could land with 20,000, which would settle the business without bloodshed. I answered, that if it were possible, it would undoubtedly be best, and referred him to my memorials for proof; that it was my own opinion, nevertheless, if the bringing transports would endanger the success of the entire business, I thought it best to secure the men-of-war, supposing they could carry but 5,000 men, instead of 8,500, which he had calculated, as with that force we should be able to fight it out. He replied he hoped we would have the transports also, and so it rested. For my part, under present circumstances, I would prefer the men-of-war with 6 or 7,000 men; and with

* Arthur O'Connor, for instance.—*Editor.*

that force to begin with, I should have no doubt of success; however, the business is in better hands. Colonel Shee then told me that the General wished to find somebody who would go directly to Ireland, as he had a safe American who would sail at a minute's warning, and also bring back the person who might go, and he was very desirous of intelligence of the state of the country at this moment. I mentioned Mc Sheehy, and he immediately went for the General, who came, and we agreed that if Mc Sheehy had no objection, he should be despatched to-morrow. I went immediately and found Mc Sheehy, to whom I opened the business, as from myself; and he agreed without difficulty to go, if the General desired it. I informed the General of his assent, at dinner, and he desired me to thank him in his name, and desire him to hold himself in readiness for to-morrow, which I did accordingly, and to-morrow we shall see what are his instructions. Mc Sheehy has behaved very well in this business.

7. The General has been out on a boating party all day, until six o'clock in the evening. On his return, he desired me to find Mc Sheehy, which I did accordingly, and he told him that he must sail that night, as every thing was ready, and gave him verbal instructions, which in my mind were very insufficient, and it is the first time I have had reason to find fault with Hoche. He desired him to go to such persons as I should name, and learn from them as much as he could, on the actual state of the country at this moment, the temper of the people,

the number and disposition of the troops, whether the French were expected or desired, and if so, in what part particularly. I asked him, was Mc Sheehy to tell them nothing in return? He said he must go into no particulars, but tell them, in general, that the dispositions of France were highly favourable to Ireland, and that both the Government and people were anxious for their emancipation. He then gave Mc Sheehy twenty louis, and we parted. I brought Mc Sheehy to my lodgings, and made him change his dress from head to foot, equipping him with shirts, boots, stockings, waistcoats, coat and cloak, all either Irish, or made after the Irish fashion. I then gave him the address of Oliver Bond and Richard Mc Cormick. I desired him to call on the former first, and tell him he came from me at Brest; and, to satisfy Bond, I desired him to say that when Jackson was seized, and Hamilton Rowan and Dr. Reynolds escaped, he advised me to do the same, and offered me money for that purpose, if I wanted it. For Mc Cormick, I desired him to tell him that a few days before I left Dublin for America, I took him alone into his garden, and acquainted him with my plan of pushing on, if possible, for France, and that I had also, about the middle of December last, written to him by my brother from Philadelphia, acquainting him with my progress. That, I think, will satisfy both that he has seen me. I desired him, in addition to the General's orders, to tell them that he had known me in Paris for some time; that I was now at Brest; that I had the rank of Adjutant General in the army of the Republic, and that I was in good repute with the General and Government. I desired him further to say that an expedition was in great forwardness at Brest; that I had read some months back, with great concern, an account in a London paper of the arrestation of John Keogh, and within these few days, a second account of the arrestation of Sam. Neilson, Russell, and my other friends at Belfast; that I would, on my part, move heaven and earth to procure their deliverance, and that I particularly recommended and entreated of them to profit of every possible delay which the forms of the law could give, in order to postpone their trial; and I desired him to press this particularly, as I had the strongest hopes that, in a short time, we should be there to rescue them; finally, I desired him to collect as many newspapers as he could, for three or four months back, particularly the Northern Star, which Bond would furnish him with, as being agent for that paper in Dublin. I then walked with him down to the quay, where I saw him join the Captain, who was in waiting, it being 8 o'clock, and a fine moonlight night. If they have good weather and fair wind, they may be easily in Dublin in four days; two days will suffice for Mc Sheehy's business, and four to return, makes ten; however, I will allow a fortnight, and attend the expiration of that term with the utmost impatience. In this business I chose Bond, from his honesty and his close connection with Belfast, and Mc Cormick for a thousand reasons, especially his being secretary to the Catholics, and his perfect knowledge of the state of the public mind in Dublin. I hope Mc Sheehy will acquit himself well; he has not much to do, and I encouraged him as much as I could. Here is a fortnight now dead loss! D—n it for me! I had like to forget an odd circumstance. The General desired Mc Sheehy to learn particularly who were the members in the new Parliament for county Derry. I observed, the new Parliament would not be called until next year. The General then said, "Well, learn who are the candidates, and for *Derry*, remember, not *Kerry*." I do not, for my part, understand this. In my mind, it is of mighty little importance, who are either members or candidates for one place or the other; perhaps Hoche has a mind to set up himself. Seriously, I do not see the drift of his question at all. Well, I will even leave it, as I always do in similar cases, to explain itself, for "*Quod supra nos, nil ad nos.*"

8. Grimel, the merchant who procured the American vessel for the General, tells me that Mc Sheehy was off last night by half past nine, so that business, so far, goes on well.

9. This day a young man was brought to head-quarters, who had been taken on board an American, bound from Limerick to Portugal. His name is Barry St. Leger; he is an Irishman by birth, but has been bred at Charleston, South Carolina, where his father is a man of property. He left Limerick the 14th October, and the account he gives is

perfectly satisfactory; a great part of it I know myself to be true. He says that every body in Ireland expects the French; that the gentry are making preparations to receive them; that every magistrate is raising twenty men, who are to preserve the peace in place of the militia, should these last be ordered to the coast; but he adds also, what I very well believe, that it is universally supposed the militia would join the French immediately, and that a great majority of them are even sworn to do so; that every day persons are arrested, and that just before his departure, he heard that J. Bagwell, M. P. for the county Tipperary, had been taken up, and a Lord *Dosforth*, as he pronounced it, in county Armagh.—For this last circumstance, he must be mistaken. There is Lord Gosford, Governor of that county; but he, I am sure, is far from being an enemy to the Government. I rather suppose he is at the head of the Peep-o'-Day Boys, and in that case, so much the worse for him, if we arrive. The result of this young man's account is, that Ireland is in a state of the highest fermentation, and that nothing but our presence is wanting to settle the affair at a blow. He spoke very rationally, and in consequence, I begged of the General to have him released from prison, so that he has now the liberty of the town. There is another remarkable circumstance. The officers of the navy are continually talking of the fleets that England has in the Channel, and that lying Scotch rascal, whom we examined the other day, said that he saw three (two with his eyes, and the third I suppose by the second sight). Now, St. Leger, in coming from Limerick to Brest, has necessarily sailed entirely round the South of Ireland, (the very station where the English fleet must necessarily be,) and he saw nothing. The privateer that took him, on the 22d October, sounded the night before under Cape Clear, and he saw nothing. The two English sailors whom we examined with the Scotchman, and who came at the same time, and nearly in the same track, saw nothing, and almost every day, prizes arrive and enter Brest, without meeting a single vessel. Now, if the English be in force in the Channel, how can all this possibly happen? And if they be not, what precious time are we losing here, and my poor friends in peril of their lives. Well, well! I am half mad with vexation at these eternal delays.

10. Saw the *Legion Noire* reviewed; about 1,800 men. They are the banditti intended for England, and sad blackguards they are. They put me strongly in mind of the Green-boys of Dublin.

12. Examined, at Mr. Shee's apartment, an American captain, who is only five or six days from London. He gives us no great encouragement. His account is, that Sir J. Jervis is off Ushant, as he heard, with eleven or twelve sail of the line; and he, himself, coming down Channel, fell in with three different little squadrons, two of four ships and one of three, which were standing to the westward under easy sail, and were going, as he supposed, to join Admiral Jervis. If that be so, they will keep us

here as long as they please, for, when united, they will make twenty-two sail of the line, and our expedition is but twelve. In that case, our only chance is to wait for the first hard gale of wind which may blow them off the coast, and then make a run for it.

13. Went, by order of the General, among the prisoners of war at Pontanezen, near Brest, and offered their liberty to as many as were willing to serve aboard the French fleet. Sixty accepted the offer, of whom fifty were Irish. I made them drink heartily before they left the prison, and they were mustered and sent aboard the same evening. I never saw the national character stronger marked than in the careless gaiety of these poor fellows. Half naked and half starved as I found them, the moment that they saw the wine before them, all their cares were forgotten; the instant I made the proposal, they accepted it without hesitation; the Englishmen balanced, and several of them asked, in the true style of their country, "What would I give them?" It is but justice to others of them to observe, that they said nothing should ever tempt them to fight against their King and country. I told them they were perfectly at liberty to make their choice, as I put no constraint upon any man. In the event, of about one hundred English, ten men and boys offered themselves; and of about sixty Irish, fifty as I have observed; not one Scotchman, though there were several in the prison. When I called for the wine, my English recruits begged for something to eat at the same time, which I ordered for them. Poor Pat

never thought of eating; but when his head was a little warm with the wine, he was very urgent to be permitted to go amongst the Englishmen, and flog those who refused to enter, which, of course, I prevented, though with some little difficulty. "*Arrah blood an' ounds, Captain dear, won't you let me have one knock at the blackguards?*" I thought myself on Ormond quay once more. Oh, if we once arrive safe on the other side, what soldiers we will make of our poor fellows! They all said they hoped I was going with them, wherever it was. I answered, that I did not desire one man to go where I was not ready to show the way, and they replied with three cheers. It is to be observed, that I never mentioned the object of the expedition; they entered the service merely from the adventurous spirit of the nation and their hatred of the English, without any idea that they had a chance of seeing Ireland again.

18. I have made no memorandums these four or five days, for several reasons, one of which was that I had nothing material to insert; and another, that I have been indisposed with a slight cold in my head, which has made me more stupid than ordinary. Yesterday, as all the world is beginning to embark and arrange themselves, I desired Colonel Shee to tell the General that my wish was to serve with the Grenadiers on the advanced guard, unless he had occasion for me about his person. Mr. Shee replied, that the offer did credit to my zeal, but he must see who commanded the grenadiers, that I might not find myself placed under an inferior officer. I answered,

that they were commanded by my friend Gatine, an Adjutant General; that, at any rate, my wish was to serve in the post of honour, where I could most improve myself, and that, as to the etiquette of rank, we could soon settle that, as I was willing to join as a volunteer. Mr. Shee promised to speak to the General, which he did last night. The General told him his intention was to keep me in his family, and that I should embark in the same vessel with himself (La Fraternité, a frigate); I am very glad of that, and I should be very glad also to serve with the grenadiers, but I cannot be in two places at once, "without I was a bird." Col. Shee told me the General was very well pleased with my offer. Barry St. Leger, the young fellow whom we examined a few days ago, has very spiritedly desired to come with us as a volunteer, and I have, by means of Mr. Shee, fixed him in the General's own guards; they are a most noble company of grenadiers, commanded by Capt. Bloom, (a German, as indeed are likewise almost all the privates,) and have distinguished themselves singularly in La Vendée. Bloom has promised me to take care of St. Leger, and I hope he will do well. If I had Mat and Arthur here now, I could fix them both. Well, if we get safe to the other side, I shall perhaps be able to do it there. We will see. To-day I took occasion to disburthen my mind on the state of our expedition to Col. Shee. I told him the Spanish fleet was, as we knew officially, in Toulon, where, it was true, they might annoy the English commerce in the Mediterranean, which was the only good they could do, now that Corsica was restored to the Republic; that, instead of idling in this manner at Toulon, they ought to be in Brest waters, which would secure the success of our expedition beyond the possibility of miscarriage, and, by that means, cripple the naval power of England for ever; that, it was true, the French and Spanish navies have never co-operated long, successfully; nevertheless, this did not apply to our case, as our operation was simple, and required only a superiority in the Channel for one week, which would settle the affair as well as a century; that, divided as our naval force was now, and watched as we were by the English, it was hardly possible to suppose that we should reach Ireland without falling in with their fleet; and that, if they were superior, or even equal in numbers, I gave it as my opinion that they would *infallibly* beat us: that all this risk might be prevented, and the matter reduced to absolute certainty, by the co-operation of the Spanish fleet, and that, consequently, their absence proved to me either that the French Government had little influence in Spain, or that the Spanish Government was infatuated to a degree I could not conceive, and at the reflection of which I lost all temper. That England would never forgive them the insult of escorting Richery out of Cadiz; that the consequence of this mode of making war, in detail, would be that England would beat us first, and then send a fleet into the Mediterranean, which would beat them soundly, and, in this manner, destroy us separately. Finally, I said, as I hoped, in the worst event, they would not take us all, such as escaped should push on for Ireland, and make a desperate plunge into the country. To all this long harangue, which I have detailed here very immethodically, Colonel Shee had nothing comfortable or substantial to offer in reply. After heartily damning the Spaniards, in which I was not behind him, he said, he had reason to hope we might still get over. I said I hoped it as much as he, but hardly expected it. He then said, we must not suffer ourselves to see things in too gloomy a light. I replied, that my manner of seeing things should not influence my conduct, or prevent my doing my duty in the action, if we were forced into one, but that, at the same time, I thought it right to give him my opinion at full length before our departure. The conversation then ended with a second volley of imprecations from both of us, on the inconceivable madness of the Spanish Government. If they do not pay dear for this system which they have adopted, there is not a drop of water in Brest harbour. Oh, if we had their twenty-five sail of the line, now idling in Toulon, (d—n them sempiternally!) with Richery's four or five, who have got safe into Rochefort, and our own twelve, that would make forty sail of the line, and then, indeed, our business would be a party of pleasure. But now, see how it is; the English, from the best information which we can collect, are watching us, with twenty-five sail of the line, in three divisions; it is hardly possible but we must fall in with one of them, which will delay us, in spite of us, until the others come up, and then they will flog us completely, and give the finishing blow to the French marine! and, as for the Spaniards, afterwards, they will give them no trouble. How terrible to think of all this! and, at the same time, how simply and easily it might be prevented, and our common adversary humbled for ever. Well, what I cannot remedy, it does not signify my grieving at; but, if I were King of Spain for six weeks, I think I would settle this affair. D—n them! I think I could spend this whole night in cursing them. One good thing, however, has happened within these five days: Villaret Joyeuse, the Admiral, is cashiered, and we have got another in his place. Joyeuse was giving, underhand, all possible impediment to our expedition. He made the Directory believe we were at a stand for want of seamen, and, since his departure, we have found out that there are more than enough; and, as the chiefs always give the *ton*, we find already a better spirit rising in the marine. But, what can we do with twelve ships?

22. I have been hard at work these three or four days, recruiting and writing. I have picked up about twenty very stout hands, which makes eighty in all, and cost me five louis, which the Republic owes me. I have finished my address to the Irish people, one to the militia, and one to the Irish seamen. They are all in the printer's hands, and, to

speak honestly, not one of them is any great things. I think I have lost the little facility in writing that I once had. The fact is, my mind is so anxious about our business, that I cannot write. I do not sleep at nights. The General has been ill with a severe pain in his bowels these three days; we were afraid at first he was poisoned, but it proved to be a false alarm: he was at the Comédie last night.

23. I cannot imagine what delays us now, unless it be waiting for Richery, who is said to be coming up from Rochefort. Though I have the strongest apprehensions we shall be intercepted by the English, still I wish we were at sea. There is nothing so terrible to me as suspense; and besides, the lives of my poor friends in Ireland are in extreme peril. God send we may be in time to save them, but I much fear it. Well, let me not think of that. If we fall in with the English, we must fight them at close quarters, and crowd our tops, poops, and quarter-decks with musketry. It is our only chance, but against superior numbers even this will not do. Those infernal Spaniards! They will pay dear for their folly; but what satisfaction is that to us? I was thinking last night of my poor little family till I was as melancholy as a cat. God knows whether we shall ever meet again. If I reach Ireland in safety, and any thing befalls me after, I have not the least doubt my country will take care of them, and my boys will find a father in every good Irishman; but if I should happen to be killed at sea, and the expedition should not succeed, I dread to think

on what may become of them. It is terrible! I rely on the goodness of Providence, which has often interposed to save us,—on the courage and prudence of my wife, and on the friendship of my brother, to protect them. My darling babies! I doat on them. I feel the tears gush into my eyes whenever I think of them. I repeat to myself a thousand times the last words I heard from their innocent little mouths. God Almighty bless and protect them! I must leave this subject.—I have taken a little boy, whom I found among the prisoners of war, as my servant. He is so young that he will not be of much use to me; but he was an orphan, and half naked. He was born in Dorsetshire, and his father was an Irish Quartermaster of dragoons. He is a natural son. I have rigged him out handsomely; and if he brushes my coat and takes care of my portmanteau, with the baggage, it is all I require. His name is William White.

25. Colonel Shee tells me to-day that he has it from Bruix, one of our Admirals, that we shall sail in six days. Would to God it were to-night! There is a fine steady breeze, blowing right out of the harbour. In six days it will be the first December.

The first of January I left Sandy Hook. The first of February I arrived at Havre: and, if we arrive safe at our destination, it is possible that on the first January next, I may be once more in Dublin. *Quanquam, oh!* General Clarke set off nine days ago, at a minute's warning, for Vienna, by way of Italy. That looks like peace with the Emperor;

but, thank God, I see no signs as yet of peace with England; on the contrary, Lord Malmesbury and my old lover, Charles De la Croix, are keeping up a very snappish correspondence, which the Directory publishes regularly. I have been hard at work half this day translating orders and instructions for Colonel Tate, an American officer, who offered his services, and to whom the General has given the rank of *Chef de Brigade*, and 1050 men of the *Legion Noire*, in order to go on a bucaniering party into England. Excepting some little errors in the locality, which, after all, may seem errors to me from my own ignorance, the instructions are incomparably well drawn; they are done, or at least corrected, by the General himself, and if Tate be a dashing fellow, with military talents, he may play the devil in England, before he is caught. His object is Liverpool, and I have some reason to think that the scheme has resulted from a conversation which I had a few days since with Colonel Shee, wherein I told him that if we were once settled in Ireland, I thought we might make a piratical visit in that quarter,—and, in fact, I wish it were we that should have the credit and profit of it. I should like, for example, to pay a visit to Liverpool myself, with some of the gentlemen from Ormond quay, though I must say the citizens of the *Legion Noire* are very little behind my countrymen, either in appearance or morality, which last has been prodigiously cultivated by three or four campaigns in Bretagne and La Vendée. A thousand of these desperadoes, in their black jackets, will edify John Bull exceedingly, if they get safe into Lancashire.

Every day I walk for an hour alone on the ramparts, and look down on the fleet which rides below. There are about fifty sail of ships of war, of all sizes, of which, perhaps, twenty are of the line. It is a most magnificent *coup d'œil*, but my satisfaction is always damped by two reflections: first, that my wife and our darling little babies, one of whom I have never seen, and perhaps may never see, are most probably at this moment on the ocean, exposed to all the perils of a winter passage. The remembrance of the vessel which was wrecked last February, at Havre, I may say before my eyes, and of the unfortunate French-woman, who was drowned, with her two infants, shoots across my mind a thousand times a day. And I lie awake, regularly, half the night, listening to the wind, every puff of which makes me shudder. Oh, my babies! my babies! God Almighty will, I hope, preserve you and your mother, whatever becomes of me. I doat upon you, you little things. Well, I am at work for you here, and I am going to fight for you, and, if all goes well, there will not be on earth so happy a being as I shall be, when I have you all once more in my arms. My other reflection, which also torments me, is the uncertainty of our arrival in Ireland, on account of the English fleet. Sometimes I wish for a storm of five or six days, to blow them off Brest; but then I think of my poor little family, and check myself directly. At other times, I wish to wait for those infernal blockheads, the Spaniards, if we could get them up from Toulon; but then I think of my friends who are now in prison, and whose lives may be sacrificed by our delay. Altogether, I scarcely know what to wish, and my mind is ten times more troubled and tempestuous than the ocean on which I am gazing. Fortunately, the measure does not depend upon me. I wait my orders like every one else, and, of course, I have no responsibility, but for my own personal conduct; and I hope I shall acquit myself at least without discredit. If I could command events, and were sure that Russell and the others could afford the time, what I would wish would be to delay the expedition until the arrival of the Spanish fleet, which I would instantly order up from Toulon; that operation might require, at soonest, six weeks, and our success would then be certain. But what signifies my tormenting myself about what I cannot remedy? The Spaniards won't come, and be d——d to them, and we shall be beaten first, and they after, and the liberty of Ireland, the lives of my best friends, and all my own expectations, will be sacrificed! Well, I do not care! My mind is getting hardened now, just as it was in Ireland, when I expected every day to be seized and hanged.

26. To-day, by the General's orders, I have made a fair copy of Col. Tate's instructions, with some alterations, from the rough draft of yesterday, particularly with regard to his first destination, which is now fixed to be Bristol. If he arrives safe, it will be very possible to carry it by a *coup de main*, in which case he is to burn it to the ground. I cannot but observe here, that I transcribed with the greatest

sang froid, the orders to reduce to ashes the third city of the British dominions, in which there is, perhaps, property to the amount of £5,000,000. But such a thing is war! The British burned without mercy in America; they endeavoured to starve 25,000,000 of souls in France; and, above all, they are keeping, at this moment, my country in slavery, my friends in prison, myself in exile. It is these considerations which steel me against the sense of horrors which I should otherwise shudder to think of. Yet I cannot but remark what misery the execution of the orders which I have transcribed and assisted in framing may produce, and how quietly Col. Shee and myself sat by the fire discussing how we might do the greatest possible mischief to the unfortunate wretches on whom our plans are intended to operate. Well, they may thank themselves; they are accomplices with their execrable Government, which has shown us the way in all these direful extremities, and there is not a man of them but would willingly exterminate both the French and Irish. Yet once again! The conflagration of such a city as Bristol! It is no slight affair: thousands and thousands of families, if the attempt succeeds, will be reduced to beggary! I cannot help it! If it must be, it must, and I will never blame the French for any degree of misery which they may inflict on the people of England. I do not think my morality or feeling is much improved by my promotion to the rank of Adjutant General. The truth is, I hate the very name of England; I hated her before my exile; I hate her since, and I will hate her always.

29. I have no memorandums to make that are worth a farthing; always writing and writing. I declare I am tired of my life, or, as the French say, *je m'ennuye de ma personne.* Yesterday, at dinner, the General was mentioning several deputies who, having been in the army before the Revolution, had profited of the advantages which their situation in the legislative body gave them, to promote themselves to high rank; and he added, " Well, there is Carnot, of whom they say so much, both good and evil. He was a Captain of Engineers before the Revolution, and he is a Captain of Engineers yet." It is highly honourable to Carnot.—Apropos of the General. There is a charming little aristocrat, with whom he is perfectly well, although all her relations are Chouans. In all the hurry of our expedition, he contrived to steal off, and spend two days and nights with her. Mr. Shee and I were in a mortal fright at his absence, for, knowing where he was gone, and on what business, we apprehended some of the Chouans might waylay and assassinate him. When they attempted it in the middle of Rennes, they might well execute it in a by-road, and if any thing happened to Hoche, there is an end of our business. It was very indiscreet in him, but God forbid I should be the man to accuse him, for I have been buffeted myself so often by the foul fiend, that it would be rather indecent in me to censure another, (Sings.) " 'Tis woman that

seduces all mankind." I do not think, however, (but God knows,) that under the present circumstances I would have gone a catterwauling for two days among the Chouans. Hoche has all the right in the world (and why not?) to do as he pleases with his own life, but not to knock our expedition in the head. I was very angry with him, which, as I never did a foolish thing myself in my life for the sake of a woman, was but reasonable.—It is all nonsense; for they do what they please with us, and it is in vain talking about it; however, I hope he may stop here whilst he is well.—I learn to-day that the Etat Major, myself included, does not embark in the same frigate with the General, and I am sorry for it, for divers excellent reasons. I should be very glad to have gone with him, but if I cannot, I must submit, though it vexes me confoundedly; however, I will say nothing of it, but keep my mind to myself, though I think the General ought to have taken me with him. I do not know now on what vessel I am to embark, and I am plaguy angry, if any body cared. Well, I must take to my old remedy, patience; it is not the first mortification I have met with in the business, and it certainly will not be the last. How if I should be taken by the English, for example? D—n it for me; but I can't help myself, so let the matter rest. To-day the officers of the Etat Major gave a grand dinner to four or five of the Captains f the fleet; we were about twenty at dinner, and very pleasant.

All the Captains seemed satisfied that, with the number of soldiers we have embarked, we shall be a match for the English ; but what they fear is to meet them on their return, after landing us. Would to God we were once landed; what difference does it make to the French? they may as well be blocked up in Cork as in Brest harbour; and, if we get safe, that is the worst which can happen to them. I cannot express the anxiety of my mind on this circumstance, but I believe it will be easily conceived that nothing can exceed it. Only think how deep a stake I have engaged, when one of the *last* considerations is my *life*. Once for all: I dislike mortally the idea of a sea-fight; for in the first place I expect we shall be worsted, and perhaps the expedition frustrated; and in the next place, I may be killed, and then my poor little babies will reap no advantage from my death, whereas if it was my lot to fall after our landing, I should have the consolation of being assured that my country would provide for them, and I can safely say that their future establishment is an object which occupies my mind at this important moment much more than any concern about my personal safety: not that I wish at all to make the idle rhodomontade of saying that I am indifferent about my life; very far from it: I wish to live and to be happy with my dearest love, and my friends, and to educate my darling babies; but if it should happen that I should fall in the contest, at least I wish that it should be in my own country. If I have my wish, I may say, in the words of my poor friend Russell,

> "If we meet with a privateer, or lofty man of war,
> We will not stay to wrangle, nor to chatter, nor to jar."

Poor fellow! His situation at this moment is one of my principal concerns. I trust in God we shall, after all, be yet in time, in spite of the English fleet, to rescue him and the rest of his fellow-sufferers. Well, let me change the subject. Mr. Shee showed me to-day the proclamation of the General, which is a great favour, as the second in command, General Grouchy, has not seen it yet. I need not detail the contents here, as I will take care to have a copy amongst my papers.* It is very incorrectly printed, which is a pity, and I found here and there some expressions which put me in mind of my old friend, Captain Poitier.

30. To-day Colonel Shee, who has been alarmed with some symptoms of the gout, to which he is a martyr, resolved to go on board the Fraternité, whilst he is yet able to move. He is near sixty, and with a broken constitution, as may well be supposed after thirty-six years of service,—yet he is as bold and eager in the business as if he were but five-and-twenty. I went aboard with him, and dined with the Admiral Morard de Galles, (who has succeeded Villaret Joyeuse,) and two other Admirals, Bouvet and Bruix. When I was about to leave him, I took

* This paper, as the landing was not effected, ceases to be of interest.

him aside for an instant, and told him that as we embarked on different vessels, I might, perhaps, not have another occasion to speak to him, and therefore I availed myself of this to observe, that, as it was likely we might fall in with the English, and of course have an action, I had to entreat of him, in case any thing should happen to me, and that he got safe to Ireland, to exert himself in behalf of my family, by making such a report of my services as he thought just, and as they merited. He assured me, in case of any accident, I might rely upon his zeal and friendship, and he requested, at the same time, that if a similar circumstance befel him, I would render his family the same service, which I assured him, with great truth and sincerity, I would not fail to do, and so we parted. I have a sincere regard for him, and the very best opinion both of his zeal and talents. Well, now that he is aboard, there is one step gained. It seems we (the Etat Major) embark aboard the *Indomptable*, an 80-gun ship, and the finest vessel in the squadron ; that is some comfort, however. A young Frenchman, Adjoint to Crublier, an Adjutant General, applied to me today to be my Adjoint—for Crublier, who was a great favourite with the General, has fallen, I apprehend, into some disgrace, and does not come with us. This young man's name is Dorsan, but I do not know him, and he does not speak English, so I told him I left all that to the General, and would speak to him about it, which I did accordingly, mentioning my own opinion, on which he left me at liberty to do as I pleased; so I will not take him. At night, Rapatelle, another young lad, told me he was nominated to be my Adjoint, and I like him a great deal better than the other; so I told him I would take to-night to consider of it, and let him know to-morrow the result. I like Rapatelle well enough, but he does not speak English neither, so I shall still be in a difficulty. If I had Matt here now, I could fix him in a minute, Captain and Adjoint. Well, if I get to Ireland, I must have aids-de-camp there, and then I will see what can be done. I am now Adjutant General, and, of course, I will not be put back, if I am not promoted, in my own country. Called in the evening at Grimel's, where all the Generals generally go to play cards and trictrac. General Grouchy, who is second in command, got hold of me, and we had a long talk about Ireland. He begged me to call to-morrow on the Printer of the Marine, and see if I could not find any thing geographical relating to that country, and, at all events, to call on him to-morrow at eleven, which I promised to do. General Cherin, *Chef de l'Etat Major*, told me to-night that I shall embark the day after to-morrow. So I came up stairs, and packed up my trunk, and I am now at single anchor, and this business will, at last, be brought to a decision. I have been in France exactly ten months to-night. Well, it has not been time misspent. We will see now in a few days what will come of it. At all events, I have done my best.

DECEMBER, 1796.

2. Bantry Bay Expedition—on board. Received my order to embark on board the Indomptable, of 80 guns, Capt. Bedout. Packed up directly, and wrote a long letter of directions to my wife,* in which I detailed every thing I thought necessary, and advised her, in case of any thing happening me, to return to America, and settle in Georgia or Carolina. I enclosed this under cover to Madgett, and, at two o'clock, arrived on board. We have a most magnificent vessel. To-day I command the troops, as the highest in rank; but to-morrow I shall be superseded, I expect, by the arrival of the whole Etat Major. I hope in God we are about to set out at last. I see, by a proclamation of the Lord Lieutenant, that the north of Ireland is in a flame; if we arrive safe, we shall not do much to *extinguish* it. Well, we shall see.

4. As it is now pretty certain that the English are in force off Ushant to the number of sixteen ships of the line and ten frigates, it seems hardly possible that we can make our way to Ireland without falling in with them; and, as even the most successful action must be attended with damages in our masts and rigging,—so that, even if victorious, (which I do not expect,) we may yet be prevented from proceeding on the expedition, considering the stormy season of the year, I have been devising a scheme which, I think, in the present state of things

* See Appendix.

in Ireland, can hardly fail of success. It is this: That three, or, at most, four sail of the fastest going ships should take advantage of the first favourable moment, (as a dark night and a strong gale from the north-east,) and slip out with as many troops as they can carry, including at least a company of the *Artillerie legere*, steering such a course as, though somewhat longer, should be most out of the way of the English fleet; that they should proceed round the coast of Ireland, keeping a good offing for fear of accidents, and land the men in the North, as near Belfast as possible. If we could land 2,000 men in this manner, with as many stand of arms as we could carry beside, I have no doubt but in a week we would have possession of the entire North of Ireland, and we could certainly maintain ourselves there for a considerable time, against all the force which could be sent against us; the consequence of which would be, 1st, That the whole South would be disfurnished of troops, which would, of course, be sent against us; and I also am almost certain that the British fleet would directly quit its station off Brest, where it has been now cruizing ten weeks, according to our accounts, as thinking that the mischief was already done, and that they were watching the stable when the steed was stolen; in which case, the main embarkation might immediately set off, and, landing in the South, put the enemy between two fires, and so settle the business almost without a blow. If this scheme be adopted, it is absolutely necessary that no mortal should hear of it but Morard de Galles, Hoche, and Col. Shee. The reason of my wishing not to lose an instant, and, likewise, to make the attempt with 2,000 men, contrary to the opinion I have given elsewhere in these memorandums, is, that I have seen articles within these few days in the French papers, including, among others, a proclamation of the Lord Lieutenant of Ireland, dated November 9th, by which I see that the insurrection is ready every instant to explode in the North, and that they have gone so far as to break open the magazine in Belfast and take by force ten barrels of powder. I dread, in consequence, their committing themselves before they are properly supported. If we were there, with almost any number of troops, provided we had arms and artillery, I should have no doubt of success. After deliberating these two days, which I have spent on board, and examining my scheme in all possible lights, I went to-day at two o'clock on board the Fraternité to state it to Col. Shee, who is confined to his hammock with the gout, as he expected. I explained it to him at length, and he seemed to relish it a good deal, and, as the General dines to-day on board with the Admiral, he promised he would mention it to him, and have his opinion. I should have observed, that I begged, in case it was adopted, to be permitted to go with the first embarkation. We then fixed to meet to-morrow, when he will let me know the result, and so we parted. He is a noble old fellow, at this time of life, and with that terrible malady, the gout, to expose himself with so much spirit as he manifests on this occasion. Apropos of spirit! my captain, citizen

Bedout, has fought like a lion in this war; he commanded the Tigre, which was taken by the English on the 27th June, 1795, and was wounded in four places before he struck to three three-deckers, which were on him at once. I mentioned to Col. Shee that, if my plan was adopted, I thought he should be named Commodore, which is his rank, especially as the Indomptable is a remarkably fast-sailing ship, and he seems heartily bent on our expedition, which is far from being the case with most of the marine. I must now wait till to-morrow, and, I hope in God, my scheme may be adopted, as I am sure it is our best course under the circumstances. I fear it, however; the more so, as, if it succeeds, it will undoubtedly lessen, in some degree, the eclat which would attend Hoche, if he were the first to land;—but I hope he is above such weakness as to sacrifice the success of the measure to his own reputation. We shall see. To-day the Admiral has given orders that after to-morrow no one will be allowed to go on shore, which is what the French call "*lever la planche*." The General sleeps aboard that night, so every thing now seems to "give dreadful note of preparation." I wish, however, my scheme may be adopted. I am exceedingly well off aboard, and Captain Bedout is remarkably civil and attentive; he is a Canadian, and speaks very good English.

8. The uniformity of my life, at anchor in the roads of Brest, does not furnish much matter for observation. I saw Mr. Shee yesterday, who is still in bed with the gout. He tells me that he spoke of my plan to the General, who said at once it was impos-

sible, and that he durst not take on himself the responsibility it would induce. His reasons are good. First, if our little squadron fell in with the enemy, we must, to a moral certainty, be taken. Next, if we got even clear, and that the remainder of the squadron fell in with the enemy and was beaten, which would, most probably, be the case, the whole fault would be laid on him, as having weakened the main force by the detachment; and, lastly, that from the state of our preparations, being victualled and furnished but for a short period, we must speedily sail, *coute qui coute*, so that the advantage I proposed in drawing off the English fleet would be useless, as we could not afford to wait the time necessary to suffer that circumstance to operate. This last is the best of his reasons, but I remain firmly of opinion that my scheme is, under all the circumstances, infinitely the best. If we were able to go in force, *à la bonne heure;* but as we are not, and as I have no expectation but that we shall be well beaten, and the whole expedition miscarry, I look upon my proposal as the best means to save so much out of the fire, and perhaps, with the force I speak of, we might succeed, even though the main body might miscarry. I say *perhaps*, though in fact I do not doubt it. As to the General's objection on the score of the hazard, undoubtedly there is great hazard; but, in the first place, I look upon the actual hazard to be much greater on his plan; inasmuch as four ships have an infinitely better chance of escaping the vigilance of Admiral Gardner, (who is watching us without with eighteen sail of the line,) than fifteen, of which our squadron consists (not including frigates on either side); and as to fighting, they will beat us as surely with our fifteen sail as with four, and the consequence will be, of course, the failure of our expedition. In the next place, as to the hazard, there is no possibility of executing so great a measure as that which we have in hand, without infinite hazard; and, as we are undoubtedly the weaker at sea, we are to choose those measures which offer us the least risk, and in that respect I have no doubt of the superiority of my plan. However, it is decided otherwise, and I must submit. Our force is of fifteen sail of the line, ten frigates, and seven or eight transports; that makes upwards of thirty sail—a force which can never escape the vigilance of the English, unless there should come a furious storm for two or three days, without remission, which would blow them up the Channel. And even so, by all I can see of our preparations, we are not ready to avail ourselves instantly of that circumstance, so that, in all probability, if a storm were to come to our relief, the enemy would have time to be back again to block us up, or, at least, to intercept us; besides, the elements seem to conspire against us. In the memory of man there has not been known, at Brest, so long a succession of fine weather at this season; and we have had now three weeks of favourable winds, of which, for obvious reasons, we have not been able to profit. Of course, when this weather changes, we must look for the wind in the opposite quarter, which is the prevailing wind in winter, and will block us up as effectually as the English. I am absolutely weary of my life. If the wind sets in to the westward, and continues there for any time, as is highly probable, the troops will get sickly and impatient, and what is worse, our provisions of all sorts will be exhausted; and so we shall be obliged to give up the expedition from downright poverty. Want of money is the great stumbling-block of the French Government. These are sad croaking memorandums, but, unfortunately, they are all too true.—Those abominable Spaniards! Well, they will lose their American colonies; that is some revenge, and Mr. Pitt may profit now of my scheme for the Sandwich Islands. I have now done with my proposition, which is, undoubtedly, liable to the objections made by the General: when there is only a choice of difficulties, what is the scheme which is without them!—We had a grand exercise to-day of great guns and small arms, and both troops and seamen went through their business with great activity. I should like to see the same thing on board an English man-of-war. We did not fire, but two other ships (The Nestor and the Eole,) did; it was a beautiful sight.—I saw Mr. Shee for half an hour this evening; the gout had got into his left hand, and he was dreadfully out of spirits; I think for the first time. He tells me the General thinks the marine are still trifling with him, on purpose to gain time, until the bad weather sets in; when, if it holds any time, as is highly probable, our stores of all sorts will be exhausted, and the business must be given up from pure necessity. This I apprehended myself. He also says that Bruix, a rear-admiral, who is charged with the execution of the naval department, and in whose zeal the General had great confidence, has cooled exceedingly within these few days, so much, that to-day, when the General called on him, and was pressing him on our affair, Bruix, instead of answering him, was dandling one of his little children. The excuse now is, that we are waiting for some charts or plans, which must be washed in water-colours, and will take two days; a worthy subject for delay in the present stage of the business! I begin more and more to think that we shall not get out in force. It is true the General may order us out at his peril, but it is a dreadful responsibility to take on himself; for if any accident happened to us, he would have the whole marine on his back, and, by what I see of these gentlemen, I think they would rather that all should fail, than their prophecy not be verified; and, by-the-by, it is always in their power to make us miscarry, so I think it can hardly be expected that Hoche will go those lengths. A man's own scheme is always lovely in his eyes; but I cannot help wishing that we were out safe with even four ships, according to my plan, and it seems not impossible but we may come to that at length. Our whole business now, not to speak of the English, turns on a change of the wind. In the mean time, the troops keep up their health and spirits, and are, at this moment, as well as possible, and every evening dancing on the quarter-deck. Would to God we were all in Ireland, but when will that be? We are thirteen thousand five hundred strong.

11. Went ashore yesterday to take my leave of Brest. Four of our frigates stood out of the Goulet that evening, so here are, at least, symptoms of movement. This morning went on board the Fraternité to see Colonel Shee, and, to my infinite satisfaction, saw Richery in the offing, standing in for the road, where he anchored safely in an hour after. He brings with him five ships of the line and two frigates, of which we shall have three of the line, and the crews of the two others, which are foul. It is a reinforcement of the most infinite consequence to us, and perhaps may enable us to force our way out at last. I am astonished how Richery, with his squadron, has been able to elude the vigilance of the English; he must be an excellent officer, and I presume we shall have him, of course, with us. The General comes aboard to-day, and it is not impossible, if the weather is favourable, but we may sail to-night. God send, whatever may be the event! for I am tired of this suspense.

12. The Etat Major came aboard last night; we are seven in the great cabin, including a lady in boy's clothes, the wife of a Commissaire, one Ragoneau. By what I see, we have a regular army of Commissaries, who are going to Ireland to make their fortunes. If we arrive safe, I think I will keep my eye a little upon these gentlemen. In consequence of the arrival of Richery, our squadron will be augmented with

two if not three ships, and the army with 1,700 men, which, with 13,400 already on board, will make 15,100 — a force more than sufficient for our purpose, if, as I am always obliged to add, we have the good fortune to reach our destination in safety.

14. To-day the signal is made to heave short and be ready to put to sea; the report is, we shall make sail at four o'clock. I am truly rejoiced at it. "I do agnize a natural and prompt alacrity." Called on my friend Shee, who is better; he is able to-day to write a little. Recommended my wife and family to his friendship and protection, in case of any thing happening to me. He promised me heartily to exert himself in their behalf; and I have no doubt he will keep his word; so I have done all that is now in my power to do. Saw Richery this morning, which I am glad of, as I like to observe the countenances of men who have distinguished themselves. *Evening.*—Having nothing better to employ me, I amuse myself scribbling these foolish memorandums. In the first place, I must remark, the infinite power of female society over our minds, which I see every moment exemplified in the effect which the presence of Madame Ragoneau has on our manners; not that she has any claim to respect, other than as she is a woman, for she is not very handsome, she has no talents, and (between friends) she was originally a *fille de joye* at Paris. Yet we are all attentive and studious to please her; and I am glad, in short, she is aboard, as I am satisfied she humanizes us not a little. General Watrin paid us a visit this

evening, with the band of his regiment, and I went down into the great cabin, where all the officers mess, and where the music was playing. I was delighted with the effect it seemed to have on them. The cabin was ceiled with the firelocks intended for the expedition, the candlesticks were bayonets stuck in the table, the officers were in their jackets and *bonnets de police*—some playing cards, others singing to the music, others conversing—and all in the highest spirits—once again I was delighted with the scene. At lengh Watrin and his band went off, and, as it was a beautiful moonlight night, the effect of the music on the water, diminishing as they receded from our vessel, was delicious. We are still at anchor—bad! bad!

15. At 11 o'clock this morning the signal was made to heave short, and I believe we are now going to sail in downright earnest. There is a signal also at the point for four sail of enemies in the offing; it is most delicious weather, and the sun is as warm and as bright as in the month of May—"I hope," as Lord George Brilliant says, "he may not shine *through* somebody presently." We are all in high spirits, and the troops are as gay as if they were going to a ball: with our 15,000, or more correctly, 13,975 men, I would not have the least doubt of our beating 30,000 of such as will be opposed to us; that is to say, if we reach our destination. The signal is now flying to get under weigh, so, one way or other, the affair will be at last brought to a decision, and God knows how sincerely I rejoice at it.

The wind is right aft. Huzza! At one we got under weigh, and stood out of the Goulet until three, when we cast anchor by signal in the Bay de Camaret, having made about three leagues. Our ship, I think, would beat the whole fleet; we passed, with easy sale, a frigate, *La Surveillante*, under her top-gallant sails, and nothing was able to come near us. We are now riding at single anchor, and I hope we shall set off to-morrow.

16. At twelve to-day the *Fougueux*, a 74, ran foul of us, but we parted without any damage on either side. When we were as close as possible, with the muzzles of our guns touching, I clearly saw the impossibility of boarding a ship of the line, from the distance between the gunwale of the one and the other. At two, a signal to get under weigh. At half after two, made sail, the wind still favourable, but slack. Settled our *role de combat*. Chasseloup and Vaudray, with their Adjoints, are on the lower deck; Simon and I, with ours, on the main deck; Cherin, I believe, with the Captain. I had rather be on the quarter-deck or poop, where I could see something; however, I said nothing. We are all in full regimentals, with our laced hats, &c. which is to encourage the troops. I believe our ship will behave well; but it will be still better if we reserve our valour for the shore. At all events, two or three days must, I think, settle the affair.

17. Last night passed through the Raz, a most dangerous and difficult pass, wherein we were within an inch of running on a sunken rock, where we must

every soul have inevitably perished. I knew nothing about it, for my part, till this morning, and I am glad of it. Captain Bedout told me he had rather stand three such engagements as that wherein he was taken, than pass again through the Raz at night, so it seems, the affair was serious; if we had struck, we should have gone to pieces in a quarter of an hour, as the tide runs furiously at the rate of not less than ten knots an hour. Ours is the first squadron that has passed through the Raz, which even single ships avoid, unless in case of necessity. This morning, to my infinite mortification and anxiety, we are but eighteen sail in company, instead of forty-three which is our number. We conjecture, however, that the remaining twenty-five have made their way through the Yroise, and that we shall see them to-morrow morning; at the same time, we much fear that some of our companions have perished in that infernal Raz. We have nothing for it now but to wait till to-morrow. *At night.*—This day has passed without any event; the weather moderate, the wind favourable, and our eighteen sail pretty well together. Two of the Admirals and the General are with the absent: God send they may have escaped the Raz. Rear Admiral Bouvet, and General Grouchy, second in command, are with us. I believe there is a rendezvous fixed in case of separation, so to-morrow we shall see. We run on an average five or six knots an hour, course W. N.W.

18. At nine this morning, a fog so thick that we cannot see a ship's length before us. "Hazy weather, master Noah;" d—n it, we may be, for

aught I know, within a quarter of a mile of our missing ships, without knowing it; it is true we may also, by the same means, miss the English, so i may be as well for good as evil, and I count firmly upon the fortune of the Republic. How, after all, if we were not to join our companions? What will Grouchy and Bouvet determine? We are enough to make the attempt, but we must then steer for the North of Ireland. If it rested with me, I would not hesitate a moment, and, as it is, I will certainly propose it, if I can find an opening.

> "If we are marked to die, we are enough
> To do our country loss; and if to live,
> The fewer men, the greater share of honour."

This confounded fog continues without interruption. *At night.*—Foggy all day, and no appearance of our comrades. I asked General Cherin what we should do in case they did not rejoin us. He said that he supposed General Grouchy would take the command with the troops we had with us, which, on examination, we found to amount to about 6,500 men. I need not say that I supported this idea with all my might. The Captain has opened a packet containing instructions for his conduct in case of separation, which order him to cruize for five days off Mizen Head, and, at the end of that time, proceed to the mouth of the Shannon, where he is to remain three more; at the end of which time, if he does not see the fleet, or receive further orders by a frigate, he is to make the best of his way back to Brest.

But we must see, in that case, whether Bouvet and Grouchy may not take on themselves to land the troops. I am glad to see that Cherin is bent on that plan, notwithstanding the interference of his Aid-de-camp Fairin, who put in his word, I thought, impertinently enough.

19. This morning, at eight, signal of a fleet in the offing; *Branlebas general;* rose directly and made my toilet, so now I am ready, *ou pour les Anglais, ou pour les Anglaises.* I see about a dozen sail, but whether they are friends or enemies, God knows. It is a stark calm, so that we do not move an inch even with our studding sails: but here we lie rolling like so many logs on the water. It is most inconceivably provoking; two frigates that were ordered to reconnoitre, have not advanced one hundred yards in an hour, with all their canvass out; it is now nine o'clock; — a calm, and in the middle of December! Well, it cannot last long. If this fleet prove to be our comrades, it will be famous news; if it be the English, let them come; we will do our best, and I think the Indomptable will not be the worst-fought ship in the squadron. This calm! this calm! it is most terribly vexatious. At half-past ten we floated near enough to recognize the signals, and, to my infinite satisfaction, the strange fleet proves to be our comrades, so now *nous en sommes quittes pour la peur*, as the French say; counted sixteen sail, including the Admiral's frigate: so the General is safe. The wind, which favoured us thus far, is chopped about, and is now right in our

teeth; that is provoking enough. If we had a fair wind, we should be in Bantry Bay to-morrow morning. At half-past one, hailed by a lugger, which informed us of the loss of the Seduisant, a seventy-four of our squadron, the first night of our departure, with five hundred and fifty men of the ninety-fourth demi-brigade, of whom she saved thirty-three. It happened near the same spot where we were in such imminent danger. I was mistaken above in saying that the Fraternité was with the squadron which joined us; it is Admiral Neilly's frigate, and we know nothing of the other, which circumstance has thrown us all into the greatest anxiety. Admiral Morard de Galles, General Hoche, General Debelle, and Colonel Shee, are aboard the Fraternité, and God knows what is become of them. The wind, too, continues against us, and, altogether, I am in terrible low-spirits. How if these d——d English should catch us at last, after having gone on successfully thus far? Our force, on leaving Brest water, was as follows: Indomptable, 80 guns; Nestor, Cassard, Droits de l'Homme, Tourville, Eole, Fougueux, Mucius, Redoutable, Patriote, Pluton, Constitution, Trajan, Watigny, Pegaze, Revolution, and the unfortunate Seduisant of 74 guns (17 sail of the line); La Cocarde, Bravoure, Immortalité, Bellone, Coquille, Romaine, Sirene, Impatiente, Surveillante, Charente, Resolue, Tartare, and Fraternité, of 36 guns (13 frigates); Scevola and Fidele *armés en flutes;* Mutine, Renard, Atalante, Voltigeur, and Affronteur, corvettes; and Nicodeme, Justine, Ville d'Orient, Suffren, Experiment, and Alegre, transports; making, in all, 43 sail. Of these there are missing, this day, at three o'clock, the Nestor and Seduisant, of 74; the Fraternité, Cocarde, and Romaine frigates, the Mutine and Voltigeur, corvettes; and three others, transports.

20. Last night, in moderate weather, we contrived to separate again; and this morning, at eight o'clock, we are but fifteen sail in company, with a foul wind, and hazy. I am in horrible ill humour, and it is no wonder. We shall lie beating about here, within thirty leagues of Cape Clear, until the English come and catch us, which will be truly agreeable! Let me not think: I amuse myself at night, when the rest are at cards, walking alone in the gallery, and singing the airs that my poor love used to be fond of:

> "The wandering tar, that not for years has pressed
> The widow'd partner of his day of rest,
> On the cold deck, far from her arms remov'd,
> Still hums the ditty that his Susan lov'd."

I feel now the truth of these beautiful lines. Well, hang sorrow! At *ten*, several sail in sight to windward; I suppose they are our stray sheep. It is scandalous to part company twice in four days in such moderate weather as we have had; but sea affairs, I see, are not our forte. Captain Bedout is a seaman, which, I fancy, is more than can be said for nine-tenths of his *confreres*.

21. Last night, just at sunset, signal for seven sail in the offing; all in high spirits, in hopes

that it is our comrades; stark calm all the fore part of the night; at length a breeze sprung up, and this morning, at daybreak, we are under Cape Clear, distant about four leagues; so I have, at all events, once more seen my country; but the pleasure I should otherwise feel at this is totally destroyed by the absence of the General, who has not joined us, and of whom we know nothing. The sails we saw last night have disappeared, and we are all in uncertainty. It is most delicious weather, with a favourable wind, and every thing, in short, that we can desire, except our absent comrades. At the moment I write this, we are under easy sail, within three leagues, at most, of the coast, so that I can discover here and there patches of snow on the mountains. What if the General should not join us! If we cruise here five days, according to our instructions, the English will be upon us, and then all is over. We are thirty-five sail in company, and seven or eight absent. Is that such a separation of our force, as, under all the circumstances, will warrant our following the letter of our orders, to the certain failure of the expedition? If Grouchy and Bouvet be men of spirit and decision, they will land immediately, and trust to their success for justification. If they be not, and if this day passes without our seeing the General, I much fear the game is up. I am in undescribable anxiety, and Cherin, who commands aboard, is a poor creature, to whom it is vain to speak; not but I believe he is brave enough, but he has a little mind. There cannot be imagined a situation more provokingly tantalizing than mine at this moment, within view, almost within reach of my native land, and uncertain whether I shall ever set my foot on it. We are now (nine o'clock,) at the rendezvous appointed; stood in for the coast till twelve, when we were near enough to toss a biscuit ashore; at twelve tacked and stood out again, so now we have begun our cruise of five days in all its forms, and shall, in obedience to the letter of our instructions, ruin the expedition, and destroy the remnant of the French navy, with a precision and punctuality which will be truly edifying! We opened Bantry Bay, and, in all my life, rage never entered so deeply into my heart as when we turned our backs on the coast. I sounded Cherin as to what Grouchy might do; but he turned the discourse; he is *Taata Enos.** Simon is entirely of my opinion, and so is Captain Bedout; but what does that signify? At half after one, the Atalante, one of our missing corvettes, hove in sight, so now again we are in hopes to see the General. Oh, if he were in Grouchy's place, he would not hesitate one moment. Continue making short boards; the wind foul.

22. This morning, at eight, we have neared Bantry Bay considerably, but the fleet is terribly scattered; no news of the Fraternité; I believe it is the first instance of an Admiral in a clean frigate, with moderate weather, and moon-light nights, parting

* See Cook's Voyages.

company with his fleet. Captain Grammont, our first Lieutenant, told me his opinion is that she is either taken or lost, and, in either event, it is a terrible blow to us. All rests now upon Grouchy, and I hope he may turn out well ; he has a glorious game in his hands, if he has spirits and talent to play it. If he succeeds, it will immortalize him. I do not at all like the countenance of the Etat Major in this crisis. When they speak of the expedition, it is in a style of despondency, and, when they are not speaking of it, they are playing cards and laughing ; they are every one of them brave as to their persons, but I see nothing of that spirit of enterprise, combined with a steady resolution, which our present situation demands. They stared at me this morning when I said that Grouchy was the man in the whole army who had least reason to regret the absence of the General, and began to talk of responsibility and difficulties, as if any great enterprise was without responsibility and difficulties. I was burning with rage ; however I said nothing, and will say nothing until I get ashore, if ever I am so happy as to arrive there. We are gaining the Bay by slow degrees, with a head-wind at east, where it has hung these five weeks. To-night we hope, if nothing extraordinary happens, to cast anchor in the mouth of the Bay, and work up to-morrow morning ; these delays are dreadful to my impatience. I am now so near the shore that I can see distinctly two old castles, yet I am utterly uncertain whether I shall ever set foot on it. According to appearances,

Bouvet and Grouchy are resolved to proceed; that is a great point gained, however. Two o'clock:—we have been tacking ever since eight this morning, and I am sure we have not gained one hundred yards; the wind is right a-head, and the fleet dispersed, several being far to leeward. I have been looking over the schedule of our arms, artillery, and ammunition; we are well provided; we have 41,160 stand of arms, twenty pieces of field artillery, and nine of siege, including mortars and howitzers; 61,200 barrels of powder, 7,000,000 musket cartridges, and 700,000 flints, besides an infinite variety of articles belonging to the train; but we have neither sabres nor pistols for the cavalry; however, we have nearly three regiments of hussars embarked, so that we can dispense with them. Messieurs of the Etat Major continue in the horrors; I find Simon the stoutest of them, and Fairin, Cherin's aid-de-camp, the worst; he puts me in mind of David in the Rivals,—"But I am fighting Bob, and d—n it, I won't be afraid." I continue very discreetly to say little or nothing, as my situation just now is rather a delicate one; if we were once ashore, and things turn out to my mind, I shall soon be out of my trammels, and, perhaps, in that respect, I may be better off with Grouchy than with Hoche. If the people act with spirit, as I hope they will, it is no matter who is General, and, if they do not, all the talents of Hoche would not save us; so it comes to the same thing at last. At half-past six, cast anchor off Beer Island, being still four leagues from our landing-place; at work with General Cherin, writing and translating proclamations, &c. all our printed papers, including my two pamphlets, being on board the Fraternité, which is pleasant!

23. Last night it blew a heavy gale from the eastward with snow, so that the mountains are covered this morning, which will render our bivouacs extremely amusing. It is to be observed, that of the thirty-two points of the compass, the E. is precisely the most unfavourable to us. In consequence, we are this morning separated for the fourth time; sixteen sail, including nine or ten of the line, with Bouvet and Grouchy, are at anchor with us, and about twenty are blown to sea; luckily the gale set from the shore, so I am in hopes no mischief will ensue. The wind is still high, and, as usual, right a-head; and I dread a visit from the English, and altogether I am in great uneasiness. Oh! that we were once ashore, let what might ensue after; I am sick to the very soul of this suspense. It is curious to see how things are managed in this "best of all possible worlds." We are here, sixteen sail, great and small, scattered up and down in a noble bay, and so dispersed that there are not two together in any spot, save in one instance, and there they are now *so close*, that if it blows to-night as it did last night, they will inevitably run foul of each other, unless one of them prefers driving on shore. We lie in this disorder, expecting a visit from the English every hour, without taking a single step for our defence, even to the common one of having a frigate in the harbour's

mouth, to give us notice of their approach: to judge by appearances, we have less to dread here than in Brest water, for when we were there, we had four corvettes stationed off the *goulet*, besides the signal posts. I confess this degree of security passes my comprehension. The day has passed without the appearance of one vessel, friend or enemy; the wind rather more moderate, but still a-head. To-night, on examining the returns with Waudré, Chef d'Etat Major of the Artillery, I find our means so reduced by the absence of the missing, that I think it hardly possible to make an attempt here, with any prospect of success; in consequence, I took Cherin into the Captain's room, and told him frankly my opinion of our actual state, and that I thought it our duty, since we must look upon the main object as now unattainable, (unless the whole of our friends returned to-morrow, and the English gave us our own time, which was hardly to be expected,) to see what could be best done for the honour and interest of the Republic, with the force which remained in our hands; and I proposed to him to give me the *Legion des Francs*, a company of the *Artillerie legere*, and as many officers as desired to come volunteers in the expedition, with what arms and stores remained, (which are now reduced, by our separation, to four field pieces, 20,000 firelocks at most, 1,000 lb. of powder, and 3,000,000 cartridges,) and to land us in Sligo Bay, and let us make the best of our way; if we succeeded, the Republic would gain infinitely in reputation and interest; and if we failed, the loss would be trifling, as the expense was already incurred, and as for the legion, he knew what kind of desperadoes it was composed of, and for what purpose—consequently, in the worst event, the Republic would be well rid of them; finally, I added that though I asked command, it was on the supposition that none of the Generals would risk their reputation on such a desperate enterprise, and that if another was found, I would be content to go as a simple volunteer. This was the outline of my proposal, which I pressed on him with such arguments as occurred to me, concluding by observing that, as a foreigner in the French service, my situation was a delicate one; if I were simply an officer, I would obey in silence the orders of my superiors; but having, from my connexions in Ireland, obtained the confidence of the Directory so far as to induce them to appoint me to the rank of *Chef de Brigade*, and of General Hoche, who had nominated me Adjutant General, I thought it my duty, both to France and Ireland, to speak on this occasion, and that I only offered my plan as a *pis aller*, in case nothing better suggested itself. Cherin answered that I did very right to give my opinion, and that as he expected a council of war would be called to-morrow, he would bring me with him, and I should have an opportunity to press it. The discourse rested there, and to-morrow we shall see more, if we we are not agreeably surprised, early in the morning, by a visit from the English, which is highly probable. I am now so near the shore, that I can in a manner touch the sides of Bantry Bay with my right and left hand; yet God knows whether I shall ever tread again on Irish ground. There is one thing which I am surprised at, which is the extreme *sang froid* with which I view the coast. I thought I should have been violently affected, yet I look at it as if it were the coast of Japan; I do not, however, love my country the less for not having romantic feelings with regard to her. Another thing, we are now three days in Bantry Bay; if we do not land immediately, the enemy will collect a superior force, and perhaps repay us our victory of Quiberon. In an enterprise like ours, every thing depends upon the promptitude and audacity of our first movements, and we are here, I am sorry to say it, most pitifully languid. It is mortifying, but that is too poor a word; I could tear my flesh with rage and vexation, but that advances nothing, and so I hold my tongue in general, and devour my melancholy as I can. To come so near, and then to fail, if we are to fail!—and every one aboard seems now to have given up all hopes.

24. This morning the whole Etat Major has been miraculously converted, and it was agreed, in full council, that General Cherin, Colonel Waudré, (Chef d'Etat Major of the Artillery,) and myself, should go aboard the Immortalité, and press General Grouchy, in the strongest manner, to proceed on the expedition, with the ruins of our scattered army. Accòrdingly we made a signal to speak with the Admiral, and in about an hour we were aboard. I must do Grouchy the justice to say,

that the moment we gave our opinion in favour of proceeding, he took his part decidedly, and like a man of spirit: he instantly set about preparing the *ordre de bataille*, and we finished it without delay. We are not more than 6,500 strong, but they are tried soldiers, who have seen fire, and I have the strongest hopes that, after all, we shall bring our enterprise to a glorious termination. It is a bold attempt, and truly original. All the time we were preparing the *ordre de bataille*, we were laughing most immoderately at the poverty of our means, and I believe, under the circumstances, it was the merriest council of war that was ever held; but "*Des Chevaliers Francais tel est le caractère.*" Grouchy, the commander in chief, never had so few men under his orders since he was Adjutant General; Waudré, who is Lieutenant-colonel, finds himself now at the head of the artillery, which is a furious park, consisting of one piece of eight, one of four, and two six-inch howitzers; when he was a Captain, he never commanded fewer than ten pieces, but now that he is in fact General of the Artillery, he prefers taking the field with four. He is a gallant fellow, and offered, on my proposal last night, to remain with me and command his company, in case General Grouchy had agreed to the proposal I made to Cherin. It is altogether an enterprise truly *unique;* we have not one guinea; we have not a tent; we have not a horse to draw our four pieces of artillery; the General in chief marches on foot; we leave all our baggage behind us; we have nothing but the arms in our hands, the clothes on our backs, and a good courage ; but these are sufficient. With all these original circumstances, such as I believe never were found united in an expedition of such magnitude as that we are about to attempt, we are all as gay as larks. I never saw the French character better exemplified than in this morning's business. Well, at last I believe we are about to disembark ; God knows how I long for it. But this infernal easterly wind continues without remorse, and though we have been under weigh three or four hours, and made I believe three hundred tacks, we do not seem to my eyes to have gained one hundred yards in a straight line. One hour and a half of good wind would carry us up, and perhaps we may be yet two days. I learn from a pilot whom I found aboard the Admiral, that my friend Hutchins lives within two miles of Bantry, and is now at home, so perhaps I may see him to-morrow ; I wonder what kind of a meeting we shall have ! When I saw him last he was a right good fellow ; but so many changes happen in twenty months ! At all events, he will be, I dare say, not a little surprised to see me with a blue coat on my back, and a national cockade in my hat. At six, cast anchor, having gained I think not less than fifty yards, to speak within bounds. The rapidity of our progress is the more amazing, when it is considered that we have been not much more than eight hours in covering that space of ground, and besides, we have a cool refreshing breeze from the east, which is truly delightful.

Well, time and tide wait for no man. I may now say with the Probationary Odes, "sometimes it blows, sometimes it freezes, just as it pleases." Well, let it blow and be hanged! I do not wonder to-night at Xerxes whipping the sea; for I find myself pretty much in the mood to commit some such rational action. To return to our expedition; the more I think of it, the more I find it amusing; as Johnson says, "the negative catalogue of our means is extremely copious." In addition to what I have mentioned already, we have no horses for our cavalry. Huzza! I apprehend we are to-night 6,000 of the most careless fellows in Europe, for every body is in the most extravagant spirits on the eve of an enterprise which, considering our means, would make many people serious. I never liked the French half so well as to-night, and I can scarcely persuade myself that the loungers of the Boulevards and the soldiers I see about me are of the same hemisphere. To judge the French rightly, or at least to see the bright part of their character, you must see them not in Paris, but in the camp. It is in the armies that the Republic exists. My enemy, the wind, seems just now, at eight o'clock, to relent a little, so we may reach Bantry by to-morrow. The enemy has now had four days to recover from his panic, and prepare to receive us; so much the worse, but I do not mind it. We purpose to make a race for Cork, as if the devil were in our bodies, and when we are fairly there, we will stop for a day or two to take breath, and look about us. From Bantry to

Cork is about forty-five miles, which, with all our efforts, will take us three days, and I suppose we may have a brush by the way, but I think we are able to deal with any force that can, at a week's notice, be brought against us. We are not the best-dressed body of men in Europe. I think I have seen a Captain of the Guards in St. James's Park, who would burn for as much as one of our demi-brigades. "There's not a rag of feather in our army; good argument, I hope, we will not fly." *Apropos*, of that quotation. It is inconceivable how well that most inconceivable of all writers, Shakspeare, has hit off the French character in his play of Henry V. I have been struck with it fifty times this evening; yet it is highly probable he never saw a French officer in his life. Well, I have worked hard to-day, not to speak of my boating party aboard the Admiral, against wind and tide, and in a rough sea. I have written and copied fifteen letters, besides these memorandums; pretty well for one day. I think I will stop here. I have but one observation to add: there is not, I will venture to say, one grenadier in the Compagnie Bloom, that will not sleep to-night in his hammock more contentedly than the Archbishop of Dublin in a down bed. I presume our arrival has put several respectable characters in no small fuss, but time will show more of that.

25. These memorandums are a strange mixture. Sometimes I am in preposterously high spirits, and at other times I am as dejected, according to the posture of our affairs. Last night I had the strongest

expectations that to-day we should debark, but at two this morning I was awakened by the wind. I rose immediately, and, wrapping myself in my great coat, walked for an hour in the gallery, devoured by the most gloomy reflections. The wind continues right a-head, so that it is absolutely impossible to work up to the landing-place, and God knows when it will change. The same wind is exactly favourable to bring the English upon us, and these cruel delays give the enemy time to assemble his entire force in this neighbourhood, and perhaps (it is, unfortunately, more than perhaps) by his superiority in numbers, in cavalry, in artillery, in money, in provisions, in short in every thing we want, to crush us, supposing we are even able to effectuate a landing at last, at the same time that the fleet will be caught as in a trap. Had we been able to land the first day and march directly to Cork, we should have infallibly carried it by a *coup de main;* and then we should have had a footing in the country, but as it is—if we are taken, my fate will not be a mild one; the best I can expect is to be shot as an *emigré rentré,* unless I have the good fortune to be killed in the action; for most assuredly if the enemy will have us, he must fight for us. Perhaps I may be reserved for a trial, for the sake of striking terror into others, in which case I shall be hanged as a traitor, and embowelled, &c. As to the embowelling, "*je m'en fiche;*" if ever they hang me, they are welcome to embowel me if they please. These are pleasant prospects! Nothing on earth could sustain me now, but the consciousness that I am engaged in a just and righteous cause. For my family, I have, by a desperate effort, surmounted my natural feelings so far, that I do not think of them at this moment. This day, at twelve, the wind blows a gale, still from the east, and our situation is now as critical as possible, for it is morally certain that this day or to-morrow on the morning, the English fleet will be in the harbour's mouth, and then adieu to every thing! In this desperate state of affairs, I proposed to Cherin to sally out with all our forces, to mount to the Shannon, and, disembarking the troops, make a forced march to Limerick, which is probably unguarded, the garrison being, I am pretty certain, on its march to oppose us here; to pass the river at Limerick, and, by forced marches, push to the North. I detailed all this on a paper which I will keep, and showed it to Captain Bedout, and all the Generals on board, Cherin, Simon, and Chasseloup. They all agreed as to the advantages of the plan, but after settling it, we find it impossible to communicate with the General and Admiral, who are in the Immortalité, nearly two leagues ahead, and the wind is now so high and foul, and the sea so rough, that no boat can live; so all communication is impracticable, and to-morrow morning it will, most probably, be too late; and on this circumstance perhaps the fate of the expedition and the liberty of Ireland depends. I cannot conceive for what reason the two commanders-in-chief are shut up together in a frigate. Surely they should be on board the flagship. But that is not the first misfortune resulting from this arrangement. Had General Hoche remained, as he ought, on board the Indomptable, with his Etat Major, he would not have been separated and taken by the English, as he most probably is; nor should we be in the difficulties we now find ourselves in, and which most probably to-morrow will render insurmountable. Well, it does not signify complaining. Our first capital error was in setting sail too late from the bay of Camaret, by which means we were obliged to pass the Raz in the night, which caused the loss of the Seduisant, the separation of the fleet, the capture of the General, and above all, the loss of time resulting from all this, and which is never to be recovered. Our second error was in losing an entire day in cruizing off Bantry bay, when we might have entered and effected a landing with thirty-five sail, which would have secured every thing; and now our third error is, the having our Commander-in-Chief separated from the Etat Major, which renders all communication utterly impossible. My prospects at this hour are as gloomy as possible. I see nothing before me, unless a miracle be wrought in our favour, but the ruin of the expedition, the slavery of my country, and my own destruction. Well, if I am to fall, at least I will sell my life as dear as individual resistance can make it. So now I have made up my mind. I have a "merry Christmas" of it to-day.

26. Last night, at half after six o'clock, in a heavy gale of wind still from the east, we were surprised by the Admiral's frigate running under our

quarter, and hailing the Indomptable, with orders to cut our cable and put to sea instantly; the frigate then pursued her course, leaving us all in the utmost astonishment. Our first idea was that it might be an English frigate, lurking in the bottom of the bay, which took advantage of the storm and darkness of the night to make her escape, and wished to separate our squadron by this stratagem; for it seems utterly incredible, that an Admiral should cut and run in this manner, without any previous signal of any kind to warn the fleet, and that the first notice we should have of his intention should be his hailing us in this extraordinary manner, with such unexpected and peremptory orders. After a short consultation with his officers, (considering the storm, the darkness of the night, that we have two anchors out, and only one spare one in the hold,) Captain Bedout resolved to wait, at all events, till to-morrow morning, in order to ascertain whether it was really the Admiral who hailed us. The morning is now come, the gale continues, and the fog is so thick that we cannot see a ship's length a-head; so here we lie in the utmost uncertainty and anxiety. In all probability we are now left without Admiral or General; if so, Cherin will command the troops, and Bedout the fleet; but, at all events, there is an end of the expedition. Certainly we have been persecuted by a strange fatality, from the very night of our departure to this hour. We have lost two commanders-in-chief; of four admirals not one remains; we have lost one ship of the line, that we know of, and probably many others of which we know nothing; we have been now six days in Bantry Bay, within five hundred yards of the shore, without being able to effect a landing; we have been dispersed four times in four days; and, at this moment, of forty-three sail, of which the expedition consisted, we can muster of all sizes but fourteen. There only wants our falling in with the English to complete our destruction; and to judge of the future by the past, there is every probability that will not be wanting. All our hopes are now reduced to get back in safety to Brest, and I believe we shall set sail for that port the instant the weather will permit. I confess, myself, I now look on the expedition as impracticable. The enemy has had seven days to prepare for us, and three, or perhaps four days more before we could arrive at Cork; and we are now too much reduced, in all respects, to make the attempt with any prospect of success—so, all is over! It is hard, after having forced my way thus far, to be obliged to turn back; but it is my fate, and I must submit. Notwithstanding all our blunders, it is the dreadful stormy weather and easterly winds, which have been blowing furiously, and without intermission, since we made Bantry Bay, that have ruined us. Well, England has not had such an escape since the Spanish Armada, and that expedition, like ours, was defeated by the weather; the elements fight against us, and courage is here of no avail. Well, let me think no more about it; it is lost, and let it go! I am now a Frenchman, and must regulate my future plans accordingly. I hope the Directory will not dismiss me the service for this unhappy failure, in which, certainly, I have nothing personally to reproach myself with; and, in that case, I shall be rich enough to live as a peasant. If God Almighty sends me my dearest love and darling babies in safety, I will buy or rent a little spot, and have done with the world for ever. I shall neither be great, nor famous, nor powerful, but I may be happy. God knows whether I shall ever reach France myself; and, in case of the contrary, what will become of my family? It is horrible to me to think of. Oh! my life and soul, my darling babies, shall I ever see you again? This infernal wind continues without intermission, and now that all is lost, I am as eager to get back to France as I was to come to Ireland.

27. Yesterday several vessels, including the Indomptable, dragged their anchors several times, and it was with great difficulty they rode out the gale. At two o'clock, the Revolution, a seventy-four, made signal that she could hold no longer, and, in consequence of the Commodore's permission, who now commands our little squadron, cut her only cable and put to sea. In the night, the Patriote and Pluton, of 74 each, were forced to put to sea, with the Nicomede *flute*, so that this morning we are reduced to seven sail of the line and one frigate. Any attempt here is now desperate, but I still think, if we were debarked at the mouth of the Shannon, we might yet recover all. At ten o'clock, the Commo-

dore made signal to get under weigh, which was delayed by one of the ships, which required an hour to get ready. This hour we availed ourselves of to hold a council of war, at which were present, Generals Cherin, Harty, and Humbert, who came from their ships for that purpose; Adjutant-Generals Simon, Chasseloup, and myself; Lieut.-Col. Waudré, commanding the artillery, and Favory, Captain of Engineers, together with Commodore Bedout, who was invited to assist; General Harty, as senior officer, being President. It was agreed that our force being now reduced to 4,168 men, our artillery to two four-pounders, our ammunition to 1,500,000 cartridges and 500 rounds for the artillery, with 500 pounds of powder—this part of the country being utterly wild and savage, furnishing neither provisions nor horses, and especially as the enemy, having *seven* days' notice, together with *three* more which it would require to reach Cork, supposing we even met with no obstacle, had time more than enough to assemble his forces in numbers sufficient to crush our little army; considering, moreover, that this province is the only one of the four which has testified no disposition to revolt; that it is the most remote from the party which is ready for insurrection; and, finally, Captain Bedout having communicated his instructions, which are, to mount as high as the Shannon, and cruize there five days;—it was unanimously agreed to quit Bantry Bay directly, and proceed for the mouth of the Shannon, in hopes to rejoin some of our scattered companions; and when we are there, we will determine, according to the means in our hands, what part we shall take. I am the more content with this determination, as it is substantially the same with the paper which I read to General Cherin and the rest the day before yesterday. The wind, at last, has come round to the southward, and the signal is now flying to get under weigh. At half after four, there being every appearance of a stormy night, three vessels cut their cables and put to sea. The Indomptable, having with great difficulty weighed one anchor, we were forced, at length, to cut the cable of the other, and make the best of our way out of the bay, being followed by the whole of our little squadron, now reduced to ten sail, of which seven are of the line, one frigate, and two corvettes or luggers.

28. Last night it blew a perfect hurricane. At one this morning, a dreadful sea took the ship in the quarter, and stove in the quarter-gallery and one of the dead-lights in the great cabin, which was instantly filled with water to the depth of three feet. The cots of the officers were almost all torn down, and themselves and their trunks floated about the cabin. For my part, I had just fallen asleep when wakened by the shock, of which I at first did not comprehend the meaning; but hearing the water distinctly rolling in the cabin beneath me, and seeing two or three of the officers mount in their shirts, as wet as if they had risen from the bottom of the sea, I concluded instantly that the ship had struck and was filling with water, and that she would sink

directly. As the movements of the mind are as quick as lightning in such perilous moments, it is impossible to describe the infinity of ideas which shot across my mind in an instant. As I knew all notion of saving my life was vain, in such a stormy sea, I took my part instantly, and lay down in my hammock, expecting every instant to go to the bottom; but I was soon relieved by the appearance of one of the officers, Baudin, who explained to us the accident. I can safely say that I had perfect command of myself during the few terrible minutes which I passed in this situation, and was not, I believe, more afraid than any of those about me. I resigned myself to my fate, which I verily thought was inevitable, and I could have died like a man. Immediately after this blow, the wind abated, and, at daylight, having run nine knots an hour under one jib only, during the hurricane, we found ourselves at the rendezvous, having parted company with three ships of the line and the frigate, which makes our *sixth* separation. The frigate Coquille joined us in the course of the day, which we spent standing off and on the shore, without being joined by any of our missing companions.

29. At four this morning, the Commodore made the signal to steer for France: so, there is an end of our expedition for the present; perhaps for ever. I spent all yesterday in my hammock, partly through sea-sickness, and much more through vexation. At ten, we made prize of an unfortunate brig, bound from Lisbon to Cork, laden with salt, which we sank.

31. On our way to Brest. It will be well supposed I am in no great humour to make memorandums.* This is the last day of the year 1796, which has been a very remarkable one in my history.

January 1, 1797. At eight this morning made the island of Ushant, and at twelve opened the *Goulet*. We arrive seven sail: the Indomptable, of 80; the Watigny, Cassard, and Eole, 74; the Coquille, 36; the Atalante, 20, and the Vautour lugger of 14. We left Brest forty-three sail, of which seventeen were of the line. I am utterly astonished that we did not see a single English ship of war, going nor coming back. They must have taken their measures very ill not to intercept us, but perhaps they have picked up some of our missing ships. Well, this evening will explain all, and we shall see now what is become of our four Admirals, and of our two Generals-in-Chief.

THE PERIOD OF GENERAL TONE'S ATTACHMENT TO THE ARMY OF SAMBRE ET MEUSE.

JANUARY, 1797.

31. It is exactly one month to-day, since I wrote a line by way of memorandum. It will be well sup-

* Amidst all the agitation of my father's mind, during the ill-fated and tantalizing expedition of Bantry Bay, he was aware that his wife and three infant children, whom he had left at Princeton, in New Jersey, on his departure from America, were, amidst the storms of that wintry season, on their way to rejoin him.

posed I had no great inclination, nor in fact have I had much to say. On our arrival at Brest, after a day or two, there was a little intrigue set on foot against General Grouchy, with a view to lessen the merit of his services, in consequence of which he determined to send me to Paris with his despatches for the Directory and Minister of War. Simon was joined with me in commission, and Fairin was also despatched by Cherin, who is at the head of this cabal. Grouchy desired me to state fairly what I thought of his conduct, during our stay in Bantry

The feelings of the most affectionate of husbands and of fathers in such a situation can be better conceived than expressed. In fact, embarked on an American vessel for Hamburgh, we almost crossed him in the British Channel, in the last days of December; and, after a tedious and rough passage of two months, my mother, with her infant family, landed at the mouth of the frozen Elbe, and proceeded to Hamburgh in an open post waggon. In that commercial city, devoted to the British interest, the first news she received was that of the failure of the expedition, embellished with a thousand exaggerations. Her anxiety may well be conceived: obliged to conceal it, as well as her name, her only consolation was, that she did not hear that of Tone mentioned. Already in weak and shattered health, she was seized with a nervous fever, and remained in the most cruel perplexity, amongst strangers, whose very language she did not understand. She wrote instantly to Paris, addressing her letter to Mr. Madgett, and the answer to this letter, which came in due time, was the first news she received of her husband's safety.

Written under such circumstances of disappointment and anxiety, this portion of my father's journal, which extends to the period when we joined him in Holland, was not kept with the same regularity as the former.—*Editor.*

Bay, to the Government; and I was not a little pleased with this proof of his good opinion. We set off on the fifth of January, at night, and arrived, without accident, at Paris on the 12th. We went immediately to the Minister of War, and delivered our letters; we saw him but for an instant; thence we went to the Directory, where we were introduced and had an audience for above half an hour, at which all the Directors assisted. They were of opinion on that day, from the latest account, that Hoche had effected a landing with that part of the army which had been separated off Bantry Bay, and in consequence we expected orders immediately to return to Brest.

Several days elapsed in this manner, waiting continually for news of the General, until at length, on the 15th, he arrived with the Revolution, 74, at La Rochelle; so that put at once an end to my expectations of any thing further being attempted, at least for the present. About the 21st, the General arrived at Paris, and I had the consolation to learn from his aid-de-camp, Poitou, that my friend Mr. Shee was safe, and in tolerable health. He had suffered dreadfully from the gout, never having quitted his bed during the whole voyage of a month, but once, for a quarter of an hour. The morning after his arrival, I saw the General for five minutes. He received me very favourably, and asked me particularly about M'Sheehy's expedition, which I detailed to him, and, by his orders, gave him an abstract in writing next morning. He asked me what I was doing at Paris. I told him I was sent by General Grouchy, with his despatches, and that I was waiting farther orders. Four or five days after, the General was named to the command of the army of *Sambre et Meuse*, which was decisive with regard to our expedition. I began now to think of my own situation and of that of my family, of whom it is at length surely time to speak. On my arrival at Paris, I found a letter from my wife at Madgett's dated at Hamburgh, and informing me of her safe arrival there, about the 20th of December, with my sister and the children, my brother having decided to settle in America. The transports of joy I felt at the news of her arrival were most dreadfully corrected by the account she gave me of her health, which threw me into the most terrible alarms. I wrote to her instantly, to remain at Hamburgh until further orders, and by no means to think of exposing herself, in her present weak state, and our dear little babies, to a journey from Hamburgh, in this dreadful season, a great part of the road being through a wild country, where there is no better accommodation for travelling than open waggons. In my wife's letter there is an account of an affair relative to my sister. A person who came over in the same ship, a young Swiss merchant, just beginning the world, with little or no property, thought proper to fall in love with her; in consequence, I received by the same conveyance which brought my wife's letter, one from him, informing me of his situation and circumstances, of his love for my sister and her's for him, and praying my consent. There was an air of candour and honesty in his letter which gave me a good opinion of him, nor did I consider myself at liberty to stand in the way of her happiness, which my wife mentioned to me was deeply interested. I wrote, therefore, giving my full consent to the marriage, and trust in God they may be as happy as I wish them. It is certainly a hazardous step in favour of a man whom I do not know; but as she is passionately fond of him, and he of her, as he perfectly knows her situation, and has by no means endeavoured to disguise or exaggerate his own, I am in hopes they may do well. At all events, I have acted with the best intentions, and to the best of my judgment, under the circumstances. They will, I believe, settle in Hamburgh; so there is one more of our family dispersed. I am sure if there were five quarters of the globe, there would be one of us perched on the fifth. Towards the end of the month I received a second letter from my wife, dated December 27th, with a postscript from my little Maria, being the first line I have seen of her writing. It brought the tears fast in my eyes. Thank God! my dearest love's health is a little better, for I have been most miserable ever since I received the first letter. I hope, however, mine may arrive in time, as well as a second, which I despatched three days after the first, to prevent her leaving Hamburgh. But to return to my affairs. On the 30th, I wrote to General Hoche, on the subject of my present situation, praying him to apply to the Government to permit me to retire from the service, preserving my pay and appointments, and, at the same time, offering, at any future period, when I might be useful, to resume my situation. The same evening I had a note from the General, desiring to see me early the next morning, and accordingly this day, 31st January, I went to the Hotel of the Minister of War, where he is lodged, at eight o'clock. On my calling on his aid-de-camp, Poitou, who makes his correspondence, Poitou showed me my letter, with a note in the margin, written by the General: "*Faire une copie pour être addressée au Directoire, avec la demande de sa conservation, motivée sur l'utilité dont il peut être; lui faire une réponse flatteuse, et lui temoigner ma satisfaction de sa conduite.*" Nothing, certainly, can be more agreeable to me. Poitou also showed me, in confidence, the copy of the General's letter to the Directory in my favour, which is worded in the most flattering and strongest manner. So I am in hopes I shall succeed in my application. From Poitou, I went to the General's apartment, who received me like a friend; which I remarked the more, because his manner to his officers in general is cold and dry. He told me he had written to the Directory, and that I should carry the letter myself to General Dupont, who transacts General Clarke's business in his absence; that Dupont would present me to the Directory in consequence, and he hoped the affair would be settled to my satisfaction. I returned him my acknowledgments, and in the course of what I said, I mentioned the arrival of my wife and family at Hamburgh, and my intention of going thither to bring them to France. The General seemed struck when I mentioned Hamburgh, and asked me again, was I going thither? I replied, it was my intention as soon as I had settled the affair he was so good as to undertake for me. "Well then," said he, "perhaps we may find something for you to do there; there is a person there whom perhaps you may see." I told him, that there, or any where else, where I could be useful to my own country and the Republic, I was ready to go, at an hour's warning. I added, that, when I asked my retreat for the present, I begged him to remember, that, if ever our business was resumed, under any form, I was as ready and desirous as ever to take my share in it, and that I did not at all despair of having the honour of serving once more under his orders. "The affair," replied he, "is but suspended. You know our difficulties for money; the repair of our fleet, and the nècessary preparations, require some considerable time, and, in the mean time, there are 15,000 men lying idle below, and, in fact, we cannot even feed them there. The Directory has resolved, in the mean time, to employ them usefully elsewhere, and has accepted my services; but be assured, the moment the enterprize is resumed, that I will return with the first *patrouille* which embarks." I expressed the satisfaction which this assurance gave me; and, after a conversation of about half an hour, in which I found him as warm and steady as ever in the business, I took my leave; and to-morrow I am to have my letter for the Directory. This conversation with Hoche has given me spirits to recommence these memorandums; for, in fact, my mind has been in a state of stupor ever since I landed at Brest from our unfortunate expedition. Perhaps Providence has not yet given us up. For my part, my courage, such as it is, is not abated one single jot, though I see by an article in the English papers, that they were in hopes to have caught the vessel on board which I was embarked, in which case, they were kind enough to promise that I should be properly taken care of. They may go and be hanged, and "I do not value their chariot of a rush." Buonaparte has beaten the Austrians for the five-and-fortieth time this campaign; killed 7,000 and taken 20,000. I mention this, because it may bring about a peace with the Emperor, in which case we shall have nothing to do but lay alongside of England; and perhaps we are not done with her yet. As soon as my affair here is settled, I will set off for Hamburgh, and bring my dear, dear love, and our little ones, and I think I will plant myself at Nanterre, beside my friend Mr. Shee, in order to keep the communication open with General Clarke, when he returns; and may be, I may be able to do a little mischief yet. I feel this moment like a man who is just awakened from a long terrible dream. Who is my lover that I am to see at Hamburgh, in God's name? I feel once more my ancient propensities revive. We shall see.

February, 1797.

8. Yesterday morning I heard of the arrival of my friend Mr. Shee, from Rochelle. I ran off immediately and found him at General Clarke's apartments. He was delighted to see me. It seems they had a dreadful voyage of it in the Fraternité. They sailed at one time four-and-twenty hours, unnoticed, in the very middle of the English fleet. We soon came to our business, in which he seems as hearty as ever; he tells me he hopes the Government will renew it by-and-by on a grand scale; and that we shall have the co-operation, so long wished-for, of the Spanish marine. If that be so, all may yet be recovered. He tells me also, that he had seen General Hoche, and spoken to him about me in the strongest manner; that the General had the best opinion of me, and had applied personally to the Directory and to General Dupont, (in whose department such business lies during the absence of General Clarke,) to have me continued on the tableau of the army; that the General had also told him of my desire to go to Hamburgh to bring my wife and family to France; on which Mr. Shee observed, that I might be more usefully employed elsewhere, and that he knew me so well, that he would take upon himself to answer for me, no personal considerations should prevent my going where I could be of most service to the cause. I told Mr. Shee that I waived going to Hamburgh, notwithstanding the state of my wife's health, and was ready, in an hour, to go wherever the General

might think proper to order me. I then mentioned to him General Grouchy's motives for sending me to Paris, and begged of him, if he found an opportunity, to express to General Hoche the favourable opinion I held of Grouchy's conduct. Mr. Shee told me he was very glad I had mentioned that circumstance, as it gave him the key to one or two things which appeared unaccountable to him; that Grouchy was, at present, rather down in the General's opinion, which he now saw must be in consequence of the cabal I spoke of, but that he would endeavour, discreetly, to set him right; so I am in hopes I have been of use to my lover Grouchy in this business. I do not know very much of him, but he behaves like a gentleman; and his conduct in Bantry Bay was as spirited as I could desire, and, besides, I hate the dirty spirit of cabal which is working against him. I then left Mr. Shee, having fixed to call on him again this morning, which I did accordingly; but we had not much conversation, being interrupted by a young General who lost a leg at Rastadt, in the last campaign on the Rhine; however, I gave him M'Sheehy's report, Grouchy's proclamation to the Irish, and my own opinion at the council of war held in Bantry Bay; I also gave him a memorandum of the names of the Northern Star, Dublin Evening Post, and Cork Gazette, which I strongly pressed him to have procured for the Directory; and he went immediately to speak to General Dupont on the subject. I am to see him to-morrow at twelve. On my return, I was hailed by General Hoche, who was driving through the Rue Montmartre, and informed me that my affair was settled; so now I am fixed in the French service, if nothing better offers in my own country. I returned the General my acknowledgments, and so we parted. Altogether, things do not look so gloomy just now as they did a fortnight ago. If the Spaniards and the Directory act with spirit and decision, all may yet do well, and Ireland be independent. As to myself, I can at least exist on my appointments, and if I had my family here, I could be as happy as the richest man in Europe; but the state of my dearest love's health keeps me in the most mortal inquietude. Two nights successively I have started out of my sleep, in a cold sweat, with horrible dreams concerning her. I have read her two letters a thousand times, and there is not a phrase regarding her health that I have not turned a thousand different ways to torment myself; in short, I am truly miserable on her account. To-morrow I will demand of Mr. Shee, whether I am to be employed here or not; if not, the moment I receive my appointments I will set out to meet her. If I am employed, I think I will order her to stay at Hamburgh till the first of May, which is about three months, and then come in a neutral vessel to Havre, or Dunkirk, and so to Paris. I see in the English papers that, in a late debate in the Irish Parliament, the Lord Chancellor, (my old friend Fitzgibbon, who is now Earl of Clare,) did me the favour to abuse me twice by name, as the father of the United

Irishmen. I thought *he* had forgotten *me*, but if we had got safe into Ireland, with the blessing of God, I would have refreshed his memory. In the same debate, he called General Hoche "*a monster*," so, at least, I had the pleasure to be abused in good company. I wrote a witty note, in an unknown language, which I please myself to call French, to the General thereupon, consoling him for the disgrace, &c. I think I am growing sprightly once more, but God knows the heart!

18. General Hoche set off for the army on the 13th. Before his departure, he asked Mr. Shee, whether I should like to come to the army of Sambre et Meuse? To which he answered as before, that he was sure I should be ready to go wherever the General thought I could be useful; on which the General desired him to propose it to me. This was in consequence of a conversation I had with Mr. Shee, in which I mentioned to him that I thought we might be able, in consequence of my sister's marriage, (which had been fixed for the 12th inst.) to open a communication with Ireland through Hamburgh; at which General Hoche caught directly. It was fixed, therefore, that I should make this campaign with the army of Sambre et Meuse, in order to be near his person; and he made application accordingly to the Directory, for my brevet as Adjutant General, and an order to join forthwith. I learned, in the Minister's bureau, that I am designed as the officer "charged with the General's foreign correspondence." That has a lofty

sound! Bruix, who is Major General de l'Armée Navale, and, in fact, conducted the naval part of our expedition, is arrived at Paris, in order to confer with the Directory and Minister of Marine. He tells Mr. Shee, that if the Government will grant 8,000,000 livres for the navy, he will engage, in six months, to have thirty-five sail of the line ready to put to sea: 8,000,000 livres is about 350,000*l*. I trust and rely the money will be found; and indeed Truguet, the Minister, told Mr. Shee that he had made out some part already, and hopes to secure the remainder. The Spaniards, I believe, will give us twenty-five sail of the line; and if we can make out even twenty-five more, that will make fifty sail. Come, all is not desperate yet. In the meantime, I see in the English papers, that Government is arresting all the world in Ireland. Arthur O'Connor, who it seems is canvassing for county Antrim, is taken up; but, I believe, only for a libel. It seems he was walking with Lord Edward Fitzgerald when he was arrested. It is not for nothing that these two young gentlemen were walking together. I would give a great deal for an hour's conversation with O'Connor. I see he has thrown himself, body and soul, into the revolution of his country. Well, if we succeed, he will obtain, and deserves, one of the first stations in the Government. He is a noble fellow, that is the truth of it. I am now waiting for my brevet and order to join, and eke, for my *gratification d'entrée en campagne*. which amounts to 800 livres, together with two months' pay, which will make, *en numeraire,* 330 livres more; and my trunk has not yet arrived from Brest, and will not be here this month, and before that time I may be at Cologne, where our head-quarters are fixed; and in my trunk are two gold watches and chains, and my flute, and my papers, and all that makes life dear to me; and so I am in perplexity and doubtful dilemma. I must see and spin out the time, if possible, till my trunk arrives, or I shall be in a state of anxiety thereupon, which will be truly alarming. I called on my friend Monroe yesterday. He is recalled, and the Directory have refused to acknowledge Pinckney, who was named to succeed him. Monroe leaves Paris in ten days for America, and I want to write by him to Dr. Reynolds, and to my brother. If Matt were here now, I could name him my Adjoint directly. I think I will leave his coming *to his own option.*—He can at any time return to America; so I believe I *will write to him to come at once.*

22. I see by the courier of the 14th instant, that Robert and William Simms are arrested for publishing Arthur O'Connor's letter, as it should seem, for the account is rather confused. I collect from another paragraph in the same paper, that they were released on the 9th; but O'Connor remains in custody. He has proposed himself as candidate for county Antrim, and I have no doubt will be returned; and it is for a letter to the electors of that county that he has been arrested. Government will move heaven and earth to keep him out. There is now scarcely one of my friends in Ireland but is in

prison, and most of them in peril of their lives; for the system of terror is carried as far there, as ever it was in France in the time of Robespierre. I think I will call on Carnot to-day, and propose to him to write to Dr. Reynolds, to have some person on whom we can depend, sent over from Ireland, in order to confer with the Government here. It may be easily done, and my letter will go in perfect safety by Monroe. *Allons!*

23. Called on General Dupont yesterday, in order to go with him to Carnot. Instead of bringing me, he took upon himself to give me instructions, as to what I should write. I found his instructions very frivolous. I will write now on my own plan.

24. This day I called on Monroe, and gave him a letter of eight pages for Dr. Reynolds, in which I give a detailed account of our late expedition, and assure him of the determination of the French Government to persevere in our business. I likewise offer him a rapid sketch of the present posture of the great powers of Europe, in order to satisfy him of the permanency of the Republic, together with a brief view of our comparative resources as to England. Finally, I desire him (observing the most profound secrecy and rigid caution) to write to Ireland, (and by preference, if possible, to R. S.,) to send a proper person to Hamburgh, addressed to the French Resident there, in order to come on to Paris and confer with the Directory. I calculate, if nothing extraordinary happens to delay him, that that person may be here about the middle of July next;

finally, I desire him to assure my friends that we have stronger hopes than ever of success, and to intreat them, in the mean time, to remain quiet, and not, by a premature explosion, give the English Government a pretext to let loose their dragoons upon them. Such is the substance of my letter, which I have every reason to hope will go safe.

25. Walked to Nanterre to see my friend Shee, with whom I will spend two days.

26. At work with Mr. Shee, writing a memorial relating to our business, which is to be given to Lacuée, of the Council of Ancients, with whom I am a little acquainted. He is particularly connected with Carnot, which is the reason we address ourselves to him. It is in the form of a letter from Mr. Shee to General Clarke.

27. Returned this day to Paris.

28. Called on Lacuée with the memorial. Found him busily engaged with his Secretary. Left him the paper, and fixed to call on him in two or three days.

MARCH, 1797.

3. I lead the life of a dog here in Paris, where I am as much alone as in the deserts of Arabia. This night, in downright wretchedness, I am come to a tavern, where I write this memorandum in a little box by myself. It is miserable. I wonder, shall I ever be so happy as to see my dearest love and our little ones once more! My mind is overgrown with docks and thistles, for want of cultiva-

tion, and I cannot help it, for I have not a soul to speak to, whom I care a farthing about. There are about half a dozen Irishmen here in Paris that I have seen; but they are sad vulgar wretches, and I have been used to rather better company in all respects. Well, let me change the subject. I have been lately introduced to the famous Thomas Paine, and like him very well. He is vain beyond all belief, but he has reason to be vain, and for my part I forgive him. He has done wonders for the cause of liberty, both in America and Europe, and I believe him to be conscientiously an honest man. He converses extremely well; and I find him wittier in discourse than in his writings, where his humour is clumsy enough. He read me some passages from a reply to the Bishop of Llandaff, which he is preparing for the press, in which he belabours the prelate without mercy. He seems to plume himself more on his theology than his politics, in which I do not agree with him. I mentioned to him that I had known Burke in England, and spoke of the shattered state of his mind, in consequence of the death of his only son Richard. Paine immediately said that it was the Rights of Man which had broken his heart, and that the death of his son gave him occasion to develope the chagrin which had preyed upon him ever since the appearance of that work. I am sure the Rights of Man have tormented Burke exceedingly; but I have seen myself the workings of a father's grief on his spirit, and I could not be deceived. *Paine has no children!*—

Oh! my little babies! if I was to lose my Will, or my little Fantom! Poor little souls, I doat upon them, and on their darling mother, whom I love ten thousand times more than my own existence. They are never out of my thoughts. But, to return to Paine: he drinks like a fish—a misfortune which I have known to befall other celebrated patriots. I am told, that the true time to see him to advantage is about ten at night, with a bottle of brandy and water before him, which I can very well conceive. I have not yet had that advantage, but must contrive, if I can, to sup with him at least one night before I set off for the army. Three days ago I saw sixty stand of the Emperor's colours, presented by General Augereau, of the Army of Italy. They were taken in Mantua; and the President of the Directory, Rewbell, presented the General in return, with the colours of the 62d demi-brigade, which Augereau had carried over the bridge of Lodi under the fire of the enemy, and which had been voted to him in consequence by the *Conseil des Cinq Cents.* It was a glorious spectacle; and what rendered it more interesting, the father and mother of Augereau (his father an old soldier, and his mother a *bonne bourgeoise,*) were close beside him at the moment, and his brother attended him as his aid-de-camp. What a crowd of ideas did this group produce instantaneously in my mind! Well, if we had succeeded in our expedition——but no matter. "*Tout ce qui c'est differé,—n'est pas perdu.*" We shall see yet what turn things may take. The colours were carried by sixty old soldiers, and I was delighted with the *fierté* with which these veterans presented themselves. I find the spirit of enthusiasm abate daily in my mind. "*Le temps et le malheur ont fletri mon ame.*" Yet I could not be insensible to this spectacle, which brought the tears into my eyes more than once. I thought of my own father; how proud he would be of me, if we were to succeed in Ireland. Well, all in good time.

5. Gave Mr. Monroe a letter for my brother, under cover to Dr. Reynolds, in which I recommend to him to come to France, but without pressing him very strongly. I wish to God he were here to-night. Monroe will set off in four or five days.

10. Received a letter from Mary, informing me of her marriage, and written evidently with a contented heart. I trust in God she will be happy. Enclosed was a letter from my poor dear love, about whose health I am in most dreadful anxiety. She has removed to the suburbs of Hamburgh, where I hope she will be better. Maria wrote to me a little P. S. She writes like a little angel. Answered the two letters immediately, but the post will not serve till the thirteenth. Received my *gratification d'entrée en campagne*, 800 L = 32*l.* sterling.

12. Applied to-day and got an order for my arrears since the 1st Nivose. In the margin of the order I observed the following note: "*Nota. L'activité et la grande utilité de cet officier, ont été attestées par le Bureau des officiers generaux.*" This is very handsome.

20. Dined to-day with Cherin, who sets off to-night for the army of Sambre et Meuse. I hope to follow him in a week at farthest, as I am promised my *frais de route* by that time. Came home after dinner, and sat some time alone, and devoured with the spleen. Opened my desk, and read over all my dearest love's letters. They are my constant refuge, but latterly I am most terribly alarmed for her health. If I were so miserable as to lose her, I do not think I could ever survive it, and then what would become of our dearest little babies? Darling little things, I doat on them! My poor Maria! there are two postscripts of her writing; it is impossible to express how much I love them all; shall I ever have the happiness to see them again? Well, I must not think of that now. Sent out for a lemon and sugar, and determined to play the part of Lord B. "I must have my punch." Oh that my dearest love were at the other side of the little table where I am writing this! "*Quanquam oh!*" There is one thing which I have had occasion to remark to-night, and a thousand times before, since my arrival in France, viz. "That it is not good for man to be alone." If I had my dear and unfortunate friend Russell beside me, to consult on every occasion, I should no doubt have conducted myself infinitely better, and, at all events, I should have had infinitely more enjoyment. I have read a good deal latterly, but with very little profit. In reading, an observation has struck me; very well; but I have nobody to communicate it to; I cannot discuss it, nor follow

it up to its consequences: in an hour it is lost, and I remember it no more; whereas if I had a friend to whom I could open myself, it would have become a principle. All this is not my fault. Of all the privations I have ever suffered, that which I most sensibly feel, is the want of a friend since my arrival in France, to whom I could open my heart. If William, if Matt, if Russell, were here, what a difference would it make in my situation to-night. Well, I will go to my dreary bed: I declare I am weary of my existence.

24. Received this day a letter from my sister, which has thrown me into the greatest distress. I much fear that I shall lose my best-beloved wife: I cannot write.

25. Wrote to my wife and sister, promising to join them in a month if possible; took my place in the Diligence for Liege for the 29th, having received my *frais de route* yesterday.

JOURNEY TO COLOGNE.

29. Set off from Paris at three in the afternoon, in the Diligence, for Liege: travelled all night.

30. Breakfast at Soissons; supper at Rheims, which, from the little I saw of it, seems to me a delightful spot; visited the Cathedral where the Kings of France used to be consecrated; it is a noble Gothic structure, but I fancy it will be some time before that ceremony will be again performed there; drank some excellent red champaign, which is called Vin Rosé, and set off; travelled all night again.

APRIL, 1797.

1. Slept at Rocroy, famous for the battle gained in 1643, by the great Condé, in which he annihilated the Spanish infantry, and thereby changed the destiny of Europe. I should have observed that we crossed the Meuse at Mezieres, where it is not very considerable. I have now traversed Champagne, and have seen nothing remarkable; it is a flat country, interesting only from the high state of its cultivation. Rheims is the best thing in it.

2. Slept at Givet, immediately over which is Charlemont, a place I should judge impregnable from its situation on a rock, great part of which is inaccessible. There are three noble barracks at Givet, one for cavalry and two for infantry. In the beginning of the war the Austrians penetrated as far as the hills opposite Givet, but, upon observing Charlemont with their perspectives, it held out so little temptation to them, that they soon retired. Crossed the Meuse again, which is beginning to grow interesting: the banks on each side rise boldly, and, in many places, are covered with wood. Passed a chateau belonging to the *ci-devant* Duke de Beaufort, who has had the good sense not to emigrate; it is a most delicious spot, on the edge of the river, highly fertile and cultivated, and is well contrasted by the lofty rocks which rise bare and perpendicular on the opposite bank to an uncommon height. Entered the Forest of Ardennes, which brought Touchstone immediately to my mind: "Well, now I am in Ardennes; the

more fool I! when I was at home, I was in a better place."

3. Breakfasted at Dinant, on the road to which, close to the edge of the Meuse, is a remarkable sugar-loaf rock, which rises to an immense height. The road passes between this sugar-loaf and an immense pile of rocks on the other side; and there is not, I am sure, a foot more than the breadth of the carriage; the passage was opened by Louis the XIV. Opposite to Dinant is Bouvines; this country is a sort of classic ground for a French officer. Since I have last crossed the Meuse, things are beginning to wear a Flemish appearance; passed through Ciney, where there was a fair, not very unlike an English or Irish one; slept at Freneux.

4. Crossed the Meuse again, and arrived at Liege about ten o'clock; on the road near Liege is a most magnificent abbey of Benedictines, which is, in fact, a palace. At present, however, the French have laid their ungodly hands on the revenues, so I do not know how the Reverend Fathers make it out. The approach to Liege put me in mind of that to Birmingham; not that the face of the country is the same, but that, in both cases, there is a great number of neat country-boxes, extremely well kept; that the fields are well dressed, and the gardens highly cultivated, a proof that the inhabitants are at their ease, as is generally the case in great manufacturing towns. Liege itself is a melancholy dirty spot; the palace of the Prince Bishop has the air of a convent; it is a square building, the inside of which forms a court,

round which runs an arcade, where there are little shops of divers sorts; by-the-by even in the Palais Royal, at Paris, the ground floor of the Duke of Orleans' apartments is laid out in shops, which has often surprised me. An English nobleman would not suffer the interior of his palace to be so shabbily occupied. Supped in company with a Pole named Mokosky, who was secretary to Kosciusko; found him extremely interesting, which might, in some degree perhaps, result from the similarity of our situations, each of us being banished from our country, and seeking refuge in France, from the same motives: sate late with him; the only pleasant evening I have had on my journey; I like him very much; he idolizes Kosciusko, and speaks of him as of a being of superior order: his conversation brought a thousand ideas fresh into my mind.

Arrived yesterday at Cologne, where, as yet I see nothing remarkable. Went with the Adjutant General Gastines, with whom I travelled to the *Quartier General.* The General busy, and could not see us, but sent to invite us to dinner. Dinner very pleasant. I should be as happy as an Emperor, if it were not for the increasing anxiety I feel for my dearest life and soul, which, at every instant, shoots across my mind. If ever I feel myself for a moment disposed to enjoy any thing, that cruel idea recurs to me, and sinks me at once. My situation is most cruel at this moment; just at the opening of the campaign I am obliged, if I can without disgrace, to quit the army, or, if I stay, I risk the death of my wife, to me the most terrible of all events, and leave my three little children at Hamburgh without the protection of father or mother, dependant solely on the friendship of my sister, who is herself dependant on her husband, to whom I am an utter stranger. It is terrible! I have already written twice to my dearest love, that I will, if possible, proceed from Cologne to join her. I must now see how that can be done with honour; if it cannot be done with honour, it is not my fault; and, in that case, if we must all perish, we must, and there is no remedy. My mind is distracted to-night with a thousand opposite thoughts, and I know not where to fix. I am most truly miserable!

8. Mr. Shee is at *Bonn*, five leagues from this. He is appointed by the General President of the Committee of Administration of the *Pays Conquis.* Took leave of the General, and set off for Bonn at two o'clock, in the Diligence. Found Mr. Shee ill with the gout, in his bed, and his brother-commissioners at work about him. Fixed to see him early to-morrow, when I will, if I can, settle with him what I am to do under the present painful circumstances.

9. Called on Mr. Shee early, and mentioned to him my present situation. After turning it in all possible lights, we agreed that I should write a letter to the General, suggesting the necessity of opening a communication with Ireland, and offering, in case he had not otherwise disposed of me, to go in person to Hamburgh for that purpose. Wrote the letter

accordingly, which Mr. Shee translated, and I signed. Left Mr. Shee with his commissioners, and walked about Bonn, which is a charming little town. It was the residence of the Elector of Cologne, who has a most superb palace; indeed, except the Chateau de Versailles, it is by much the finest I ever saw: the King of England has nothing like it.

10. Found Mr. Shee early engaged. All the places in the Diligence for Cologne were taken to-day, so I must wait till to-morrow. Confound it! I am in the utmost impatience to know what decision the General will take with regard to my application.

11. Returned to-day to Cologne, and dined at the Quartier General. Gave my letter to Poitou; so to-morrow, I suppose, I shall have an answer. One way or other, I shall know my destination soon.

12. Saw the General to-day, for an instant, before dinner. He told me he had read my letter, approved of the plan, and had, in consequence, desired Poitou to make out a permission for me to go to Hamburgh. I did not like the word, "*permission*," and therefore took an opportunity to speak to him again after dinner, when I told him that I did not desire to go to Hamburgh unless he himself thought it advisable, and requested, that in that case, he would give me an order, specifically, for that purpose, as otherwise it might appear that I had applied for a *congé* at the very opening of the campaign, which was not the case. He entered into my view of the business di-

rectly, and promised me to have the order made accordingly; so I am in hopes that affair will be settled to my mind. I took this occasion to ask him if he had any particular directions to give me, or any particular person to whom he wished I should address myself. He told me not:—that all I had to do was to assure my friends that both the French Government and himself, individually, were bent as much as ever on the emancipation of Ireland; that preparations were making for a second attempt, which would be concluded as speedily as the urgency of affairs would admit; that it was a business which the Republic would never give up, and that if three expeditions failed, they would try a fourth, and ever until they succeeded. He desired me also to recommend that this determination should be made known through the medium of the patriotic prints in Ireland, in order to satisfy the people that we had not lost sight of them. I then took my leave, and we wished each other mutually a good voyage. I am very well satisfied with the turn which this affair is likely to take, and especially, I am infinitely indebted to General Hoche for his kindness to me personally. On leaving the General I called on Poitou, and mentioned to him what I had said about the order. I likewise wrote a line to the General, requesting my *frais de route*; but I doubt my success in this application, as our military chest here is heinously unfurnished. At all events, I have money enough to carry me to Hamburgh. Come, all is not lost that is in danger. I have now the General's word that our business will be undertaken again.

13. To-day the General set off for Coblentz. Met several of my *connaissances expeditionnaires*, among the rest Waudré, of the *artillerie legere*, who was with me on board the Indomptable, and whom I liked very much. He asked me, "was I of the army of *Sambre et Meuse?*" And when I told him I was, "*Eh bien!* said he, *c'est un brave de plus.*" It was handsomely said of him. It seems, in the distribution of officers, I am charged, being attached to the Etat Major, with the *Arméments, equippement et habillement des troupes.*" I know no more than my boot what I shall have to do, but I know that I have at least 80,000 men to arm, clothe, and equip. "By'r lakin, a parlous fear!" I have not got my order, nor my *frais de route* yet, but Poitou has promised to send me at least the order from Bonn, and I have written a line to Mr. Shee respecting the money, but I have no violent hopes of success. It costs me a very hard struggle to leave the army just now, and nothing under heaven but the state of my poor love's health could induce me to make such a sacrifice; but when that is at stake, every other consideration must give way. I would sacrifice my soul for her.

16. I have been lounging these three days about Cologne; stupid enough. Yesterday I entered a church alone, for I visit all the churches; there happened to be no one in the place but myself, and as I was gazing about, I perceived the corner of a green silk curtain behind a thick iron lattice lifted

up, and some one behind it. I drew near, in order to discover who it might be, and it proved to be a nun, young I am sure, and I believe handsome, for I saw only her mouth and chin, but a more beautiful mouth I never saw. We continued gazing on one another in this manner for five minutes, when a villanous overgrown friar entering to say his mass, put her to the rout. Poor soul, I pitied her from the very bottom of my heart, and laying aside all grosser considerations, should have rejoiced to have battered down the gates of the convent, and rescued her from her prison. These convents are most infernal institutions; but, at the peace, I trust the Republic will settle that business here, where, by-the-by, the people are dreadfully superstitious. All this last week we have had nothing but religious processions, particularly on the 14th, being Good Friday. Went to-day, being Easter Sunday, and heard High Mass in the Cathedral, but the ceremony was very modest; I fancy they have concealed their plate and ornaments for fear of us, and they are very much in the right of it. After mass, went to another church, and heard a Capuchin friar preach. Crossed the Rhine to-day, on the *pont volant*, and took possession of the *rive droite* in the name of the Republic. "Thus far we have advanced into the bowels of the land." There is great talk of an armistice with the Emperor, but I doubt it; it is too good news to be true. If we had once peace with him, we could bend all our attention, and all our resources, on England. I wonder I have heard nothing yet about my order.

17. This day Fairin, aid-de-camp to General Chérin, brought me the order for my departure, enclosed in a very friendly letter from the General-in-Chief. I do not see any thing concerning my *frais de route*, so, I presume, that part of the business is refused. It is well it is no worse. Walked out in the evening to a guinguette, delightfully situated on the banks of the Rhine, and drank a bottle of Hock. *Pas mal!*

18. Wrote this morning to my dearest love, and to Mr. Shee, to notify my intended departure. I think I will go no farther than the frontiers of Hanover, where I have desired my family to meet me. Called on General Coulanges, *Sous-Chef de l'Etat Major*, to apprise him of my departure. Took my place in the Diligence for Nimeguen, from whence I shall proceed, by Utrecht, to Amsterdam. By the time my voyaging is finished, I shall have made a pretty handsome tour of it.

JOURNEY THROUGH HOLLAND.

20. Set out from Cologne, at five in the morning, "by most of the clocks," on my way to join my dearest love. Dined at Neuss, an inconsiderable town. At three reached Crevelt, the most beautiful village I ever saw; the country all around it is flat, but highly cultivated: as to the place itself, it is a most delicious spot; there is a considerable manufactory of silk goods carried on there, which greatly enlivens it; the inhabitants, it is easy to see, are rich and comfortable. Four leagues; travelled all night.

21. Passed Guelders, the capital of the Duchy of that name, in a broken slumber. I can assure all those whom it may concern, that a German post-waggon is not the most eligible contrivance for sleeping in. I am at this moment *ereinté*, as the French say. Breakfasted at Cleves, and made my toilette to refresh me. Shaved by a surgeon for three-pence, for, in Germany, the ancient fraternity between the barbers and surgeons still subsists. Thought of Partridge's lamentation on their separation.—Set off again in my waggon at one. At four entered the territory of the Batavian Republic. At six reached Nimeguen, which is my first halt. Secured my place in the Utrecht Diligence for to-morrow morning. Walked about the town for an hour; I am enchanted with it. I never saw any thing so neat and well kept, and a young German, who is my fellow-traveller, assures me that, as we proceed, I shall find the cleanliness and exactitude increase. Passed by two or three *corps-de-garde*—the Dutch troops very handsome fine fellows, and extremely well kept. It is to be remembered though, that our ragamuffins made them fly like chaff before the wind. The Dutch officers wear gold-laced hats, like the British, and our Generals; the French plan is better in all respects. Saw several young Dutch women at their doors and windows, who seem to me to be charming creatures, dressed well, and with taste. I find that I had a very erroneous idea of Holland. Well, after all, there is nothing like travelling to dispel prejudice; with which observation, as it is perfectly origi-

nal, and I am sure never occurred to any body before, I will conclude this day's journal.

22. Set out from Nimeguen in the Utrecht Diligence, between seven and eight. A Dutch officer of dragoons, who travels with me, tells me, in a barbarous jargon, worse than my own, that a letter is just arrived at the Municipality, with the news that an armistice with the Emperor for four months is agreed upon. I hope in God the news is true; it would make a marvellous change for the better in our affairs. I am exceedingly pleased with my tour; there is something, after all, in the view of Holland, notwithstanding its monotony, which to me, at least, is not disagreeable. The features of a Dutch landscape are an immense tract of meadows, (till the view is lost in the distance,) intersected either by deep and wide ditches, or by fences of wicker made as neat as basket-work; large plantations of willows; small brick farm-houses, covered with red tiles, and in excellent order; here and there a chateau of a Seigneur, surrounded by a garden in the true Dutch taste. I am not sure that for a small garden, this taste is a bad one; its neatness, exactitude, and regularity, agree admirably with what one expects to find there. It is true it has not the picturesque beauty of an English garden, but it has, notwithstanding, its own merits, and, in short, I like it well enough *in miniature*. In a Dutch garden all is straight lines and right angles; in an English, all is sinuosity. The Dutch garden is that of a mathematician, the English that of a poet. No

question the English taste is far superior; but all I contend for is, that the Dutch is not without its beauties, and by no means merits the indiscriminating ridicule which is attempted to be thrown upon it. But I am writing an essay upon gardening, about which I know nothing. To return; I never saw such neat farming as in Holland; the English brag very much of their farming, and, to hear them talk, they are the first agriculturists in the world, as well as the bravest, wittiest, wisest, and greatest people which has ever existed. I am no practical farmer, but, to my eye, every thing in a Dutch farm is, beyond all comparison, neater than in an English one, and especially that striking and important article, the fences, to form which it is that they make such immense plantations of willows; the pasturage seems most luxuriant, and every thing, in short, in a Dutch farm wears the appearance of ease and plenty. There is, however, a striking contrast between the neatness and beauty of the farm-houses, and the mean and rustic appearance of the owners. I saw several very ordinary-looking boors lodged in mansions which, with us, would suit a gentleman of from three hundred to one thousand pounds sterling a year. A great number of these cottages have apiaries of twenty, thirty, forty, and one or two that I remarked, of above one hundred hives. I cannot see, or rather I see plainly enough, why our poor peasantry have not bees, which require so little expense, and of which their children, (whereof they never fail to have plenty,) might take care. I made the same remark with regard to the orchards in Normandy, when I first arrived in France; but he who can barely find potatoes for his family, is little solicitous about apples; he whose constant beverage is water, dreams neither of cider nor mead. Well, if we succeed, maybe we may put my poor countrymen on somewhat a better establishment. We shall see. But to return. The storks here, who are never disturbed, build on the barns and churches; I saw several at work on their nests; it is a superstition of the country. Breakfasted at Wyck. On the back of our postwaggon was painted a representation of Noah's ark; I thought it no bad allusion to the interior of the machine, and if the painter intended it, I give him credit. At seven in the evening arrived at Utrecht, of which I saw almost nothing, as I alighted at one gate, and traversed, without stopping, a part of the city to the canal from whence proceeded the barge for Amsterdam. The quarter through which I passed put me strongly in mind of Philadelphia, which, to my eye, it resembles exceedingly in the exterior of the houses, the footways paved with brick, the trees planted in the streets, the fountains, and even the appearance of the inhabitants, which is very like that of the American Quakers. I am very apt to see analogies and likenesses between places and individuals, which I fancy exist often in my imagination only; be that as it may, Utrecht put me strongly in mind of Philadelphia.—At eight, set off in the Trakschuyt, a villanous barge, which is to the grand canal packet-boat what a German postwaggon is to a neat, well-hung English chariot. The grand cabin, which is very small, being hired, I was stowed away amongst the common lumber. We were about thirty passengers, one-half Jews, every man with his pipe in his mouth. I was suffocated! I thought my entry into the boat would have been solemnized by a battle. Having nothing but French money, when I came to pay for my passage, the skipper refused my coin, which threw me into unspeakable confusion. A young Jew, seeing my difficulty, offered to change me a piece of five livres into Dutch money. I thanked him, and accepted his offer. (It is to be observed that at par the Dutch sol is exactly double the French, consequently, 100 French sous should procure 50 Dutch.) But my Jew knew the course of exchange too well for that traffic, and, taking my piece of 100 sous, gravely handed me 38 *sous d'Hollande*, by which I should have lost exactly 24 sous. I was at first rather surprised at his impudence, but, recollecting myself immediately, looked him mildly in the face, and, with great gravity, required him instantly to refund. Jew as he was, this threw him out of his play, and he immediately offered me four *sous d'Hollande* more. I told him that I perceived he was a Hebrew, and that if he would give me one hundred, he should not have the piece; on which he submitted. All this is matter of inducement. (How the deuce came I to remember so much law?) Immediately after, a man would enter the boat perforce, and sat himself down in the lap of another, who repelled him with great violence, and threw him upon me, just as I was endeavouring to compose myself to sleep, of which I had great need. I rose immediately, and, seizing him by the collar, was proceeding to inflict an unheard-of chastisement upon him, when my Jew, who had not digested his affront and his loss, thought proper to interfere, on which I instantly quitted my antagonist and attacked the Hebrew with great violence. All the world knows that a Dutch Trakschuyt is a most inconvenient scene for a battle: for, to go no farther, it is, in the first place, impossible to stand upright therein, and we were, besides, stowed away in bulk like so many herrings. I could, therefore, do little more than swear and call names, which I did in broken French, to the great astonishment of the Dutchman and terror of the Israelite, which latter I threatened with I know not what degree of punishment, making him an example for ever to all the posterity of Abraham. He demanded pardon with great marks of contrition, which I at length accorded him, and the intruder, who was the first cause of the dispute, being turned out by common consent, the tranquillity of the packet-boat was restored. My sleep was, however, fled, and the smoking continued with great perseverance, so that I was devoured with *ennui.* Opposite me was placed a fat Dutchman, with his mistress, I believe; so, to divert myself, and support the honour of the Republic, I determined to act the Celadon with Mademoiselle, who did not know one word of French. That did not, however, prevent me from making great way in her good graces, and Hans, who perceived he was losing ground fast, very wisely determined to renounce the contest, to which he found himself unequal, pulled his cap down over his eyes, and composed himself to sleep. I laid my head down, without ceremony, in the lap of Mademoiselle, and in five minutes was as fast as a church. The lady followed the example of her two lovers, and, in this manner, at five in the morning we reached Amsterdam. I certainly had no right in the world to teaze poor Hans; but, " *Des Chevaliers Français tel est le caractère;*" besides, that he seemed " not to be made of penetrable stuff." I will not venture to say as much of Mademoiselle, who, by-the-by, was very pretty.

23. At six, reached the *Auberge l'Etoile* in the Neuss or Neiss, for I am not sure of the orthography, and got immediately into bed, of which I had great occasion: for I have not had a good night's sleep since I left Cologne. Rose at ten. " Mem. Hands, but not face." It is, to-day, Sunday. Dined at the *table d'hote* very agreeably, at one; drank a bottle of " delicate wine of Lucena," or rather, indeed, most excellent claret, and set out alone to see the lions. The *Stadthuys;* a most magnificent building, which perfectly satisfied the conception I had formed of it. Beside it is the *New Church*; so called, I presume, because it *was* new when it was built by the Spaniards, before the foundation of the Dutch Republic. Assisted at divine service, with which I was much pleased. The people here seemed

devout, but I remarked that the congregation consisted entirely of persons advanced in life, or of children. I believe I was the youngest man in the church. Walked round by the quays, which are kept, as every thing else in Holland, with astonishing neatness. Looked into the cellars where the sailors eat. The cleanliness of every thing in them might tempt the appetite of a prince. I thought of George's quay, and "Ship's kettles cooked here," with some little humiliation. In point of cleanliness, to speak the truth, we are most terribly behind the Dutch. Coffee-house and the papers. It is fated that my national pride is to be humbled to-day. In the Leyden Gazette I had the mortification to read the following observation, relative to the peaceful disarming of the province of Ulster: "*Quelques menaçantes que soyent souvent les dispositions des Irlandais, rarement on les a vu produire de bien terribles effets.*" The devil of it is, that the observation is too well-founded. Fitzgibbon was right when he said, that "We were a people easily roused and easily appeased."

25. Rose at nine. "Chid Ralph for mislaying my tobacco-stopper." Wrote to my dearest love, appointing to meet her at Groninguen, the third or fourth of next month. At the Coffee House, found English papers down to the fourteenth instant; nothing material, but it was a great enjoyment to me. Several United Irishmen acquitted, whose names, however, are not mentioned. There is a schism in the yeomanry corps, many of whom are disgusted

by the tyranny exercised over the people of the North, and especially by some proclamations lately published by General Lake, which I should be glad to see, and which appear to be very violent. There have been, in consequence, resolutions, counter-resolutions, and protests; in short, there is a feud in the enemy's camp, and the English Government can count no more upon the yeomanry corps. Mr. Pitt has despatched Mr. Hammond to Vienna, either to negotiate, or, as I rather think, to prevent the Emperor from negotiating, with the French. The outcry for peace is universal, and petitions pouring in from all parts to that effect. There is one from the city of Dublin, moved by Grattan, and seconded by Ponsonby, at an aggregate meeting of the citizens, and carried without a dissenting voice. I see those illustrious patriots are at last forced to bolt out of the House of Commons, and come amongst the people, as John Keogh advised Grattan to do long since. An attempt was made to declare the county Armagh in a state of disturbance, but the scheme was defeated; and, altogether, there seems to be a faint appearance of a better spirit rising in that unfortunate country. I do not, however, build an inch high upon it. The King and Pitt seem determined to die hard. He has refused to receive the address of the city of London, sitting on the throne; and the Livery, to the number of 5,000, have voted unanimously, that it is the inherent right of the city to present their petitions in this manner, and so they are at issue. If they carry their point, (which they will not) the King will be obliged to give an answer, which is the ground of the dispute.

26. Having three or four days to dispose of, I resolved to see the *Convention Batave*, and in consequence set off this morning at five, in the Trakschuyt, for the Hague. At Haerlem saw a regiment of Dutch troops preparing for the parade; uniform blue, faced red, and the men in general of a very fine appearance; their arms, clothes, and accoutrements, in excellent order. Travelled as far as Leyden with a Dutch Admiral, who had the politeness to invite me into the state cabin, which he had hired for himself: I do not know his name, but he spoke very good French; "much better French than you or *I*, Gentlemen of the Jury." I found his conversation very agreeable; his uniform was blue, with a red cape and cuffs, embroidered in gold, and a white ostrich feather all round his hat. He is just returned from the Texel, where there are fifteen sail of the line, ready and full manned for sea. That would be very good, but unfortunately the Dutch seamen have manifested such a terrible spirit of mutiny, insubordination, and ill-will, that there is no reckoning upon them; witness their running away with the Jason frigate, and their infamous behaviour under Admiral Lucas, at the Cape of Good Hope. By-the-by, I have never been thoroughly satisfied with regard to the conduct of the said Admiral in that expedition. God knows but it may be a present of fifteen sail of the line that we are making to the English. I asked the Admiral what

he thought of Cordova's battle with Jarvis the other day, when, with twenty-seven sail of the line, he contrived to be beaten by fifteen, and to lose four ships, and whether he thought it was through cowardice or ignorance. The Dutchman bluntly answered me, "Both." And I believe he was right. He also told me, that the celebrated navigator Bougainville, is named to the command of the fleet at Brest. I am heartily glad of it.—To return to my voyage. All along the banks of the canal I observed a prodigious number of wild fowl, which, indeed, could hardly be called wild: for they let us pass within twenty yards of them, without seeming to take notice of us. Having been, in the days of my youth, something of a sportsman, I felt my ancient propensities begin to revive. There were green and grey plover, redshanks, snipes, and hares, without number. They are little disturbed: for the law here is, that every man is to sport only on his own ground; and I conclude the Dutch are either too busy or too lazy to follow much that amusement. I wonder, shall I ever have a day's partridge-shooting in Ireland again? The last day I was out, was with my dear friend Russell. Poor fellow! God knows what may be his situation this day, or whether he has not been sacrificed by that infernal Government of Ireland. Well, let me think no more of that. The banks of the canal, as we approached the Hague, are covered with villas, as thick as they can stand, and kept with an astonishing neatness; under the local difficulties of situation, it is astonishing how much they have contrived to make of their country. They have "turned diseases to commodity;" but to judge of this, it is necessary to be on the spot, and see what they have done. Nothing short of Dutch patience, perseverance, and resolution, could have commenced, continued, and concluded, the astonishing works which are executed every where in Holland. A Dutchman cultivates his garden with a precision inconceivable, and brings it to a state of absolute perfection; and within fifty yards he has a windmill built for pumping off the water, which is constantly at work; and were it to cease, he and his garden would be inundated in twenty-four hours. I have remarked twenty villas, built literally in the water, to which the master entered by a bridge; and they were the neatest boxes I ever saw.—Arrived at the Hague at five o'clock. My journey of thirteen leagues has lasted twelve hours. To Monastereven, from Dublin, which is pretty nearly the same space, it occupies nearly, as well as I can remember, the same time, and costs five shillings. In the Dutch canal there are no locks; the boat, which is much inferior to our packet-boats, in size, beauty, and in all respects, is drawn by one horse, who makes regularly about three miles an hour: so that here they say, indifferently, "Such a place is so many leagues, or, so many hours off." Set up at the Seven Churches, which, however, the intelligent reader, who knows his Geography, will be careful not to confound with a place of the same denomination in county Wicklow, which is called by the natives Glendalough. Dined at the *Table d'hote* with nine members of the Dutch Convention, very plain and respectable-looking men, who put me exceedingly in mind of my old, and much and ever-respected masters of the General Committee. I feel the tears gush into my eyes, and my pulse beat fast, in writing that sentence. After dinner, walked out alone, to see the town; visited sundry places, of which I know not yet the names; found myself at last in a wood, intersected by a noble avenue, on the right side of which was a Dutch regiment, (the uniform blue, faced white,) at exercise, and on the left, a battalion of French. The Dutch exercise, beyond all comparison, with more precision than our troops; they are taller and stouter men, better dressed and kept, their arms and accoutrements in better order. At fifty yards distance, to see them together, there is no man who, at the first blush, would not give the preference to the Dutch. But I looked closer at them when the exercise was over, and discovered at once in the French something of a fire and animation that spoke that ardent and impetuous courage which is their chief characteristic, and which the others totally wanted. I would not, after that glance, hesitate one instant, with our little battalion, to attack the Dutch regiment, which was at least twice as strong, and we would beat them. It was very amusing to me to observe the *fierté* of our soldiers, as they marched by the others; there was a saucy air of civil superiority, which made me laugh excessively, both then and ever since. The physiognomy of the

French is sharp, quick, and penetrating; that of the Dutch, round, honest, and unmeaning; the step, air and manner of the former are free and assured; they are the true stuff whereof to make soldiers. There are, however, some important points to be considered. You must leave the French grenadier permission to wear a very large cravat, if it be the fashion, tied just as he likes. His hat is likewise his absolute property, in the disposition of which he is by no means to be interrupted or constrained; he must try it on in every possible shape and form, and wear it absolutely in that position which best becomes, as he conceives, the cast of his figure. When satisfied in these important, indeed indispensable points, he is ready for every thing, and Cæsar himself is not so brave as these *petit maitres*: for every soldier in France is a *petit maitre*. I have seen them, God knows, ragged enough, but I never saw them but with their cravat well and fashionably arranged, and their hat cocked and put on with an air.

27. Visited this morning the *Convention Batave*; it is held in the palace of the *ci-devant* Stadtholder, in the room which was formerly the ball-room, the orchestras whereof are converted into *tribunes*, as they are called here and in France, and galleries with us. The tribunes are open, and no introduction by a member is necessary. The room is handsome, but has nothing particularly striking. The members were extremely decorous in their manner and appearance, and order is sufficiently kept; infinitely better, for example, than in the *Conseil des*

Cinq Cents, but not quite as well as in the English House of Commons. I observed very few members who were not at least thirty-five years of age, and most of them seemed to me to be forty and upwards; they wear no distinctive mark of any kind. Altogether, I was extremely pleased with the decorum and appearance, both of the assembly and auditors. The tribunes were full, but not crowded; there were some women of a decent appearance, and in the tribune opposite to the President (which is reserved for the friends of the members,) there were some, very handsome and well-dressed.—When I entered, the house was (as we should say) in committee on some ordinary business: at twelve it resumed, and the question for discussion was, whether the Dutch people should or should not be obliged, by the constitution, to pay the clergy? I know not what *may* be, but I know very well what *ought* to be, their decision. In France, where there is no religion, there is no salary fixed by law for the priests. In America, where there is a great deal of religion, there is no salary settled by law for the clergy. The Catholic priests and the Dissenting ministers of Ireland are paid by the voluntary subscriptions of their hearers; and after all these examples, I have no doubt as to the inconvenience of a church establishment. By-the-by, there are several of the clergy members of the *Convention Batave:* I saw to-day one Catholic priest, and three Protestant ministers sitting in their places, and the priest spoke in the debate: I know not what he said, but he made the assembly laugh heartily. There are likewise some of the noblesse in the convention, and I find they do not vote as a caste; some of them are patriots, and others aristocrats. All this information was given me by an honest Dutch patriot, who, seeing me in French uniform, was so good as to do the honours of the assembly, and point out to me the most distinguished members, particularly Van Kastacle, who is the leader of the democratic interest. He likewise informed me that, under the intended constitution, the clergy are to be excluded from seats in the legislature: and said he wished to God they would exclude the lawyers also, who were intriguers and caballers, and, from being more in the habit of public speaking, and confounding right and wrong, were often able to confute and silence honester and abler men than themselves. I could not help laughing internally at this sketch of my *ci-devant* brethren of the Dutch bar. I find a lawyer is a lawyer all over the world. The most scandalously corrupt and unprincipled body, politically speaking, that I ever knew, was the Irish bar; I was a black sheep in their body, and I bless God that I am well rid of them! rot them! I hate the very memory of the four courts, even at this distance. Well, with God's blessing, no man will ever see me again in a black gown and nonsensical big wig; so let the profession of the law go and be hanged—I am happily done with it. To return: I have now seen the Parliament of Ireland, the Parliament of England, the Congress of the United States of America, the *Corps Legislatif* of France, and the *Convention Batave;* I have likewise seen our shabby volunteer Convention in 1783, and the General Committee of the Catholics in 1793; so that I have seen, in the way of deliberative bodies, as many I believe as most men; and of all those I have mentioned, beyond all comparison the most shamelessly profligate and abandoned by all sense of virtue, principle, or even common decency, was the legislature of my own unfortunate country; the scoundrels!—I lose my temper every time I think of them.—Having dined at my *auberge,* I went to the coffee house, and read the Paris papers, viz. the Royalist ones, which were the only ones I could find: excessively disgusted with their dulness and impudence: the liberty of the press is not yet understood in France; the indecent attacks which are made with impunity on the Government are scandalous and abominable. In England there is not one of those scoundrelly journalists, but would be sent to Newgate for two years, for one fiftieth part of the libels which are published day after day in Paris, with the most perfect impunity; yet the rascals cry out that they are *enslaved,* and call the Directory tyrants and oppressors, whereas the proof that the most unbounded liberty, or, to speak more properly, the most *outrageous license,* exists in France, is, that such audacious libels are published, and that the authors are not sent instantly to the galleys. All over Europe, there is not a tyrant whose subjects dare outrage him with such impunity; and it is hard that, in the only Government emanating from the choice of the people, liberty should be made the instrument of her own destruction. But, would I destroy the liberty of the press? No! but I would most certainly restrain it within just and reasonable limits. All fair and cool discussion I would not only permit, but encourage; but the infamous personalities, the gross and vulgar abuse that disgrace the Paris journals, I would most severely punish. Liberty of the press, somebody has very well said, is like the liberty to carry a stick, which no man should be hindered from doing; but if he chooses to employ it in breaking his neighbour's head, or his windows, it is no breach of his liberty to make him answer for the mischief he has committed. In short, I am of opinion—and if ever I have the opportunity I will endeavour to reduce that opinion to practice—that the Government of a Republic, properly organized, and freely and frequently chosen by the people, should be a *strong* Government. It is the interest and security of the people themselves, and the truest and best support of their liberty, that the Government which they have chosen should not be insulted with impunity; it is the people themselves who are degraded and insulted in the persons of their Government. I would, therefore, have strong and severe laws against libels and calumny, and I do not apprehend the least danger to the just and reasonable liberty of the press, from the execution of such laws, where the magistrates, the judges, and the jury, are freely named by the people. The very same laws which, under the English constitution I regard as tyrannical and unjust, I would in a free republic preserve, and even strengthen. It is because the King names the judges and the sheriffs; because the sheriffs pack the juries; and for a thousand other obvious reasons, that I regard the English trials, in many instances, as mockery of justice; it is not that in theory the law is *bad*, but that in practical execution it is *tyrannical;* and, as I have already said, I do not see why tyrants alone should be protected by the laws, and liberty left unprotected and defenceless. I hope I am deceived; but I much fear the French Government will have reason sorely to repent their extravagant caution with regard to infringing the liberty of the press. It is less dangerous for a Government to be feared, or even hated, than despised; and I do not see how one which suffers itself, day after day, without remission, to be insulted in the most outrageous manner, with the most perfect impunity, can avoid, in the long run, falling into disrepute and contempt. In America, such gross indecency would not be suffered to pass unpunished; and surely, if rational liberty exists upon the earth, it is in the United States. "Here endeth the first lesson on the liberty of the press." I have now disburthened my soul of the indignation which was kindled in it by those abominable libels.—To return; walked forth into the wood in quest of the palace of the *ci-devant* Stadtholder, but could not find it, so that must be for tomorrow. Returned to my *auberge*, somewhat afflicted with the blue devils; remembered one of Voltaire's precepts in such cases. "*Ou bien buvez; c'est un parti fort sage;*" determined to put it in practice. Got off my boots and coat, got into my wrapper and slippers, and determined to enjoy myself. I do not see why I should come to the Hague, without tasting some Holland gin. "The liquor, when alive, whose very smell I did detest and loathe." Called for gin, water, and sugar, "on which the waiter disappeared, and returned instantly with the noggin." Performed the part of Lord B. with infinite address; drank "to the health of my dearest love;" "our friends in Ireland;" "the French Republic, with three times three;" "a speedy Republic to Ireland, with loud and universal acclamations;" "General Hoche, and the army of Sambre et Meuse." *The evening concluded with the utmost festivity.*

28. As I am about to leave the Hague to-morrow, bought the Traveller's Guide, in order to amuse myself in the boat by reading what I ought to have seen whilst I was there. I do not much see the good sense of my purchase, but I perceive I am of that class, (respectable at least for its numbers,) who are celebrated for their facility in parting with their money, of which, by-the-by, it may be supposed I am not just now afflicted with a prodigious quantity. Dinner as usual, but the company more mixed: at the lower end of the table sat a member of the Convention, worth a *plum*, and a staunch patriot; next him, in order, were three plain men, "said they were farmers—indeed looked like farmers, in boots, and spattered." They and the

representative of the Convention had a long discussion. I observed he listened to them with great attention, and took notes of their remarks. This is as it ought to be. After dinner strolled out about the Hague: "People may say this and that of being in Newgate, but, for my part, I find *Holland* as pleasant a place as ever I was in in my life." It is delicious. I am tempted, as I walk about the Hague, to cry out "Thou almost persuadest me to be a Dutchman." Whoever may be Ambassador from the Republic of Ireland to Holland, will not be the worst off of the future *Corps Diplomatique*. Returned to the auberge; demanded of the waiter "if he could help me to a glass of *genever*, or so?" (I defy man, woman, or child, to track me in that quotation.) The waiter produced the needful—Lord B., &c.

29. Set off this morning, in the trakschuyt, for Amsterdam. Travelled with the citizen Van Amstel, a deputy to the Convention, whom I had already met at dinner, and who had been pointed out to me when I went to the assembly, by my Dutch acquaintance, "whose name I know not, but whose person I reverence," as a most excellent patriot and republican. We soon found one another out; he tells me that the Committee for Foreign Affairs have received an express from General Daendels, Commander-in-chief; that the preliminaries of the peace between the French Republic and the Emperor are certainly signed, and that they have no doubt but that the fact is so; if so, it is most excellent news, indeed the best we could desire; but I have a

mighty good rule, from which I will not now depart, which is, to believe all excellent news always four-and-twenty hours after all mankind is convinced of its certainty. He gives me another piece of intelligence, which, if it be true, I regard as scarcely of less importance than the peace with the Emperor, viz. That there has been a mutiny aboard the English fleet; that the seamen had nearly thrown their Admiral overboard, and that they had tried, condemned, and hanged one of their comrades for opposing their measures. This is too good news to be true, and I long most anxiously to see it explained. It has been communicated to the *Comité des Relations Exterieurs* from Hamburgh, so I shall probably learn the truth when I meet my family at Groninguen. At our parting, Van Amstel requested to see me on my return to the Hague, and offered his services, if he could be of any convenience to me there, on which "I flourished my hands three times over my head in the most graceful manner," and took my leave. I think I will ask him to introduce my dearest love into the grand gallery of the Convention.

30. Set off on my journey to Groninguen, where I have to give my wife and babies a meeting; crossed the Zuyderzee in the night; it took us just twelve hours.

May, 1797.

1. Arrived at Lemmer at eight in the morning, and set off instantly in the trakschuyt for Strobosch; a delightful day and beautiful breeze all the way;

immense quantities of game all along the canal. Planned a voyage, to be executed, (God knows when) by my wife, Russell, and myself; to hire a trackschuyt for a month certain, to go where we liked, and stop when we liked, to live aboard our boat, to bring guns, fishing tackle, &c. and in this manner make a tour through a great part of Holland. It would be delicious: "A very pretty journey indeed, and besides where is the money?" Oh Lord! Oh Lord!

2. Slept last night at Strobosch in a six-bedded room, the other five beds being occupied by five snoring Dutchmen; genteel and agreeable! Arrived at Groninguen at twelve o'clock; the town extremely neat, like all the Dutch towns, but not as handsome as most of those I have seen; put up at the Nieuwe Münster.

6. Tormented with the most terrible apprehensions on account of the absence of my dearest love, about whom I hear nothing; walked out every day to the canal, two or three times a day to meet the boats coming from Lieuschans, whence she will arrive: No love! no love! I never was so unhappy in all my life.

7. At last, this day, in the evening, as I was taking my usual walk along the canal, I had the unspeakable satisfaction to see my dearest love, and our little babies, my sister, and her husband, all arrive safe and well: it is impossible to describe the pleasure I felt. Here is an end of my journals now, for some time at least. Since I came to France,

which is now above fourteen months, I have continued them pretty regularly for the amusement of my dearest love. As we are now together once more, they become unnecessary; we must wait for another separation.*

PERIOD OF GENERAL TONE'S ATTACHMENT TO THE BATAVIAN ARMY.

Cologne, May 26. I see to-day, in the Journal General, an article copied from an English paper, dated about a fortnight ago, which mentions that a discovery had been made in Ireland of a communication between the discontented party there and the French; that one of the party had turned traitor and impeached the rest, and that, on his indication, nearly fifty persons, in and near Belfast, had been arrested, one of them a dissenting clergyman; that their papers had been all seized, and that, on the motion of Mr. Pelham, the English Secretary, they were to be submitted to the inspection of a

* On the very day of my father's departure from the army, was fought the famous battle of Neuwied; and before he reached Amsterdam, the war was concluded, and Hoche stopt in his career of victory by the news of the truce with Austria, concluded by Buonaparte. My father's meeting with his family was short and delightful. He travelled with us about a fortnight through Holland and Belgium, left us at Brussels; and on the 26th of May was already returned to head-quarters at Cologne, whilst we proceeded on to Paris. The important events which ensued are contained in the following Journal, which he resumed with a new spirit on his arrival.—*Editor*.

Secret Committee of the House of Commons. All this looks very serious. There has been a formal message from the Government on this business. For my part, all I can say is, that, if communication has been had, it was without my knowledge; but even so I am heartily glad of it; the dissenting clergyman is Sinclair Kilburne, as I saw in a newspaper at Amsterdam; but I wonder who was the traitor; methinks I should be curious to see him!

JUNE, 1797.

4. *Friedberg.* In the Moniteur of the 27th is a long article, copied from the English papers of the 18th May, and containing the substance of the report made by the Secret Committee above mentioned; most of the facts contained in it I was already acquainted with; the organization is, however, much more complete than when I left Ireland. The most material fact is, that above 100,000 United Irishmen exist in the North of Ireland, and that they have a large quantity of arms (and at least eight pieces of cannon and one mortar) concealed. I presume that martial law is proclaimed long before this, as I see, in the Frankfort Gazette, an article from England of the 23d May, (viz. five days after that in the Moniteur,) which mentions two or three skirmishes between the army and some detached proportion of the people, who are denominated the *rebels*, in which the army had, of course, the advantage. I do not at all believe that the people are prepared for a serious and general insur-

rection, and, in short, (why should I conceal the fact?) I do not believe they have the spirit. It is not fear of the army, but fear of the law, and long habits of slavery, that keep them down; it is not fear of the General, but fear of the Judge. In the mean time, it seems Marquis Cornwallis is named to the command in Ireland, and that Lord O'Neil, Mr. Conolly, and the Duke of Leinster, have resigned their regiments. The example of the last has been followed by all the officers of the Kildare militia; this last circumstance is, in some degree, consolatory.

11. The sedition continues aboard the English fleet, and has reached the army. For the present, however, they seem to be appeased, but at the expense of dismissing a number of officers of the navy who were obnoxious to the seamen, and increasing the pay both of seamen and soldiers. When a Government is forced to such concessions, it seems to me an inevitable symptom of decaying empire. Martial law is proclaimed in Dublin, and I see that the presses of the Northern Star have been broken and burnt in Belfast by the Donegal militia.

Written aboard the Vryhéid of 74 *guns, commanded by Admiral Dewinter, at the Texel, July* 10, 1797.

[It is a long time since I have made a memorandum, notwithstanding I have been fully employed: but the fact is, I have had too much business. All

I can now do is to make an imperfect abstract of what has passed, that is most material, in the last month.]

12. *Quartier General* at Friedberg. This evening the General called me into the garden and told me he had some good news for me. He then asked, "did I know one Lewines?" I answered I did, perfectly well, and had a high opinion of his talents and patriotism. "Well," said he, "he is at Neuwied, waiting to see you; you must set off to-morrow morning; when you join him, you must go together to Treves, and wait for farther orders." The next morning I set off, and, on the 14th, in the evening, reached Neuwied.

14. Here I found Lewines waiting for me. I cannot express the unspeakable satisfaction I felt at seeing him. I gave him a full account of all my labours, and of every thing that had happened since I have been in France, and he informed me, in return, of every thing of consequence relating to Ireland, and especially to my friends now in jeopardy there. I cannot pretend to detail his conversation, which occupied us fully during our stay at Neuwied, and our journey to——

17. *Treves;* where we arrived this day. What is most material is, that he is sent here by the Executive Committee of the United People of Ireland, to solicit, on their part, the assistance in troops, arms, and money, necessary to enable them to take the field, and assert their liberty; the organization of the people is complete, and nothing is wanting

but the *point d'appui*. His instructions are to apply to France, Holland, and Spain. At Hamburgh, where he passed almost two months, he met a Señor Nava, an officer of rank in the Spanish navy, sent thither by the Prince of Peace, on some mission of consequence; he opened himself to Nava, who wrote off, in consequence, to his court, and received an answer, general, it is true, but in the highest degree favourable;—a circumstance which augurs well is, that, in forty days from the date of Nava's letter, he received the answer, which is less time than he ever knew a courier to arrive in, and shows the earnestness of the Spanish Minister. Lewines' instructions are to demand of Spain 500,000*l.* sterling, and 30,000 stand of arms. At Treves, on the 19th, Dalton, the General's aid-de-camp, came express with orders for us to return to——

21. *Coblentz;* where, on our arrival, we met General Hoche. He told us that, in consequence of the mission of Lewines, he had sent off Simon, one of his Adjutant-generals, who was of our late expedition, in order to press the Executive Directory and minister of the Marine; that he had also sent copies of all the necessary papers, including especially those lately prepared by Lewines, with his own observations enforcing them in the strongest manner; that he had just received the answers of all parties, which were as favourable as we could desire; but that the Minister of the Marine was absolutely for making the expedition on a grand scale, for which two months, at the very least, would still

be necessary; to which I, knowing Brest of old, and that two months, in the language of the Marine, meant four at least, if not five or six, remarked the necessity of an immediate exertion, in order to profit of the state of mutiny and absolute disorganization in which the English navy is at this moment, in which Lewines heartily concurred; and we both observed that it was not a strong military force that we wanted at this moment, but arms and ammunition, with troops sufficient to serve as a *noyau d'armeé*, and protect the people in their first assembling; adding, that 5000 men, sent now, when the thing was feasible, would be far better than 25,000 in three months, when, perhaps, we might find ourselves again blocked up in Brest Harbour; and I besought the General to remember that the mutiny aboard the English fleet would most certainly be soon quelled, so that there was not one minute to lose; that, if we were lucky enough to arrive in Ireland before this took place, I looked upon it as morally certain, that, by proper means, we might gain over the seamen, (who have already spoken of steering the fleet into the Irish harbours,) and so settle the business, perhaps, without striking a blow. We both pressed these, and such other arguments as occurred, in the best manner we were able; to which General Hoche replied, he saw every thing precisely in the same light we did, and that he would act accordingly, and press the Directory and Minister of the Marine in the strongest manner. He showed Lewines, Simon's letter, which contained the assurance of the Directory, "that they would make no peace with England wherein the interests of Ireland should not be fully discussed agreeably to the wishes of the people of that country." This is a very strong declaration, and has most probably been produced by a demand made by Lewines in his memorial, "that the French Government should make it an indispensable condition of peace, that all the British troops be withdrawn from Ireland, and the people left at full liberty to declare whether they wished to continue the connexion with England or not." General Hoche then told us not to be discouraged by the arrival of a British negotiator, for that the Directory were determined to make no peace but on conditions which would put it out of the power of England longer to arrogate to herself the commerce of the world, and dictate her laws to all the maritime powers. He added, that preparations were making also in Holland for an expedition, the particulars of which he would communicate to us in two or three days, and in the meantime, he desired us to attend him to Cologne; for which place we set off, and arrived on the 24th.

25. At nine o'clock at night the General sent us a letter from General Daendels, Commander-in-chief of the army of the Batavian Republic, acquainting him that every thing was in the greatest forwardness, and would be ready in a very few days; that the army and the navy were in the best possible spirit; that the Committee for Foreign Affairs (the Directory per interim of the Batavian Republic) de-

sired most earnestly to see him without loss of time, in order to make the definitive arrangements; and especially they prayed him to bring with him the deputy of the people of Ireland, which Daendels repeated two or three times in his letter. In consequence of this, I waited on the General, whom I found in his bed in the *Cour Imperiale*, and received his orders to set off with Lewines without loss of time, and attend him at——

27. The *Hague;* where we arrived accordingly, having travelled day and night. In the evening we went to the *Comédie*, where we met the General in a sort of public incognito; that is to say, he had combed the powder out of his hair, and was in a plain regimental frock. After the play, we followed him to his lodgings at the Lion d'Or, where he gave us a full detail of what was preparing in Holland. He began by telling us that the Dutch Governor-general Daendels, and Admiral Dewinter, were sincerely actuated by a desire to effectuate something striking to rescue their country from that state of oblivion and *decadence* into which it had fallen; that, by the most indefatigable exertions on their part, they had got together, at the Texel, sixteen sail of the line, and eight or ten frigates, all ready for sea, and in the highest condition; that they intended to embark 15,000 men, (the whole of their national troops,) 3,000 stand of arms, 80 pieces of artillery, and money for their pay and subsistence for three months; that he had the best opinion of the sincerity of all parties, and of the courage and conduct

of the General and Admiral; but that here was the difficulty:—The French Government had demanded that at least 5,000 French troops, the *elite* of the army, should be embarked, instead of a like number of Dutch, in which case, if the demand was acceded to, he should himself take the command of the united army, and set off for the Texel directly; but that the Dutch Government made great difficulties, alleging a variety of reasons, of which some were good; that they said the French troops would never submit to the discipline of the Dutch navy, and that, in that case, they could not pretend to enforce it on their own, without making unjust distinctions, and giving a reasonable ground for jealousy and discontent to their army; "but the fact is," said Hoche, "that the Committee, Daendels and Dewinter, are anxious that the Batavian Republic should have the whole glory of the expedition, if it succeeds; they feel that their country has been forgotten in Europe, and they are risking every thing, even to their last stake—for, if this fails, they are ruined—in order to restore the national character. The demand of the French Government is now before the Committee; if it is acceded to, I will go myself, and, at all events, I will present you both to the Committee, and we will probably then settle the matter definitively." Both Lewines and I now found ourselves in a considerable difficulty. On the one side, it was an object of the greatest importance to have Hoche and his 5,000 grenadiers; on the other, it was most unreasonable to propose any thing which could hurt the feelings of the Dutch people, at a moment when they were making unexampled exertions in our favour, and risking, as Hoche himself said, their last ship and last shilling to emancipate us. I cursed and swore like a dragoon; it went to my very heart's blood and midriff to give up the General and our brave lads, 5,000 of whom I would prefer to any 10,000 in Europe; on the other hand, I could not but see that the Dutch were perfectly reasonable in the desire to have the whole reputation of an affair prepared and arranged entirely at their expense, and at such an expense. I did not know what to say. Lewines, however, extricated himself and me with considerable address. After stating very well our difficulty, he asked Hoche whether he thought that Daendels would serve under his orders, and, if he refused, what effect that might have on the Batavian troops? I shall never forget the magnanimity of Hoche on this occasion. He said he believed Daendels would not, and, therefore, that the next morning he would withdraw the demand with regard to the French troops, and leave the Dutch Government at perfect liberty to act as they thought proper. When it is considered that Hoche has a devouring passion for fame; that his great object, on which he has endeavoured to establish his reputation, is the destruction of the power of England; that he has, for two years, in a great degree, devoted himself to our business, and made the greatest exertions, including our memorable expedition, to emancipate us; that he sees, at last, the business likely to be accomplished by another, and, of course, all the glory he had promised to himself ravished from him; when, in addition to all this, it is considered that he could, by a word's speaking, prevent the possibility of that rival's moving one step, and find, at the same time, plausible reasons sufficient to justify his own conduct,—I confess his renouncing the situation which he might command is an effort of very great virtue. It is true he is doing exactly what an honest man and a good citizen ought to do; he is preferring the interests of his country to his own private views; that, however, does not prevent my regarding his conduct, in this instance, with great admiration, and I shall never forget it. This important difficulty being removed, after a good deal of general discourse on our business, we parted late, perfectly satisfied with each other, and having fixed to wait on the Committee to-morrow in the forenoon. All reflections made, the present arrangement, if it has its dark, has its bright sides also, of which hereafter.

28. This morning, at ten, Lewines and I went with General Hoche to the Committee for Foreign Affairs, which we found sitting. There were eight or nine members, (of whom I do not know all the names,) together with General Daendels. General Hoche having, on the part of the French Government, renounced all desire of participating in the expedition, at which declaration the most lively satisfaction was manifested, (particularly by General Daendels,) they told us that they hoped all would be ready

in a fortnight, and Citizen Hahn (who appeared to possess great influence) observed, at the same time, that, as there was an English squadron which appeared almost every day at the mouth of the Texel, it was very much to be desired that the Brest squadron should, if possible, put to sea, in order to draw off at least a part of the British fleet, because, from the position of the Texel, the Dutch fleet was liable to be attacked in detail, in sailing out of the port; and even if they beat the enemy, it would not be possible to proceed, as they must return to refit. To this, General Hoche replied, that the French fleet could not, he understood, be ready before two months, which put this out of the question; and as to the necessity of returning to refit, he observed that, during the last war, the British and French fleets had often fought, both in the East and West Indies, and kept the seas after—all that was necessary being to have on board the necessary articles of *rechange;* besides, it was certainly the business of the Dutch fleet to avoid an action by all possible means. General Daendels observed that Admiral Dewinter desired nothing better than to measure himself with the enemy; but we all, that is to say, General Hoche, Lewines, and myself, cried out against it, his only business being to bring his convoy safe to its destination. A member of the committee (I believe it was Van Leyden) then asked us, supposing every thing succeeded to our wish, what was the definite object of the Irish people? To which we replied categorically, that it was to throw off the yoke of England, break for ever the connection now existing with that country, and constitute ourselves a free and independent people. They all expressed their satisfaction at this reply, and Van Leyden observed that he had travelled through Ireland, and, to judge from the luxury of the rich and extreme misery of the poor, no country in Europe had so crying a necessity for a revolution. To which Lewines and I replied, (as is most religiously the truth,) that one great motive of our conduct in this business, was the conviction of the wretched state of our peasantry, and the determination, if possible, to amend it. The political object of our visit being now nearly ascertained, Hahn, in the name of the committee, observed that he hoped either Lewines or I would be of the expedition, as our presence with the General would be indispensable. To which Hoche replied, "that I was ready to go," and he made the offer, on my part, in a manner peculiarly agreeable to my feelings. It was then fixed that I should set off for the army of Sambre et Meuse for my trunk, and especially for my papers, and that Lewines should remain at the Hague, at the orders of the committee, until my return, which might be seven or eight days. The meeting then broke up.

On our return to the *auberge* with Hoche, we took occasion to express our admiration of the singularly disinterested conduct which he had manifested on this occasion. He then told us his plan; that the Minister of the Marine, thus far, had not been lucky, counting from his expedition against Sardinia in the beginning of the war; that he had the greatest desire to do something which might give eclat to his administration; that he, General Hoche, had ceded to the wish of the Dutch Government, principally because he would press no measure, however grateful to himself, which might cool their zeal in this great business; and in the next place, because he knew that the instant the Dutch fleet was at sea, Truguet's vanity would be piqued, and that he would move heaven and earth to follow them—and instead of waiting to complete the expedition on a great scale, according to his present system, would despatch, instantly, whatever was ready for sea; so that, in all probability, if we reached Ireland, the French army would be there in a fortnight after us. He told us, likewise, that the Dutch army was not now what it had been in the commencement of the war; that they had numbers of French among them, particularly in the *artillerie legere;* that they had also a great quantity of Austrians, especially of the garrison of Luxembourg; and especially that Daendels was an excellent officer, and as brave as Cæsar, on whom we might rely; that he would send all such plans and papers as might be of service to him in this business, and, finally, that he hoped we should all speedily meet in Ireland.

JULY, 1797.

1. Arrived at Cologne, where I found the General. He told me that, as he had expected, the Minister of Marine was piqued, and had given orders, in consequence, to prepare every thing at Brest with the greatest possible expedition; that he had, if necessary, £300,000 at the disposal of the Minister; that he had just received orders from the Directory to proceed instantly to Paris, by way of Dunkirk; that from Paris he would set off for Brest, where every thing would be ready in a fortnight, and in a month he hoped to be in Ireland. He then ordered me £50 sterling, with directions to return immediately to the Hague with a letter for General Daendels. I told him, that if he expected to be ready so soon, it was my wish not to quit him. He replied, he had considered it, and thought it best I should accompany Daendels, on which I acquiesced. I then took occasion to speak on a subject which had weighed very much upon my mind,—I mean the degree of influence which the French might be disposed to arrogate to themselves in Ireland, and which I had great reason to fear would be greater than we might choose to allow them. In the Gazette of that day there was a proclamation of Buonaparte's, addressed to the Government of Genoa, which I thought most grossly improper and indecent, as touching on the indispensable rights of the people. I read the most obnoxious passages to Hoche, and

observed, that if Buonaparte commanded in Ireland, and were to publish there so indiscreet a proclamation, it would have a most ruinous effect; that in Italy such dictation might pass, but never in Ireland, where we understood our rights too well to submit to it. Hoche answered me—"I understand you, but you may be at ease in that respect; Buonaparte has been my scholar, but he shall never be my master." He then launched out into a very severe critique on Buonaparte's conduct, which certainly has latterly been terribly indiscreet, to say no worse of it; and observed that, as to his victories, it was easy to gain victories with such troops as he commanded, especially when the General made no difficulty to sacrifice the lives of his soldiers, and that these victories had cost the Republic 200,000 men. A great deal of what Hoche said was very true, but I could see at the bottom of it a very great jealousy of Buonaparte. I am also sorry to see the latter losing so fast that spirit of moderation, which did him as much honour at first as his victories. Hoche and I then talked of our own business: He said we must calculate on being opposed, at the landing, by 8 or 10,000 men; that, if they were not there, so much the better, but we must *expect* them; that the British would probably act as they did in America last war—retreat, and burn the towns behind them; that he did not desire more than twelve, or, at most fifteen thousand troops, and had made his arrangements so that the maintenance of that force should not cost the Irish people above

12,000,000 livres, equal to £500,000 sterling. He then promised to send me his instructions for carrying on the war in La Vendée, which would exactly apply to our case in Ireland; and, giving me a letter for General Daendels, in which, amongst other things, he demanded for me the rank of Adjutant General in the service of the Batavian Republic, we embraced each other and parted. He set off that evening for Bonn, and I the next morning, at five, for the Hague, where I arrived on the morning of the fourth.

4. Instantly on my arrival I waited on General Daendels, whom I found on the point of setting out for the Texel. He read the letter, and told me every thing should be settled with regard to my rank, and that I should receive two months' pay in advance, to equip me for the campaign. His reception of me was extremely friendly. I staid with Lewines at the Hague three or four days, whilst my regimentals, &c. were making up, and at length, all being ready, we parted, he setting off for Paris, to join General Hoche, and I for the Texel, to join General Daendels.

8. Arrived early in the morning at the Texel, and went immediately on board the Admiral's ship, the Vryheid, of 74 guns, a superb vessel. Found General Daendels aboard, who presented me to Admiral Dewinter, who commands the expedition. I am exceedingly pleased with both one and the other; there is a frankness and candour in their manners which is highly interesting.

10. I have been boating about the fleet, and aboard several of the vessels; they are in very fine condition, incomparably better than the fleet at Brest, and I learn from all hands that the best possible spirit reigns in both soldiers and sailors. Admiral Duncan, who commands the English fleet off the Texel, sent in yesterday an officer with a flag of truce, apparently with a letter, but in fact to reconnoitre our force. Dewinter was even with him: for he detained his messenger, and sent back the answer by an officer of his own, with instructions to bring back an exact account of the force of the enemy.

11. This day our flag of truce is returned, and the English officer released. Duncan's fleet is of eleven sail of the line, of which three are three-deckers. I do not yet exactly know our force, either by sea or land, but I must endeavour to learn it.

13. I have had a good deal of discourse to-day with General Daendels, and I am more and more pleased with him. His plan is, to place such of our people as may present themselves at first in the cadres of the regiments which we carry out, until our battalions are 1,000 each; that then we may form a corps, and he will give us proper officers to discipline and organize it; that he will keep the main army of 18 or 20,000 men in activity, and leave the security of our communications, the guarding of passes, rivers, &c. to the national troops, until they are in a certain degree disciplined. A great deal of this is good, but we must be brought

more forward in the picture than that, for every reason in the world. I replied, that the outline of his plan was just, but that cases might occur where it would be necessary to depart from it occasionally. For instance, if the militia were to join us, they ought not, nor would they consent, to be incorporated in the Dutch battalions. Daendels said, "certainly not; that he knew what the *esprit de corps* was too well to think of it; that the militia battalions would, in that case, become themselves cadres of regiments;" so that affair will be settled to the satisfaction of all parties. We then spoke of the administration, and I gave him an idea how we had been circumstanced in that regard in the Brest expedition, where we had a little army of commissaries, ready to eat up the country, who would sacrifice the liberty of Ireland, the interests of the Republic, and the honour of the General, for half-a-crown; and I did not restrain myself in speaking of those gentry as they deserve. Daendels replied, that his instructions were to leave all the details of supplying the army to the Irish people; that he brought with him but five commissaries, who were to superintend the forage, the bread, the meat, &c., and that all their proceedings should be subject to his own immediate inspection, and nothing stand good that was not authorized by his signature; that he prided himself more on his character for administration than for military talents, and that I might rely on it we should have no difficulties on that head. I was very glad to hear all this, the more because I have confidence in him. If the Brest expedition had succeeded, we should have had d——d work with those scoundrelly administrations, but I had made up my mind on that head, as to what we should do. With the Dutch I have by no means the same uneasiness, and this is one of the circumstances where we gain by the present expedition. But enough of this for the present. "All is for the best in this best of all possible worlds."

14. General Daendels showed me to-day his instructions from the Dutch Government. They are fair and honest, and I have no doubt he will act up to them. The spirit of them is, always to maintain the character of a faithful ally, and not to interfere in the domestic concerns of the people; to aid them, by every means in his power, to establish their liberty and independence, and to expect no condition in return, but that we should throw off the English yoke, and that, when all was settled on that score, we should arrange our future commerce with the Dutch Republic, on the basis of reciprocal advantage and accommodation. Nothing can be more fair and honourable, and I am convinced, from what I see of Daendels, and the frankness of his character, that he will act up to his instructions. The report to-day is, that we shall get under weigh to-morrow, and I see a bustle in the ship, which seems to confirm it; but I follow my good old rule, to ask no questions. Several boats full of troops have passed us to-day, going on board the different vessels; the men are in the highest spirits, singing

national songs, and cheering the General as they pass; it is a noble sight, and I found it inexpressibly affecting. Daendels assures me, that in the best days of the French Revolution he never witnessed greater enthusiasm than reigns at present in the army. It is, to be sure, glorious, the prospect of this day.

Our line of battle comprises fifteen sail of the line, ten frigates and sloops, and twenty-seven transports. Our land force I do not yet accurately know. To-day, (indeed at this present writing,) I can see from the cabin windows ten sail of English ships of war, little and big, who have presented themselves off the mouth of the Texel. It put me in mind of the Goulet of Brest, where I have been often regaled in the same manner; but nobody here seems to mind them.

15. The human mind, or, at least, my mind, is a singular machine. I am here in a situation extremely interesting, and on the result of which every thing most dear to me as a man and a citizen depends, and yet I find myself in a state of indifference, or rather apathy, which I cannot myself comprehend. My sole amusement is reading an odd volume of Voltaire's, which I found by chance; and, for our expedition, I declare I think no more of it than if it were destined for Japan. General Daendels showed me a letter from General Dupont, announcing the immediate departure of General Hoche for Brest; he also told me that he and I would go on board a sloop of war, and not mount

the Admiral's ship until the issue of the affair (if any there may be) between the two fleets is determined. I am not sorry for this arrangement.

16. The General tells me just now that a spy, sent out by the Admiral, returned last night with news that the English fleet is strong twenty-four sail of the line. A few days ago, he said nineteen, but he explains that, by saying that five sail had been detached to assist at the execution of Parker, the mutineer. The Admiral's opinion is, that the fellow is a double spy, and that the story of twenty-four sail is a lie, in which I join him. In the Morning Chronicle of the 6th instant, is an article which mentions that Admiral Duncan had demanded a reinforcement, and that, in consequence, three sail had set off to join him, which, with ten or eleven that he had before, and, perhaps, two which he might draw from the Dogger Bank, (where they are stationed to protect the fishery,) may bring him up to fifteen or sixteen sail; and this calculation agrees with the reports made to the Government, and those of neutral vessels which have lately entered. Be that as it may, the Admiral summoned this morning all the Admirals and Captains of the fleet, and gave them their last instructions, which were, that the frigates of 44 guns should fall into the line; that they should fight to the last extremity, even to sinking of their vessels, in which case they were to take to their boats; that, if any Captain were to attempt to break the line and hang back, the others should immediately fire on him. This is resolute

of Dewinter, and I have every reason to think his fleet will second him. He has, in the mean time, sent off a courier to the Government, to announce all this, and, if the wind springs up in our favour, we will set off instantly, without waiting for the answer.

17. Yesterday evening the Admiral told me his plan, as above set forth. He is a fine fellow, that is the God's truth. Received yesterday a letter from my dearest love, dated the 9th. Thank God! she and the babies are well and in spirits. To-day, I received two letters, one from Madgett, and the other, (dated the 13th June,) from Napper Tandy, to which I have written two answers, which I will not despatch till we are just setting off. The wind is as foul as the devil. At Brest we had, against all probability, a fair wind for five days successively, during all which time we were not ready; and, at last, when we did arrive at our destination, the wind changed and we missed our blow. Here all is ready, and nothing is wanting but a fair wind. We are riding at single anchor. I hope the wind may not play us a trick. It is terribly foul this evening. Hang it, and d—n it for me! I am in a rage, (which is truly astonishing,) and can do nothing to help myself. Well! well!

18. The wind is as foul as possible this morning; it cannot be worse. Hell! hell! hell! Allah! Allah! Allah! I am in a most devouring rage! Well, what can't be cured must be endured, as our ancestors have wisely remarked. An officer, sent out in dis-

guise to reconnoitre, is just returned; his report is favourable; he saw the English fleet, strong twelve sail of the line, and seven or eight frigates; one of the frigates bore down on the Admiral, and spoke him, on which he instantly made signal, and the whole squadron stood to the S. W. I do not conceive what could be the reason of that manœuvre, for it leaves us clear, if the wind would let us stir out. Perhaps they are going to reinforce the fleet before Brest, perhaps something has happened again at the Nore. I should have mentioned yesterday, in its place, that when the Admiral had determined to fight the enemy in the manner I have recited, he supposed them to be, at least, nineteen sail of the line strong, which does the more honour to his courage. It is most terrible to be locked up by the wind, as we are now.

19. Wind foul still. Horrible! horrible! Admiral Dewinter and I endeavour to pass away the time, playing the flute, which he does very well; we have some good duets, and that is some relief. It is, however, impossible to conceive any thing more irksome than waiting, as we now are, on the wind: what is still worse, the same wind which locks us up here, is exactly favourable for the arrival of reinforcements to Duncan, if Lord Spencer means to send him any. Naval expeditions are terrible for their uncertainty. I see, in the Dutch papers, (for I am beginning, with the help of a dictionary, to decypher a little,) that the Toulon fleet is at sea since the 20th June, strong, six sail of the

line, (two of 80, and four of 74 guns,) and six frigates. I wish them safe and well in Brest harbour. There never was, and never will be, such an expedition as ours, if it succeeds; it is not merely to determine which of two despots shall sit upon a throne, or whether an island shall belong to this or that State; it is to change the destiny of Europe—to emancipate one, perhaps three, nations; to open the sea to the commerce of the world; to found a new empire; to demolish an ancient one; to subvert a tyranny of six hundred years. And all this hangs to-day upon the wind! I cannot express the anxiety I feel. Well, no matter! I can do nothing to help myself, and that aggravates my rage. Our ships exercise at great guns and small arms, one or other of them, every day; they fire, in general, incomparably well, and it is a noble spectacle.

20. This evening I had the pleasure to count nineteen sail of British vessels, which passed the mouth of the Texel, under an easy sail. The General assures me, however, that there are not above twelve sail of the line among them, according to the comparison of the best accounts which have been received. Wind foul, as usual. The following is a state of our army. Infantry, eighteen battalions, of 452 men, 8,136; Chasseurs, four battalions, at 540 men, 2,160; Cavalry, eight squadrons, 1,650; Artillery, nine companies, 1,049; Light Artillery, two companies, 389; Etat Major, 160; total, 13,544. It is more than sufficient. Would to God we were all arrived, safe and well, at our destination.

23. I pass my time here in an absolute torpor. When I was at Brest I was bad enough, but at least we had some conversation. But here—well! &c. The Admiral tells me to-day, that he had a letter from London, dated the 16th, which mentions, that Lord Bridport has put in for fresh provisions, and that three of his ships are still in revolt; that his destination is for before Brest; that Sir Edward Pellew is arrived at Falmouth, and that his report is, that the French fleet appears in a state not likely soon to put to sea—which, by the by, Dewinter believes to be the case, and attributes to want of money; that Duncan has applied for a reinforcement, but that the reply was, that they must first finish the trial of the mutineers, in order to reduce the rest to a sense of their duty, from whence I infer that they are afraid as yet to send the ships at the Nore to sea: however, the Warrior, of 74 guns, is arrived, which brings Duncan up to thirteen sail of the line: the report in England is, that we have twenty, (I wish we had) besides frigates, with 15,000 troops embarked, and 30,000 stand of arms; but that our destination is a secret. The wind is, to-day, at N. W., which is not quite so execrable as yesterday and the day before. With a N. N. E. the Admiral says we might get out; ergo, we want yet six points of the compass. D—n it to all eternity for me! Was there ever any thing so terrible? Wrote to my wife on the 21st instant.

28. Yesterday we had a sort of fair wind, but which came so late, and so feeble, that we could not

weigh anchor; at eight in the evening it came round to the west as bad as ever, and, to-day, it is not much better. I am weary of my life. The French are fitting out a squadron at Brest, which it now appears is to be only of twelve sail of the line. Lord Bridport's fleet is twenty-two sail; ergo, he may detach, with perfect security, seven sail to reinforce Duncan, who will then have at least nineteen sail against our fifteen; ergo, he will beat us, &c. Every thing now depends upon the wind, and we are totally helpless. Man is a poor being in that respect. Fifty millions of money cannot purchase us an hour of fair wind, and talents and courage avail no more than money. But I am moralizing like an ass. "D—n morality, and let the constable be married." Well, "'Tis but in vain for soldiers to complain," (for the 595th time.)

29. This morning the wind is fair, but so little of it that we cannot stir. About mid-day it sprang up fresh, but the tide was spent, and it was too late:—to sail out of the Texel, there must be a concurrence of wind and tide. The Admiral went ashore to-day, and mounted the Downs with his perspective glass, like Robinson Crusoe; he counted twenty-five sail of three-masted vessels, and six luggers, or cutters, of the English, at anchor; he concludes they are about fifteen or sixteen of the line, the rest frigates. He tells me also, that his idea is, if there is any thing like parity of success, in case of an action, Admiral Duncan will not push the fight to extremity, as he is on an enemy's coast, and if any of his ships are dis-

masted, he must leave them; in which case, the action will be a cannonade until night, when both parties will draw off, sing *Te Deum*, and claim the victory; when he will immediately push off with his convoy, and such of his ships as will be in state to keep the sea. I like Dewinter's behaviour very much; there is nothing like *fanfaronade* in it; and I fancy Duncan will have warm work of it to-morrow morning. The wind to-night is excellent, and blows fresh; if it holds, (as I trust in God it may,) to-morrow, at eight o'clock, we shall be under weigh, being the hour of the tide. God knows how earnestly I long for that moment! I hear nothing of our mounting a cutter, as the General mentioned to me, so I may happen to be taken in a sea-fight, against my expectation. Well, if it must be, it must be; but I had rather not. I do not love your sea-fights at all; however, happy go lucky! We shall see what is to be done in that case. (Sings.) "Madam, you know my trade is war!" &c.

AUGUST, 1797.

1, 2.—Every thing goes on here from bad to worse. On the 30th, in the morning early, the wind was fair, the signal given to prepare to get under weigh, and every thing ready, when, at the very instant we were about to weigh anchor and put to sea, the wind chopped about and left us. The Admiral, having some distrust of his pilots, (for it seems the pilots here are all *Orangists,)* made signal to all the chiefs of the fleet, to know if they thought it possible to get out with the wind which then blew, (E. S. E.) but their answer was unanimous in the negative, so there was an end of the business. In an hour after, the wind hauled round more to the S. and blew a gale, with thunder and lightning; so it was well we were not caught in the shoals which environ the entry of this abominable road. At last it fixed in the S. W. almost the very worst quarter possible, where it has remained steadily ever since. Not to lose time, the Admiral sent out an officer with a letter addressed to Admiral Duncan, but, in fact, to reconnoitre the enemy's force. He returned yesterday with a report that Duncan's fleet is of seventeen sail of the line, including two or three three-deckers, which is pleasant. It is decided that we all remain on board the Vryheid and take our chance, which is very brave and foolish: for there is no manner of proportion between the good to be obtained and the hazard to be run—a rule by which I am fond to examine questions. If General Daendels is killed, our expedition will be at least greatly embarrassed, and, perhaps, fail totally thereby; and as to my personal concerns, if I get knocked on the head, and the expedition does not take place after, (both which circumstances are, at least, probable,) what will become of my dearest love and our little babies, left without protection or support? With all submission, it is a very idle point of honour of General Daendels; but it is determined, so there is an end of it. One thing more;—If we should happen to be taken, the rest will be prisoners of war, but how will it be with me in that case? "*C'est une chose à voir.*" We shall see.

Wrote to General Hoche, Lewines, and my wife. Wind still S.W. I am, to-day, twenty-five days aboard, and at a time when twenty-five hours are of importance. There seems to be a fate in this business. Five weeks, I believe six weeks, the English fleet was paralyzed by the mutinies at Portsmouth, Plymouth, and the Nore. The sea was open, and nothing to prevent both the Dutch and French fleets putting to sea. Well, nothing was ready; that precious opportunity, which we can never expect to return, was lost; and now that, at last, we are ready here, the wind is against us, the mutiny is quelled, and we are sure to be attacked by a superior force. At Brest it is, I fancy, still worse. Had we been in Ireland at the moment of the insurrection at the Nore, we should, beyond a doubt, have had, at least, that fleet, and God only knows the influence which such an event might have had on the whole British navy! The destiny of Europe might have been changed for ever; but, as I have already said, that great occasion is lost, and we must now do as well as we can. "*Le vin est tiré, il faut le boire.*"

4. Wind foul. Proposed, to-day, to the Admiral, to try an experiment in firing shells from the lower-deck guns. He said he thought it would not answer, but that he would try, notwithstanding. Nine at night, tried the shell with a thirty-six pounder, and found it answer famously. The Admiral, I fancy, will profit of this circumstance, in case of an

action with the English, and I am in hopes it will produce a considerable effect.

5. This morning arrived aboard the Vryheid, Lowry, of county Down, member of the Executive Committee, and John Tennant, of Belfast. I am in no degree delighted with the intelligence which they bring. The persecution in Ireland is at its height, and the people there, seeing no prospect of succour, which has been so long promised to them, are beginning to lose confidence in themselves, and their chiefs, whom they almost suspect of deceiving them. They ground their suspicions on the great crisis of the mutiny being suffered to pass by, without the French Government making the smallest attempt to profit of it, and I can hardly blame them. They held out till the 24th of June, the last day allowed by the British Government in the proclamation offering a general pardon, and, that day being arrived, they have almost entirely submitted, and taken the oath of allegiance; most of them have likewise given up their arms, but it appears that the number of firelocks was much less than was imagined. In consequence of all this, the Executive Committee has doubled its efforts. M'Neven was despatched from Dublin to France, and sailed from Yarmouth on the 7th July; of course he is, I reckon, long before this in Paris. Lowry, Tennant, and Bartholomew Teeling, came together to Hamburgh, where they arrived about a fortnight ago, and finding the letter I wrote to my sister, acquainting her with my being here, Teeling

immediately sailed for England, and I am in hopes he will get back safe,—in which case his arrival will give courage to the people; the other two came here. All this is very disagreeable, but, in fact, the matter depends upon one circumstance. If either the Dutch or the French can effectuate a landing, I do not believe the present submission of the people will prevent their doing what is right; and if no landing can be effectuated, no part remains for the people to adopt, but submission or flight. By what Lowry and Tennant tell me, there seems to me to have been a great want of spirit in the leaders in Dublin. I suspected it very much from Lewines' account, though I saw he put the best side out; but now I am sure of it. However, I did not say so to them, for the thing is passed, and criticising it will do no good, but the reverse. The people have been urgent more than once to begin, and, at one time, eight hundred of the garrison offered to give up the barracks of Dublin, if the leaders would only give the signal; the militia were almost to a man gained over, and numbers of these poor fellows have fallen victims in consequence. It is hard to judge at this distance, but it seems to me to have been an unpardonable weakness, if not downright cowardice, to let such an occasion slip. With eight hundred of the garrison, and the barracks to begin with, in an hour they would have had the whole capital, and by seizing the persons of half a dozen individuals, paralyzed the Government, and, in my opinion, accomplished the entire revolution by a single proclamation. But, as I said already, it is hard to judge at a distance. Keogh, I know, is not fit for a "*coup de main;*" he has got, as Lewines tells me, M'Cormick latterly into his hands, and besides, Dick is now past the age of adventure. I am surprised that Emmet did not show more energy, because I know he is as brave as Cæsar of his person. It seems to me to have been such an occasion missed as we can hardly expect to see return. Lowry and Tennant say there are now at least 80,000 men in Ireland, of British troops, including the militia and yeomanry corps, who, together, may make 35,000; but in this account I am sure there is great exaggeration: for they spoke very much by guess, and a number that is guessed, as Johnson remarks, is always exaggerated. I suppose, however, there may be fifty, or 55,000 of all kinds; and it is not that force, composed as I know it is, that would make me despair of success, if we could once get out of this d——d hole, of which I see no sign; and to comfort me still more, I learn that, in general, the westerly winds, which lock us up, prevail during the whole of this month, before the end of which time we shall have eaten up our provisions, and probably be encumbered with sick: for it can hardly be supposed the troops will keep their health so long, cooped up as they are in transports, where they are packed like herrings. Add to this the chance of a peace being concluded with England, and I think I am not too gloomy in saying that nothing can well be more unpromising than the appearance of things to-day.

8. Wind foul. We have now been detained here so long, that our hopes of undertaking the expedition to Ireland are beginning exceedingly to relax, and I more than suspect the General is speculating on one elsewhere, for I have remarked him, within these three days, frequently examining a map of England, particularly the eastern coast, about Yarmouth, and he has asked me several questions which lead that way. As Lowry and Tennant travelled that road very lately, I learn from them that there are few or no troops on that coast, except a small camp at Ipswich, about half way, or sixty-nine miles from London. In consequence, last night, when the General and I were walking alone on the quarter-deck, and cursing the wind, he began to mention his apprehensions on the score of our provisions running short, as well as the danger of attempting the passage north-about so late in the season, and he began to moot again the point about Yarmouth. I said, that if unfortunately we were detained so far in the season as to render the Irish expedition utterly impracticable, it was undoubtedly desirable to do something in England, as well for the glory of the Dutch arms, as that all the expense hitherto incurred in the affair might not be lost. That in such case my idea was to run over to the English coast, and debark the army, not at Yarmouth, but at Harwich, or nearer London if possible; to carry nothing with us but bread for six days and ammunition; to make

a desperate plunge by forced marches for the capital, where I did not consider it impossible to arrive before the enemy could be in sufficient force to oppose us, supposing the eastern coast to be as unfurnished of troops as Lowry and Tennant had represented. That if we were once there, we might defy all the force of England; for if they were assembled to the number of 100,000 in Hyde Park, we could at all times make conditions by threatening, in case they drove us to extremity, to set fire to the city at the four corners, and defend ourselves afterwards to the last man; that I had no doubt, but with such a pledge in our hands, we might make our own terms; and I dwelt a good deal (I cannot say with any great success,) on the glory of such a desperate enterprize, if we had the good fortune to succeed, which seemed to me, though very far from certain, yet at least so possible as to deserve serious consideration. I mentioned likewise, as a subordinate circumstance, that if we once reached London we should, to a certainty, find a strong reinforcement, inasmuch as a large portion of the mob, and those very desperate fellows, consisted of Irishmen, to the amount of many thousands, who, I was sure, would desire nothing more than to have their will of the English. All these arguments seemed, however, to make no great impression on Daendels, who still recurred to his Yarmouth scheme. He seems to me to expect some co-operation there, on what grounds I know not; but I fancy he will find himself egregiously deceived. If any thing can be done in England, it must be, in my mind, by a "*coup de main*," whereas he talks of maintaining himself for some time in the country, which, with 14,000 men, is flat nonsense. He asked me if he were to land on the eastern coast, would it not be possible for any of the Irish to effectuate a landing on the other side, cross the country and join him—when he would give them arms? To this most extravagant of all questions, I contented myself with declaring gravely, that I looked upon it as impracticable. To be sure it is most egregious nonsense to suppose for an instant that such a measure could, by any possibility, be executed by a body of unarmed men, without a single ship prepared to carry them over. Far from invading England, I wish to heaven they were able to take the field in their own country. I cannot conceive how such a wild idea could, for a moment, enter Daendels' head; yet he seemed to be in earnest. To return to my scheme. I think that Charles XII. with 14,000 men would execute it, supposing he could effectuate the landing; but I readily admit that it requires much such a head and heart as his to attempt the enterprize. Certain it is, that we will not try it. Daendels' answer at length was, that he was of opinion the Dutch Government would not consent to it, and that, even if they did, it would require too much time, as he must, in that case, new model the army—which I do not understand. I think Hoche, with 15,000 French grenadiers, would effectuate it, but for the Dutch I cannot pretend to say; it seems to me, however, at least *possible*. From Harwich to London, the distance is but seventy-two miles, which could be made by forced marches in three days, supposing we had horses to draw the artillery, which, in that case, we must bring with us. But this is raving, for the thing will not be done; so there is an end of it.

9. This morning, the General, Lowry, Tennant, and myself, took a walk ashore for a couple of hours. He examined them particularly as to what they knew of the state of the public mind in Scotland, and the possibility of meeting support from the patriots in that country, in case the expedition to Ireland were so long delayed as to become impracticable, and that he should decide, in consequence, to try an attack on Scotland. They answered him very rationally: it seems emissaries have been sent from the north of Ireland to that country, to propagate the system of the United Irishmen, and that they have, to a certain degree, succeeded in some of the principal manufacturing towns, such as Paisley and Glasgow, where societies are already organized, and, by the last accounts, they had even advanced so far as to have formed a provincial committee: nevertheless, they observed that these facts rested on the veracity of the agents sent from the north, the Scotch having sent none of their body in return; that they could not pretend to say whether the Scotch patriots were up to such a decided part, as to take arms in case of an invasion, but their opinion rather was, that they were not so far advanced. As to the possibility of assistance from Ireland, on which head Daendels ex-

amined them pretty closely, they were decidedly of opinion that it was utterly impracticable, and not to be thought of. Certainly it is a most extravagant expectation. After discussing the question fully, we parted, the General returning aboard the Vryheid, and Lowry, Tennant, and I, setting off for the Texel, where they are tolerably lodged in a little village. We walked over a great part of the island, which is by nature one of the most barren, uncomfortable spots that can be imagined; but such are the inconceivable efforts of liberty and good government, that this ungrateful soil is in a great degree reclaimed, enclosed, and drained, covered with flocks and herds, filled with neat and snug dwellings, and supporting five little towns, which are beautiful in their kind. The population is inconceivable for the extent, and the peasants all well fed and clothed. I thought of Ireland a thousand times, with her admirable soil and climate, and the vast advantages which nature has showered down upon her, and which are all blasted by the malignant influence of her execrable government, till my blood boiled within me with rage and vexation. Well, I cannot help it; so let me think no more, if possible, on that melancholy subject.

12. The General has been making an excursion ashore and is not yet returned. The wind is as foul as ever, and I begin fairly to despair of our enterprise. To-night Admiral Dewinter took me into secret and told me he had prepared a memorial to his Government, stating that the design originally

was, to be ready for the beginning of July, and that every thing was, in consequence, embarked by the 9th: that the English fleet at that time consisted, at the very most, of thirteen sail of the line, which could not make any effectual opposition; that contrary winds having prevailed ever since, without an hour's intermission, the enemy had had time to reinforce himself to the number of seventeen sail of the line, so that he had now a superiority in force over the Dutch fleet, which, of course, rendered the issue of an engagement, to a certain degree, doubtful; that, by this unforeseen delay, which might, and probably would, continue still longer, a great additional consumption of provisions had taken place, so that, in a very few days, there would be barely sufficient for the voyage north-about; that the season was now rapidly passing away, and, if the foul wind continued a fortnight longer, the voyage would become highly dangerous, if not utterly impracticable, with a fleet encumbered with so many transports, and amounting to nearly seventy sail, of all kinds; and that, in consequence, even a successful action with the English would not ensure the success of the enterprise, which the very season would negative; that, for all these reasons, his opinion was, that the present plan was no longer advisable, and, in consequence, he proposed that it should be industriously published that the expedition was given up; that the troops should be disembarked, except from 2,500 to 3,000 men, of the élite of the army, who, with twenty or thirty pieces of artillery, and all the arms and ammunition, should remain on board the frigates, and one or two of the fastest sailing transports; that, as the vigilance of the enemy would probably be relaxed in consequence, this flotilla should profit of the first favourable moment to put to sea and push for their original destination, where they should land the men, arms, and artillery, and he would charge himself with the execution of this plan; that by this means, even if they failed, the Republic would be at no very great loss, and, if they succeeded, must gain exceedingly; that she would preserve her grand fleet, which was now her last stake, and, during the winter, would be able to augment it, so as to open the next campaign, (in case peace was not made *ad interim*,) with twenty sail of the line in the North sea. These are, most certainly, very strong reasons, and unfortunately the wind gives them, every hour, fresh weight. I answered, that I did not see at present any solid objection to propose to his system; and that all I had to say was, that, if the Batavian Republic sent but a corporal's guard to Ireland, I was ready to make one. So here is our expedition in a hopeful way. Twice, within nine months, has England been saved by the wind. It seems as if the very elements had conspired to perpetuate our slavery and protect the insolence and oppression of our tyrants. What can I do at this moment? Nothing. The people of Ireland will now lose all spirit and confidence in themselves and their chiefs, and God only knows whether, if we were even able to effectuate a landing with 3,000 men, they might act with courage and decision. I hope they would, and believe it; yet, after all, it is uncertain, their hopes have been so often deceived, and they have suffered such a dreadful persecution in consequence of what they have already done in this business; yet their sufferings must have only still more exasperated their minds, and I cannot suppose that, if they saw the arms, they would not instantly seize and turn them on their oppressors. I cannot doubt it. At all events, we should at least know the worst, and, if they had not courage to assert their liberty, they deserve to suffer their present slavery and degradation. But once again I do not believe it! I shall, in consequence, as far as in me lies, support the Admiral's plan, the more as it is, I see now, our only resource, and feeble as it is, it is still better than nothing. We must now begin, if at all, like the French in La Vendée. Well, we have a good cause, and they had a bad one; we are the people, and they were but a faction of two provinces; we have powerful means, and, on the present plan, we must use them *all*. All things considered, I do not know but there is something in the proposed expedition more analogous to my disposition and habits of thinking; which is a confession, on my part, more honest than wise; for I feel very sensibly that there is no common sense in it: but after all, it is my disposition, and I cannot help it. I am growing utterly desperate, and there are times in which I would almost wish for death, if it were it not for the consideration of my wife and my darling little babies, who depend for their existence upon mine.

13. The General returned last night from his excursion, and this morning he mentioned to me the Admiral's plan, in which he said he did not well see his way, and was proceeding to give me his reasons, when we were interrupted by General Dumonceau, our second in command, and a heap of officers, who broke up our conversation. When he renews it, I will support Dewinter's plan, as far as I am able. The wind is as foul as ever, viz: S. W.; in or near which point it has now continued thirty-six days that I am aboard, viz: since the 8th of July last. At night:—The General and I have been poring over the map of England, and he has been mooting a plan, which, in my mind, is flat nonsense, viz: to land at or near Lynn, in Lincolnshire, with his 14,000 men, where he thinks he could maintain himself until the fleet could return and bring him a reinforcement of as many more, and then march upon London and stand a battle. It is hardly worth while combating a scheme which will certainly never be adopted; it is sufficient to observe, that his plan necessarily includes that he must be absolute master of the sea during the whole time necessary for its execution, which, without going farther, is saying enough. Besides, I presume it is hardly to be expected that, with even 28,000 men, (supposing he had horses to mount his cavalry and draw his artillery, which he would not have,) he would

be able to force his way for above one hundred miles through an enemy's country, who would have time more than sufficient to collect his forces and make the necessary disposition to give him a warm reception.

14. The General is gone off again, on a party of pleasure, to North Holland. He invited me to accompany him, but I have no stomach for pleasure or enjoyment of any kind, so I refused, and set off for the Texel to see Lowry and Tennant, and talk over the Admiral's new plan, in order to have their opinion thereupon. After dinner we walked out to a pretty little farm, about a mile from the town, where they are lodged, and sat down on a hillock, where we had a view of the fleet riding at anchor below. I then told them that I looked upon our expedition, on the present scale, as given up, and I stated the reasons assigned by Dewinter, and which are unanswerable. I then communicated his plan, and desired their advice and opinion on the whole, and especially as to the material fact, whether they thought the people would join us, if they saw no more than 3,000 men. After a long consultation, their opinion, finally, was, that the scheme was practicable, but difficult; and that, by great exertions and hazards on the part of their chiefs, the people might be brought forward; but that for that, it was indispensable the landing should be effected in the counties of Down or Antrim, but especially the former, where there were, in June last, twenty-four regiments of a thousand men each, ready or-

ganized, with all their officers and sub-officers. They mentioned, at the same time, that if the expedition had taken place three months ago, with five hundred men, it could not have failed of success; but public spirit was exceedingly gone back in that time, and a great number of the most active and useful chiefs were either in prison or exile, which would considerably increase the difficulty of carrying the present system into execution. I saw they were a good deal dejected by the change of the plan, and consequent diminution of our means, and did my best to encourage them. At last we all got into better spirits, consoling ourselves with the reflection that, if we succeeded with so slender a force, the glory of our success would be the greater, and if we failed, there would be less reason to reproach us. We agreed that we should be, at our landing, in the case of men who have burned their ships—that we had no retreat, but must conquer or die; and we counted a good deal (and I think with reason,) on the spirit of enthusiasm which we should be able to raise in the people. We likewise agreed, that we would stop at no means necessary to ensure our success, rather than turn back one inch from our purpose. After this discussion, we returned to the inn, where we supped, and, after divers *loyal* and *constitutional* toasts, retired to bed at a very late hour.

15. As it will require from three weeks to a month to arrange matters for the expedition on the present plan, Lowry and Tennant have determined

to go on to the Hague, and if they have time, to Paris, in order to see Mac Neven and Lewines, and to join with them in endeavouring to procure assistance from France; and especially, if possible, to obtain a small armament to co-operate with that from the Texel, and which, by spreading the alarm, and distracting the attention of the enemy, must produce the most beneficial effects. It is likewise their wish that I should accompany them, and if I had the time and money to spare, I should like it well enough, and I think it might do good. In consequence, it was determined this morning, that I should return immediately aboard the Vryheid, and propose the measure to Admiral Dewinter. I returned accordingly, but the Admiral was not on board. Late in the evening he returned, and I told him of our project, which he approved highly, and will give Lowry and Tennant letters of introduction to the Dutch Government. I said nothing of my going until I see the General, who is not yet returned from his party.

16. Went to the Texel to see Lowry and Tennant, and spent the day.

17. We all three came aboard the Vryheid, in order to settle about our journey to the Hague, and on our arrival found things as unpleasantly situated as possible. I see clearly there is a coolness pretty far advanced between the Admiral and the General, whose manner towards each other is marked with a manifest dryness which bodes no good. The General was the first who spoke to me. He said, that

with 4000 men, he would undertake the enterprize, but not with less. I then addressed myself to the Admiral, to whom I communicated what the General had said with regard to the number of troops which he thought indispensable. The Admiral answered at once, that it was impossible, and that 2500 was the very utmost that he would undertake to transport; and that even that force would require eighteen sail to carry them, viz.: six frigates, which might carry 600 men; six large transports, 1800, and the remaining 100, in six luggers and cutters. I think this calculation not reasonable. In short, our expedition seems now, independent of all other reasons, to be aground on the same shoal where so many others have been shipwrecked; I mean the disagreement between the land and sea service, about which I can no longer doubt. It is pleasant!

20. Yesterday morning the General set off for the Hague in one carriage, and Lowry, Tennant, and I, in another. We arrived safe this evening, *per varios casus, per tot discrimina rerum.*

21. Breakfasted with the General. He told me, in the first place, that the Government had rejected the plan proposed by the Admiral, and persisted in their original design; that, however, in consideration of the lateness of the season, he had prepared a memorial for a new arrangement, which is shortly this: To sail out and fight Admiral Duncan. If the issue of the battle be favourable, to pass over immediately 15,000 men, or as many more as we

can send, in every thing that will swim, to Scotland; to seize, in the first instance, on Edinburgh, and march right on Glasgow, taking every possible means to alarm the enemy with the idea that we meant to penetrate by the North of England, which is to be done by detaching flying parties, making requisitions, &c. on that side; to maintain ourselves, meantime, behind the canal which joins the Frith of Forth to the Clyde; to collect all the vessels in the latter, and pass over the army to the North of Ireland; to send round, whilst these military operations were going on by land, the frigates, and such transports, (as few as possible,) as might be necessary, to carry over the artillery, stores, &c. Finally, that the English would probably be alarmed by all this for their own country, and perhaps recal a part of their troops from Ireland, which would very much facilitate the success of the enterprize.

26. The General has submitted his plan to General Dejean, (commanding the army of the North,) who approves of it entirely, provided the frigates can get round to meet us; but of this, barring some unforeseen accident, I think there can be little doubt, inasmuch as the Admiral himself, who seems at present cool enough in all that concerns the expedition, has already, in his *projet* of the 10th instant, not only given his opinion in favour of the possibility of effectuating, with frigates, the passage north-about, but even offered to command the expedition. The General's plan is now before the

Government, with General Dejean's approbation, and he tells me, he has strong hopes it will be adopted.

30. The General set off, 27th August, on his return to the Texel, where we followed him next day, and arrived on the 30th.

September, 1797.

1. A new system, rendered indispensable by the course of events, has been mentioned to me to-day by the General, which will probably oblige me to make a course to the head-quarters of the army of *Sambre and Meuse,* and from thence to Paris. Admiral Duncan's fleet has been reinforced to twenty-one sail of the line, so that, even if the wind come round in our favour, it would be madness in us to venture an action, with such a terrible inferiority of force; in addition to which, we have now, in consequence of the delays occasioned by the wind, not above ten days' provisions remaining for the troops on board. The plan proposed is, in fact, but an improvement on the last one, viz. to land the troops, and quarter them in the neighbourhood, so as to be able to collect them in forty-eight hours; to appear to have renounced the idea of the expedition, but in the mean time to re-victual the fleet with all diligence and secrecy, which may occupy probably a month; to endeavour even to reinforce it by one or two vessels, who might, in that time, be got ready for sea. All this will bring us to the time of the equinox, when it will be impossible for the

enemy (who will besides, it is probable, have relaxed in his vigilance, in consequence of these manœuvres,) to keep the sea. When all is ready, the troops are to be reimbarked with the greatest expedition, and a push to be made instantly for Scotland, as already detailed. "Capot me, but it wears a face." Such is the present idea, which we shall probably lick into more shape. The General talks of sending me to the Hague to confer with the Dutch Government and General Dejean; from thence to Wetzlar, to communicate with Hoche; and from thence to Paris, to open the affair to the Minister of Marine. "A very pretty journey indeed; and, besides, where's the money?" Well, I do not see how I can be so well employed during this vacant month; so, in God's name, I am ready.

3. This day the General gave me my instructions to set off to join General Hoche, at Wetzlar, and give him a copy of the memorial containing the plan already mentioned. He gave me, besides, verbal instructions to the following import; namely, that it might be expedient to follow up the first debarkation by a second of 15,000 of the French troops now in the pay of Holland; with which reinforcement, the army, being brought up to 30,000 men, could maintain itself in Scotland in spite of any force that could be brought against it; that it might even penetrate into England, and by that means force the enemy to a peace; that 25,000 might be employed on this service, and the remaining 5,000 detached into Ireland, from whence it was

morally certain that a great portion of the troops would be withdrawn to defend England itself: that, if General Hoche would, in that case, take the command of the united armies, he (Daendels) desired nothing better than to serve under him; if not, he was ready to serve under any other French General, (being a senior officer,) in which case each army was, as to all matters of discipline, administration, &c. to remain under their respective chiefs. He mentioned Chaumont as a proper person, in case Hoche declined to command the expedition; Macdonald* to command the French troops; and himself, of course, the Dutch. He desired me likewise, but this was matter of great confidence, to tell Hoche that, in case he approved of the plan, he should write to the Directory, recommending to them to press the Dutch Government strongly to the adoption of it; that, to this effect, the Directory should write a letter to the Committee for Foreign Affairs at the Hague, flattering and praising them extremely for what they had hitherto done, and the great exertions they had made, and exhorting them to continue the same laudable zeal; reminding them that France was now negotiating with England, and if it were not for the interests of her allies, could have an honourable peace in an hour; that the success of the enterprise in question would exceedingly strengthen her hands, and infallibly secure the restitution of all the Dutch possessions in both In-

* Now Duke of Tarentum.

dies; finally, to make them feel that it was incumbent on them to make every effort on their part to second the Republic, at a time when she was exposing herself to war, merely for their interests—when she could, by renouncing them, secure that peace so necessary to herself, in all respects, at this moment. In addition to all this, Daendels desired me to explain to Hoche the necessity of a greater degree of communication on the part of the French Government; that of the Batavian Republic being in utter ignorance of the state of preparations at Brest and elsewhere, and whether any or what degree of support or co-operation might be expected, which naturally threw a certain degree of damp, and had a sinister effect, on their operations. With these instructions, I set off the same day with Lowry and Tennant, who determined to take this opportunity to go to Paris.

12. The last eight days I spent on the road 'twixt Alkmaer and Wetzlar. At Brussels, we heard the first rumour of the conspiracy of Pichegru, CARNOT, and the downfal of the Royalists, on the 18th Fructidor.

13. This day I saw General Hoche, who is just returned from Frankfort; he has been very ill with a violent cold, and has still a cough, which makes me seriously uneasy about him; he does not seem to apprehend any thing himself, but I should not be surprised, for my part, if, in three months, he were in a rapid consumption. He is dreadfully altered, and has a dry, hollow cough, that it is distressing to

the last degree to hear. I immediately explained to him the cause of my arrival, gave him Daendels' plan and the map of Scotland, and such further elucidation as I was able in conversation. He shook his head at the idea of a second embarkation at the mouth of the Clyde, and observed that, if we got safe into Scotland, the British would immediately detach a squadron of frigates into the Irish channel, which would arrive, to a moral certainty, before the Dutch frigates, (which were, according to the plan proposed, to go North-about,) and that they would thus cut us off from all communication with Ireland. As to the officers whom Daendels named, he observed that "Chaumont was as much of a General as he was that bottle," pointing to one that stood on the table before him; "that, as to Macdonald, he was a good officer, but he knew he would not go." I replied, as to the second embarkation, I was entirely of his opinion, and looked upon it as inexecutable; that, nevertheless, I thought well of the project, as a measure against England. He then told me that he would take it into his serious consideration, and let me know the result in three or four days; in the mean time, I am to attend his orders.

17. The General's health is in a most alarming state, and nobody here seems to suspect it, at least to the extent that I do. Urgent as the affair is on which I am here, I have found it impossible to speak to him about it; and God knows when, or whether I may ever, find an opportunity, which, in addition

to my personal regard and love for him, is a circumstance which very much aggravates my uneasiness. To-day he has been removed by four grenadiers from one chamber to another: for he is unable to walk. It is terrible to see a fine handsome fellow, in the very flower of youth and strength, so reduced. Wrote yesterday to General Daendels, to apologize for my silence, letting him know that I found it as yet impossible to speak to General Hoche about our affair; partly on account of the state of his health, and partly on account of his being so occupied, as well by the command of the two armies of the Rhine and Sambre et Meuse, as by the late events in Paris; promising, at the same time, to write again in three or four days, and entreating him, meanwhile, to continue his preparations on the system we had settled at my departure from the Texel.

19. My fears, with regard to General Hoche, were but too well founded. He died this morning at four o'clock. His lungs seemed to be quite gone. This most unfortunate event has so confounded and distressed me, that I know not what to think, nor what will be the consequences. Wrote to my wife, and to General Daendels, instantly. Yesterday Simon, by the General's orders, after communicating with me, wrote to the Minister for Foreign Affairs and of the Marine, but I know not to what effect.

21. The death of General Hoche having broken my connection with the army of Sambre et Meuse, where I have no longer any business, I applied this

day (20th) for an order to set off for Paris, which I obtained instantly from General Lefebvre, who commands in chief *per interim.* Set off at four o'clock and travelled all night; arrived at twelve, on the 21st, at Coblentz, and at night at Bonn.

22. This is the 1st Vendemiaire, the anniversary of the establishment of the French Republic. Called early on my friend Mr. Shee, whom I found occupied in preparing for the fête which is to be celebrated on the occasion. At twelve, assisted at the fête, and dined afterwards with the *Commission Intermediaire*, the Municipality of Bonn, the constituted authorities, &c.: drank sundry loyal and constitutional toasts, but not *too many*, as appears by this journal, which I am peaceably writing at my inn. After dinner, Mr. Shee told me he had just received intelligence, from a quarter on which he very much relied, that the negotiation with England was knocked on the head, which, if it be true, as is highly probable, is excellent news. Settled to call upon him to-morrow early, and show him sundry papers, &c., and came home soberly and wrote to General Daendels. I had promised a very pretty woman at dinner, "whose name I know not, but whose person I reverence," to meet her to-night at a grand ball given by the Municipality; but I will deceive her like a false traitor, and go to my innocent bed; yet she is very pretty for all that, and speaks very pretty German French, and I am sure has not one grain of cruelty in her composition, and besides, "*à la guerre, comme à la guerre*;" but then, I must set off to-morrow, and so, "Oh, cruel fate! that gave

thee to the Moor!" Besides, I have just received a delightful letter from my dearest love, written three months ago, which has put me out of conceit with all women but herself, so, as before, I will go to my virtuous bed.

PERIOD OF GENERAL TONE'S ATTACHMENT TO THE ARMÉE D'ANGLETERRE.

N. B. *November* 21. It is, to-day, upwards of two months since I made a memorandum; which is downright scandalous: for many important circumstances have happened in that time. The only good in my journals is, that they are written at the moment, and represent things exactly as they strike me; whereas, when I write after an interval of some time —— But I am going into an essay on journal writing, instead of my business. Let me endeavour to take up, as well as I can, from memory, the thread of my history.

October 1, or thereabouts, I arrived in Paris, where I had the satisfaction to find my wife and little babies in health and spirits; went to Lewines, who is in high favour here with every body: he is all but acknowledged as Minister from Ireland, and I am heartily glad of it; for I have an excellent opinion of his integrity and talents. He has the *entrées libres* with Barras, Pléville Lepelley (Minister of the Marine,) and Talleyrand Perigord, (Minister for Foreign Affairs,) whom I saw in Philadelphia, when we were both in exile. In a day or two we went together to the Minister for the Marine, in order to ask him to give me a note of introduction to Barras, but were not able to beat it into his head that we did not want him to present me formally to the Directory, as an agent from some foreign power: on which I set him down in my own mind for a dunce. In consequence of his refusal, we determined to go ourselves to the Luxembourg, which we did accordingly, two or three evenings after. We found Barras at home, giving favourable audience to Madame Tallien, with whom he retired into an inner room, where they continued, I have no doubt, very seriously employed, for about half an hour. On his return, we presented ourselves, and I delivered him the memorial which General Daendels had entrusted me with for General Hoche, and, at the same time, detailed to him fully all the verbal instructions I had received from General Daendels. He heard me very attentively, and told me in reply that he expected General Debelle, brother-in-law to General Hoche, in town every day, who had the thread of our affairs in his hands; and that, on his arrival, I should address myself to him.

5, (or thereabouts.) General Debelle arrived; and I immediately waited on him, agreeably to Barras's orders. After telling him all that I was instructed to do, he desired me to make a note of it, which I did accordingly, and delivered to him a day or two after. Some short time after, he told me that most probably it would be Simon, who was with us in the expedition to Bantry Bay, who would be charged with the command. I saw clearly the fact, that

Debelle knew nothing of the determination of the Government: he set off for the army in a day or two after, and I have not seen him since. As it was now time to think a little of my own affairs, I applied to General Hédouville to obtain me an order to stay in Paris, in order to follow up the business wherewith I was charged by Generals Hoche and Daendels, and to receive the arrears of my appointments which are due to me.

The day after its proclamation, I saw an *arrêté* of the Directory, ordaining the formation of an army, to be called *L'armée d'Angleterre;* and appointing Buonaparte to command it. Bravo! This looks as if they were in earnest. General Desaix, of the army of the Rhine, (who distinguished himself so much by his defence of Kehl against Prince Charles, in the last campaign) is ordered to superintend the organization of the army until the arrival of Buonaparte.

It is singular enough, that I should have forgotten to mention in its place the famous battle, fought on the 11th of October, between the English fleet, under Admiral Duncan, and the Dutch, commanded by Dewinter. There never was a more complete victory than that gained by the English. The fleets were equal in number, but they had the advantage in number of guns and weight of metal. It was well I was not on board the Vryheid. If I had, it would have been a pretty piece of business. I fancy I am not to be caught at sea by the English—for this is the second escape I have had; and by land I mock myself of them.

NOVEMBER, 1797.

8. My brother Matthew joined me from Hamburgh, where he arrived about a month ago. It is a great satisfaction to me, and I hope he arrives just in time to take a part in the expedition.

9. This day General Hédouville brought me to General Berthier, and presented me to him, recommending me in the warmest manner We had very little conversation, but he promised to speak of me to General Buonaparte, whom he sets off to join in three or four days. Two days after, I called, and left for him a memorial of about five lines, addressed to Buonaparte, offering my services, &c. It is droll enough I should be writing to Buonaparte.

20. Yesterday General Hédouville presented me to Desaix, who is arrived within these few days. I could not possibly desire to meet a more favourable reception; he examined me a good deal as to the localities of Ireland, the face of the country, the facility of finding provisions; on which I informed him as well as I could. He told me that he had not directly the power himself to name the officers who were to be employed in the army of England, but that I need not be uneasy, for I might rely I should be of the number. His expression, at parting, was "*Laissez moi faire, nous arrangerons tout cela.*" So I may happen to have another offer at John Bull before I die. God knows how I desire it. I like Desaix at least as well, if not better, than any of his *confrères* I have yet seen. There is a soldier-like

frankness and sincerity in his manner, from which I augur every thing favourable.

25. This day we, viz. Lewines, Lowry, Tennant, Orr, Teeling, and myself, gave a grand dinner, at Méots, to Generals Desaix, Hédouville, Watrin, Mermet, Dufalga, and one or two of their aids-de-camp. Watrin and Mermet we asked as being friends of General Hoche, and embarked in the expedition of last year. Our dinner was superb, and every thing went off very well; we had the fort of Kehl represented in the dessert, in compliment to Desaix.

29. This day received my arrears for four months, so now I am at my ease as to cash—2,330 livres.

December, 1797.

10. This day was a grand fête, to receive the ratification of the treaty of peace by the Emperor, which has been brought up by Buonaparte in person to the Directory. It was superb, and I was particularly pleased with the President Barras's speech, wherein reigns a spirit of the most determined hostility to England. As far as I can observe, all parties in France are sincerely united in this sentiment.

12. Called this day, with Lewines, on General Desaix, and gave him Taylor's map of Ireland. He tells us to be under no anxiety; that the French Government will never quit the grasp which they have got of England, till they humble her to the dust; that it is their wish, and their interest (that of all France as well as of Ireland); that the Government now

had means, and powerful ones, particularly money, and they would devote them all to this great object; it might be a little sooner or a little later, but that the success of the measure was inevitable. Barras has lately, in one or two different conversations, gone as far with Lewines as Desaix with me.

21. General Desaix brought Lewines and me this morning and introduced us to Buonaparte, at his house in the Rue Chantereine. He lives in the greatest simplicity; his house is small, but neat, and all the furniture and ornaments in the most classical taste. He is about five feet six inches high, slender and well made, but stoops considerably; he looks at least ten years older than he is, owing to the great fatigues he underwent in his immortal campaign of Italy. His face is that of a profound thinker, but bears no marks of that great enthusiasm and unceasing activity by which he has been so much distinguished. It is rather, to my mind, the countenance of a mathematician than of a general. He has a fine eye, and a great firmness about his mouth; he speaks low and hollow. So much for his manner and figure. We had not much discourse with him; and what little there was, was between him and Lewines, to whom, as our Ambassador, I gave the *pas*. We told him that Tennant was about to depart for Ireland, and was ready to charge himself with his orders if he had any to give. He desired us to bring him the same evening, and so we took our leave. In the evening we returned with Tennant, and Lewines had a good

deal of conversation with him; that is to say, *insensed* him a good deal on Irish affairs, of which he appears singularly uninformed: for example, he seems convinced that our population is not more than two millions—which is nonsense. Buonaparte listened, but said very little. When all this was finished, he desired that Tennant might put off his departure for a few days, and then, turning to me, asked whether I was not an Adjutant General? To which I answered, that I had the honour to be attached to General Hoche in that capacity. He asked me where I had learned to speak French? To which I replied, that I had learned the little I knew since my arrival in France, about twenty months ago. He then desired us to return next evening but one, at the same hour, and so we parted. As to my French, I am ignorant whether it was the purity or barbarism of my diction which drew his attention, and as I shall never inquire, it must remain as an historical doubt, to be investigated by the learned of future ages.

23. Called this evening on Buonaparte, by appointment, with Tennant and Lewines, and saw him for about five minutes. Lewines gave him a copy of the memorials I delivered to the Government, in February 1796,* (nearly two years ago,) and which fortunately have been well verified in every material fact, by all that has taken place in Ireland since. His manner is cold, and he speaks very

* See Appendix.

little; it is not, however, so dry as that of Hoche, but seems rather to proceed from languor than any thing else. He is perfectly civil, however, to us; but from what we have yet seen or heard from him, it is impossible to augur any thing good or bad. We have now seen the greatest man in Europe three times, and I am astonished to think how little I have to record about him. I am sure I wrote ten times as much about my first interview with Charles de la Croix, but then I was a greenhorn; I am now a little used to see great men, and great statesmen, and great generals, and that has, in some degree, broke down my admiration. Yet, after all, it is a droll thing that I should become acquainted with Buonaparte. This time twelve months, I arrived in Brest, from my expedition to Bantry Bay. Well, the third time, they say, is the charm. My next chance, I hope, will be with the *Armée d'Angleterre*—*Allons! Vive la Republique!* I make no memorandums now at all, which is grievous; but I have nothing to write.

January, 1798.

1. I wish myself the compliments of the season; a merry Christmas and a happy new Year. The Minister of Foreign Affairs has written to the Minister of Police, that whereas Pitt may probably endeavour to slide in some of his emissaries under the character of Refugee United Irishmen, none be permitted to remain but such as *I* may vouch for—which shows they have some confidence in me;

and the Minister of Police has given his order in consequence.

2 to 6. Called on my old friend General Clarke, who is at last returned to Paris: his close connection with Carnot has thrown him out of employment, and I am heartily sorry for it; for I have a very good opinion of him. He is, however, very well with Buonaparte, to whom he tells me he has spoken of me in the strongest manner, for which I feel sincerely obliged.

13. Saw Buonaparte this evening with Lewines, who delivered him a whole sheaf of papers relative to Ireland, including my two memorials of 1795, great part of which stands good yet. I took this opportunity to mention the desire all the Refugee United Irishmen, now in Paris, had to bear a part in the expedition, and the utility they would be of in case of a landing in Ireland. He answered that they would all be undoubtedly employed, and desired me to give him in, for that purpose, a list of their names. Finally, I spoke of myself, telling him that General Desaix had informed me that I was carried on the tableau of the *Armée d'Angleterre*: he said "I was." I then observed that I did not pretend to be of the smallest use to him whilst we were in France, but that I hoped to be serviceable to him on the other side of the water; that I did not give myself to him at all for a military man, having neither the knowledge nor the experience that would justify me in charging myself with any function;—"*Mais vous êtes brave,*" said he, inter-

rupting me. I replied that, when the occasion presented itself, that would appear. "*Eh bien,*" said he, "*cela suffit.*"

FEBRUARY, 1798.

1. The number of Irish refugees is considerably increased. Independent of Lewines, Tennant, and Lowry, of whom I have spoken, there are Teeling of Lisburn, Orr of Derry, M'Mahon of County Down, Macan and Burgess of County Lowth, Napper Tandy, and my brother. There is also one Maguire, who was sent by Reynolds from Philadelphia, in consequence of my letter to him by Monroe, and one Ashley, an Englishman, formerly Secretary to the Corresponding Society, and one of those who was tried with Thomas Hardy, in London, for high treason. We all do very well except Napper Tandy, who is not behaving correctly. He began some months ago by caballing against me with a priest of the name of Quigley, who is since gone off no one knows whither; the circumstances of this petty intrigue are not worth my recording. It is sufficient to say that Tandy took on him to summon a meeting of the Irish refugees, at which Lewines and I were to be arraigned, on I know not what charges, by himself and Quigley. Lewines refused to attend, but I went; and when I appeared, there was no one found to bring forward a charge against me, though I called three times to know "whether any person had any thing to offer." In consequence of this manœuvre, I have had no com-

munication since with Tandy, who has also lost ground, by this mean behaviour, with all the rest of his countrymen; he is, I fancy, pestering the Government here with applications and memorials, and gives himself out for an old officer, and a man of great property in Ireland, as I judge from what General Murat said to me in speaking of him the other night at Buonaparte's. He asked me did I know one Tandy, "*un ancien militaire, n'est-ce pas?*" I said I did know him, but could not say that he was exactly "*un ancien militaire*," as he had never served but in the volunteer corps of Ireland, a body which resembled pretty much the *Garde Nationale* of France at the beginning of the Revolution." "*Mais c'est un très riche proprietaire?*"—I told him I believed he was always in easy circumstances; and there the discourse ended. By this I see how he is showing himself off here. He has got lately a coadjutor in the famous Thomas Muir, who is arrived at Paris, and has inserted two or three very foolish articles relating to the United Irishmen in the Paris papers, in consequence of which, at a meeting of the United Irishmen now in Paris, (with the exception of Tandy,) it was settled that Lowry, Orr, Lewines, and myself, should wait upon Muir, and, after thanking him for his good intentions, intreat him not to introduce our business into any publications which he might hereafter think proper to make. Accordingly, we waited on him a few days since; but of all the vain, obstinate blockheads that ever I met, I never saw his equal. I could scarcely conceive such a degree of self-sufficiency to exist. He told us roundly that he knew as much of our country as we did, and would venture to say he had as much the confidence of the United Irishmen as we had; that he had no doubt we were very respectable individuals, but could only know us *as such*, we having shown him no powers or written authority to prove that we had any mission; that he seldom acted without due reflection, and when he had once taken his party, it was impossible to change him; and that, as to what he had written relative to the United Irishmen, he had the sanction of, he would say, the most respectable individual of that body, who had, and deserved to have, their entire confidence and approbation, and whose authority he must and did consider as justifying every syllable he had advanced. This most respectable individual of the body, we presume to be Tandy: for we did not ask his name. So that, after a discussion of nearly three hours, we were obliged to come away *re infectâ*, except that we gave Mr. Muir notice, that he had neither license nor authority to speak in the name of the people of Ireland, and that if we saw any similar productions to those of which we complained, we should be obliged to take measures that would conduce neither to his ease nor respectability: for that we could not suffer the public to be longer abused. On these terms we parted very drily on both sides. The fact is, Muir and Tandy are puffing one another here for their private advantage; they are supporting themselves by indorsing each other's credit, and issuing, if I may so say, accommodation-bills of reputation. This conversation has given the *coup de grace* to Tandy with his countrymen here, and he is now, in a manner, completely *in Coventry*. He deserves it. These details are hardly worth writing, but as there may be question of the business hereafter, I thought I might as well put them down.

10. Lewines was the other night with Buonaparte, when a conversation took place, which I think, from his relation of it, worth recording. Since the 18th Fructidor, the Jacobins are, in a certain degree, more tolerated by Government than formerly, and some of their leaders, who had been tried at Vendome with Babœuf, venture to show themselves a little.—On that evening, a person called on the General from the Minister of Police, and spoke to him for a considerable time in a low voice, so that Lewines did not hear what he said, but it appears by the sequel that it was probably relative to some overtures from the chiefs of that party: for Buonaparte, all at once, sprang into the middle of the room, with great heat, and said, "What would these gentlemen have? France is revolutionized! Holland is revolutionized! Italy is revolutionized! Switzerland is revolutionized! Europe will soon be revolutionized! But this, it seems, is not enough to content them. I know well what they want; they want the domination of thirty or forty individuals, founded on the massacre of three or four millions; they want the constitution of 1793, but

they shall not have it, and death to him who shall demand it! We did not fail to reduce them to order when we had but 1,500 men, and we will do it much easier now, when we have 30,000. We will have the present constitution, and no other; and we have common sense and our bayonets to maintain it. I know these persons, in order to give themselves some little consequence, affect to spread reports of some pretended disunion between the Government and the Legislative Body. It is false. From the foundation of the Republic to this day, there never was, perhaps, a moment when there reigned such perfect harmony between the constituted authorities; and I may add, since it seems they are so good as to count me for something in the affair, that I am perfectly in union of sentiment and esteem with the Government, and they with me. He that fears calumny is below me. What I have done has not been done in a *boudoir*, and it is for Europe and posterity to judge me. No! we will not have the assistance of those gentlemen who call themselves chiefs and leaders of the people; we acknowledge no chiefs nor leaders but those pointed out by the Constitution,—the Legislative Body and the Executive Directory; and to them only will we pay respect or attention. For the others, we know very well how to deal with them, if necessary; and, for my part, I declare, for one, that if I had only the option between royalty and the system of those gentlemen, I would not hesitate one moment to declare for a King. But we will have neither the one nor the other; we will have the Republic and the Constitution, with which if those persons pretend to interfere, they shall soon be made sensible of their absolute nullity." He spoke to this effect, as Lewines reported to me, but in a strain of the greatest animation and with admirable eloquence.

11. In conversation, to-day, with Gen. Clarke, I mentioned to him how happy I was when the news of the armistice between Buonaparte and the Austrians arrived, as I began to be extremely uneasy at his situation. Clarke assured me I was quite right in that respect; that the fact was, the division of Joubert was completely beaten out of the Tyrol by the peasants, with no better arms than chance furnished, down to clubs and sticks, with which they charged the French like madmen, and drove before them the very same troops who had so often defeated the best-disciplined forces of Austria:—of such an uncertain nature is the courage of armies, and so much are they disconcerted by a mode of fighting different from that to which they have been accustomed! that the Venetians were rising *en masse* and Trieste was retaken, so that the communication with Italy was exceedingly embarrassed; that, if the army had met with the least check in front, it was ruined, and every step that Buonaparte advanced increased his difficulties and multiplied the probabilities against him. I was glad to hear my own opinion confirmed by Clarke, who is a military man of experience and character, and especially, who was on the spot at the moment.

MARCH, 1798.

1. An event has taken place, of a magnitude scarce, if at all, inferior in importance to that of the French Revolution. The Pope is dethroned and in exile. The circumstances relating to this great event are such as to satisfy my mind that there is a special Providence guiding the affairs of Europe at this moment, and turning every thing to the great end of the emancipation of mankind, from the yoke of religious and political superstition under which they have so long groaned.

3. I have seen lately in the paper called the *Bien Informé*, two articles relating to Napper Tandy, which are most ridiculous rhodomontades. They describe him as an Irish general to whose standard 30,000 United Irishmen will fly the moment he displays it, and other trash of the like nature. This must come directly or indirectly from himself; for I remember some time ago, at a dinner given to him, Madgett, and myself, by Aherne, as soon as he got warm with wine, he asserted he would answer, himself, for raising all the yeomanry of Ireland, who were at least 30,000 men—precisely the number above stated. This is sad pitiful work, puffing a man's self in this manner, especially when it is *not true.*

4. On the 19th February last, (as I see in the Courier of the 26th,) Lord Moira made a motion of great expectation in the Irish House of Lords, tending to condemn the vigorous measures which have

been pursued by the British government in that country, and to substitute a milder system. I was exceedingly disappointed at his speech, which was feeble indeed, containing little else than declamation, and scarcely a single fact, at a time when thousands of crimes of the most atrocious nature have been perpetrated for months over the whole face of the country. In times like ours, half friends are no friends. A man in his situation, who can tell the truth with safety, (or even with danger,) and does not, is a feeble character, and his support is not worth receiving. He must speak out ALL, boldly, or be silent. Independent of this, which I cannot but consider as a timid and unmanly suppression of facts which, on this great occasion especially, should be sounded through Europe if possible by every man having a drop of genuine Irish blood in his veins, there is introduced a strained compliment to the virtues of the King, and a most extravagant and fulsome eulogium on the magnanimity of his Royal Highness George Prince of Wales, which completely disgusted me. A pretty time, indeed, to come out with a panegyric on the royal virtues, and the virtues of the princely heir, when his ministers and his army are laying the country waste with fire and with sword. " I hate such half-faced fellowship." His lordship, at the conclusion of this milk-and-water harangue, comes to his conciliatory plan, which is to check the army in their barbarities, and to grant Catholic Emancipation and Parliamentary Reform. It is really amusing to see the various shifts and struggles, turns, twists and wry faces, the noble Lord makes, before he can bring himself to swallow this last bitter pill. This kind of conduct will never do well at any time, but it is downright folly in times like the present. His Lordship has mortally offended one party, and not at all satisfied the other, as will always be the case in similar circumstances. I am sorry for all this, because I esteem him personally; politically I must give him up, the more so, as HE OUGHT TO HAVE KNOWN BETTER. But if Lord Moira speaks in this half-and-half style, the Chancellor, on the other side, appears not to have been so reserved; he openly calls the United Irishmen *rebels*, and says they should be treated as such; he mentions me by name, as having been Adjutant-General in Hoche's expedition, and again in the armament at the Texel, and says I am at this very moment an accredited envoy at Paris from that accursed Society, who had also, as he is pleased to say, their envoys at Lisle, by whose insidious and infernal machinations it was, that Lord Malmesbury's negotiation was knocked on the head. He also makes divers commentaries on a well-known letter written by me to my friend Russell in 1791, and which, one way or other, he has brought regularly before the House at least once a session ever since, and which figures in the secret report made by Secretary Pelham, in the last. From all these facts, and divers others which he enumerates, he infers, that the design of the United Irishmen is to separate Ireland from Great Britain, and that, consequently, all measures to destroy that infamous conspiracy are fair and lawful; of which opinion the House of Lords was also, Lord Moira's motion being rejected by a large majority. I can hardly, I think, be suspected of partiality to the Chancellor, but I declare I have a greater respect for his conduct on this occasion, than for that of Lord Moira. He is at least an open and avowed enemy; he takes his party, such as it is, like a man who expects no quarter, and is, therefore, determined to give none. Had Lord Moira brought as much sincerity to the attack on that most atrocious of all Governments, as the Chancellor did to its defence, though I am far from thinking he would have been able to influence the decision of the House of Lords, he would at least have been able to scandalize it to all Europe. Instead of that, he has trimmed, and by trimming has lost himself: for, to repeat it once more, in terrible times as ours now are, a man must speak out the whole truth or be silent.

But to return to my friend Fitzgibbon. Though his speech be sincere, I cannot think it very wise, under all the circumstances of the case. If the people of Ireland had any doubts as to the determination of the French Government to support them, he has taken care to remove them all, by dwelling on the reception their envoys have met with here. If the United Irishmen, groaning so long under a horrible persecution, might be supposed to relax a little in their resolution, he has been so kind as to raise their drooping spirits, by showing them that a simple emissary from their society has had such influence with the Executive Directory as to outweigh all the offers of his Majesty's Ministers to obtain peace, and even to cause the sending away of his ambassador, in a manner certainly not the most grateful to his feelings; in short, he has let out the grand secret, that there is a regular communication between the Patriots (or, as he is pleased to call them, the rebels,) of Ireland and the French Executive; that the independence of our country is the common object of both, which they are determined to pursue in concert, until it is attained; and that all the efforts of Government, to stop the progress of this most fearful event, have been and continue to be vain. That this candid avowal of such important facts, coming from such authority, is likely to raise the spirits of the adherents to the English Government, and to extinguish all hope in the breasts of the patriots, is, I confess, more than I can bring myself to believe. On the whole, I do not think the Chancellor's speech that of a profound and temperate statesman; such as it is, however, I will take care to submit, or cause it to be submitted, to Buonaparte and one or two other Republicans here, who I think will be edified by the contents thereof. With regard to what he says of Lewines and myself, who, I presume, are the envoys of this pernicious Society that he alludes to, his information, wherever he got, or however he came by it, is correct enough; what relates to me, is quite right; and as to Lewines, though he certainly was not at Lisle, artfully undermining Lord Malmesbury, I do admit he was doing his best to defeat him at the Luxembourg and elsewhere, and I hope and believe with success. What weight his representations may have had, we cannot exactly know, not being in the secrets of the Directory; but without vanity, he may reasonably conclude that some weight they certainly had, and if it was they which turned off my Lord Malmesbury, according to the Chancellor's assertion, Lewines may boldly say that he has, in that instance, deserved well of his country. The fact is, he and I have both done our best here to serve the cause of liberty in Ireland, but we have neither done as much good, nor as much evil, as Fitzgibbon is pleased to lay to our charge, and, for example, in the present instance, I do not think in my conscience that it was we who hunted Lord Malmesbury out of the country.—*Allons!*

20. It is with the most sincere concern and anxiety that I see in the late English papers, that Arthur O'Connor has been arrested at Margate, endeavouring to procure a passage for France; the circumstances mentioned indicate a degree of rashness and indiscretion on his part which is astonishing. It seems he set off from London in company with four others, viz. Quigley the Priest, who was some time since in Paris, and of whom I have no great reason to be an admirer; Binns of the Corresponding Society; Alley, also of the Corresponding Society; and his servant, of the name of Leary. Quigley called himself at first, Captain Jones, and afterwards Colonel Morris,

the others passed for his servants. Their first attempt was at a place called Whitstable, where the vigilance of the Custom-house officers embarrassed them. They then hired a cart, which they loaded with their trunks, (of which it seems they were sufficiently provided,) and crossed the country on foot for twenty-five miles to Margate. It does not appear that they made much mystery of their intended destination; but be that as it may, at Margate they were arrested by the Bow-street runners, Fugin and Rivet, who had followed them *à la piste* from London. From Margate they were brought back with their luggage to the Metropolis, where they were examined, two or three successive days, before the Privy Council, and finally committed to the Tower. Since their committal, several other persons have been arrested, particularly a Colonel Despard, a Mr. Bonham, and a Mr. Evans. It is inconceivable, that five men should attempt such an enterprize, and with such a quantity of luggage; it is equally incredible, that they should bring papers with them, of which the newspapers say several have been found, and especially one in the great-coat pocket of Quigley, purporting to be an address from the Executive Directory of England to that of France, and desiring the latter to give credit to Quigley, as being "the worthy citizen whom they had lately seen." These last expressions stagger me, or I should not believe it possible any man living would leave a paper of such consequence in such a careless extraordinary place. Other newspapers, however, say that no papers have been found, but the expressions above quoted shake me a good deal. It is also reported that O'Connor has said, his friends may be easy about him, as he has nothing to fear. God send it may be so, but I am very much afraid he will find it otherwise. It is dreadful to think of a man of his situation, character, and talents, being caught in so extraordinary and unaccountable a manner. I cannot conceive it. Time, and time only, will explain whether there is any treachery in the business. It is certain, Government had notice of their intentions before they set off: for the Bow-street officers left London as soon as they did. The report is, that they will be tried at Maidstone by a special commission, consisting of Justices Buller, Heath, and Lawrence; which is expected to sit before the 10th of April. I expect that event with the most anxious solicitude, but fear the very worst, for a thousand reasons.

24. This day I received my orders to set off for head-quarters at Rouen, where I am to remain in the suite of the Etat Major, till further orders. There is at least one step made.

25. Received my letters of service from the War Office, as Adjutant General in the Armée d'Angleterre. This has a lofty sound to be sure, but God knows the heart! Applied to the Minister at War for leave to remain a few days in Paris, to settle my family, which he granted.

26. I see in the English papers of March 17th, (from Irish papers of the 13th,) news of the most

disastrous and afflicting kind, as well for me individually as for the country at large. The English Government has arrested the whole committee of United Irishmen for the province of Leinster, including almost every man I know and esteem in the city of Dublin. Amongst them are Emmett, M'Neven, Dr. Sweetman, Bond, Jackson, and his son; warrants are likewise issued for the arrestation of Lord Edward Fitzgerald, M'Cormick, and Sampson; who have not however yet been found. It is by far the most terrible blow which the cause of liberty in Ireland has yet sustained. I know not whether in the whole party it would be possible to replace the energy, talents, and integrity, of which we are deprived by this most unfortunate of events. I have not received such a shock from all that has passed since I left Ireland. What a triumph at this moment for Fitzgibbon! These arrestations, following so close on that of O'Connor, give rise to very strong suspicions of treachery in my mind. I cannot bear to write or think longer on this dreadful event. Well, if our unfortunate country is doomed to sustain the unspeakable loss of so many brave and virtuous citizens, woe be to their tyrants, if ever we reach our destination. I feel my mind growing every hour more and more savage. Measures appear to me now justified by necessity, which, six months ago, I would have regarded with horror. There is now no medium. Government has drawn the sword, and will not recede, but to superior force—*if ever that force arrives.* But it does not signify threatening. Judge of my feelings as an individual, when Emmett and Russell are in prison, and in imminent peril of a violent and ignominious death. What revenge can satisfy me for the loss of the two men I most esteem on earth? Well, once more, it does not signify threatening. If they are sacrificed, and I ever arrive, as I hope to do, in Ireland, it will not go well with their enemies. This blow has completely deranged me—I can scarce write connectedly.

29. The last arrestations seem to be followed up by others.—Government will now stop at nothing.

31. Called with Lewines on Talleyrand, the Minister for Foreign Affairs, to take leave previous to my setting off for the army, and met with a gracious reception. I took that opportunity to tell him, I had reason to think that Lewines and I, as is the fact, were exposed to some little dirty intrigues here, and all we desired was, that he would judge us, not after any calumnious report, but after our conduct, such as he himself had observed it. He replied, we might make ourselves easy on that head; that he had heard nothing disadvantageous with regard to us, but even if he had, he should pay it no attention—the opinion of Government being made up in our favour. This is pleasant, the more so as poor Lewines and I have been tormented latterly with dirty cabals and factions, which I scorn to commit to paper. We have, God knows, done our best to content every body, but we find it impossible, whilst one of us is Adjutant General, and the other is well received, and with attention by the French Govern-

ment. I solemnly declare I believe these are our sole offences, but, also, they are offences not to be forgiven. I hate such pitiful work, and I am heartily glad I am getting off to the army, where I shall be out of the reach of it. If I would dirty my paper with them, I could record some anecdotes which are curious enough, were it only for their singular meanness; but I will not; let them die and rot; my conduct will stand the test, and to that I trust. When a man knows he has nothing to accuse himself of, it is not very difficult to bear the malevolence of others, with which profound observation I dismiss this chapter.

APRIL, 1798.

2. Lewines waited yesterday on Merlin, who is President to the Directory for this Trimestre, presented him with a letter of introduction from Talleyrand, and pressed on him (as far as he could with propriety) the necessity of sending succours to Ireland the earliest possible moment, especially on account of the late arrestations. Merlin replied, that, as to the time or place of succour, he could tell him nothing, it being the secret of the State; but, though he could not enter into the details of the intended expedition, he would tell him thus much to comfort him, "*That France never would grant a peace to England on any terms, short of the independence of Ireland.*" This is grand news. It is far more *direct and explicit* than any assurance we have yet got. Lewines made the proper acknowledgments, and then ran off

to me to communicate the news. The fact is, whatever the rest of our countrymen here may think, Lewines is doing his business fairly and well, and like a man of honour. I wish others of them whom I could name, had half as good principles.

3. Lewines is determined to take a journey to Holland, or perhaps to Hamburgh, on his private affairs; he will probably set off about the same time I do: he has been now on the Continent for the public business above fifteen months, at his own expense, to the amount of at least *500l.* sterling; during which time his colleagues at home have not thought proper to remit him one farthing; and it is now in order to raise money that he is going to Holland. It is to me unaccountable how men under whose good faith and authority he came here can so neglect their engagements; the rather as M'Neven, when *he* was here, undertook to remind them of their duty, and that proper remittances should be made. It is the less excusable, as several of the individuals concerned are not only in easy, but in affluent circumstances. So, however, it is, and, what is better, Lewines is accused here by some of his countrymen and fellow-sufferers of neglecting, if not sacrificing the public cause to his own private interests; in which accusation, by the by, I have the honour to find myself included; but as to that, "*je m'en fiche. Allons!*" To be sure, if any thing could shake the determination of a man who has made up his mind on our question, it would be the pitiful and mean persecution which he and I find ourselves exposed to

here, for some time back. There is no sort of *désagrément* that we have not suffered. Well, it is no matter; that will all pass away, and, in the long run, it will be seen whether we have not, each of us in his vocation, done our best for the country. Certain it is, however, that the pleasure I formerly felt in pursuing this great object is considerably diminished by recent experience. But once more, no matter: it is my duty to go on, and go on I will, arrive what may. I hope yet to do some good and prevent some mischief, and I foresee sufficient grounds to exercise me, both at one and the other. At all events, I will do my duty and discharge my conscience; and then come what may, I can abide the consequences.

4. This day, at three o'clock (having previously received my letters of service, order to join, *frais de route*, &c.), I set off for the head-quarters of the *Armée d Angleterre* at Rouen.

5. After travelling all night, arrived at twelve to-day, and took up my lodgings at the Maison Wattel. Met General Kilmaine by accident, who invited me to dinner; where I found General Lemoine, and Bessieres, Commandant of the guides of Buonaparte, &c. &c. Comedy in the evening.

6. Strolling about the town, which is large, ugly, and dirty. It wears, however, a great appearance of manufacturing and commercial activity, which, I have no doubt, in time of peace is considerably augmented. The Cathedral is a beautiful relic of Gothic architecture. I have seen the inside of Westminster

Abbey, and of Notre Dame, at Paris, as well as several others in Germany and elsewhere, but I prefer the inside of the Cathedral of Rouen to them all. It is a magnificent *coup d'œil.* But, what is provoking, between the body of the church and choir some pious Archbishop, who had more money than taste, has thrown a very spruce colonnade, of pure Corinthian architecture, which totally destroys the harmony of the building, and ruins what would otherwise produce a magnificent effect. This little specimen of Grecian architecture is more truly *Gothic* than all the rest of the edifice.

7. On a second inspection of the Cathedral this day, I find that the *Corinthian* colonnade, which is described in terms of such just indignation in yesterday's journal, turns out to be *Ionic;* but all 's one for that. The Archbishop I still hold to be a blockhead in all the dialects of Greece and all the orders of architecture.

8. Heard part of a sermon, this being Easter Sunday. Sad trash! a long parallel, which I thought would never end, between Jesus Christ and Joseph, followed by a second, equally edifying, comparing him with the prophet Jonas, showing how the one lay three nights in the tomb, and the other three nights in the belly of a great fish, &c.; at all which I profited exceedingly. The church was full of women, but I did not see twenty men. I wonder how people can listen to such abominable nonsense. —Apropos, I should have mentioned in its place that Lewines called a day or two before we left

town on Buonaparte, to endeavour to interest him in behalf of our unfortunate friends now under arrest, and try whether it would be feasible to obtain a declaration from the Directory, similar to that which they issued in the case of the patriots of the *Pays de Vaud*, for whose safety they made the aristocracy of Berne personally responsible. Buonaparte replied, that the case was totally different: with regard to the Swiss, France was in a situation to follow up the menace by striking instantly; with England, it was not so. She was a power of the first rank, and the Republic must never threaten in vain. Under these circumstances, he thought any interposition on the part of the French Government in favour of the Irish patriots might injure them materially, by inflaming still more the English Government against them, and could, at the same time, do them no possible service. In this reasoning Lewines was obliged to acquiesce, and, in fact, the argument is unanswerable.

20. Walked out this evening along the river, to see the *bateaux plats* which are building here for the descent. There are ten of them, four of which are launched. I judge the whole might be ready in three weeks or a month at farthest; they cost 13,000 livres apiece, or 541*l.* 13*s.* 4*d.* sterling. Apropos, of the expedition. I am utterly at a loss what to think since my departure from Paris. Desaix, whom I hoped to find here, seems certainly to be at Toulon; and the report in the papers of this day, as well as in my brother Matthew's letter, is, that Buonaparte is to set off in three days to join

him, and take the command of the inconceivable armament which is preparing in the ports of the Mediterranean, the destination of which nobody knows. It is certain that Buonaparte's guides set off from this on the road to Paris, three days ago. In the mean time, it seems General Kilmaine commands, *per interim*, the army of England. All this I confess utterly *deroutes* me. "I am lost in sensations of troubled emotions." The prevailing opinion in the Paris papers is, that Egypt is the object of this armament, and that the Turk is to concur with us in the expedition. If it were not for our own business, I should like extremely, in that case, to be with General Desaix: but that is "castle building." What if, when all was embarked, Buonaparte were suddenly to turn to the right on Gibraltar, and surprise Lord St. Vincent with a visit one of these fine mornings? but I am afraid he won't:—the thing is, however, possible.

24. The last Paris papers mention that Buonaparte is decidedly set off to take the command of the expedition which is preparing in the Mediterranean. It is, I learn, to consist of three divisions, one to embark at Toulon, commanded by Buonaparte in person; another at Genoa, by Kleber; and the third at Civita Vecchia, by Desaix. The object declared is Egypt and Syria.

25. William Hamilton, who married J. Russell's daughter, is arrived, a few days since, in Paris. He was obliged to fly to London, in consequence of the arrestation of O'Connor and his party. On his way

he met Lewines at Brussels; and also saw, in an English paper of the 3d, that the revolution in Ireland was commenced, having broken out in the south, and that General Abercrombie and the army were in full march to suppress it. Both he and Lewines believe it. For my part, I do not—it is, at most, some partial insurrection; and so much the worse. I wrote, however, to General Kilmaine, to request an order to join him at Paris, in case the news was true, which, however, I am sure it is not. My brother writes me word that there is a person waiting for Lewines at the Hague, who has made his escape with plans, charts, and other military information, and that Lewines is expected with him in Paris every day. Who can this be? I wish Lewines was returned.

26. I see in the Paris papers to-day, extracts from English ones, of a late date, by which it appears, as I suspected, that the news of an insurrection in Ireland was, as yet, premature; nevertheless, things in that country seem to be drawing fast to a close.

27. I am sadly off for intelligence here, having nothing but the imperfect extracts in the Paris papers. I see to-day, and am very glad to see it, that my friend Sir Lawrence Parsons has resigned the command of the King's County militia, in consequence of the sanguinary measures about to be adopted by the English Government, in which he will take no share. His example should be imitated by every country gentleman in Ireland; but they have neither the sense nor the virtue to see that. Alarming as

the state of Ireland really and truly is to the English Government, I have no doubt on my mind that it is their present policy to exaggerate the danger as much as possible, in order to terrify the Irish gentry out of their wits, and, under cover of this universal panic, to crush the spirit of the people and reduce the country to a state of slavery more deplorable than that of any former period of our deplorable history. They take a chance against nothing. They see that Ireland will escape them without a struggle, if they adopt lenient measures: they therefore prefer force. If it succeeds, well and good; if it fails, still Ireland is the material sufferer: it is she that bears all the actual calamities of war; and if England must, at last, renounce her sovereignty, at least she will desolate what she cannot subdue. It is a most infernal policy, but no new one for her to adopt. In this point of view, the conduct of the English Government, though atrociously wicked, is by no means deficient in system and arrangement. They have begun by seizing almost the whole of the chiefs of the people; and now they are about to draw the sword, in order to anticipate the possibility of assistance, and to reduce them to that state, that, if assistance should at length arrive, they may be unable to profit by it. In this last design, however, I am sure they will find themselves mistaken; the spirit is, I think, too universally spread to be checked now, and the vengeance of the people, whenever the occasion presents itself, will only be the more terrible and sanguinary. What miserable slaves are the gentry of Ireland! The only accusation brought against the United Irishmen by their enemies is, that they wish to break the connexion with England, or, in other words, to establish the independence of their country; an object in which, surely, the men of property are most interested. Yet the very sound of independence seems to have terrified them out of all sense, spirit, or honesty. If they had one drop of Irish blood in their veins, one grain of true courage or genuine patriotism in their hearts, they should have been the first to support this great object; the people would have supported them; the English Government would never have dared to attempt the measures they have since triumphantly pursued, and continue to pursue: our Revolution would have been accomplished without a shock, or perhaps one drop of blood spilled, which now can succeed, if it does succeed, only by all the calamities of a most furious and sanguinary contest—for the war in Ireland, whenever it takes place, will not be an ordinary one. The armies will regard each other, not as soldiers, but as deadly enemies. Who, then, are to blame for this? The United Irishmen, who set the question afloat, or the English Government and their partisans, the Irish gentry, who resist it? If independence be as good for a country as liberty for an individual, the question will be soon decided. Why does England so pertinaciously resist our independence? Is it for love of us? is it because *she* thinks *we* are better as we are? That single argument, if it stood alone, should determine every honest Irishman. But, it will be said, the United Irishmen extend their views farther; they go now to a distribution of property, and an Agrarian law. I know not whether they do or no. I am sure, in June, 1795, when I was forced to leave the country, they entertained no such ideas. If they have since taken root among them, the Irish gentry may accuse themselves. Even then they made themselves parties in the business; not content with disdaining to hold communication with the United Irishmen, they were among the foremost of their persecutors; even those who were pleased to denominate themselves patriots were more eager to vilify, and if they could to degrade them, than the most devoted and submissive slaves of the English Government. What wonder, if the leaders of the United Irishmen, finding themselves not only deserted, but attacked, by those who, for every reason, should have been their supporters and fellow-labourers, felt themselves no longer called upon to observe any measures with men only distinguished by the superior virulence of their persecuting spirit? If such men, in the issue, lose their property, they are themselves alone to blame, by deserting the first and most sacred of duties—duty to their country. They have incurred a wilful forfeiture, by disdaining to occupy the station they might have held among the People, and which the People would have been glad to see them fill: they left a vacancy, to be seized by those who had more courage, more sense, and more honesty; and not only so, but, by this base and interested desertion, they furnished their enemies with every argument of justice, policy, and interest, to enforce the system of confiscation. Besides, if the United Irishmen succeed, there is no rational man can doubt, but a very short period will suffice to do away the evils inseparable from a contest; and that, in seven years, or less, after the independence of Ireland is established, when she can apply all her energy to cultivate her natural resources—her trade, commerce, agriculture, and manufactures, will be augmented to a degree amply sufficient to recompense her for the sacrifices she will be undoubtedly obliged to make, in order to purchase her liberty. The example of America is an evidence of this truth, and England knows it well; it is one reason why she is so eager in the contest. On the other hand, if the English party succeed, and the United Irishmen are put down, what will be the consequence to Ireland?—Her eternal prostration at the feet of her tyrant, without a prospect of ever being able to rise. What then is to be said of a faction, to whom defeat is extermination, and whose victory would be but the perpetuation of their slavery? At least, the United Irishmen have a great and glorious object to terminate their prospect, and which sanctifies almost any means they may take to attain it. The best that can be said, in palliation of the conduct of the English party, is, that they are content to sacrifice the liberty and independence of their country to the pleasure of revenge, and their own personal security. They see Ireland only in their rent-rolls, their places, their patronage, and their pensions. There is not a man among them who, in the bottom of his soul, does not feel that he is a degraded being, in comparison of those whom he brands with the name of incendiaries and traitors. It is this stinging reflection which, amongst other powerful motives, is one of the most active in spurring them on to revenge. Their dearest interests, their warmest passions, are equally engaged. Who can forgive the man that forces him to confess he is a voluntary slave, and that he has sold, for money, every thing that should be most precious to an honourable heart?—That he has trafficked in the liberties of his children, and his own, and that he is hired and paid to commit a daily parricide on his country? Yet, these are charges which not a man of that infamous caste can deny to himself, before the sacred tribunal of his own conscience. At least, the United Irishmen, as I have already said, have a grand, a sublime object, in view. Their enemies have not, as yet, ventured, in the long catalogue of their accusations, to insert the charge of interested motives. Whilst this is the case, they may be feared and abhorred, but they can never be despised; and I believe there are few men who do not look upon contempt as the most insufferable of all human evils. Can the English faction say as much? In vain do they crowd together, and think, by their numbers, to disguise or lessen their infamy. The public sentiment, the secret voice of their own corrupt hearts, has already condemned them. They see their destruction rapidly approaching, and they have the consciousness that, when they fall, no honest man will pity them. "They shall perish like their own dung; those who have seen them shall say, Where are they?"

May, 1798.

17. Having obtained leave of absence for two decades, I have spent the last twenty days deliciously, with my family, at Paris. During that time, we received a letter from my brother William, dated from Poonah, the 7th of January, 1797, (sixteen months ago,) at which time he was in health and spirits, being second in command of the infantry of the Peschwa, or chief of the Mahratta State, with appointments of 500 rupees a month, which is about 750*l*. sterling a year. I cannot express the pleasure which this account of his success gave us all; great as has been his good fortune, it is not superior to his merit. Six years ago he went to India a private soldier, unknown, unfriended, and unprotected; he had not so much as a letter of introduction: but talents and courage like his were not made to rust in obscurity; he has forced his way to a station of rank and eminence, and I have no doubt that his views and talents are extended with his elevation. The first war in India, we shall hear more of him. His letter was enclosed in one from my mother to Mary, by which I see she and my father are in health and spirits. Two or three days after the receipt of Will's letter, we were agreeably surprised

by one from poor Arthur, of whom we had no news for a long time. His letter is dated from Hamburgh, where Meyer had shown him all possible kindness and friendship. We answered it immediately, desiring him to come directly to Paris, where I judge he may arrive in about a month. Poor fellow, he is but sixteen years of age, and what a variety of adventures has he gone through! It is now two years and a half since he and I parted at Philadelphia, when I sent him home in the Susannah, Captain Baird, to notify to my friends my immediate departure for France. It was a delicate commission for a boy of his age, and he seems to have acquitted himself well of it; at least, I have heard no complaint of his indiscretion. When the first arrestations took place in Ireland, in September, 1796,—when my dear friend Tom Russell, Neilson, and so many others, were arrested in Belfast,—those of my friends in Dublin who were in the secret, dreading the possibility of the Government seizing on Arthur, and either by art or menaces wringing it from him, fitted him out, and sent him again to America, with the consent of my father and mother, who were with reason afraid for his personal safety. In America (where he arrived after my wife and family had sailed for Europe,) he met with Mat., and after some little time embarked on board a sloop bound for the West Indies; on his return from this voyage, he again met with Mat., who was on the point of sailing for Hamburgh, in consequence of my instructions. At Philadelphia they parted, and what poor Arthur's adventures have been since, I know not. He is, however, safe and sound, having supported himself these two years without assistance from any body. When I saw him last, he was a fine manly boy, with a beautiful countenance. I hope and trust he will do well; if we ever come to have a navy in Ireland, he is the very stuff of which to make a *Jean du Bart*. I do not yet know what we shall or can do for him; but when he arrives, we shall see. Perhaps I may be able to accomplish something through Admiral Bruix, who is now Minister of the Marine. I am not superstitious; yet I cannot but remark the singularity of the circumstance, that Mary, Mat., Arthur, and myself with my family, should, after such a diversity of strange events, be all re-assembled in France on the eve of this great expedition; and that, precisely at the same time, we should have the happiness of hearing from my father and mother, and especially from Will, after a silence of above four years. It is one of the singular traits in the history of our family, and increases the confidence I feel, that we shall all meet together yet, well and happy.

18. Dined to-day with Adjutant General Rivaud, *Chef d'Etat Major par interim* of the army of England; there were, also, General Marescot of the Engineers, and Adjutant Generals Boulant and Dugommier: the dinner was very pleasant; all the war was talked over, the characters of the Generals canvassed, &c. It is certain that Houchard might have taken the Duke of York, and his whole army, at the time of his famous retreat, or rather flight,

from before Dunkirk. There was but one passage open by which he could possibly escape, and Jourdan, with his division, was within half a league of it, when Houchard's orders overtook him, commanding him to halt instantly, on pain of immediate destitution. In consequence, he was obliged to stop short, and had the mortification to see the English army defile quietly before him, every man of whom he could have made prisoner. By this account it appears that Houchard, at least, was justly condemned. On the whole, I got over this day pretty well.

19. I do not know what to think of our expedition. It is certain that the whole left wing of the army of England is, at this moment, in full march back to the Rhine; Buonaparte is God knows where; and the clouds seem thickening more and more in Germany, where I have no doubt Pitt is moving heaven and hell to embroil matters, and divert the storm which was almost ready to fall on his head. Nearer home there has been an expedition, the failure of which has vexed me, not on account of the importance of the affair, (for it was a trifle,) but for the sake of example. A flotilla of about thirty gun-boats, under the command of Muskein, (an officer who had made himself a reputation in this kind of *petite guerre,*) sailed from Lahogue to attack the *Isles Marcou;* he had on board a detachment of the 4th demi-brigade. It appears, however, that, on their arrival before the Islands, five sail only attacked, and the remainder kept out of the range of

fire; in consequence, after a cannonade of three or four hours, the five sail were obliged to fall back, having lost six men killed and fifteen wounded. I am sorry for this, principally on two accounts: first, as it may have a bad effect on the spirit of the troops, and perhaps disgust them with maritime expeditions; and, secondly, on the score of reputation. "What!" may the English well say; "you are going to conquer England, and you cannot conquer the Isles Marcou!" It is a bad business, take it any way.

21. Rivaud, *Chef de l'Etat Major*, tells me this morning that the English have landed about 10,000 men near Ostend, undoubtedly with a view to bombard it, and burn the shipping and small craft preparing there for the expedition: I believe the number must be extremely exaggerated; be that as it may, he says 6,000 French are already collected, and that is more than enough to render a good account of 10,000 English. Championnet commands in that division; and Bessieres is in the town, where there is a garrison of about 700 men, which is not, by any means, enough. If they suffice, however, to prevent the enemy from succeeding by a *coup de main*, that will be sufficient: for a very few days will bring together a force which will make the English remember the attack with a vengeance. In the mean time, Rivaud has dispatched expresses to the Directory and to General Kilmaine, Commander-in-chief. To-morrow will let us know more of the matter.

23. Yesterday passed without any news; to-day the Journals announce that the English have attempted to bombard Ostend; that to this effect, they landed 4,000 men, who were almost immediately attacked and defeated. Rivaud, in speaking of this affair, made a remark which I think worth recording. He said the French generals of to-day undoubtedly had not the extent and variety of knowledge of those under the old regime; but they made up for that deficiency by superior intrepidity; and where the chiefs are intrepid, the French soldier, who is intrepidity itself, will always follow them, and undoubtedly beat any troops they meet with. I have no doubt but Rivaud is right.

25. Buonaparte is at Toulon and embarked since the 14th; his speech to his army I read to-day, and there are two sentences in it which puzzle me completely. In the first, at the beginning of the address, he tells the troops that they form a wing of the Army of England; in the second, towards the end, he reminds them that they have the glory of the French name to sustain in countries and seas the *most distant.* What does that mean? Is he going, after all, to India? Will he make a short cut to London by way of Calcutta? I begin foully to suspect it. He has all his *savans* embarked with him, with their apparatus; that can hardly be for England. As for Egypt, of which so much has been said, I never paid much attention to the report. If it be for India, I wish to God I were with him; I might be able to co-operate with Will, and perhaps

be of material service; but what would become of my family in my absence? I am in more perplexity at this moment than I have been in since my arrival in France. I have a good mind to write to the Minister at War, or of the Marine, whom I know. Why not to Barras? *Allons!* I will write to Bruix—happy go lucky!

26. I have changed my mind, and written this day a letter to General Kilmaine, acquainting him with Will's present situation in India, and offering to go thither, if the Government thinks that my services can be useful, requesting secrecy and a speedy answer. I know not how this may turn out. It is a bold measure; my only difficulty is about my family; but if the Directory accepts my offer, I hardly think they will refuse to pay my wife one half of my appointments during my absence; if they do that, I will go cheerfully; notwithstanding that the age for enterprize is almost over with me. My blood is cooling fast. "My May of life is falling to the sear, the yellow leaf." It would be singular, if after all, I were to go out to India.

28. The English having appeared in force before Havre, and attempted to throw some bombs into the city, Adjutant-General Rivaud, (*Chef de l'Etat Major,*) determined to send me off at a moment's warning to join General Bethencourt, who commands the division. In consequence, having received orders, and made up my kit, I set off post, and ran all night.

29. Arrived this morning at Havre, waited on General Bethencourt, who received me very politely.

30. This morning at four o'clock, there was a heavy cannonade to the southward, which continued at intervals until ten. The weather is hazy, so that we can see nothing distinctly. I walked out on the batteries three or four times, but could make nothing of it; I fear, however, the worst for our corvettes. Dined with General Bethencourt, and made after dinner the tour of the ramparts with him.

31. My fears were too true about the corvettes. They fell in with a squadron of five English frigates, and immediately the captain of the Vesuve of thirty-two guns, took fright and ran his ship ashore; his name is l'Eccolier. He fired but two broadsides. His comrade, however, who commanded the Confiante, and whose name is Pevrieux, fought his ship in another-guess manner; he engaged the Diamond within pistol-shot for three hours, and it was not until the rest of the squadron were closing fast around him, that he ran his ship ashore, where he continued to defend himself for two hours; so that the English could not succeed in their attempt to burn her: but she is dismasted and torn to pieces by their shot. This affair is the more honourable for him, as the Diamond carries twenty-four pounders, and his ship twelve-pounders.

JUNE, 1798.—HAVRE.

1. Read this morning an article in a Paris Journal which astonishes me more than I can express. It states that General Daendels has fled from the Hague, and has been proclaimed a deserter by the Dutch Government. It seems orders were given to arrest him, which he avoided by flying into France, and it is supposed he is now in Paris. The true reason is said to be his having given his opinion too unguardedly on the measures of his Government. This is the whole of the article, and I confess it astonishes me most completely. Judging from my own experience, I would say that Daendels is an honest man and a good citizen, if there is one existing; and I learn by a letter from Lewines, dated May the 4th, and which is obscure in some parts, from a prudent caution, that parties run exceedingly high in Holland, so that I must conclude he is a victim to his principles. Go now and make revolutions!—Daendels was obliged to fly to France ten years ago, from the fury of the Orange faction; in his absence he was beheaded in effigy. In 1794, he returned triumphant with Pichegru, (another memorable instance of the caprices of fortune,) and was appointed to the chief command of the Batavian army. Now, in 1798, he is again obliged to fly to France, with the disgraceful epithet of deserter attached to his name, to avoid, as I conclude from circumstances, the fury of the Democratic party. It is with me a great proof of a man's integrity, when, in times of

revolution, he is sacrificed alternately by both parties; but certainly what he gains on the score of principle, he loses on that of common sense. In order to do any good, with any party, a man must make great sacrifices, not only of his judgment, but what is much worse, I fear of his conscience also. If he cannot bring his mind to this, there is but one line of conduct for him to pursue, which is to quit the field. He is the best politician, and the honestest man, who does the most good to his country and the least evil: for evil there will be, in his despite, and he must be at times himself the instrument thereof, whatever it cost him. He must keep a sort of running account with his conscience, where he is to set off the good against the bad, and if the balance be in his favour, it is all he can expect. This is but a melancholy speculation for a man at the beginning of his political career, but I am afraid that it will be found, in effect, the only practicable one. I see also in the papers, that they have begun to arrest the women in Ireland, for wearing United Irish rings. Will the men submit to this, or is it humanly possible for them to resist?

4. Yesterday I received a letter from Adjutant-General Rivaud, informing me that I might return to Rouen when I pleased. I answered it to-day, letting him know that as the enemy continued still before the place, I considered it my duty to remain until further orders. Nominated the citizens Fayolles, Captain of Infantry, and Favory, of the Engineers, to be my Adjoints, and despatched the

letters of nomination to the Minister at War. So now I am fairly afloat. "If I had bought me a horse in Smithfield, I were manned, horsed, and wived." I had like to have forgotten. This is his Majesty's birth-day. (Sings.) "*God save great George our King.*" I feel myself extremely loyal on the sudden, methinks. Well, "God knows the heart. Many a body says *well,* that thinks *ill,*" &c. &c. &c.

5. Last night went my rounds as Adjutant-General, in all the forms. "I brought in the boar's head, and quitted me like a man." I do not see, myself, that this quotation is extremely apposite; but no matter. I like the idle activity of a military life well enough, and if I were employed in an Irish army, I should make a tolerable good officer; but the difference of the language here is terribly against me. However, I made myself understood at all the outposts, which is sufficient for my purpose. *Vive la Republique!* I do not know what that sally is for, I am sure. The report in Havre this morning is, that the Toulon fleet has beaten an English squadron in the Mediterranean, and taken four sail of the line. "Would I could see it, quoth blind Hugh."

8. Citizen Fayolles, my Adjoint, is arrived from Rouen, so I am something more at my ease. Yesterday the enemy appeared before Havre, and from their manœuvres we expected an attack. In consequence, all the batteries were manned and the furnaces heated. I was stationed in the *Batterie*

Nationale. About three o'clock in the afternoon, they bore down upon us, within two cannon shot; but after some little time, hauled their wind and stood off again; so we were quit for the fright. As they passed the battery, at the *Pont la Hève*, they threw about half a dozen shells, to answer as many shot the battery had fired at them, *à tout volée*, but neither the one nor the other did any damage.

It was a fine sight, and I should have enjoyed it more, had it not been for certain "speculations on futurity and the transmigration of souls," which presented themselves to my fancy at times. I defy any man to know whether he is brave or not, until he is tried, and I am very far from boasting of myself on that score; but the fact is, and I was right glad of it, that when I found myself at my battery, and saw the enemy bearing right down upon us, and as I thought to begin the cannonade, though I cannot say with truth that I was perfectly easy, yet neither did I feel at all disconcerted; and I am satisfied, as far as a man in that situation can judge of himself, that I should have done my duty well, and without any great effort of resolution. The crowd and the bustle, the noise, and especially the conviction that the eyes of the cannoniers were fixed on the *chapeau galonnée*, settled me at once; it is the etiquette in such cases, that the General stands conspicuous on the parapet, whilst the canoniers are covered by the *epaulement*, which is truly amusing for him that commands. Nevertheless, I have no doubt that it is easier to behave well on the parapet, exposed to all the fire, than in the battery, where the danger is much less. I had time to make all these, and divers other wise remarks during my stay: for it was six in the evening before the English stood off; and, on the faith of an honest man, I cannot truly say I was sorry when I saw them decidedly turn their backs. Huzza! *Vive la Republique!* "Thus far our arms have with success been crowned. For though we have not fought, yet have we found no enemy to fight withal." Huzza! Huzza!

12. Yesterday I read in the French papers, an account of the acquittal of Arthur O'Connor at Maidstone, and of his being taken instantly into custody again. Undoubtedly Pitt means to send him to Ireland, in hopes of finding there a more complaisant jury. Quigley, the priest, is found guilty; it seems he has behaved admirably well, which I confess was more than I expected; his death redeems him. Alley, Binns, and Leary, the servant, are also acquitted and discharged. O'Connor appears to have behaved with great intrepidity. On being taken into custody, he addressed the judges, desiring to be sent to the same dungeon with his brother, who, like him, was acquitted of high treason, and, like him, was arrested in the very court. The judge, Buller, answered him coldly, that their commission expired when the sentence was pronounced, and that the court could do nothing farther in the business. He was instantly committed. My satisfaction at this triumph of O'Connor is almost totally

destroyed by a second article in the same paper, which mentions that Lord Edward Fitzgerald has been arrested in Thomas-street, Dublin, after a most desperate resistance, in which himself, the magistrate, one Swan, and Captain Ryan, who commanded the guard, were severely wounded. I cannot describe the effect which this intelligence had on me; it brought on, almost immediately, a spasm in my stomach, which confined me all day. I knew Fitzgerald very little, but I honour and venerate his character, which he has uniformly sustained, and, in this last instance, illustrated. What miserable wretches by his side are the gentry of Ireland! I would rather be Fitzgerald, as he is now, wounded in his dungeon, than Pitt at the head of the British Empire. What a noble fellow! Of the first family in Ireland, with an easy fortune, a beautiful wife, a family of lovely children, and the certainty of a splendid appointment under Government if he would condescend to support their measures, he has devoted himself wholly to the emancipation of his country, and sacrificed every thing to it, even to his blood. My only consolation is the hope that his enemies have no capital charge against him, and will be obliged to limit their rage to his imprisonment. Poor fellow! He is not the first Fitzgerald who has sacrificed himself to the cause of his country. There is a wonderful similarity of principle and fortune between him and his ancestor Lord Thomas, in the reign of Henry VII., who lost his head on Tower-hill for a gallant but fruitless attempt to recover the independence of Ireland. God send the catastrophe of his noble descendant be not the same. I dread every thing for him, and my only consolation is in speculations of revenge. If the blood of this brave young man be shed by the hands of his enemies, it is no ordinary vengeance which will content the People, whenever the day of retribution arrives.

13. I have been running over in my mind the list of my friends, and of the men whom, without being so intimately connected with them, I most esteem. Scarcely do I find one who is not or has not been in exile or prison, and in jeopardy of his life. To begin with Russell and Emmett, the two dearest of my friends, at this moment in prison on a capital charge. M'Neven and J. Sweetman, (my old fellow-labourers in the Catholic cause;) Edward Fitzgerald, Arthur and Roger O'Connor, (whom, though I know less personally, I do not less esteem;) Sampson, Bond, Jackson, and his son,—still in prison; Robert and William Sims, the men in the world to whose friendship I am most obliged, but just discharged; Neilson, Hazlitt, M'Cracken, the same; M'Cormick, absconded; Rowan and Dr. Reynolds in America; Lewines, Tennant, Lowry, Hamilton, Teeling, Tandy, &c. and others, with whom I have little or no acquaintance, but whom I must presume to be victims of their patriotism, (not to speak of my own family) in France, Germany, and elsewhere. Stokes disgraced on suspicion of virtue. It is a gloomy catalogue for a man to cast his eyes over. Of all my political connexions I see but John Keogh who has

escaped, and how he has had that inconceivable good fortune, is to me a miracle.

16. Last night, at the *Comédie*, I had a conversation with General Kilmaine, who has been here these two days, which did not much encourage me, on the present posture of our affairs. He began on the subject of my letter of the 26th May, offering to go to India. I told him it was not a thing that I pressed, or wished to give for more than it was worth; my object was merely to inform the Government that, if nothing were likely to be done in Europe, and an attempt were to be made in India, if they thought that, under the circumstances, my services could be of any use, I was ready to go in twenty-four hours. General Kilmaine answered, that a short time would let us see the object of Buonaparte's plan; that, in the mean time, there was a supplementary armament preparing at Toulon, of two ships of the line, with some frigates and transports, and, if it were destined for India, we would then see what was to be done. This conversation naturally introduced the subject of the grand expedition against England or Ireland, of which, from Kilmaine's report, I do not see the smallest probability. The Marine is in a state of absolute nullity: the late Minister, Pleville Lepeley, towards the end of his ministry, had disarmed all the ships of the line, so that when he was pressed by the Directory, it appeared that nothing was ready, and, in consequence, after about a month's shuffling, he was obliged to resign. I mentioned that I had better hopes of the present Minister, Bruix, who, besides

being a man of acknowledged talents and activity, was, in a certain degree, bound in honour to try the expedition, having taken so active a part in conducting the last, and been even indirectly implicated by his enemies in its failure, which ought naturally to pique him to make the greatest exertions. Kilmaine said, "that was all true; but what could Bruix do? In the first place, he had no money; in the next, the arsenals of Brest were empty, and what stores they had in other ports they could not convey thither, from the superiority of the naval force of the enemy, which kept every thing blocked up; finally, that of fourteen sail of the line now in the port of Brest, there were but three in a state to put to sea; that the Government, towards the end of Pleville Lepeley's ministry, being apparently uninformed of the real state of the Marine, had ordered him (Kilmaine) to have the army prepared; in consequence of which he had marched about 17,000 men towards the coast, where they still remained, viz. six demi-brigades of infantry, one regiment of dragoons, one of hussars, and one of chasseurs, besides the artillery; but that there was no manner of appearance of any thing being done by the Marine." All this is as bad as can be. I then asked whether he could tell me the determination of the Government with regard to the cadres of regiments formed by General Hoche for the last expedition, and whether the Irishmen now in Paris were to be employed in them? He said he had spoken of it twenty times to the Directors; that, in fact, the existence of those cadres was authorized by no law, and if there was any question about them, the consequence would be their immediate suppression; that, if the expedition took place, the matter would be managed; but, in the mean time, nothing could be done, the constitution being express against employing foreigners, and that jealousy carried so far, that the Directory were obliged to refuse the offer of a regiment of hussars, made to them by the Cisalpines; which fact I remember myself, and, in truth, cannot blame the French for adopting a principle so reasonable. I then mentioned that the situation of those young men now in Paris was very painful, and that I was afraid, if something were not done in their behalf, they would be reduced to great difficulties. He said he felt all that; at the same time, the conduct of many of the Irish in Paris was such as to reflect credit neither on themselves nor their country. That there was nothing to be heard of amongst them but denunciations, and if every one of them, separately, spoke truth, all the rest were rascals. At the same time, there was one thing in their favour; hitherto they had asked nothing for themselves, which, in some degree, saved their credit—except one, named O'Finn, who appeared in the light of a mere adventurer; that Tandy had also applied for assistance, and that he (Kilmaine) believing the poor old man to be in distress, had signed a paper to the Minister at War, requesting he might be employed. I answered, that I was heartily sorry for the account he gave me of the conduct of our countrymen, which I had some reason to believe he had not exaggerated, having been denounced myself more than once, for no other offence, as I believe in my conscience, than the rank I held in the French army, which caused heart-burnings amongst them; that the misfortune was, they came into France with their ideas mounted too high; from having had a certain degree of influence among the people at home, and finding themselves absolutely without any in France, their tempers were soured, and their ill humour vented itself in accusations of each other. I then took occasion to ask the General, whether, in the worst event, of a general peace, (leaving Ireland under the British yoke,) he thought the French Government would do any thing for the Irish patriots, who had suffered so much in their cause; and who, by the number of men they employed, and the quantity of money they had cost England, had served as a powerful diversion in favour of the Republic, without putting her to the expense of one shilling; and I mentioned the example of England, after the revocation of the edict of Nantz, who had received with open arms, and given all possible encouragement to the French Protestants, with far less reason than in the present instance. The General answered, that, in the event I mentioned, he had no doubt but the French Government would give every possible encouragement to the Irish Refugees. I then observed to him, that I had been thinking, whether the islands in the Gulf of Venice, Corfu, &c. did not offer a convenient occasion for affording a settlement, and especially as their destiny was yet unsettled—

at the same time, that I merely threw it out as a hint for him to think of, having myself no definite ideas on the subject. He said he would turn it in his mind, and so our conversation ended. All this is as discouraging as it can well be. I am sworn not to despair: it is my motto; but if it were not for that, I know not what I should do to-day. I should have observed in its place, that General Kilmaine told me, denunciations of the Irish had even reached the Government, and had of course lowered the nation in their esteem; he added that Lewines, however, was not implicated, of which I am heartily glad. I did not ask him how it was with regard to myself.

18. The news I have received this morning, partly by the papers, and partly by letters from my wife and brother, are of the last importance. As I suspected, the brave and unfortunate Fitzgerald was meditating an attack on the capital, which was to have taken place a few days after that on which he was arrested. He is since dead in prison; his career is finished gloriously for himself, and, whatever be the event, his memory will live for ever in the heart of every honest Irishman. He was a gallant fellow. For us, who remain as yet, and may perhaps soon follow him, the only way to lament his death is to endeavour to revenge it. Among his papers, it seems, was found the plan of the insurrection, the proclamation intended to be published, and several others, by which those of the leaders of the People who have thus far escaped have been implicated, and several

of them seized. Among others, I see Tom Braughall, Lawless, (son of Lord Cloncurry,) Curran, (son of the Barrister,) Chambers and P. Byrne, printers, with several others, whom I cannot recollect. All this, including the death of the brave Fitzgerald, has, it appears, but accelerated matters; the insurrection has formally commenced in several counties of Leinster, especially Kildare and Wexford; the details in the French papers are very imperfect, but I see there have been several actions. At Monastereven, Naas, Clain, and Prosperous, (the three last immediately in my ancient neighbourhood,) there have been skirmishes, generally, as is at first to be expected, to the advantage of the army; at Prosperous, the Cork Militia were surprised and defeated. The villains—to bear arms against their country. Kilcullen is burnt; at Carlow, four hundred Irish, it is said, were killed; at Castledermot, fifty; in return, in County Wexford, where appears to be their principal force, they have defeated a party of six hundred English, killed three hundred, and the Commander, Colonel Walpole, and taken five pieces of cannon. This victory, small as it is, will give the people courage, and show them that a red coat is no more invincible than a grey one. At Rathmines, there has been an affair of cavalry, where the Irish had the worst, and two of their leaders, named Ledwich and Keogh, were taken, and, I presume, immediately executed. I much fear that the last is Cornelius, eldest son to my friend, J. Keogh, and a gallant lad; if it be so, I shall regret him sincerely; but how many other valuable lives must be sacrificed, before the fortune of Ireland be decided! Dr. Esmonde, and eight other gentlemen of my County, have been hanged; at Nenagh, the English whip the most respectable inhabitants, till their blood flows into the kennel. The atrocious barbarity of their conduct is only to be excelled by the folly of it; never yet was a rebellion, as they call it, quelled by such means. The eighteen thousand victims sacrificed by Alva in the Low Countries in five years, and on the scaffold, did not prevent the establishment of the liberty of Holland. From the blood of every one of the martyrs of the liberty of Ireland will spring, I hope, thousands to revenge their fall. In all this confusion of events, there is one circumstance which looks well. The English Government publish, latterly, no detailed accounts, but say, in general, that all goes well, and that a few days will suffice to extinguish the rebellion; at the same time they are fortifying the pigeon-house in Dublin, in order to secure a retreat for the Government in case of the worst, which does not savour, extremely, of the immediate extinction of the rebellion.

19. This evening, at five, set off by command for Rouen, having taken leave of General Bethencourt last night, who loaded me with civilities. Arrived at five in the evening, and met General Rivaud. General Kilmaine is also arrived; so I shall see him to-morrow. General Grouchy, who commanded the *Armée expeditionnaire* in Bantry Bay, and to whom I was much attached, is also here.

20. To-day is my birth-day. I am thirty-five years of age; more than half the career of my life is finished, and how little have I yet been able to do. Well, it has not been, at least, for want of inclination, and, I may add, of efforts. I had hopes, two years ago, that, at the period I write this, my debt to my country would have been discharged, and the fate of Ireland settled for good or evil. To-day it is more uncertain than ever. I think, however, I may safely say I have neglected no step to which my duty called me, and in that conduct I will persist to the last. Called this morning on General Groüchy —I find him full of ardour for our business; he has read all the details, and talks of going to Paris in two or three days, to press the Directory upon that subject. His idea is to try an embarkation aboard the corvettes and privateers of Nantes; on which, he thinks, at least 3000 men with 20,000 muskets can be stowed, and he speaks as if he meant to apply for the command of this little armament. What would I not give that he should succeed in the application? I once endeavoured to be of service to General Grouchy, when I saw him unjustly misrepresented, after our return from Bantry Bay, and he does not seem to have forgotten it: for nothing could be more friendly and affectionate than his reception of me to-day. We talked over the last expedition. He said he had shed tears of rage and vexation fifty times since, at the recollection of the opportunity of which he had been deprived; and there was one thing which he never would pardon in himself—that

he did not seize Bouvet by the collar, and throw him overboard, the moment he attempted to raise a difficulty as to the landing. He also mentioned his intention to apply for me to be his Adjutant General, of which I am very glad, and added, that, as he believed he would have the command of the fourth division of the Army of England, (besides the command of the cavalry,) in which Nantes was included, in case the Government relished his offer, he would be at hand to execute our plan, making, at the same time, a great parade at Brest, and elsewhere, to divert the attention of the enemy. In short, he shows the same zeal and ardour in our cause that I had occasion to remark in him during the late expedition; and I look on it as a fortunate circumstance for me to be attached to him. From General Grouchy I went to visit the General-in-chief, Kilmaine, and mentioned to him, that, under the circumstances, (especially as there was no appearance of any event at Havre,) I had thought it my duty to return near him, to receive his orders. He said I did very right, but he was sorry, at the same time, to tell me, that he was much afraid the Government would do nothing; and he read me a letter from the Minister of Marine, which he had received this very morning, mentioning, that, in consequence of the great superiority of the naval force of the enemy, and difficulty of escaping from any of the ports during the fine season, the Directory were determined to adjourn the measure until a more favourable occasion. I lost my temper at this, and told him that if the affair was adjourned, it was lost. The present crisis must be seized, or it would be too late; that I could hardly hope the Irish, unprovided as they were of all that was indispensable for carrying on a war, could long hold out against the resources of England, especially if they saw France make no effort whatsoever to assist them; that, thus far, they had been devoted to the cause of France, for which, if they had not been able to do much, at least they had sufficiently suffered; but who could say, or expect, that this attachment would continue, if, in the present great crisis, they saw themselves abandoned to their own resources? that now was the moment to assist them—in three months it might be too late, and the forces then sent, if the Irish were overpowered in the mean time, would find themselves unsupported, and, in their turn, be overpowered by the English. General Kilmaine answered, that he saw all that as well as I did; but what could he do? He had pressed the Directory again and again on the subject, but they were afraid to incur the charge of sacrificing a handful of the troops of the Republic, and would not try the enterprize except on a grand scale.

Quigley has been executed, and died like a hero! If ever I reach Ireland, and we establish our liberty, I will be the first to propose a monument to his memory; his conduct, at the hour of his death, clears every thing. "Nothing in his life became him, like the leaving of it."—Poor Pamela—she is in London, which she has been ordered to quit in three days. The night of her husband's arrestation, she was taken in labour, and—will it be believed hereafter? not one physician could be found in Dublin, hardy enough to deliver her. The villains! the pusillanimous and barbarous scoundrels! It was a lady, who was not even of her acquaintance, that assisted her in her peril. I do not think there is a parallel instance of inhumanity in the annals of mankind. She is said to be inconsolable for the death of Fitzgerald. I well believe it—beautiful and unfortunate creature! Well, if Ireland triumphs, she shall have her full share of the victory, and of the vengeance. There is, also, under the head of Waterford, 2d June, an article which gives me the highest satisfaction, inasmuch as it proves that, notwithstanding the death, exile, and arrestation of so many leaders of the Irish, enough are still at large to conduct their affairs and give them a consistency which I was afraid they wanted. It is an extract from the proclamation of the Supreme Committee, (as it is called in the French papers,) consisting of three articles. The first invites all Irishmen, absent from their native country, to return instantly, or, if that be impossible, to transmit all succour in their power, (in money or otherwise,) in order to assist their countrymen in throwing off the yoke of English tyranny. The second enjoins all Irishmen in the British service to quit it instantly, under pain of forfeiting their rights as Irish citizens.—All Irish in the British service, now employed in Ireland, who shall be taken with arms in their hands, to be shot instantly. The third is a solemn promise to recompense all soldiers and seamen who abandon the enemy to join the standard of their country: all ships brought in, to be the property of the captors, and preference to be given in the distribution of the national property to such as shall act in conformity with the present proclamation. These three articles are of the highest importance, as they show the existence of something like regular authority among the Irish. It is curious that they are contained, almost verbatim, in the memorial I delivered to the Executive Directory, two years ago. (*Vide second Memorial, Articles* 2, 3, 4.*) I am anxious to see the effect this will produce. If the Irish can hold out till winter, I have every reason to hope that the French will assist them effectually. All I dread is, that they may be overpowered before that time. In all this business I do not see one syllable about the North, which astonishes me more than I can express.

30. Having determined to set off for Paris, in consequence of the late news from Ireland, I got leave of absence, for a fortnight, from General Kilmaine. My Adjoint, Citizen Favory, called on me the next morning after my arrival, to inform me that the Minister of War had despatched an order for me to come to Paris in all haste. I waited upon him in consequence. He told me it was the Minister of Marine who had demanded me, and gave me, at the same time, a letter of introduction for him.

CÆTERA DESUNT.

* See Appendix

CONCLUSION.

BY THE EDITOR.

In order to give a clear and full narrative of the third and last expedition for the deliverance of Ireland, it will be necessary to ascend somewhat higher. When Carnot, the only able and honest man in the Councils of the Directory, was proscribed, and when General Hoche died, the friends of a revolution in that Island lost every chance of assistance from France. Those two great statesmen and warriors, earnest in the cause, of which they perceived the full importance to the interests of their country and to the extension of Republican principles, had planned the expeditions of Bantry Bay and of the Texel, on the largest and most effective scale which the naval resources of France and Holland could afford. The former failed partly by the misconduct of the navy, and partly by the indecision of Grouchy, —of that honest but wavering man who twice held the fate of Europe in his hands, at Bantry Bay and at Waterloo, and twice let it slip through them, from want of resolution. The second failed only through the fault of the elements.

On the death of Hoche, the French Government recalled, to succeed him, the most illustrious of their warriors; he who afterwards wielded the destinies of Europe, and who then, under the name of General Buonaparte,* was already acknowledged the first Commander of the age: and yet it was an age fertile in great Chiefs. But he who, before the age of thirty, had already achieved the immortal campaigns of Italy; subdued that beautiful country; founded one Republic (the Cisalpine,) and extinguished another (Venice); humbled the power of Austria, and compelled her, by his private authority,† to liberate Lafayette from the dungeons of Olmutz and acknowledge the French Republic by the treaty of Campo

* The petty and impotent malice of that great man's adversaries was very unlucky in the choice of the nicknames by which they chose to call him. When the English would only address the Royal prisoner, whose title they had fully acknowledged in the Conferences of Chatillon, by the appellation of General Buonaparte, they gave him the most illustrious name which appears on the pages of history from the days of antiquity, and one which shines, perhaps, with purer lustre than that of the Emperor Napoleon. When the French Royalists pretended that *Nicholas*, and not *Napoleon*, was his real name, they were probably ignorant that the meaning of the word, in Greek, is derived from Victory.

† The Directory were so far from approving of this noble act, that they would not even allow Lafayette to return to France. It was not till Napoleon became First Consul, and was thereby enabled to grant this permission, that it was obtained. It was one of the first acts of his administration.

Formio;—was more than a mere General. It is, however, with extreme reluctance that I feel myself called upon, by the nature of my subject, to point out any errors in the conduct of the sovereign, chief, and benefactor, under whom I bore my first arms and received my first wounds; of him who decorated me with the insignia of the legion of honour, and whom I served with constant fidelity and devotion to the last moment of his reign. But the imperious voice of truth compels me to attribute to the influence and prejudices of General Buonaparte, at that period, the prime cause of the failure of the third expedition for the liberation of Ireland.

The loss of Hoche was irreparable to the Irish cause. Although he died in the prime of his youth—and his deeds, eclipsed by those of his still greater rival, are now nearly forgotten—at that period they were competitors in glory, and formed two opposite parties in the army. The Generals and officers of the two schools continued, for a long time, to view each other with dislike. Both these great men were ambitious; both eager for their personal fame, and for that of France; and bent on raising her to an unequalled rank amongst nations. But Hoche was an ardent and sincere Republican; he could sacrifice his own hopes and prospects to the cause of liberty, as he nobly proved, when he resigned at Daendels the command of the Texel expedition. Buonaparte always associated in his mind the power of France and his own aggrandizement; nor could he be satisfied with *her* being raised to the pinnacle of power and prosperity, unless *he* was the guide of her march and the ruler of her destinies. Admirably formed by nature for a great administrator and organizer, he meditated already in his mind those vast creations which he afterwards accomplished, and which required an unlimited authority for their execution; he loved the prompt obedience and regulated order of absolute power, and felt a secret dislike to the tumultuous and wavering conflicts of a Republican Government, whose energy is so frequently counteracted by the disunion of its parties and the necessity of persuading instead of commanding. In short, he never was a Republican. This feeling he could scarcely disguise, even then when it was most necessary to conceal it: for no man who ever rose to such power, perhaps, ever made so little use of dissimulation. Stern, reserved, and uncommunicative, he repelled with haughty disdain the advances of the Jacobins; and the Emperor Napoleon, the future sovereign and conqueror, might already be discerned in the plain and austere General of the Republic.*

But circumstances, at this precise period, rendered that conduct the best which he could pursue. The enthusiasm of democracy was extinct in France; the people were weary of the successive revolutions which had placed so many weak and

* He was the first man who dared to drive from his doors the "Dames de la Halle," or fishwomen of Paris, when they came to congratulate him on his victories. One must be familiar with the history of the Revolution to appreciate this fact.

worthless characters at the head of affairs, and longed for the firm hand and the bit and bridle of a ruler. The mean and rapacious members of the Directory, who, in expelling their colleague Carnot, had driven all credit and respectability from their councils, sought support, and thought to make this young and popular Chief their instrument. He was courted by every party. He felt, however, the public pulse, and judged that a premature attempt would be hopeless. It was then that, giving up for the moment his designs in Europe, he began to meditate a brilliant project for his personal glory and aggrandizement in the East; a plan to regenerate those regions, and be the founder of a new Empire, by means of the victorious arms of France. This plan was only defeated by the battle of the Nile, and the resistance of St. Jean d'Acre.

To the enterprize against Ireland, the favourite object of Hoche, and to prosecute which he was ostensibly summoned, he felt a secret but strong repugnance. Though the liberation of that country might prostrate for ever the power of England and raise the Republic to the pinnacle of fortune, (a circumstance for which he did not yet wish, as it would render his services needless,) it offered no prospects of aggrandizement to him; it strengthened that Republican cause which he disliked; and the principles of the Irish leaders, when he investigated the business, appeared to him too closely allied to those of the Jacobins. Neither did he ever sufficiently appreciate the means and importance of that country; his knowledge of it, as may be seen in my father's memoirs, was slight and inaccurate. The Directors, who began to fear him and wished to get rid of him, entered willingly into his views, when he proposed to use this expedition only as a cover and direct their real efforts to the invasion of Egypt. It is asserted that he said, on the occasion, "What more do you desire from the Irish? You see that their movements already operate a powerful diversion." Like every selfish view, I think this was a narrow one. The two most miserable and oppressed countries of Europe always looked up to Napoleon for their liberation. He never gratified their hopes; yet, by raising Ireland, he might have crushed for ever the power of England, and by assisting Poland, placed a curb on Russia. He missed both objects, and, finally, fell under the efforts of Russia and of England. And it may be observed, as a singular retribution, that an Irishman commanded the army which gave the last blow to his destinies.

When my father was presented to him, and attached to his army as Adjutant General, he received him with cold civility, but entered into no communications. His plans were already formed. Ostensibly a great force was organized on the Western Coasts of France, under the name of the Army of England; but the flower of the troops were successively withdrawn and marched to the Mediterranean; the eyes of Europe were fixed on these operations, but, from their eccentricity, their object could not be discovered. My father, despatched (as may be seen in his Journals,) to head-quarters at Rouen, and employed in unimportant movements on the coast, in the bombardment of Havre, &c., heard, with successive pangs of disappointment, that Buonaparte had left Paris for the South; that he had arrived at Toulon; that he had embarked and sailed with a powerful expedition in the beginning of June. But his destination remained as mysterious as ever. General Kilmaine was left in command of the disorganized relics of the army of England, from whence all the best troops were withdrawn. That officer, an Irishman by birth, and one of the bravest Generals of the army of Italy, whose cavalry he commanded in the preceding campaigns, was, from the shattered state of his health and constitution, unfit to conduct any active enterprize.

When Buonaparte departed from the coast of France, all fortune and conduct seemed to disappear with him from the councils of the Republic. The Directors were neither cruel nor bloody, like the government which had preceded them; but the Jacobins, though they might well be feared and hated, could not be despised. The rapacity of the Directors disgusted all the friends and allies of France; their prodigality wasted its resources—their weakness encouraged its internal enemies—their improvidence and incapacity disorganized its armies and fortresses, and left them defenceless against the reviving efforts of adversaries who were humbled, but not subdued. Suwarrow and Prince

Charles soon turned the fate of arms; Austria re-entered the lists; and, in the short space of about two years, the very existence of that Republic which Hoche and Napoleon had left triumphing and powerful was in jeopardy; her conquests were gone, her treasury was empty, her armies were naked, disorganized, and flying on all sides. Such was the state of France when the Conqueror of Egypt returned to save and restore it.

In the mean time, the Irish cabinet succeeded in its infernal purpose of driving the People to premature insurrection. The leaders of the United Irishmen had organized a plan for a general rising. But traitors were found in their councils; they were all arrested; the gallant Lord Edward Fitzgerald killed, and the capital secured. Nevertheless, the exasperated peasantry in Kildare, Carlow, and some districts in the North, rose in arms against the intolerable excesses of the soldiery quartered upon them. But these partial insurrections of naked crowds, without arms or leaders, without union or concert, (which my father had so often deprecated,) could lead to no result. They were successively crushed by the overpowering forces directed against them, and the reign of terror was established without check or limitation. The state of France, in the worst days of Robespierre, was never more prostrate, nor did its government pursue its bloody measures with a more unsparing hand. The whole population were abandoned to the absolute discretion of an infuriated, licentious, and undisciplined soldiery; the meanest agents of authority exercised a power without control; individuals were half-hanged, whipped, and picketed, to extort confession, without trial, in the very capital, in the courts of the castle, and under the roof of the Viceroy; the country blazed with nightly conflagrations, and resounded with the shrieks of torture; neither age nor sex was spared, and the bayonets of the military drove men, women, and children, naked and houseless, to starve in the bogs and fastnesses; those who trusted to the faith of capitulations were surrounded and slaughtered by dragoons in the very act of laying down their arms; and no citizen, however innocent or inoffensive, could deem himself secure from informers.

The noble resistance of the small county of Wexford deserves to be particularly noticed. It was such as to alarm for a moment the Irish Government about the success of their measures. That little district, comprising about 150,000 souls, surrounded by the sea and mountains, and secluded from the rest of the Island, had imbibed but a small share of the prevailing revolutionary spirit, for its population had not much communication with their neighbours, and were remarkably quiet and happy. It is stated by Mr. Edward Hay, that before the insurrection, it did not contain above two hundred United Irishmen. It may, perhaps, have been deemed, from this very circumstance, that, if an insurrection could be provoked within its limits, the People, less organized and prepared than in the districts of the North, would be subdued more easily, and afford, with less risk, a striking example to the rest of the Island. The soldiery were let loose, and committed for some time every excess on the innocent peasantry. A noble lord, who commanded a regiment of militia, was distinguished by the invention of the pitch cap; another officer, worthy to serve under him, by the appellation of "The Walking Gallows." But why recal facts, which are engraved on the hearts and in the memory of every Irishman? At length, goaded to madness, the Wexfordians, to the number of 20 or 30,000, rose in arms, with pikes, staves, and scythes, and in two or three actions, seized on the chief towns, and drove the soldiery out of the county. Their moderation towards their persecutors, in the moment of victory, was as remarkable as their courage in the field. Their forbearance, and even their delicate and chivalrous generosity towards the ladies and families of the aristocracy who fell into their hands, was most amiable and admirable.* The noble lord abovementioned was taken, and even he was rescued by their leaders from the infliction of the pitch cap, which he so well deserved. In recompense, he engaged, on the close of the insurrection, to obtain a capitulation for them, if they would let him loose, and afterwards sat on the court-martial which condemned them to be hanged. It required all the means and all the efforts of the Irish Government, to

* The comment of some patrician ladies on this forbearance, was, "That the croppies wanted gallantry."

subdue this small district. At one time, they trembled in the walls of Dublin, lest the Wexfordians should penetrate there. Several battles were fought, with various success, and it was not till the royal forces surrounded them on all sides, that they broke through their toils, and threw themselves into the mountains of Wicklow, where their leaders successively capitulated Provoked and irritated as these innocent people were, it is remarkable that only two instances of cruelty (the massacre of their prisoners at Scullabogue, and on the bridge of Wexford,) occurred on their side, during the insurrection:—and these were both perpetrated by runaways from their main army, whilst the remainder were fighting.

The indignation of the unfortunate Irish was just and extreme against that French Government which had so repeatedly promised them aid, and now appeared to desert them in their utmost need. When Lord Cornwallis, who was sent shortly after to put an end to the system of terror which desolated the country, succeeded to the Viceroyalty, 2,000 volunteers from this very county of Wexford offered their services to fight the French, and formed the flower of the British army which invaded Egypt under General Abercrombie. Their petition, a model of native simplicity, energy, and indignation, is recorded in the Appendix of Hay's History of the Wexford Insurrection.

But, weak and improvident as the Directors were, they must be acquitted of the charge of betraying their allies. The fact was, that their treasury and arsenals were empty, the flower of their army and navy were gone to Egypt, the remainder were totally disorganized ; in short, when the insurrection broke out in Ireland, they were entirely unprepared to assist it. Their indolence and incapacity had suffered every thing to fall to decay, and their peculations and profusion had wasted their remaining means. The feelings of my father on the occasion may be more easily conceived than expressed. On the 20th of May, Buonaparte had embarked from Toulon. On the 23d, the insurrection broke out. As the news of each arrest, and of each action, successively reached France, he urged the Generals and Government to assist the gallant and desperate struggle of his countrymen, and pressed on them the necessity of availing themselves of the favourable opportunity which flew so rapidly by. They began their preparations without delay ; but money, arms, ammunition, and ships, all were wanting. By the close of June, the insurrection was nearly crushed, and it was not till the beginning of July that my father was called up to Paris, to consult with the Ministers of the War and Navy Departments on the organization of a new expedition At this period his Journal closes, and the public papers, my mother's recollections, and a few private letters, are my sole documents for the remaining events.

The plan of the new expedition was to despatch small detachments from several ports, in the hope of keeping up the insurrection, and distracting the attention of the enemy, until some favourable opportunity should occur for landing the main body, under General Kilmaine. General Humbert, with about 1,000 men, was quartered for this purpose at Rochelle; General Hardy, with 3,000 at Brest, and Kilmaine with 9,000 remained in reserve. This plan was judicious enough, if it had been taken up in time. But, long before the first of these expeditions was ready to sail, the insurrection was completely subdued in every quarter; the people were crushed, disarmed, disheartened, and disgusted with their allies; and the Irish Government had collected all its means, and was fully prepared for the encounter. Refugees from that unfortunate country, of every character and description, arrived in crowds, with their blood boiling from their recent actions and sufferings. When they saw the slowness of the French preparations, they exclaimed, that they wanted nothing but arms, and that, if the Government would only land them again on the coast, the people themselves, without any aid, would suffice to reconquer their liberty. This party, more gallant than wise, were chiefly led by an old sufferer in the cause, James Napper Tandy. Their zeal was often indiscreet and unenlightened, and they did more mischief than good. Napper Tandy boasted, that 30,000 men would rise in arms on his appearance, and the Directory were puzzled by these declarations, which contradicted my father's constant assertion, that 10,000 or 15,000 French troops would be absolutely necessary in the beginning of the contest.

The final ruin of the expedition was hurried by

the precipitancy and indiscretion of a brave, but imprudent and ignorant officer. This anecdote, which is not generally known, is a striking instance of the disorder, indiscipline, and disorganization which began to prevail in the French army. Humbert, a gallant soldier of fortune, but whose heart was better than his head, impatient of the delays of his Government, and fired by the recitals of the Irish refugees, determined to begin the enterprise on his own responsibility, and thus oblige the Directory to second or to desert him. Towards the middle of August, calling the merchants and magistrates of Rochelle, he forced them to advance a small sum of money, and all that he wanted, on military requisition; and, embarking on board a few frigates and transports, with 1000 men, 1000 spare muskets, 1000 guineas, and a few pieces of artillery, he compelled the Captains to set sail, for the most desperate attempt which is, perhaps, recorded in history. Three Irishmen accompanied him, my uncle Matthew Tone, Bartholomew Teeling, of Lisburn, and Sullivan, nephew to Madgett, whose name is often mentioned in these memoirs. On the 22d of August they made the coast of Connaught, and, landing in the bay of Killala, immediately stormed and occupied that little town.

Strange and desperate as was this enterprise, had it been prosecuted with the same spirit and vivacity with which it was begun, it might have succeeded, and Humbert, an obscure and uneducated soldier, have effected a Revolution, and crowned his name with immortal glory. The insurrection was scarcely appeased, and its embers might soon have been blown into a flame; but, landing in a distant, wild, and isolated corner of the island, instead of pressing rapidly at once, as he was strongly advised, to the Mountains of Ulster, (the centre of the United Irish organization,) and calling the people to arms, he amused himself, during a fortnight, in drilling the peasantry of the neighbourhood, who flocked to his standard, and enjoying the hospitality of the bishop of Killala. That prelate rendered a most signal service to the Irish Government by thus detaining the French General. At the battle of Castlebar, he defeated a numerous corps which had been directed in all haste against him, under General Lake. On this occasion I have heard, but cannot vouch for the authenticity of the anecdote, that, as soon as his Irish auxiliaries had fired their muskets, they flung them away as useless, and rushed to the charge with their pikes. For a few days a general panic prevailed; but the Viceroy, Cornwallis, marched in person; all the forces of the kingdom were put in motion, and Humbert was speedily surrounded and confined behind the Shannon, by twenty times his numbers. At length he perceived the trap into which he had fallen, and attempted, what he should have done at first, to force his way over that river, and throw himself into the mountains of the North. But encircled, on the 8th of September, at Ballinamuck, by an entire army, his small band, after a gallant resistance, were compelled to lay down their arms. The French were received to composition, and shortly exchanged; but the Irish were slaughtered without mercy, and the cruelties afterwards exercised on the unresisting peasantry will render the name of General Lake remembered for ages in those remote districts of Connaught. Of the Irish who had accompanied Humbert, Sullivan escaped, under the disguise of a Frenchman, and Matthew Tone and Teeling were brought in irons to Dublin, tried, and *executed*.

The news of Humbert's attempt, as may well be imagined, threw the Directory into the greatest perplexity. They instantly determined, however, to hurry all their preparations, and send off at least the division of General Hardy, to second his efforts, as soon as possible. The report of his first advantages, which shortly reached them, augmented their ardour and accelerated their movements. But such was the state of the French navy and arsenals, that it was not until the 20th of September that this small expedition, consisting of one sail of the line and eight frigates, under Commodore Bompart, and 3,000 men, under General Hardy, was ready for sailing. The news of Humbert's defeat had not yet reached France.

Paris was then crowded with Irish emigrants, eager for action. In the papers of the day, and in later productions, I have seen it mentioned, that no fewer than twenty-four United Irish leaders embarked in General Hardy's expedition; and Lewines, an agent of the United Irish in Paris, is specified by name. This account is erroneous. The mass of the United Irishmen embarked in a small and fast-sailing boat, with Napper Tandy at their head. They reached, on the 16th September, the Isle of Raghlin, on the Northwest coast of Ireland, where they heard of Humbert's disaster; they merely spread some proclamations, and escaped to Norway. Three Irishmen only accompanied my father in Hardy's flotilla: he alone was embarked in the Admiral's vessel, the Hoche, the others were on board the frigates. These were Mr. T. Corbett and Mac Guire, (two brave officers, who have since died in the French service), and a third gentleman, (connected by marriage with his friend Russell,) who is yet living, and whose name it would, therefore, be improper in me to mention.

In Curran's Life, by his Son, I find an anecdote mentioned which must have been derived from the authority of this gentleman. It is stated that, on the night previous to the sailing of the expedition, a question rose amongst the United Irishmen engaged in it, whether, in case of their falling into the enemy's hands, they should suffer themselves to be put to death, according to the sentence of the law, or anticipate their fate by their own hands? That Mr. Tone maintained, with his usual eloquence and animation, that in no point of view in which he had ever considered suicide, could he hold it to be justifiable; that one of the company suggested that, from political considerations, it would be better not to relieve, by any act of self-murder, the Irish Government from the discredit in which numerous executions would involve it; an idea which Mr. Tone highly approved. This anecdote is substantially correct; but the gentleman did not understand my father.

At the period of this expedition, he was hopeless of its success, and in the deepest despondency at the prospect of Irish affairs. Such was the wretched indiscretion of the Government, that before his departure, he read himself in the *Bien Informé*, a Paris newspaper, a detailed account of the whole armament, where his own name was mentioned in full letters, with the circumstance of his being embarked on board the Hoche. There was, therefore, no hope of secrecy. He had all along deprecated the idea of these attempts on a small scale. But he had also declared, repeatedly, that, if the Government sent only a corporal's guard, he felt it his duty to go along with them; he saw no chance of Kilmaine's large expedition being ready in any space of time, and, therefore, determined to accompany Hardy. His resolution was, however, deliberately and inflexibly taken, in case he fell into the hands of the enemy, never to suffer the indignity of a public execution. He did not consider this as suicide—an act which in usual cases he regarded as a weakness or frenzy,—but merely as choosing the mode of his death:—and, indeed, his constitutional and nervous sensitiveness at the slightest idea of personal indignity, would have sufficed to determine him never to bear the touch of an executioner. It was at dinner, in our own house and in my mother's presence, a little before leaving Paris, that the gentleman above mentioned proposed, that the Irish should leave to the Government all the shame and odium of their execution. The idea struck him as ludicrous, and he applauded it highly: "My dear friend," he said, "say nothing more, you never spoke better in your life." And after the gentleman's departure, he laughed very heartily at his idea of shaming the Irish Government, by allowing himself to be hanged; adding, that he did not at all understand people mooting the point whether they should or should not choose their own deaths, or consulting on such an occasion. That he would never advise others, but, "please God, they should never have his poor bones to pick." *(Vide Win. Jenkins.)* This conversation may have been repeated at Brest, but such were certainly my father's feelings on the subject.

At length, about the 20th of September, 1798, that fatal expedition set sail from the Baye de Camaret. It consisted of the Hoche, 74; Loire, Resolue, Bellone, Coquille, Embuscade, Immortalité, Romaine, and Semillante, frigates; and Biche schooner and aviso. To avoid the British fleets, Bompart, an excellent seaman, took a large sweep to the Westward, and then to the North-east, in order to bear down on the Northern coast of Ireland, from the quarter whence a French force would be least expected. He met, however, with contrary winds, and it appears that his flotilla was scattered; for, on the 10th of October, after twenty days' cruise, he arrived off the entry of Loch Swilly, with the Hoche, the Loire, the Resolue, and the Biche. He was instantly signalled; and, on the break of day, next morning, 11th of October, before he could enter the bay or land his troops, he perceived the squadron of Sir John Borlase Warren, consisting of six sail of the line, one razee of sixty guns, and two frigates, bearing down upon him. There was no chance of escape for the large and heavy man of war. Bompart gave instant signals to the frigates and schooner, to retreat through shallow water, and prepared alone to honour the flag of his country and liberty, by a desperate but hopeless defence. At that moment, a boat came from the Biche for his last orders. That ship had the best chance to get off. The French officers all supplicated my father to embark on board of her. "Our contest is hopeless," they observed, "we shall be prisoners of war, but what will become of you?" "Shall it be said," replied he, "that I fled, whilst the French were fighting the battles of my country?" He refused their offers, and determined to stand and fall with the ship. The Biche accomplished her escape, and I see it mentioned in late publications, that other Irishmen availed themselves of that occasion. This fact is incorrect, not one of them would have done so; and besides, my father was the only Irishman on board of the Hoche.

The British Admiral despatched two men of war, the razee, and a frigate, after the Loire and Resolue, and the Hoche was soon surrounded by four sail of the line and a frigate, and began one of the most obstinate and desperate engagements which have ever been fought on the ocean. During six hours she sustained the fire of a whole fleet, till her masts and rigging were swept away, her scuppers flowed with blood, her wounded filled the cock-pit, her shattered ribs yawned at each new stroke and let in five feet of water in the hold, her rudder was carried off, and she floated a dismantled wreck on the waters; her sails and cordage hung in shreds, nor could she reply with a single gun from her dismounted batteries to the unabating cannonade of the enemy. At length she struck. The Resolue and Loire were soon reached by the English fleet; the former was in a sinking condition--she made, however, an honourable defence; the Loire sustained three attacks, drove off the English frigates, and had almost effected her escape; at length, engaged by the Anson, razee of sixty guns, she struck after an action of three hours, entirely dismasted. Of the other frigates, pursued in all directions, the Bellone, Immortalité, Coquille, and Embuscade, were taken, and the Romaine and Semillante, through a thousand dangers, reached separate ports in France.

During the action, my father commanded one of the batteries, and, according to the report of the officers who returned to France, fought with the utmost desperation, and as if he was courting death. When the ship struck, confounded with the other officers, he was not recognized for some time; for he had completely acquired the language and appearance of a Frenchman. The two fleets were dispersed in every direction; nor was it till some days later, that the Hoche was brought into Loch Swilly, and the prisoners landed and marched to Letterkenny. Yet rumours of his being on board must have been circulated, for the fact was public at Paris. But it was thought he had been killed in the action, and I am willing to believe that the British officers, respecting the valour of a fallen enemy, were not earnest in investigating the point. It was at length a gentleman, well known in County Derry as a leader of the Orange party and one of the chief magistrates in that neighbourhood, Sir George Hill, who had been his fellow-student in Trinity College, and knew his person, who undertook the task of discovering him. It is known that, in Spain, Grandees and Noblemen of the first rank pride themselves in the functions of familiars, spies, and informers of the Holy Inquisition; it remained for Ireland to offer a similar example. The French officers were invited to breakfast with the Earl of Cavan, who commanded in that district; my father sat undistinguished amongst them, when Sir George Hill entered the room followed by police officers. Looking narrowly at the company, he singled out the object of his search, and stepping up to him, said, "Mr. Tone, I am *very happy* to see you." Instantly rising, with the utmost composure, and disdaining all useless attempts at concealment, my father replied, "Sir George, I am happy to see you; how are Lady Hill and your family?" Beckoned into the next room by the police officers, an unexpected indignity awaited him. It was filled with military, and one General Lavau, who commanded them, ordered him to be ironed, declaring that, as on leaving Ireland, to enter the French service, he had not renounced his oath of allegiance, he remained a subject of Britain, and should be punished as a traitor. Seized with a momentary burst of indignation at such unworthy treatment and cowardly cruelty to a prisoner of war, he flung off his uniform, and cried, "These fetters shall never degrade the revered insignia of the free nation which I have served." Resuming then his usual calm, he offered his limbs to the irons, and when they were fixed, he exclaimed, "For the cause which I have embraced, I feel prouder to wear these chains, than if I were decorated with the star and garter of England." The friends of Lord Cavan have asserted that this extreme, and I will add, *unmanly* and *ungenerous* severity, was provoked by his outrageous behaviour when he found that he was not to have the privileges of a prisoner of war. This supposition is not only contradicted by the whole tenour of his character, and his subsequent deportment, but no other instances of it have ever been specified than those noble replies to the taunts of General Lavau. Of the latter, I know nothing but these anecdotes, recorded in the papers of the day. If, as his name seems to indicate, he was a French emigrant, the coincidence was curious, and his conduct the less excusable.

Another version of this story, which I have seen for the first time in the London New Monthly Magazine, states that Mr. Tone was recognised by, or, according to another account, had the imprudence to make himself known to, an old acquaintance at Lord Cavan's table, who speedily informed his lordship of the guest who sate at his board. The first circumstantial account is the one which reached us in France; but, in my opinion, the difference between the two stories is very trifling. It regards only the fashion in which Sir George Hill gave in his information.

From Letterkenny he was hurried to Dublin without delay. In the same Magazine I find that, contrary to usual custom, he was conveyed during the whole route fettered and on horseback, under an escort of dragoons. Of this farther indignity, I had never heard before. During this journey, the unruffled serenity of his countenance, amidst the rude soldiery, and under the awe-struck gaze of his countrymen, excited universal admiration. Recognizing, in a group of females which thronged the windows, a young lady of his acquaintance; "There," said he, "is my old friend Miss Beresford; how well she looks!" On his arrival, he was immured in the Provost's prison, in the Barracks of Dublin, under the charge of the notorious Major Sandys, a man whose insolence, rapacity, and cruelty, will long be remembered in that city, where, a worthy instrument of the faction which then ruled it, he enjoyed, under their patronage, a despotic authority within its precincts (*See Curran's Speeches, Hevey versus Major Sirr.*)

Though the reign of terror was drawing to a close, and Lord Cornwallis had restored some appearance of legal order and regular administration in the kingdom, a prisoner of such importance to the Irish Protestant ascendancy party, as the founder and leader of the United Irish Society, and the most formidable of their adversaries, was not to be trusted to the delays and common form of law. Though the Court of King's Bench was then sitting, preparations were instantly made for trying him summarily before a Court-Martial. But before I give an account of this trial and of the nature of his defence, it will be necessary to remove some erroneous impressions on these subjects which I have seen stated, both in Curran's Life, by his son, and in the very fair and liberal comments of the London New Monthly Magazine. A prevailing notion in both these works is that, from my father's early dislike to legal studies and inaccurate acquaintance with the English laws, he considered his French commission as a protection, and pleaded it in his defence. It is impossible to read his speech on the trial, and preserve this idea. Though he used to laugh at his little proficiency in legal lore, he knew perfectly well that the course he had deliberately taken subjected him to the utmost severity of the British laws. Nor was he ignorant that, by the custom of the land and the very tenor of those laws, his trial, as it was conducted, was informal. He never was legally condemned: for, though a subject of the crown, (not of Britain, but of Ireland,) he was not a military man in that kingdom: he had taken no military oath, and, of course, the court-martial which tried him had no power to pronounce on his case, which belonged to the regular criminal tribunals. But his heart was sunk in despair at the total failure of his hopes, and he did not wish to survive them. To die with honour was his only wish, and his only request to be shot like a soldier. For this purpose, he himself preferred to be tried by a Court-Martial, and proffered his French commission, not to defend his life, but as a proof of his rank, as he stated himself on the trial.

If farther proof were required that my father was perfectly aware of his fate, according to the English law, his own Journals, written during the Bantry Bay expedition, afford an incontestable one. (*See Dec.* 26, 1796.) But my father also knew that political considerations will often supersede the letter of the laws. The only chance on which he had formerly relied was, that the French Government would interfere, and claim him with all its power and credit; to that, and to threats of severe retaliation, he knew that the British Cabinet would yield, as they did about a year afterwards in the case of Napper Tandy,—a curious fact (and which is not generally known, perhaps not even to that gallant soldier himself,) is, that Sir Sidney Smith was detained by Carnot in the Temple for that very purpose, like a prisoner of state rather than a prisoner of war.

The time of my father's trial was deferred a few days, by the officers appointed to sit on the Court-Martial receiving marching orders. At length, on Saturday, 10th November, 1798, a new court was assembled, consisting of General Loftus, (who performed the functions of President,) Colonels Vandeleur, Daly, and Wolfe, Major Armstrong, and a Captain Curran; Mr. Paterson performed the functions of Judge-Advocate.

At an early hour, the neighbourhood of the barracks was crowded with eager and anxious spectators. As soon as the doors were thrown open, they rushed in and filled every corner of the hall.

Tone appeared in the uniform of a *Chef de Brigade* (Colonel). The firmness and cool serenity of his whole deportment gave to the awe-struck assembly the measure of his soul:—nor could his bitterest enemies, whatever they deemed of his political principles and of the necessity of striking a great example, deny him the praise of determination and magnanimity.

The members of the Court having taken the usual oath, the Judge-Advocate proceeded to inform the prisoner that the Court-Martial before which he stood was appointed by the Lord Lieutenant of the Kingdom, to try whether he had or had not acted traitorously and hostilely against his Majesty, to whom, as a natural-born subject, he owed all allegiance, from the very fact of his birth in that Kingdom: and, according to the usual form, he called upon him to plead guilty or not guilty.

Tone.—"I mean not to give the Court any useless trouble, and wish to spare them the idle task of examining witnesses. I admit all the facts alleged, and only request leave to read an address, which I have prepared for this occasion."

Col. Daly.—"I must warn the prisoner that, in acknowledging those *facts*, he admits, to his prejudice, that he has acted *traitorously* against his Majesty. Is such his intention?"

Tone.—"Stripping this charge of the technicality of its terms, it means, I presume, by the word 'traitorously,' that I have been found in arms against the soldiers of the King, in my native country. I admit this accusation in its most extended sense, and request again to explain to the Court the reasons and motives of my conduct."

The Court then observed, that they would hear his address, provided he confined himself within the bounds of moderation. He rose, and began in these words:—

"Mr. President, and Gentlemen, of the Court-Martial: I mean not to give you the trouble of bringing judicial proof, to convict me, legally, of having acted in hostility to the Government of his Britannic Majesty in Ireland. I admit the fact. From my earliest youth, I have regarded the connexion between Ireland and Great Britain as the curse of the Irish nation; and felt convinced that, whilst it lasted, this country could never be free nor happy. My mind has been confirmed in this opinion by the experience of every succeeding year, and the conclusions which

I have drawn from every fact before my eyes. In consequence, I determined to apply all the powers which my individual efforts could move, in order to separate the two countries.

"That Ireland was not able, of herself, to throw off the yoke, I knew. I therefore sought for aid wherever it was to be found. In honourable poverty, I rejected offers which, to a man in my circumstances, might be considered highly advantageous. I remained faithful to what I thought the cause of my country, and sought in the French Republic an ally, to rescue three millions of my countrymen from———"

The President here interrupted the Prisoner, observing, that this language was neither relevant to the charge nor such as ought to be delivered in a public court. One member said, it seemed calculated only to inflame the minds of a certain description of people (the United Irishmen), many of whom might probably be present; and that, therefore, the Court ought not to suffer it. The Judge-Advocate said, he thought that if Mr. Tone meant this paper to be laid before his Excellency in way of *extenuation*, it must have quite a contrary effect, if any of the foregoing part was suffered to remain.

Tone "I shall urge this topic no further, since it seems disagreeable to the Court; but shall proceed to read the few words which remain."

Gen. Loftus. "If the remainder of your address, Mr. Tone, is of the same complexion with what you have already read, will you not hesitate, for a moment, in proceeding, since you have learned the opinion of the Court?"

Tone. "I believe there is nothing in what remains for me to say, which can give any offence. I mean to express my feelings and gratitude towards the Catholic body, in whose cause I was engaged."

Gen. Loftus. "That seems to have nothing to say to the charge against you, to which only you are to speak. If you have any thing to offer in defence or extenuation of that charge, the Court will hear you; but they beg that you will confine yourself to that subject."

Tone. "I shall, then, confine myself to some points relative to my connexion with the French army. Attached to no party in the French Republic, without interest, without money, without intrigue, the openness and integrity of my views raised me to a high and confidential rank in its armies. I obtained the confidence of the Executive Directory, the approbation of my Generals, and, I venture to add, the esteem and affection of my brave comrades. When I review these circumstances, I feel a secret and internal consolation, which no reverse of fortune, no sentence in the power of this Court to inflict, can ever deprive me of, or weaken in any degree. Under the flag of the French Republic I originally engaged, with a view to save and liberate my own country. For that purpose, I have encountered the chances of war, amongst strangers: for that purpose, I have repeatedly braved the terrors of the ocean, covered, as I knew it to be, with the triumphant fleets of that

Power which it was my glory and my duty to oppose. I have sacrificed all my views in life; I have courted poverty; I have left a beloved wife unprotected, and children whom I adored, fatherless. After such sacrifices in a cause which I have always conscientiously considered as the cause of justice and freedom—it is no great effort, at this day, to add 'the sacrifice of my life.'

"But I hear it said, that this unfortunate country has been a prey to all sorts of horrors. I sincerely lament it. I beg, however, it may be remembered, that I have been absent four years from Ireland. To me, these sufferings can never be attributed. I designed, by fair and open war, to procure the separation of the two countries. For open war I was prepared; but if, instead of that, a system of private assassination has taken place, I repeat, whilst I deplore it, that it is not chargeable on me. Atrocities, it seems, have been committed on both sides. I do not less deplore them; I detest them, from my heart; and to those who know my character and sentiments, I may safely appeal for the truth of this assertion. With them, I need no justification.

"In a cause like this, success is every thing. Success, in the eyes of the vulgar, fixes its merits. Washington succeeded, and Kosciusko failed.

"After a combat nobly sustained, a combat which would have excited the respect and sympathy of a generous enemy, my fate was to become a prisoner. To the eternal disgrace of those who gave the order, I was brought hither in irons, like a felon. I mention this for the sake of others; for me, I am indifferent to it; I am aware of the fate which awaits me, and scorn equally the tone of complaint and that of supplication.

"As to the connexion between this country and Great Britain, I repeat it, all that has been imputed to me, words, writings, and actions, I here deliberately avow. I have spoken and acted with reflection and on principle, and am ready to meet the consequences. Whatever be the sentence of this Court, I am prepared for it. Its members will surely discharge their duty; I shall take care not to be wanting to mine."

This speech was pronounced in a tone so magnanimous, so full of a noble and calm serenity, as seemed deeply and visibly to affect all its hearers, the members of the Court not excepted. A pause ensued of some continuance, and silence reigned in the hall till interrupted by Tone himself, who inquired, whether it was not usual to assign an interval between the sentence and execution? The Judge-Advocate answered, that the voices of the Court would be collected without delay, and the result transmitted forthwith to the Lord Lieutenant. If the prisoner, therefore, had any farther observations to make, now was the moment.

Tone. "I wish to offer a few words, relative to one single point—to the mode of punishment. In France, our *Emigrés,* who stand nearly in the same situation in which, I suppose, I now stand before you, are condemned to be shot. I ask, that the

Court should adjudge me the death of a soldier, and let me be shot by a platoon of grenadiers. I request this indulgence, rather in consideration of the uniform which I wear (the uniform of a *Chef de Brigade* in the French army,) than from any personal regard to myself. In order to evince my claim to this favour, I beg that the Court may take the trouble to peruse my commission and letters of service in the French army. It will appear from these papers, that I have not received them as a mask to cover me, but that I have been long and *boná-fide* an officer in the French service."

Judge-Advocate. "You must feel that the papers you allude to, will serve as undeniable proofs against you."

Tone. "Oh!—I know it well—I have already admitted the facts, and I now admit the papers as full proofs of conviction."

The papers were then examined: they consisted of a brevet of *Chef de Brigade*, from the Directory, signed by the Minister of War; of a letter of service, granting to him the rank of Adjutant-General; and of a passport.

General Loftus. "In these papers you are designated as "serving in the Army of England."

Tone. "I did serve in that army, when it was commanded by Buonaparte, by Desaix, and by Kilmaine, who is, as I am, an Irishman. But I have also served elsewhere." Requested if he had any thing farther to observe, he said, nothing more occurred to him, except the sooner his Excellency's approbation of their sentence was obtained, the better. He would consider it as a favour, if it could be obtained in an hour.

General Loftus then observed, that the Court would, undoubtedly, submit to the Lord Lieutenant the address which he had read to them, and, also, the subject of his last demand. In transmitting the address, he, however, took care to efface all that part of it which he would not allow to be read; and which contained the dying speech and last words of the first apostle of Irish union, and martyr of Irish liberty, to his countrymen. Lord Cornwallis refused the last demand of my father, and he was sentenced to die the death of a traitor, in forty-eight hours. on the 12th of November. This cruelty he had foreseen: for England, from the days of Lewellyn of Wales and Wallace of Scotland to those of Tone and Napoleon, has never shown mercy or generosity to a fallen enemy. He then, in perfect coolness and self-possession, determined to execute his purpose and anticipate their sentence.

The next day was passed in a kind of stupor. A cloud of portentous awe seemed to hang over the City of Dublin.—The apparatus of military and despotic authority was every where displayed; no man dared to trust his next neighbour, nor one of the pale citizens to betray, by look or word, his feelings or sympathy. The terror which prevailed in Paris under the rule of the Jacobins, or in Rome during the proscriptions of Marius, Sylla, and the Triumviri, and under the reigns of Tiberius, Nero, Caligula, and Domitian, was never deeper, or more universal, than that of Ireland at this fatal and shameful period. It was, in short, the feeling which made the People, soon after, passively acquiesce in the Union, and in the extinction of their name as a Nation. Of the numerous friends of my father, and of those who had shared in his political principles and career, some had perished on the scaffold, others rotted in dungeons, and the remainder dreaded, by the slightest mark of recognition, to be involved in his fate. One noble exception deserves to be recorded.

John Philpot Curran, the celebrated orator and patriot, had attached himself in his political career to the Whig party; but his theoretical principles went much farther: and when the march of the Administration to despotism was pronounced—when the persecution began—I know that, in the years 1794 and 1795, and particularly at the Drogheda assizes the former year, and on occasion of the trial of Bird and Hamill (where they were both employed as counsel) he opened his mind to my father; and that on the main point—on the necessity of breaking the connexion with England—they agreed. Curran prudently and properly confined himself to those legal exertions at the bar, where his talents were so eminently useful, and where he left an imperishable monument to his own and to his country's fame. It was well that there remained one place, and one man, through which the truth might sometimes be heard. He avoided committing himself in the

Councils of the United Irishmen; but, had the project of liberating Ireland succeeded, he would have been amongst the foremost to hail and join her independence. On this occasion, joining his efforts to those of Mr. Peter Burrowes, he nobly exerted himself to save his friend.

The sentence of my father was evidently illegal. Curran knew, however, very well that, by bringing the case before the proper tribunal, the result would ultimately be the same—that he could not be acquitted. But then, the delays of the law might be brought in play, and the all-important point, of gaining time, would be obtained. The French Government could not, in honour, but interfere, and the case, from a mere legal, would become a political one. In politics my father had many adversaries, but few personal enemies; in private and public life, he was generally beloved and respected; his moderation, too, was known and appreciated by those who feared a Revolution, and trusted to him as a mediator, if such an event was to take place. In short, it did not appear a matter of impossibility to have finally saved him, by some agreement with the Government. Determined to form a bar for his defence, and bring the case before the Court of King's Bench, then sitting, and presided by Lord Kilwarden, a man of the purest and most benevolent virtue and who always tempered justice with mercy, Curran endeavoured, the whole day of the 11th, to raise a subscription for this purpose. But *terror* had closed every door; and I have it from his own lips that even among the Catholic leaders, many of them wealthy, no one dared to subscribe. Curran then determined to proceed *alone*. On this circumstance no comment can be expected from the son of Theobald Wolfe Tone. Those men had behaved nobly towards him in former times, almost as perilous. The universal dread must be their excuse.

On the next day, 12th November, (the day fixed for his execution,) the scene in the Court of King's Bench was awful and impressive to the highest degree. As soon as it opened, Curran advanced, leading the aged father of Tone, who produced his affidavit that his son had been brought before a bench of officers, calling itself a Court-Martial, and sentenced to death. "I do not pretend," said Curran, "that Mr. Tone is not guilty of the charges of which he is accused. I presume the officers were honourable men. But it is stated in this affidavit, as a solemn fact, that Mr. Tone had no commission under his Majesty; and, therefore, no Court-Martial could have cognizance of any crime imputed to him, whilst the Court of King's Bench sate in the capacity of the Great Criminal Court of the land. In times when war was raging, when man was opposed to man in the field, Courts-Martial might be endured; but every law authority is with me, whilst I stand upon this sacred and immutable principle of the Constitution, that martial law and civil law are incompatible, and that the former must cease with the existence of the latter. This is not, however, the time for arguing this momentous question.

My client must appear in this Court. He is cast for death this very day. He may be ordered for execution whilst I address you. I call on the Court to support the law, and move for a *Habeas Corpus*, to be directed to the Provost-Martial of the barracks of Dublin, and Major Sandys, to bring up the body of Tone."

Chief Justice. "Have a writ instantly prepared."

Curran. "My client may die, whilst the writ is preparing."

Chief Justice. "Mr. Sheriff, proceed to the barracks, and acquaint the Provost-Marshal that a writ is preparing to suspend Mr. Tone's execution, and see that he be not executed."

The Court awaited, in a state of the utmost agitation and suspense, the return of the Sheriff. He speedily appeared, and said, "My Lord, I have been to the barracks, in pursuance of your order. The Provost-Marshal says he must obey Major Sandys; Major Sandys says he must obey Lord Cornwallis." Mr. Curran announced, at the same time, that Mr. Tone, the father, was just returned, after serving the habeas corpus, and that General Craig would not obey it. The Chief Justice exclaimed, "Mr. Sheriff, take the body of Tone into custody—take the Provost-Marshal and Major Sandys into custody, and show the order of the Court to General Craig."

The general impression was now, that the prisoner would be led out to execution, in defiance of the Court. This apprehension was legible in the countenance of Lord Kilwarden, a man who, in the worst of times, preserved a religious respect for the laws, and who, besides, I may add, felt every personal feeling of pity and respect for the prisoner, whom he had formerly contributed to shield from the vengeance of Government, on an occasion almost as perilous. His agitation, according to the expression of an eye-witness, was magnificent.

The Sheriff returned at length with the fatal news. He had been refused admittance in the barracks; but was informed that Mr. Tone, who had wounded himself dangerously the night before, was not in a condition to be removed. A French emigrant surgeon, who had closed the wound, was called in, and declared there was no saying for four days, whether it was mortal. His head was to be kept in one position, and a sentinel was set over him to prevent his speaking. Removal would kill him at once. The Chief Justice instantly ordered a rule for suspending the execution.

I must collect my strength to give the remaining details of the close of my father's life. The secrets of a state prison, and of such a prison as were those of Dublin, at that period, are seldom penetrated; and the facts which have reached us are few and meagre. As soon as he learned the refusal of his last request, his determination was taken with the same resolution and coolness which he exhibited during the whole transaction. In order to spare the feelings of his parents and friends, he refused to see any one, and requested only the use of writing materials. During the 10th and 11th of November he addressed the Directory, the Minister of Marine, General Kilmaine, and Mr. Shee, in France, and several of his friends in Ireland, to recommend his family to their care. I here insert a translation of his letter to the Directory, the only one of which we obtained a copy.

" From the Provost's Prison, Dublin,
" 20th *Brumaire*, 7th year of the Republic,
" (10th November, 1798).

" *The Adjutant-General Theobald Wolfe Tone, (called Smith,) to the Executive Directory of the French Republic.*

" CITIZEN DIRECTORS:

" The English Government having determined not to respect my rights as a French citizen and officer, and summoned me before a court-martial, I have been sentenced to death. In these circumstances, I request you to accept my thanks for the confidence with which you have honoured me, and which, in a moment like this, I venture to say I well deserved. I have served the Republic faithfully, and my death, as well as that of my brother, a victim like myself, and condemned in the same manner about a month ago, will sufficiently prove it. I hope the circumstances in which I stand will warrant me, Citizen Directors, in supplicating you to consider the fate of a virtuous wife and of three infant children, who had no other support, and, in losing me, will be reduced to the extreme of misery. I venture, on such an occasion, to recal to your remembrance, that I was expelled from my own country in consequence of my attempts to serve the Republic; that, on the invitation of the French Government, I came to France; that ever since I had the honour to enter the French service, I have faithfully, and with the approbation of all my chiefs, performed my duty: finally, that I have sacrificed for the Republic all that man holds dearest—my wife, my children, my liberty, my life. In these circumstances, I confidently call on your justice and humanity in favour of my family, assured that you will not abandon them. It is the greatest consolation which remains to me in dying.

"Health and respect.

"T. W. TONE, (called Smith,)

"*Adjutant-General.*"

He then, with a firm hand and heart, penned the two following letters to my mother:—

"Provost's Prison, Dublin Barracks,

"*Le* 20 *Brumaire, an* 7 (10th Nov. 1798).

"DEAREST LOVE:

"The hour is at last come when we must part. As no words can express what I feel for you and our children, I shall not attempt it; complaint, of any kind, would be beneath your courage and mine; be assured I will die as I have lived, and that you will have no cause to blush for me.

"I have written on your behalf to the French Government, to the Minister of Marine, to General Kilmaine, and to Mr. Shee; with the latter I wish you especially to advise. In Ireland, I have written to your brother Harry, and to those of my friends who are about to go into exile, and who, I am sure, will not abandon you.

"Adieu, dearest love; I find it impossible to finish this letter. Give my love to Mary; and, above all things, remember that you are now the only parent of our dearest children, and that the best proof you can give of your affection for me, will be to preserve yourself for their education. God Almighty bless you all.

"Your's ever,

"T. W. TONE.

"P.S. I think you have a friend in Wilson, who will not desert you."*

SECOND LETTER.

"DEAREST LOVE:

"I write just one line, to acquaint you that I have received assurances from your brother Edward, of his determination to render every assistance and

* Nobly did this pure and virtuous man, and he alone of all those whom my father had depended upon, fulfil the expectation of his friend. He was to my mother a brother, a protector, and an adviser, during the whole period of our distress; and when, at the close of eighteen years, we were ruined a second time by the fall of Napoleon, he came over from his own country to offer her his hand and his fortune, and share our fate in America.

protection in his power; for which I have written to thank him most sincerely. Your sister has likewise sent me assurances of the same nature, and expressed a desire to see me, which I have refused, having determined to speak to no one of my friends, not even my father, from motives of humanity to them and myself. It is a very great consolation to me, that your family are determined to support you; as to the manner of that assistance, I leave it to their affection for you, and your own excellent good sense, to settle what manner will be most respectable for all parties.

"Adieu, dearest love. Keep your courage, as I have kept mine; my mind is as tranquil this moment as at any period of my life. Cherish my memory; and, especially, preserve your health and spirits for the sake of our dearest children.

"Your ever affectionate

"T. Wolfe Tone.

"11th November, 1798."

It is said, that, on the evening of that very day, he could see and hear the soldiers erecting the gallows for him before his windows. That very night, (according to the report given by his gaolers,) having secreted a penknife, he inflicted a deep wound across his neck. It was soon discovered by the sentry, and a surgeon called in at four o'clock in the morning, who stopped the blood and closed it. He reported that, as the prisoner had missed the carotid artery, he might yet survive, but was in the extremest danger. It is said, that he murmured only in reply, "I am sorry I have been so bad an anatomist." Let me draw a veil over the remainder of this scene.

Stretched on his bloody pallet in a dungeon, the first apostle of Irish union, and most illustrious martyr of Irish independence, counted each lingering hour during the last seven days and nights of his slow and silent agony. No one was allowed to approach him. Far from his adored family, and from all those friends whom he loved so dearly, the only forms which flitted before his eyes were those of the grim gaoler and rough attendants of the prison; the only sound which fell on his dying ear, the heavy tread of the sentry. He retained, however, the calmness of his soul, and the possession of his faculties, to the last:—and the consciousness of dying for his country, and in the cause of justice and liberty, illumined, like a bright halo, his latest moments, and kept up his fortitude to the end. There is no situation, under which these feelings will not support the soul of a patriot.

On the morning of the 19th of November, he was seized with the spasms of approaching death. It is said that the surgeon who attended whispered that, if he attempted to move or speak, he must expire instantly; that he overheard him, and, making a slight movement, replied, "I can yet find words to thank you, Sir: it is the most welcome news you could give me. What should I wish to live for?" Falling back with these expressions on his lips, he expired without farther effort.

On closing this painful and dreadful narrative, I must allude to some hints which I have heard from a most respectable and well-informed quarter, that, in consequence of the attempts to withdraw him from the jurisdiction of the military tribunals, my father's end may have been precipitated by the hands of his gaolers, and that, to conceal their crime, they spread the report of his voluntary death. It is certainly not my duty to exculpate them. That his end was voluntary, his determination previous to his leaving France (which was known to us,) and the tenor of his last letters, incline me to believe:—(neither is it likely that Major Sandys, and his experienced satellites, would perform a murder in so bungling a way as to allow their victim to survive the attempt during eight days.) If this was the case, his death can never be considered as a suicide; it was merely the resolution of a noble mind to disappoint, by his own act, the brutal ferocity of his enemies, and to avoid the indignity of their touch.

But, on the other side, it cannot be denied, that the character of these men would warrant the worst conclusion. The details of my father's death and last words only reached the public ear through their reports; no one was allowed to approach him after his wound; no medical attendant to come near him, except the prison surgeon, a foreigner and French emigrant.* Why was no coroner's inquest held on

* It would be a very curious coincidence, if General Lavau, who behaved so brutally to my father on arresting him, was,

his body, as was held on Jackson's in the very court where he died? The resistance which was opposed by the military to the warrant of the Chief Justice was indecorous and violent in the extreme; nor was it till compelled by the firmness of Lord Kilwarden to give way, that they acknowledged the wound of their prisoner, though, according to their own report, it had been inflicted during the preceding night. Was it possible that, fearing the interference of the civil courts, they hastened his end? or, what would be more atrocious still, admitting the fact that he had wounded himself, did they intend to conceal it, and to glut their mean and ferocious revenge, and insult their dying enemy, (who had thought to escape their indignities,) by dragging him out, in that state, and executing him with their own hands? That their preparations continued till interrupted by the interference of superior authority; that the wound of their prisoner was anxiously concealed, as long as possible; and that no one, even afterwards, was allowed to approach and speak to him during his long agony, are certain facts.

Between these dreadful suspicions the reader must judge for himself. As for what passed within the Provost's prison, it must remain for ever amongst the guilty and bloody mysteries of that pandemonium. If charges of so black and bloody a nature can be adduced with any appearance of probability

also, a French emigrant. These men would hold him in double abhorrence, as a soldier of the French Republic, and a democrat.

against the agents of the Irish Government, the violence, cruelty, and lawless proceedings, in which they were indulged with perfect impunity by their employers, not only warrant them, but give them too tremendous a probability. As for my part, I have merely stated, as I have done through the whole of this work, in the fairest and fullest manner, the facts which have reached us, without any comment or opinion of my own.

APPENDIX

TO THE

MEMOIRS OF THEOBALD WOLFE TONE.

This Appendix comprises a selection amongst such of his Memorandums, Notes, and Letters, as we have been able to recover, and deemed illustrative of the character of the author, or of the times in which he lived. They were written with the utmost carelessness, and destined for the perusal of only one or two friends. As my father and his friends had the habit of designating each other by mock names, drawn from any trivial circumstance, the following key will be necessary to understand the fragments of his Journals.—Editor.

[The reader will also find subjoined the Two Memorials presented by the author to the French Government, of which such frequent mention is made in the body of the work; together with a most affecting and interesting letter written by him to his wife, when on the point of embarking in the Bantry Bay expedition.]

Mr. Hutton, or John Hutton,—means Mr. Tone.
P. P. Clerk of the Parish—Mr. T. Russell, his friend.
Blefescu—The City of Belfast.

The Draper,	Mr. Wm. Sinclair	*United Irish leaders in Belfast.*
The Jacobin,	Mr. Samuel Neilson	
The Tanner,	Mr. Robert Simms	
The Hypocrite,	Dr. Macdonnell	
The Irish Slave,	Mr. Macabe	
The Keeper,	Whitley Stokes*	*United Irish leaders in Dublin.*
The Tribune,	J. Napper Tandy	
The Vintner,	Mr. Edward Byrne, of Mullnaihack	
Gog,	Mr. John Keogh	
Magog,	Mr. R. M'Cormick†	

* Dean of Trinity College.
† Secretary of the Catholic Committee.

Fragments of Memorandums previous to 1791.

June 21, 1789. Fitzgibbon's want of temper and undoubted partiality will let in his resentments and his affections to bias his decisions. But Lord Earlsfort is an ignorant man, and a stupid man, and a corrupt man.

Mem. The committee for drawing up the address to the Chancellor, being headed by Egan and Tom Fitzgerald, were said by Curran to be more like a committee for drawing a waggon, than for drawing up an address.

Mem. When the Chief Baron, at the time of the King's illness, went over to London, his companions were Curran, Egan, and R. Barrett; on which Fitzgibbon remarked, that he travelled like a mountebank, with a monkey, a bear, and a sleight-of-hand man.

June 20, 1790. My idea of political sentiment in Ireland is, that, in the middling ranks, and, indeed, in the spirit of the people, there is a great fund of it, but stifled and suppressed, as much as possible, by the expensive depravity and corruption of those who, from rank and circumstances, constitute the legislature. Whatever has been done, has been by the people, strictly speaking, who have not often been wanting to themselves, when informed of their interests by such men as Swift, Flood, Grattan, &c.

Mem. Michael Smith went six years round before he made half a guinea. Downes, in the year 1783, received his first brief in a record, by the joint influence and procurement of Dudley Hussey, Dennis George, and Michael Smith; but they engaged him in every cause on that circuit, and he had merit to sustain the recommendation.

Mem. Wolfe is the Chancellor's private tutor in legal matters. Fitzgibbon has read Coke and Littleton, under his papa; he has a very intelligent clerk to note his briefs; he has Boyd to hunt his cases; and he has some talents, great readiness, and assurance; and there is Fitzgibbon.

Mem. Erskine, who, in England, is not looked upon as a very sound lawyer, knows more law than the twelve Judges of Ireland, *plus* the Chancellor.

August 4, 1790. Wogan Browne, Esq. foreman of the grand jury of county Kildare, sent down this evening to the bar-room a newspaper of the 3d, containing the resolutions of the Whig Club, in answer to a printed speech, purporting to be that of the Chancellor, on the election of Alderman James. It was enclosed in the following letter: "Mr. Wogan Browne presents his compliments to the gentlemen of the Bar; he encloses them this day's paper, which he has just now received; he requests they will return it to him, and hopes they will find in the vindication of the Whig Club, principles similar to their own; as honest and blunt men must look up to talents for the support of their most undenied rights, in times when they are so shamefully invaded."

This bold and manly epistle struck the bar of a heap. The father, a supporter of opposition in Parliament, was here only solicitous how he should escape giving an answer, which, indeed, every man, save one or two, seemed desirous to shift on his neighbour. Burn and Burrowes were decided to meet the letter boldly; Brownrigg and Lespinasse for taking no farther notice than acknowledging the receipt; the first, on the principle of preserving the harmony of the Bar; the latter, for some time, could assign no reason for his opinion, other than that he did not know who Mr. Browne was; but, at length, when pressed, he said, with equal candour and liberality, "that he did not like to receive any thing from a reformed Papist." The general sense seeming to be for something in reply which should be perfectly insipid, I grew out of patience, and proposed, I confess without hope of its being adopted, a resolution to the following purport: "That the Leinster Bar, in common with the Whig Club, and many other respectable societies, felt the warmest indignation and abhorrence of the late unconstitutional proceedings of the Privy Council, in the election of Alderman James—proceedings no less formidable to the liberties of the capital, than alarming to every city in the kingdom, as forming part of a system evidently subversive of their franchises, whether established by custom, charter, or the statute law of the land."

This resolution the majority seemed determined to conceive that I was not serious in; yet I was. However, being utterly hopeless of support, I did not press it. Two or three civil notes were proposed, of which the following, by Rochford, may serve as a sample. "The Leinster Bar present their compliments to Mr. Wogan Browne, and are thankful to him for his obliging communication of this day's paper, which they have the honour of returning."

However, the sense of shame in the majority was too high to admit so milky a composition, and, at length, after much irregular scuffling, the following was adopted as an answer, on my proposal, which I premised by stating that it had not my own approbation, as being too feeble: "The Leinster Bar return their thanks to Mr. Wogan Browne, for his early communication of the resolutions of the Whig Club. However, individually, a majority of the gentlemen present may approve of the spirit of these resolutions, yet, as many respectable members are absent, the Bar, as a body, do not feel themselves authorized to give any further opinion on the subject of Mr. Browne's letter."

The words "majority of gentlemen present," being objected

to by Mr. Moore, produced a division to ascertain the point, when nine were for continuing and five were for expunging them.

N. B. Such is the public spirit and virtue of the Leinster Bar.

Fragments of Notes, Letters, and Memorandums, of 1791.*

July 14, 1791. I sent down to Belfast resolutions suited to this day, and reduced to three heads. 1st, That English influence in Ireland was the great grievance of the country. 2d, That the most effectual way to oppose it was by a reform in Parliament. 3d, That no reform could be just or efficacious which did not include the Catholics, which last opinion, however, in concession to prejudices, was rather insinuated than asserted.

I am this day, July 17, 1791, informed that the last question was lost. If so, my present impression is, to become a red-hot Catholic; seeing that in the party, apparently, and perhaps really, most anxious for reform, it is rather a monopoly, than an extension of liberty, which is their object, contrary to all justice and expediency.

Journey to Belfast, October, 1791.

Wednesday, Oct. 11, 1791. Arrived at Belfast late, and was introduced to Digges, but no material conversation. Bonfires, illuminations, firing twenty-one guns, volunteers, &c.

12 Introduced to Mc Tier and Sinclair. A meeting between Russell, Mc Tier, Macabe, and me. Mode of doing business by a Secret Committee, who are not known or suspected of co-operating, but who, in fact, direct the movements of Belfast. Much conversation about the Catholics and their committee, &c , of which they know wonderfully little at Blefescu. Settled to dine with the Secret Committee at Drew's, on Saturday, when the resolutions, &c., of the United Irish will be submitted. Sent them off, and sat down to new-model the former copy Very curious to see how the thermometer of Blefescu has risen, as to politics. Passages in the first copy, which were three months ago esteemed too hazardous to propose, are now found too tame. Those taken out, and replaced by other and better ones. Sinclair came in; read and approved the resolutions, as new-modelled. Russell gave him a mighty pretty history of the Roman Catholic Committee, and his own negotiations. Christened Russell, *P. P. Clerk of this Parish.* Sinclair

* Towards the close of this year, and at the period of my father's first journey to Belfast, he began, as he states in his own life, to keep the regular series of those journals, of which we have recovered these fragments.—*Editor*

asked us to dine and meet Digges, which we acceded to with great affability. P. P. very drunk. Home; bed.

13. Much good jesting in bed, at the expense of P. P. Laughed myself into good humour. Rose. Breakfast. Dr. Mc Donnell. Much conversation regarding Digges. Went to meet Neilson; read over the resolutions with him, which he approved. Went to H. Joy's, to thank him for his proposing me at the Northern Whig Club. He invited Digges, P. P., and me, for Friday next, which we accepted. Made farther alterations in the resolutions, by advice of Digges.

14. Breakfasted with Digges at his lodgings. Met Capt. Seward, who carried out Mr. Pearce to America. Pearce now living in President Washington's house. Met Macabe, who is going to England. He showed P. P. and me certain curious drawings. Met Mc Tier, and showed him the resolutions, as amended. Curious discourse with a hair-dresser, (one Taylor,) who has two children christened by the priest, though he is himself a Dissenter, merely with a wish to blend the sects. Visited Jordan, who is an extraordinary young man, and lives in a baby-house. Walked all about the town, seeing sights. Four o'clock; went to dinner to meet the Secret Committee, who consist of Wm. Sinclair, Mc Tier, Neilson, Mc Leary, Macabe, Simms 1st and Simms 2d, Haslitt, Tennant, Campbell, Mc Ilvaine, P. P., and myself. P. P. and I made our declarations of secrecy, and proceeded to business. P. P. made a long speech, stating the present state and politics of the Catholic Committee, of which the people of Blefescu know almost nothing. They appeared much surprised and pleased at the information. Read the card of the Catholics and Stokes' letter. The Committee agree that the North is not yet ripe to follow them, but that no party could be raised directly to oppose them. Time and discussion the only things wanting to forward what is advancing rapidly. Agreed to the resolutions unanimously. Resolved to transmit a copy to Tandy, and request his and his fellow-citizens' co-operation, from which great benefit is expected to result to the cause, by reflecting back credit on the United Irishmen of Blefescu. Settled the mode of carrying the business through the club at large, on Tuesday next. The Secret Committee all steady, sensible, clear men, and, as I judge, extremely well adapted for serious business. Macabe asked us for Monday, Neilson for Tuesday, both which we did most graciously accept. Home at 10. P. P. in the blue devils—thinks he is losing his faculties; glad he has any to lose.

15. Digges came in to supper; had been lecturing P. P. on the state of his nerves, and the necessity of early hours; to which he agreed; and, as the first fruits of my advice and his reformation, sat up with Digges until three o'clock in the morning, being four hours after I had gone to bed

16. Sunday. Breakfast—Digges, Jordan, and Macabe. Church—a vile sermon from Bristowe, (called Caiaphas) against smuggling, &c., and about loyalty, and all that. P. P. in great sorrow and distress of mind; resolved to leave off smuggling, which is injurious to the fair trader.* Walked in the mall with Digges and P. P. The ladies, one and all, *speer* P. P. who is exceedingly fallen thereon, in his own good opinion. Put the plump question to Digges, relative to the possibility of Ireland's existence, independent of England. His opinion decidedly for independence. England would not risk a contest, the immediate consequence of which would be the destruction of her funds. Ireland supplies her with what, in case of a war, she could not possibly do without—as seamen and provisions. France would most probably assist, from the pride of giving freedom to one kingdom more. So would all the enemies of England. Nothing to be done, until the religious sects here are united, and England engaged in a foreign war. If Ireland were free, and well governed, being that she is unincumbered with debt, she would, in arts, commerce, and manufactures, spring up like an air-balloon, and leave England behind her, at an immense distance. There is no computing the rapidity with which she would rise. Digges promised to detail all this, and much more, on paper. Home. Dinner at William Sinclair's, to meet Dr. Halliday, who could not come, being suddenly called out to attend a sick bishop. Much conversation about Foster's treatment of Macabe and Pearce. Sinclair in high wrath with Foster, of whom he told scurrilous anecdotes. The loom now in America, and a capital of 500,000 dollars subscribed to carry on the manufacture of linen; workmen, the great want in America, which this loom goes precisely to obviate. America improving, silently and unnoticed, in manufactures; instance, in coarse linens, from 14*d.* to 8*d.*, of which, seven years since, there was a large export from Ireland, but which they now are able to supply themselves. Danger, therefore, by the aid of Pearce's various and inexhaustible invention, that they may proceed in like manner in other fabrics. Washington has adopted Pearce as his protegé, and declares him to be the first man in America. Great superiority of Ireland and John Foster, who can afford to fling away what America and General Washington are glad to pick up. One and all of us d—n the Government. Home. P. P. sober. Find a large packet by the mail, which we rip open in haste, and find 2000 prospectuses of the United Irishmen, instead of the pamphlet. Sat down in a pet, and wrote a tart letter to Chambers; got up in a rage, cursed, stormed. P. P. very wise, quotes Seneca, Boethius de

* Lest some ingenious commentator should take this seriously, and charge Mr. Russell with smuggling, it is proper to notice that he was then an officer in the British army.—EDITOR.

Consolatione, and many other good books; enforces the folly of anger in many shapes; I more and more enraged. Left the inn and went to sleep at Dr. M'Donnell's. P. P. not quite honest; owes me now several shillings, and makes no movement towards payment; gave him a hint, on his observing how cheap Belfast was, and that he had not changed a guinea for some days, by assuring him that I had, and found it very expensive; hope this may do. Bed.

17. Breakfast—M'Donnell, M'Aughtrey, Bryson, Digges, P. P., and I. Went to the inn; P. P. paid the bill, by which my anxiety as to my shillings is completely removed; believe I owe *him* now two or three, but shall not inquire. P.P. received a letter from C O'Connor, an Irish Papist; very good sense in it for all that; read it to all persons when and where it did behove him. Walked out with Digges and P. P. to Macabe's to dinner; the old set; nothing new under the sun. Came into town early; went to the theatre; saw a man in a white sheet on the stage, who called himself a Carmelite. P. P. whispered to me, with a very significant face, not to be too sure he was a Carmelite. Puzzled at this; turned round in a little time with my doubts to P. P.—P. P. asleep. N. B. A gentleman, indeed a nobleman, on the stage, in a white wig, vastly like a gentleman whom I had seen in the morning, walking the streets in a brown wig; one Mr. Atkins, a player. *Quere.* Was he a Lord or not? P. P. incapable of resolving my doubts. Came home before the play was half over, the parties appearing all so miserable, that I could foresee no end to their woes. Saw a fine waistcoat on the man that said he was a Carmelite, through a tear in the sheet which he had wrapped about him; afraid after all that he was no Carmelite, and that P. P. was right in his caution. Home; whiskey punch with P. P. Bed early.

18. Dined with Neilson. Went at eight to the United Irishmen; M'Tier in the chair; twenty-eight members present; the club consists of thirty-six original members; six new ones proposed. William Sinclair moved the resolutions, which were adopted unanimously. A committee of correspondence struck; the members are Sinclair, M'Tier, Haslitt, Neilson, and R. Simms, secretary. Read C. O'Connor's letter with great pleasure and satisfaction. Campbell made a flighty objection to one paragraph, relating to a renunciation of certain tenets falsely attributed to the Roman Catholics; answered with great ability by Bryson. Campbell angry because he was wrong, as is always the case; his objection overruled. P. P. and I made several orations on the state of the Roman Catholics, and the readiness of the citizens of Dublin to co-operate with the United Irishmen. The intelligence received with great applause. Broke up at eleven; came home; resolved to go to the coterie;

dressed; went with P. P. P. P. changed his mind, after a quarter of an hour's fluctuation in the lobby, and calling a council of waiters, at which the chamber-maid assisted; *pleasant, but wrong;* came back again in something very like an ill humour. At the door P. P. changed his mind again, and proposed to return to the coterie; refused him plump. P. P. severe thereupon; taxed me with many faults, one of which was giving advice; told P. P. I would do so no more. P. P. frightened; submitted. Went to bed with a resolution to attack him in my turn next morning. Could not sleep; a cat in the room; got up and turned her out; fell asleep at last.

19. Breakfast; M'Aughtrey, Digges, and Bryson. Digges took me out to ask my opinion of the United Irishmen. I told him I thought them men of spirit and decision, who seemed thoroughly in earnest. He said he thought so too. I asked him whether they any-way resembled the Committees of America in 1775, and afterwards? He said, "Precisely." In Digges' opinion, one Southern, when moved, equals twenty Northerns, but *very hard to move them.* Digges, Secretary to the Baltimore Committee, in Maryland, for some years. He appears to take very kindly to P. P. and me.—Went, at one, to the Select-men. Agreed on the mode of corresponding with the Volunteers of Dublin. Five hundred of the resolutions of the United Irishmen to be printed on little paper, for distribution. Sinclair's idea, that the citizens should every where precede the volunteers in adopting similar resolutions. Agreed that all communications, now, and for some time to come, should be through the medium rather of clubs than volunteers, inasmuch as there are now many existing corps who might be influenced to oppose our present measures regarding the Catholics, but it would be impossible to raise a club differing in principles from the United Irish; besides, when the clubs are formed, the volunteers will follow of course. Armagh not ripe for a deputation of Roman Catholics from Dublin, but every exertion to be made to prepare them, by letters, newspapers, &c. Home at ten; a rainy night. P. P. in the rain, very like King Lear in the storm; came home in the character of the banished Kent. *Mem.* P. P. got up very early in the morning, this day, and wrote three letters before I was up; on which proof of the amendment of his life, I remitted the attack which I had intended to make upon him.

21. Did not get up till one o'clock. Dressed; went in a chaise to Joy's, with Digges and P. P. An amazing battle after dinner on the Catholic question. For the Peep-of-day-boys, MM. Joy, Williamson, and A. Stewart; for the Defenders, P. P. and myself. The Defenders victorious, after a hard battle. All the arguments on the other side, common-place, vague, and indefinite. (Vide my pamphlet, in which I call my adversary Goose.) P. P. very clever; led Williamson into a

palpable absurdity, by a string of artful questions. Williamson afraid of a bug-a-boo. Joy an artful and troublesome antagonist. Stewart half way between both parties. The Peep-of-day-boys ashamed of their own positions. Agree to the justice of liberating the Catholics, but boggle at the expediency. D——d nonsense. P. P. eloquent! ready to fight Williamson. The chaise—Digges of opinion that P. P. and I were victorious. *Mem* All arguments over a bottle foolish. Home; went to bed early. P.P. at the card club, came home at two, and awaked me. P. P. perfectly polite; went to sleep at last..

22. Walked with P. P. and Jordan; Jordan a very clever young man. *Mem.* Met the man who said on the stage he was a Carmelite, walking the streets with a woman holding him by the arm; the woman painted up to the eyes; convinced, at last, that he was no Carmelite; made my apologies to P. P. who triumphed thereon.

23, Sunday. Dinner at A. Stewart's, with a parcel of squires of county Down. Fox-hunting, hare-hunting, buck-hunting, and farming. No bugs in the northern potatoes; not even known by name, &c. A farm at a smart rent always better cultivated than one at a low rent; probable enough. Went at niné to the Washington club. Argument between Bunting and Boyd, of Ballicastle. Boyd pleasant. Persuaded myself and P. P. that we were hungry. Went to the Donegal Arms and supped on lobsters. Drunk. Very ill-natured to P. P. P. P. patient.—*Mem.* To do so no more. Went to bed. Gulled P. P. with nonsense. Fell asleep.

24. Wakened very sick. Rose at nine. Breakfast at Wm. Sinclair's, per engagement; could not eat. Mrs. Sinclair nursed me with French drams, &c. Rode out with P. P. and Sinclair to see his bleach-green. A noble concern; extensive machinery. Anecdotes of the linen trade. Nearly independent of England. Seven years ago application made to Parliament for a bounty of 1½d. per yard; resisted by England, carried at last. Before the bounty, not more than thirty or forty pieces shipped direct for the West Indies from Belfast; now, always 50, 60, and 70, boxes in every ship. England threatened then to take off the duty on foreign linens, but did not venture it. Ireland able to beat any foreign linens for quality and cheapness, as appears by the American market, which gives no preference by duties, and is supplied entirely by Ireland. If England were disposed, she might, for a time, check the trade of Ireland in linens; but she would soon give up that system for her own sake, because she could not be supplied elsewhere so good and cheap. German linens preferred, out of spite, by some families in England, particularly by the royal family. All the King's and Queen's linen, German, and, of course, all their retainers. Sinclair, for experiment, made

up linen after the German mode, and sent it to the house in London which served the King, &c.; worn for two years, and much admired; ten per cent. cheaper, and 20 per cent. better, than the German linen. Great orders for *Irish German* linen, which he refused to execute. All but the royal family content to take it as mere Irish. *God save great George our King!*

25. Dinner at M'Tiers; Waddel Cunningham, Holmes, Dr. Bruce, &c. A furious battle, which lasted two hours, on the Catholic question; as usual, neither party convinced. Teazed with the liberality of people agreeing in the principle, but doubting as to the expediency. Bruce an intolerant high priest; argued sometimes strongly, sometimes unfairly; embarrassed the question by distinctions, and mixing things in their nature separate. We brought him, at last, to state his definite objection to the immediate emancipation of the Roman Catholics. His ideas are, 1st. Danger to true religion, inasmuch as the Roman Catholics would, if emancipated, establish an *inquisition*. 2d. Danger to property by reviving the Court of Claims, and admitting any evidence to substantiate Catholic titles. 3d. Danger, generally, of throwing the power into their hands, which would make this a Catholic Government, incapable of enjoying or extending liberty! Many other wild notions, which he afterwards gave up, but these three he repeated again and again, as his creed. Almost all the company of his opinion, excepting P. P., who made desperate battle, M'Tier, Getty, and me.

26. Breakfast; Digges, and Jordan. *Chat.* Jordan enraged at Bruce's theory. Walked out; saw the glass-house, foundry, &c. Dinner at Sinclair's; M'Tier, M'Aughtrey, P. P. and I. Bruce's theory again discussed. Sinclair much surprised at it. Catholic question. Assertion of Bruce relative to their behaviour at Convention; denied by P. P., who threatens to write a book. M'Tier asked what could we do against England? Sinclair hot. He and P. P. agree that the army in Ireland would be annihilated, and could not be replaced. Sinclair defies the power of England as to our trade; admits that she could check it for a time, but that, after the revolution, it would spring up with inconceivable rapidity, Ireland being unincumbered with debt. (Singular that his opinion agrees with Digges, even in the very words.) My own mind quite made up. Sinclair bleaches annually 10,000 pieces of linen. P. P. of opinion that the weakness of England should be looked to, as well as that of Ireland; also, Mr. Digges, who says, "the first shot fired by England against this country, down go her stocks." Home early. P. P. pretty well on, but not quite gone. Bed.

27. Rise for the purpose of packing. Assisted by Digges, and very much impeded by P. P. who has not yet slept off his wine, and is, besides, for certain reasons, much puzzled. Jordan

and M'Donnell stay with us. At one o'clock leave Belfast with heavy hearts, having first taken leave of every body on the road. M'Donnell sees us four miles on the road.

Hic finis longæ chartæque, viæque,—as the divine Flaccus hath it.

The poor ambassadors are reduced to the rank of private individuals—*Sic transit gloria mundi*—

P. P. and J. HUTTON.

Nov. 7, 1791. Dinner at Doyle's. Eighteen present—Tandy, Jones, Drennan, Pollock, M'Kenna, M'Nevin, M'Cormick, P. P. and Mr. Hutton, &c. All quiet at first. Tandy says that Grattan is certainly with us; also, the Duke of Leinster, almost as certain. Read the declaration of the Catholic Society for constitutional information; very much admired, and justly. Jones begins to broach opinions; thinks the question involved and complicated unnecessarily, by mixing the question of reform with the Catholic business: get the last first, and the other will follow of course. Jones opposed by Mr. Hutton, on the ground that the mere right of the Catholics is not supported by sufficient strength to induce the Protestants to come forward, and, therefore, a common interest must call forth common exertions. If a compact be once established between the parties, it is of little import which part of the question comes first; but absolutely necessary to hold out, on the one hand, reform to the Protestants, and, on the other, emancipation to the Catholics; by which the views and interests of both are inseparably consolidated and blended. Mr. Hutton very ingenious and persuasive on the occasion, and uses sundry other good arguments. Followed by Neilson, on the ground of past experience, that nothing can be done by disunited parties, and no secure bond of union but common interest; instances the convention, and concludes with many compliments to Mr. Hutton.

Letter to Mrs. Tone, from Dublin, about the Summer of 1791.

Dear Love,—I have nothing more to say, than that affairs are going on here swimmingly. We have got up a club of United Irishmen in Dublin, similar to that in Belfast, who have adopted our resolutions, with a short preface. We have pretty well secured all Connaught, and are fighting out the other two provinces. It is wonderful with what zeal, spirit, activity, and secrecy, all things are conducted. I have dined with divers Papists, and, in particular, with Lord Dunsany, who lately reformed, but is still a good Catholic in his heart. He begged the honour of my acquaintance, and I shall call on him to-morrow. My book is running like wildfire. The castle has got hold of the story, but very imperfectly. All they know is, that the disorder broke out in Belfast, and was carried there by one Toole, or Toomey, or some such name, a lawyer. I suppose they will endeavour to find out this Mr. Toole, or Toomey, or whatever his name is.

George Ponsonby is, on a sudden, grown vastly civil and attentive, ... and so much for politics. I learn, and I am sorry, that you have got a return of the pain in your head. Willy is growing too strong for you, and, therefore, I beg you may wean him immediately. He is old enough now, and you must not injure your own health for that little monkey,* especially when you know how precious your health is to me.

My stay in town is of such infinite consequence, that I am sure you would not wish me to quit, whilst things are in their present train. If you can get Mary down, I shall be very happy; I leave it to you, as I am, with my head, hands, and heart, so full of business, that I have scarcely time to subscribe myself, yours, &c.

Letter to Mrs. Tone, from Belfast, October 20, 1791.

MY DEAREST LIFE AND SOUL,—I wrote a few posts since, just to let you know that I was alive and well. I did not tell you any news, as I journalize every thing, and promise myself great pleasure from reading my papers over with you. I have christened Russell by the name of P. P., Clerk of this Parish, and he makes a very conspicuous figure in my memoirs. If you do not know who P. P. is, the joke will be lost on you. I find the people here extremely civil; I have dined out every day since I came here, and have now more engagements than I can possibly fulfil. I did hope to get away on Sunday, but I fear I shall not be able to move before Thursday. You cannot conceive how much this short absence has endeared you to me. You think it is better for us to be always together, but I am sure, from my own experience, you are wrong: for I cannot leave you now, though but for one week, that I do not feel my heart cling to you and our dear little ones. I have no more to say, but to desire my love to all of you, and am, dearest Love, ever yours. If you have not written before this, you need not write; I wish, however, I had one letter from you.

T. W. TONE.

P. S. DEAR MATTY,—As to any thing your wise husband may have said of me, I neither desire to know, nor do I care. It is sufficient, generally, "*I had a friend.*" I am at present composing a pretty moral treatise on temperance, and will dedicate it to myself, for I don't know who is likely to profit so much by it. Pray give my love to your virgin daughter and infant progeny. "God bless every body." Yours, till death,

P. P.

* Good words! Papa.—*Editor*

P. S. P. P. has been scribbling his bit of nonsense. He is a great fool, and I have much trouble to manage him. I assure you that you will be much amused by his exploits in my journal, which is a thousand times wittier than Swift's, as in justice it ought, for it is written for the amusement of one a thousand times more amiable than Stella. I conclude in the words of my friend P. P., God bless every body!

P. S. P. P. calls me "*his friend* Mr. John Hutton;" but God knows the heart. He is writing a journal, but mine is worth fifty of it.

Journals of 1792.*

July 4. Waited on Mr. F. by his desire, who told me that Mr. Conolly was just returned from England, and that he was much better affected than they had expected, but some of Fitzgibbon's people had been endeavouring to frighten him with Catholic insurrections, &c. That he was decidedly against the conduct of the House of Commons, in rejecting the petition, because, if the principles on which they justified that measure were right, they should not have granted the Catholics any thing, not even Sir Hercules Langrishe's bill. Mr. F. then said, that Mr. Conolly was a man who liked attentions, and therefore he would advise Byrne and Keogh, and some Kildare gentlemen (I mentioned Fitzgerald), to wait on him with the declaration, and any other papers; to prefer their earnest desire for the approbation and support of so very respectable a character, and express their apprehensions, lest pains might be taken to prejudice his mind against them.

Journal of the Proceedings of Mr. John Hutton on his second embassy to Belfast; also his dealings with the Catholics, including his combinations with sundry dissenting Republicans, and his plan for a general system of Irish Jacobins.

July 9. Set out posting with the Keeper of the College Lions for Belfast (Whitley Stokes). Breakfast at the Man of War; missed poor P. P. sadly. The Keeper dull. Proposed picquet; agreed to; played very fair; doubt that the Keeper is a blackleg.

10. Set off early. Arrive at Belfast at one o'clock; learn that the first company is at exercise, and dine upon Waddel Cunningham. Unpack in a hurry, and dress in regimentals; run off to the field, and leave the Keeper to fag. Meet every body. Cunningham very civil; dine in the tent, at the right hand of the Captain. After dinner the whole company turn out and dance on the field; *vastly French;* march into town in

* The journals of January, February, March, April, May, and June, 1792, are lost. From the month of July, we possess the series of those journals to the 20th of November.—*Editor.*

the evening, "all with magnanimity and benevolence." Sup with Neilson and the old set; very much tired after my journey. Bed at one o'clock.

11. Rise with great headach; stupid as a mill-horse; call on Sinclair; read over the address. Agree to meet him and Dr. White,* with whom I learn I am appointed committee-man, the next morning, at breakfast, and settle it finally. Call on the unfortunate Keeper, whom I have not seen Lord knows when; find that he gets on very well without me. Bring him to the Hypocrite and introduce him; the Hypocrite as gentle as ever; asks us to dine next day; agree thereto. Meet the Irish Slave, who is rejoiced to see me. Dine with Neilson and the old set; the Keeper comes late; conversation flat enough. More and more miss poor P. P. Bring the Keeper to the coterie. See an apparition of Jordan, who is in London; find, on speaking Latin to the said apparition, that it is Jordan himself; heartily glad to see him. Sup at the coterie; sup again at Neilson; the old set. Bed late. All this day dull as a post; no P. P. Sad! sad!

12. Rise again with headach, resulting from late hours. Go out to the Draper at Lilliput. Meet Dr. White; settle the address; many alterations. Go off at nine in the evening to meet the delegates at the Donegal Arms; fifteen present, M'Tier in the chair. Read the address from the committee; Waddel Cunningham opposes it, without assigning any reason. Neilson at him. At last out it comes. The coming down of Mr. Hutton has given great alarm, especially as he has brought with him some man from the College, whom no one knows. The company all laugh; Cunningham goes off in a pet. The address read, paragraph by paragraph, and approved unanimously, except that part which relates to the Catholics, which had H. Joy's single negative. Address to the National Assembly read and approved in like manner. Broke up. Home. Bed as usual at half past one. D—d bad hours!

13. Rise again with a headach. Go to the Donegal Arms. No Catholics by the mail; very odd. Saw them take places for last night. Will they come or not? No letters. The Jacobin party up here; Lafayette down; think they are all wrong. Belfast not half so pleasant this time as the last. Politics just as good or better; every thing else worse. Grievous want of P. P.; the Keeper not equal to him. By the by, the Hypocrite made the Keeper drunk last night. Fine doings. Miss that unfortunate Digges. Hear that several Catholics have been seen; run to try; find Magog, Weldon, and others, to a large amount. The hair of Dr. Haliday's wig miraculously grows grey with fear of the Catholics. Several comets appear

* Now of Baltimore.—*Editor.*

in the market-place. Walk the Catholics about to show them the lions. See the figure of Commerce at the insurance office; the Catholics mistake it for an image, and kneel down, take out their beads, and say their prayers before it; leave them at the Exchange, and go to dinner with Simms. The old set. Drink nothing. Go at seven to meet the Jacobins. Expect a sharp opposition to-morrow. Some of the country corps no better than Peep-of-day-boys. Antrim folks good; Down, bad. Good news from Munster: Gog preaching for three days to six bishops, who are at last converted; so the returns will go on—*ça ira!* The Draper tells Mr. Hutton that great exertions are making to impress people with the idea that he is going to ram something down their throats. Stuff, stuff! The Draper moderate; thinks it will be a work of time, &c. but still the cause gains ground daily. All this not very encouraging. Come home in not the most amiable temper. Get my belt, &c. for the review to-morrow. Generally sulky. Want P. P. in order to *advise* him; just in a humour to give advice. The Keeper dines this day in the country with the Hypocrite, and others; suppose he will make a beast of himself again. Bed. A plot! a plot! Neilson comes to my bedside at one o'clock, with orders to prepare for battle in the morning. Passing by a room in the inn, he heard Cunningham's voice very loud; the door being half open, he went in and found, to his utter astonishment, delegates from the country corps, with Waddel haranguing against the Catholics, and talking of some sedition intended to be broached the next day. Waddel taken all aback by this apparition of Neilson. Neilson abuses him, and reads the papers; the company breaks up without coming to any determination, but Neilson expects hot work in the morning. Waddel a ———. Sleep at last, about two.

14. *Era of the French Revolution!* Knocked up early by Neilson; get on my regimentals, and go breakfast with the Catholics. M'Kenna arrived. Drums beating, colours flying, and all the honours of war. Brigade formed, and march off by ten; 700 men, and make a tolerable appearance. A council of war held in a potato field, adjacent to the review-ground. Present, the Draper in the chair, the Tribune, his brother George, Dr. Crawford of Lisburn, Rev. Mr. Craig, Dr M'Kenna, and Mr. Hutton: all fools except the first and last. Crawford and Tandy frightened out of their wits. We are undone; shall be defeated; all the country corps decidedly against us, from the report of some seditious paper (the old story); better to adopt something moderate, that shall include all parties. M'Kenna very absurd; takes upon him the man of influence; says the Catholics are timid, and a repulse here would be fatal, and success of little consequence, as a declaration in favour of the Catholics was now useless, unless fol-

lowed up by some strong step. Mr. Hutton at last breaks silence; contradicts M'Kenna plump, as to the use of a declaration, in which the Draper concurs; examines the question in three lights, as being carried by a small majority, or lost, or not proposed. In the first case, if we succeed by a small majority, it is still success and a majority, which is better than a defeat. In the second, if it be lost, let it go; let us know the worst, and not be afraid to look the question in the face, nor delude ourselves and the Catholics with the idea of support, where no support is to be found. As to the third idea, which seemed to prevail most in the council, of not proposing the address, that was, of all possible measures, the worst; it carried in it all the evils of the other two, and many more; it was cowardly and foolish, more ruinous than the worst defeat: for those men who had already spread so many lies about the address would, if it was now kept back, utter a thousand more, and say it was so infamous that no man could be found hardy enough to propose it to the meeting; that, in the Catholic question, not to advance was to recede, and if, after the strong measures of the last nine months, we were now to blink it, it would at once utterly destroy all hopes or prospect of union. Unanimity was a good thing in itself, and more essentially so, as it was a means of promoting good principles; if, however, the principle must be renounced, to procure unanimity, it was not worth buying at that price. Mr. Hutton, likewise, said, that he did not see the question in so desperate a light; he would hope it might be carried, even by a large majority; but, in all events, whether carried or not, he entreated the Draper to move it boldly, and leave the event to Providence. The Draper agrees; the other members shrug up their shoulders, depart, and the council breaks up. The Draper and Mr. Hutton walk about the field; every man discourages them, but all won't do. The Draper a fine resolute fellow. Mr. Hutton says nothing of the energy, spirit, and decision of his own character, especially when contrasted with the caution and moderation of the Lisburn men, and the bladdering stuff of M'Kenna. Moderation—nonsense! March into town at three. Meet Haslitt and Neilson: take the word "Catholic" out, and put in the word "Irishmen" of every religious denomination. Procession. Meeting at the Linen Hall, astonishing full. Question moved by the Draper. Before the debate goes on five minues, satisfied that we have it hollow; the Lisburn men, and our good advisers in the field, all mistaken. More and more satisfied that their moderation is nonsense and stuff. Carry the question with about five dissenting voices, among whom are Joy and Waddel Cunningham. All hollow. Could have carried any thing. The business now fairly settled in Belfast and the neighbourhood. Huzza! Huzza! Dinner at the Donegal Arms. Every body as happy as a king, but Waddel, who looks like the Devil himself! Huzza! God bless every body! Stanislaus Augustus! George Washington! *Beau-jour* Who would have thought it this morning? Huzza! Generally drunk.—Broke my glass thumping the table. Home, God knows how or when. Huzza! God bless every body again, generally.—Bed, with three times three. Sleep at last.

16. Rise and go to breakfast with Will Simms at the Grove; all the Catholics from Dublin there. Council of war in the garden; Gog, Robert Simms, and Mr. Hutton. Gog expounds the plan of organizing the Catholic body. Mr. Hutton takes the opportunity to press an idea started by P. P. several months back, for organizing, in a similar manner, the Dissenting interest. All agree that if that could be accomplished, the business would be done. Quere; How? Simms satisfied that we have already a great majority of the thinking men through the North with us; says, however, that if Government attack the Catholic Committee, under the new system in two months, the North will not be ready to support them. Mr. Hutton explains, that we are not ready to call on any one yet for more than good wishes, and asks Simms, who is indeed a Tanner, and shall for the future be so called, what he thinks of the next 14th of July. The Tanner looks extremely wise and significant. Gog, Mr. Hutton, and he, worship each other, and *sign an article with their blood; flourish their hands three times in a most graceful manner*, (see Goldsmith's Citizen of the World), and march off into town. "Ho, but they are indeed most agreeable creatures." (Do.) Lounge till near dinner. Go to the Donegal Arms, and meet all the Catholics. M'Kenna comes in, and confesses that his behaviour at the council of war on the 14th was indefensible, and that he is sorry, &c. Dinner; M'Tier in the chair. Checquered at the head of the table, a Dissenter and a Catholic. Delightful! The four flags, America, France, Poland, Ireland, but *no England*. Bravo! *Beau-jour!* The Draper and I sit together at the foot of the table. Conversation regarding M'Kenna, who has acted very strangely. Home. Bed. Determine to set off to-morrow and see P. P. Go to sleep thinking of my journey. Keeper gone to Scotland.

17. Waked by Neilson, to see Gog, and other Catholics, before they set off. Go to the Inn. Much conversation about the Peep-of-day-boys and Defenders. My letter in the Northern Star approved of. Proposed by Neilson that the Catholics should go by Rathfriland, where the disturbances are, and meet some of the gentlemen of the neighbourhood, in order to try if any thing can be done to restore peace. He offers, in that case, to go himself, and all parties request me to go too. Vexed to the very soul at having my *expiration* to Dungannon all blown up. Rot it—sink it—d—n it—must go—cannot possibly help it. Poor P. P.—Well, "'Tis but in vain for soldiers to

complain." Agree to set off in half an hour to Rathfriland. Hope our journey may do some good, as the restoration of tranquillity is to us of the last importance. Console myself with this hope for the disappointment of not seeing P. P. but vexed d———y for all that. Set off in a very middling temper with Neilson and his wife. Arrive, at ten, at a Mr. Lowry's, near Rathfriland. Received with great politeness and hospitality. Supper. Sit up late, as usual. Bed at half past one. Sad! sad!

18. Rise, and set off with Neilson and young Lowry, to Rathfriland. In about an hour the Catholics arrive from Downpatrick. Meet Mr. Tighe, the Parson, Sam. Barber, the Dissenting Minister, Mr. Derry, the Priest, and about eighteen gentlemen of the neighbourhood. Agreed on all hands that the Protestants were the aggressors. Several have been killed on both sides. Great offence taken at the Catholics marching about in military array, and firing shots at unseasonable times. The Catholics certainly wrong in that, and must, if possible, be stopped. The majority think that if that were accomplished, the disturbances would soon die away. Some bigots think that their arms should be taken from the Catholics. God forbid! besides, the thing is in its nature impossible. Mr. Hutton proposes that the Catholics shall agree to desist from parading in bodies and firing, and the Dissenters shall declare that they will maintain the peace of the country against all who shall transgress, without *distinction of party or religion*. An amendment proposed by Neilson, that this declaration should be made by the volunteers. The idea unanimously approved, and three officers then present (Captain A. Lowry, Captain Cowen, and Captain Barber,) engage for their respective companies. A refractory priest, of the name of Fitzsimons, much blamed; the Catholics engage to have him removed. They likewise propose to have a pastoral letter from their bishop, and a circular one from the committee, to be read in every chapel, recommending peace and good order. The Catholics always ready to make peace and keep it. Cannot, on the whole, learn that they do any thing worse than meet in large bodies, and fire powder; foolish, certainly, but not wicked. They break open no houses, nor ever begin an attack. The Protestants, however, extremely alarmed at their meetings, which, therefore, must, if possible, be suppressed. The Catholic clergy have almost totally lost their influence since the people have got arms, so fatal to superstition and priestcraft is even the smallest degree of liberty. The Catholics and Mr. Hutton receive the thanks of the meeting for their public spirit in coming down on the occasion. All part on excellent terms. Mr. Hutton meditates attempting an excursion to Dungannon. Finds, on calculation, that P. P. would, most probably, be in Belfast about the time he could reach there. Gives up his scheme in a pet, and sets off with

the Catholics for Newry, on his way to Dublin. Gog converts a bishop at Newry, another at Downpatrick. Arrive at Dundalk. Gog insufferably vain, and fishing for compliments, of which Mr. Hutton, at first, is rather sparing. Gog then praises Mr. Hutton, who relents thereupon, and lays it on in return pretty thick. Nothing too gross. A great deal of wine. Bed, as usual, between one and two. Bad! Bad! Bad!

19. Set off early, and ride twelve miles on a lame hack; pleasant and respectable! Get on to Drogheda, and find the Newry stage just setting off for Dublin. Leave Gog converting another bishop, (the Catholic Primate) and drive off in the stage; no adventures; arrive in town at six in the evening. *Hic finis longæ chartæque, viæque.*—Hor.

N. B. The meeting on the 14th like the old German meetings in the woods. All the people sitting, and the armed warriors in a ring standing round. Fine effect of the unanimous *Ay* of the Assembly when passing the address. Mr. Hutton affected so that the tears stood in his eyes; sentimental and pretty.

21. *Dublin.* Ride out with Gog to Grattan, and tell him of the state of things in the North and in the South, which he approves. Talk of next Winter. He apprehends Government will make a blow at the Catholics, by committing their chairman. Mr. Hutton of opinion that the whole body should rise and go with him in that event. Grattan advises to let him go, and immediately elect another. If *he* be committed, elect another, and so on, but never to recede. Mr. Hutton asks for a committee to inquire, next session, into the state of the North, and the causes of the riots there. Grattan thinks it would do mischief, because the committee being, to a certainty, under the influence of the Castle, would misstate and garble facts, and draw conclusions which even these facts could not warrant. Mr. Hutton says that is very hard, which Grattan admits; but says the reason is obvious, that we have *no Parliament in Ireland.*

22. Meet the sub-committee; read the address, which is approved, with a clause promising protection from the General Committee to all peaceable Catholics. Think this a capital stroke, as it gives such a hold of the *bas peuple,* of whom there are in this country above 3,000,000. Meet Gog in the evening, who is in a peck of troubles. Expects Burke over in Cork every day, notwithstanding all that has been done to prevent his coming.* Burke pretends that he is come on his private affairs. *Private fiddlesticks!* Gog in a rage; determined to thwart him on all occasions, and put him down with the Catholics, which he most richly deserves for the great impropriety of

* See Vol. I. p 85.

his conduct in never communicating a syllable of information whilst acting as agent in England, though perpetually applied to for that purpose, and also for his now coming over (if he does come) against the inclination of every one concerned. Burke by far the most impudent, *opiniâtre* fellow that ever I knew. Gog wants to have a Robin not to invite him to their houses. Believe, if he comes, he will be rumped. Does he want another 2000 guineas?

23. Dined with Tom Braughall and Gog. Read a very long prancing letter from Burke, filled with nonsense about the French Revolution, on which he is as mad as his father. The issue is, that the Catholics will meet no support from ministry in England, (who seem to be bullied by ministry here) in their next application to Parliament; they must, therefore, rely on their own force. And it seems pretty evident that England, if she will not interfere on their behalf, neither will she interfere against them; so that the Catholics, and the Protestant ascendancy, are left to fight it out, *propriis aribus*, (*à la bonne heure*.) It should seem, that Government here have gone so far as to menace stopping the mutiny bills and supplies, if they are not allowed the sole management of the Catholic affairs. What will be the issue of all this?

24. In committee. Read over Burke's letter again, and receive orders to prepare an answer thereto, and also a letter to the Hon. Mr. Browne Wrote a letter to Burke, giving him his congé, regretting that ministry in England had, by adopting a determined neutrality, rendered further application to them useless, and of course deprived the Catholics of the powerful aid of his talents, and giving him a remote prospect that he might again be employed on some future emergency. All very civil and indefinite: not a bad letter. This day my appointment as Secretary to the Sub-committee, until the rising of Parliament, was confirmed unanimously by the General Committee, with a stipend for that time of 200*l*.

25. Sub-committee. Letter to Burke read, and objected to by Mr. Fitzgerald, as being too pointed a dismissal. Long conversation thereon, and alterations made. The majority of the Sub-committee cowardly. Gog stout, but overruled.

26. Rode out to Grattan's, and dined there by appointment with Gog and Hardy. Little new; but the old ground beaten over again. Talking of the late Chief Baron Burgh, Grattan said that he fell in love with daisies on his march; he stopped to pick them up, and twist them into a garland, which he flung about him, and so entered the field of battle, half a hero and half an opera-dancer. Pretty! Captain Fitzgerald, Grattan's brother-in-law, a fine young fellow. Great deal of wine; Grattan keeps us to sup.

27. Pleasant breakfast. Tell Grattan about Digges.

Grattan eager to know him. Promise to send him Digges letter on trade, &c.

31. Circular letter for the returns ready for signing. The Vintner comes in, and, after a long debate, refuses to sign. Cowardly! rascally! The fellow is worth 200,000*l.* Gog in the horrors. Dine with Warren and Archdekin. Sick all this day. Bed at nine o'clock.

August 1. "Merry be the first of August!" Breakfast in college. Boswell shows us a loom of his invention, for weaving fishing nets, which executes it completely with the fisherman's knot. He sent a sample to the Society for Encouraging the Arts in London, which had offered sixty guineas premium for such an invention. Several others put in their claim, but his was the only one which answered. He would, in consequence, have got the reward, only it was luckily discovered, in time to prevent it, that he was an Irishman, for which reason only they did refuse him. Wise and liberal. Mr. Everhard, of Sligo, comes in; gives a most melancholy account of the depression and insults under which the Catholics of that town labour; every Protestant rascal breaks their heads and windows for his amusement, and no grand jury will find their bills, nor petit jury convict their tormentors. The Catholic spirit quite broken. They do not even beat one another. Sad! sad! Busy all day folding papers, &c. for the Munster Bishops! D—d all Bishops! Gog not quite well on that point. Thinks them a good thing. Nonsense. Dine at home with Neilson and M'Cracken. Very pleasant. *Rights of man! French revolution! No Bishops!* &c. &c. &c.

2. Breakfast with Drennan and Neilson. Sub-committee. More papers. Gog not at all equal in steadiness to Magog, and as vain as the devil. Magog not a grain of a Papist, nor Warren; all the others so so enough. Meet J. Bramston just setting off for England. Dine at Sweetman's with a long set. All well. Half the county Down have returned their delegates. Bravo!

3. Sub-committee. Folding circular letters, &c. Wexford returns at last. Rent-roll of their delegates, 15,000*l.* per annum. Bravo! This makes eight counties.

Journal of the proceedings of John Hutton, Esq. on his third journey to the North of Ireland; including his artful negotiations with the Peep-of-day-boys, and sundry Peers of the realm; also, his valorous entry into, and famous retreat out of, the city of Rathfriland; interspersed with sundry delectable adventures and entertaining anecdotes.—Vive le Roi!

August 7. Set out posting on my expedition among the Peep-of-day-boys, with Gog and Neilson Pleasant journey.

Arrive in Drogheda, and dine. Settle with Neilson to meet us at Rathfriland. The first of last month kept here with solemnity: "July the first in Oldbridge Town there was a grievous battle." Sick. Bed at eight o'clock.

8. Go to the Coffee House. See the Derry Grand Jury resolutions, and the call of the county of Wexford. In a horrible rage. Sit down and write a paper for the Northern Star, signed Vindex, abusing the resolutions, &c. Show Vindex to Gog, who is as pleased as Punch; tells me he has succeeded with the Bishops, and is to dine with them. Go to Bird's, and stay amongst a parcel of girls all the evening. Puppy! Home late.

9. Walk out with Gog, and plan counter-resolutions for Derry: come home and write them. Gog takes them in his pocket to the Primate. Bird and Hamill; propose to them to offer a coalition to the Protestant ascendancy, and that instead of orange cockades, all parties should unite and wear green ones on the next first of July. A good scheme, though it is my own. They seem to think it could not be done. Let them try, however.

11. Breakfast. Hear that Mr. Barber is of opinion we ought not to go to Rathfriland, and has desired some one to write us word so. It is surmised that his reason is, lest we might be insulted by some of the bigots in that town. Cannot help it: what must be, must be, and we *must* go to Rathfriland. Buy powder and ball, and load our pistols, for fear of accidents. My balls too little; d—n it! Afraid of Capt. Swan, who is a bloody Peep-of-day-boy: endeavour to make a pun on his name: something about goose, but it won't do. "When as I sat in Babylon." Hear just now that if we go to Rathfriland we shall be houghed: "pleasant, but wrong." What is to be done? This information we have from Mr. O'Neil, of Cabra: cowardly enough, but I dare say he *heard* it. Set off for Mr. O'Neil, of Bannvale, on our way for Rathfriland. Arrive at length at that flourishing seat of liberality and public virtue. "I fear thee, O *Rathfriland*, lest that thy girls with spits, and boys with stones, in puny battle slay me." Stop at Murphy's Inn, six in number, all valiant. Get paper, and begin to write to Dr. Tighe, Mr. Barber, and Mr. A. Lowry. Stopped short by the intelligence that the Landlord will give us no accommodations! Hey! hey! The fellow absolutely refuses. He has cold beef and lamb chops, and will give us neither, but turns off on his heel. D——d fine. Well, Mr. Murphy! The dog is a Quaker. What is to be done, now, at half past four? A striking proof of the state of politics in this country, when a Landlord will not give accommodation for money to Catholics. Get a Mr. Murphy at last, brother to our hospitable landlord, and a decent man: explain the motives of our coming to him; and remind him of the conversation of 18th July last.

He seems very much ashamed of the behaviour of his brother, and, in some degree, apprehensive of our meeting some insult; which, however, he hopes may not happen. All stout. Some of us determined to make the boors of Rathfriland smoke for it, if they attack us, particularly M'Nally, who has ridden from Newry armed, merely to assist us in case of necessity; manly and decided! The *gentlemen* of the Town have learned, as we presume, that we are prepared, and therefore make no attempt to duck us, as they had lamented they did not do on our last visit. Leave Rathfriland in great force, the cavalry in the front. See about 150 Peep-of-day-boys exercising within a quarter of a mile of the town. Suppose if we had attempted to lie in the town, we should have had a battle. Arrive at Mr. O'Neil's and dine. Old gentry, and very hospitable and kind. Mr. O'Neil exceedingly hurt at being refused a dinner in Rathfriland, within sight of which he and his ancestors have lived for a century. Horrible thing, these religious discords, which are certainly fomented by the aristocrats of this country. Get off with great difficulty from O'Neil, and arrive at Newry about ten. Dismount with our four cases of pistols, very stout. "Five pound for a Peep-of-day-boy." Huzza! Huzza! Generally glad that we are come back safe. Mug porter to a large amount. God bless every body. Bed.

12. See Vindex in print, incorrect enough; made out a quotation on Captain Swan: "If he had been saucy, we would have made him a rare bird on the earth, and very much like a *black* swan." Hit this off yesterday, as we were going into Rathfriland, when I was in a fright. Was I in a fright? The truth is, I was not, and yet I was not a jot sorry when it was bed-time, and all well; "All fair," as Mr. Breslaw hath it. Dine at O'Hanlon's. After dinner ride to Rosstrevor along shore. Beautiful! Mourne, the sea, &c. Sit up very late and talk treason. Sad!

13th. Agree to push on for Belfast, where we arrive and sup with Neilson and Simms. Neilson brings us home to lodge. Bed late.

14th. Walk out and see M'Cracken's new ship, the Hibernia. Hibernia has an English crown on her shield. We all roar at him. Dine at Neilson's with the old set. The county Down getting better every day on the Catholic question. Gog and Mr. Hutton called upon to give an account of the present state of Catholics. Mr. Hutton makes a long and accurate statement, which meets the unanimous approbation of all present. The Belfast men get warm with wine and patriotism. All stout; Gog valiant; also the Irish slave; also the Tanner; also Mr. Hutton. The Catholics offer to find soldiers, if Belfast will provide officers. All fair. Lurgan green as usual. Something will come out of all this. Agree to talk the matter over to-morrow, when we are all cool. Huzza! Generally drunk. *Vive la nation!* D—n the Empress of Russia! Success to the Polish arms, with three time three. Huzza! Generally *very* drunk. Bed. God knows how. To dine to-morrow with the Tanner. Huzza! Huz—

15. Waken drunk. Breakfast with Neilson, the Jacobin, &c. More volunteer companies springing up like mushrooms, nobody knows why. All the Antrim corps well. Please God, we shall furnish them with something to think of. This country will never be well until the Catholics are educated at home, and their clergy elective. Dinner at the Tanner's; all well. The Rev. T. Birch, of *Botany Bay*, tells us that he is just returned from a meeting of eighteen Dissenting clergymen from different parts of Ulster, and had the pleasure to find them *all* well-disposed to Catholic liberty; he has no doubt but the cause is spreading most rapidly. He thinks, what I fear is true, that the Catholic clergymen are bad friends to liberty. The priest of Saintfield preached against United Irishmen, and exhorted his people not to join such clubs, on which he was immediately rebuked in the chapel by one of his congregation. All this very good. It cannot be that the rabble of Rathfriland should stop the growing liberty of Ireland. Home. Bed early.

16. The Tanner called on me to recommend two things: First, to publish the plan alluded to by the Derry Grand Jury, to which we agree, as secrecy is no longer necessary; and, secondly, that the new committee should not meet so early as October, because the longer it is delayed, the more numerous our friends in the North will be, as every day produces converts, and, therefore, if Government should attack the committee, we should have a stronger support. To this we answer, that we are sure Government will not venture on any strong measure until Parliament is sitting to back them, and it will be advisable to have the country members assembled for some little time before the danger, (if any can arise,) that they may know each other, and be accustomed to stand fire. The Tanner acquiesces in this reasoning; very glad to see him so anxious about us, and so eager to procure us *proper* support. Digges used to praise him and Getty; also the Hypocrite thinks Macabe and he the two men in Belfast most to be depended upon. Set off for Hillsborough, accompanied by the Jacobin. Write to Lord Downshire, and request permission to wait upon him; he asks us to dinner, which we decline; he then appoints seven o'clock in the evening, when we wait on him and Lord Hillsborough. Very long conversation on the subject of our mission. Lord Downshire's faculties quite gone. Lord Hillsborough 's sharp enough; a high Aristocrat. Angry at the committee's interference. No notion of any mode of settling the disturbances but by a strong hand. Talks of more regiments of light-horse,

and calls the committee and the Defenders, "Dublin Papists, and country Papists;" says our going down has done great mischief, though our motives may be good; abuses the men who formed the meeting at Rathfriland on the 18th July; says there are four thousand stand of arms in the hands of the Defenders, and, if they will pile them up in one place, he will ensure their protection; inveighs bitterly against the communications between the Catholics through the country, and against seditious publications, which he *explains* to signify Payne; says the laws have been equally administered, for that six Protestants have been hanged for Peep-of-day-boy practices, and two of them on the spot where the burglary was committed. (*This a lie.*) In short, that he will see the laws execute themselves, without our interference. On the whole, his Lordship was just civil, and no more.—Fine fencing between his Lordship and Mr. Hutton, who defends the Catholics with great address and ability; hits his Lordship several times, on the *riposte.* The ambassadors both bluff and respectful. State their case, and that they did not come until called upon; make a cut or two at the Protestant ascendancy about Rathfriland. Admit the 4,000 stand of arms, but state that they have in no one instance been used offensively. Strike a little at the new corps; to the raising of which, and the spirit of the officers, we insinuate, almost the whole of the present alarm may be attributed. Pin his Lordship to the confession that the Catholics have never, in any case, begun the attack. As to their meeting in bodies, admit it is improper, but state that they have always dispersed without doing mischief. Finally, declare our convictions that, if the Catholics could see that they had equal protection with the Protestants, peace would be immediately restored. Part from their Lordships, neither of us much pleased with the other. Set off, and arrive at Ballinahinch late. Introduced to M'Clokey, "a proper man." That neighbourhood almost totally converted, though very bad some little time back. A new corps raised there on Peep-of-day-boy principles, converted by M'Clokey, who, in return, is chosen their lieutenant. All well. The Catholics and they are now on such good terms that the Catholics lend them their arms to learn their exercise, and walk to see them parade, and both parties now in high affection with each other, who were before ready to cut each other's throats. All this done in about two months, or less, and by the exertions of one obscure man. What might not be done by the Aristocrats of the county Down, if they were actuated by the same spirit?

17. Rise as sick as a dog. Walk out to Montalto and meet Lord Moira. Breakfast with his Lordship, the Abbé Berwick,*

* The Rev. Mr. Berwick, Chaplain to his Lordship.

and Williamson, of Lisburn. Apprize them of our expedition, and ask leave to introduce Gog, which he grants with much civility; his Lordship well-disposed, and the more so as Lords Hillsborough and Annesley are adverse. He abuses Lord Annesley, who is by all accounts a mere brute, and has a trick of knocking down the Catholics on the roads, or wherever he meets them, for his amusement; scoundrel! Why do they not knock him down again, and be hanged? Bring Gog up and introduce him; invited to dinner with his Lordship, and promise accordingly. Dinner spoiled by the unexpected arrival of General Patterson and Colonel Marsh, on their way to England; stupid as the devil; the Abbé quite out of spirits. Mr. Hutton and Gog rise early and depart; leave Ballinahinch and travel in the dark to Banbridge; unpleasant enough; bad road; sleep at Banbridge.

18. Arrive at Newry about 8. Meet O'Hanlon and some others; tell them of our journey; all agree that we should publish the address to the Defenders. Write to Lord Downshire, Lord Moira, Col. Sharman, Bishop Mc Mullen, Bishop Lennon, and inclose copies of the address. Pat. O'Hanlon engages to distribute the address through Mourne, and all other parts where the disturbances are, in the County Down. Propose to set off for Dublin; prevailed upon to stay and endeavour to reconcile the Catholics of Newry, who have been bickering; agree accordingly. Meet the contending parties in the evening at the Inn. Gog makes a very lucid statement of the Catholic affairs; never heard him half so well; preaches up peace and union, and advises them to direct their animosities against the common enemy, the monopolists of the country. The whole company agree to bury all past feuds in oblivion; rise and shake hands mutually. The chairman, by order of the meeting, invites Gog and Mr. Hutton, who has played *ripieno* all the evening, to dine with the Catholics of Newry next day, to commemorate the restoration of harmony; which they agree to, though it breaks in on their system.

19. *Sunday*. Go to mass; foolish enough; too much trumpery. The king of France dethroned!! Very glad of it, for now the people have fair play. What will the army do? God send they may stand by the nation. Every thing depends upon the line they take. *Our* success depends on things which some of us are such fools as not to see. Ride to Rosstrevor; more and more in love with it; dinner; thirty people, many of them Protestants, invited on the occasion. Dr. Moody, the Dissenting minister, says grace; bravo! all very good; toasts excellent. United Irishmen mentioned again, and the idea meets universal approbation; hope it may do; wonderful to see how rapidly the Catholic mind is rising, even in this Tory town,

which is one of the worst spots in Ireland; sit till nine; set off for Dundalk, and arrive about 12.

20. Off very early, and breakfast in Drogheda; get the people together, and put them up to every thing; all stout. Set off for Dublin, and arrive at six in the evening; a good deal fatigued. This has been, on the whole, a most excellent journey, and has done infinite good. We have put our adversaries in the North completely in the wrong, and of course ourselves in the right. We have materially contributed to restore peace in the county Down; we have created a spirit in Newry, which never existed there before; we have reconciled their differences; we have generally encouraged our friends, disheartened our enemies, and puzzled Lord Hillsborough. All very good.

> Hic finis longæ chartæque viæque.—*Hor.*
> Here our long journey and my paper ends.—*Francis.*

23. Dublin. Sub-committee. Letter from Dr. Esmonde, of Kildare. Mr. Conolly friendly in a great degree, and entirely condemns the Derry resolutions.

24. Write a letter to O'Hanlon, in Newry, desiring him to collect facts relative to the disturbances in county Down; and hints about the Catholic Society and United Irish, of Newry—good letter.

27. Sunday. Tinnehinch. Read to Grattan and Hardy a manifesto which I had written on the part of the General Committee, in answer to a set of pert resolutions from county Limerick, certainly prepared by the Chancellor. Grattan thinks, it too controversial, and recommends moderation in language and firmness in action. The manifesto taken to pieces, and at least three-fourths struck out; many passages supplied by Grattan himself, Mr. Hutton taking them down from his dictation; no man bears criticism half so well as Mr. Hutton. The manifesto, as amended, not to be published until all the grand juries have spoken out. Grattan desires Mr. Hutton to take *great pains* in incorporating the new with the original matter, so that the joining may not be perceived. Consultation as to the conduct of the Catholic committee, on the subject of their petition. Mr. Hutton throws out the idea of the committee adjourning before the meeting of Parliament, which is eagerly adopted by the two members. The reasons which determine this question are: 1st, It will make the new committee-men stout, when they find themselves out of danger. 2d, When the petition, &c. is prepared, they can be of more use in the country than in town, as mediums of information to the people. 3d, It will remove the Chancellor's imputation of a Popish Congress sitting in the capital to overawe Parliament, and so put the friends to the cause in the House of Commons on strong grounds, and of course cripple their adversaries.

Grattan takes Mr. Hutton aside, and tells him that as the season for action is now approaching, it is the wish of himself and his friends that all communication between them and the Catholics should be through him, Mr Hutton; as, if they were to hold personal communication, Government would say they were agitators, inflaming the public mind, and that, instead of their being the organ of the Catholics' sentiments, the Catholics were only instruments in their hands; that the grievances of the Catholics would thereby be said not to be felt, but suggested by Grattan and his friends, to answer the purposes of a faction; all which would entail a kind of responsibility on them, and embarrass and weaken them much in the operations of next winter. Mr. Hutton very much pleased with this; and the more, as the party had absolutely refused to communicate with his great predecessor, Burke, and now refuse to communicate with the Catholics through any other medium than himself; Bravo! Break the matter gently to Gog. Gog struck all of a heap—jealous as the devil, says he sees the cause is desperate, and that Grattan is going to give them up: no such thing. Argue with him, and satisfy him tolerably; but his vanity, of which he has plenty, has got a mortal blow—poor Gog! All this may not serve Mr. Hutton in the long run. Gog has not strength of mind to co-operate fairly; must do all, or seem to do all, himself. Has worked out M'Kenna first, and now Burke, both with sufficient appearance of reason: but the fact is, a dirty personal jealousy, lest they might interfere with his own fame, is at the bottom of all. Little mind! paltry! Mr. Hutton will do what is right, *coute qui coute*. Finds himself more and more necessary to the Catholics, which is his best chance: but if Gog sets his face against him, he must go down like the others. Mr. Hutton now established as the medium of communication between the Catholics and their friends in Parliament. How long will he remain so! Proud ground! Grattan considers the Catholic question as but a means of advancing the general good—Right! But do the Catholics consider it so? The devil a bit, except one or two of them. Gog says, if they get franchise we shall see all they will do for reform. God send; but I, for one, doubt it: however, I will go on—their cause is just, independent of reform.

28. Grattan sails for England to-night. The Czar* cautions me not to lay myself under pecuniary obligations to Gog. See that he is right, and at any rate have no necessity for money just now.

September 1. Dress myself in the Belfast uniform, and go to dine at Dixon's. All the soldiers salute me as I pass, and the

* Counsellor Peter Burrowes.

sentries carry their arms: pleased as Punch at this, and a great fool for my pains. Suppose they take me for the Duke of Brunswick, or some foreign officer of distinction. Puppy!

3. Burke is come. The Catholics all angry. Fancy his reception will be mortifying enough.

5. Agree that Gog shall go into a full exposition with Burke, of the grounds of the displeasure of the Catholics. Burke, a sad impudent fellow, forcing himself upon these people. Gog thinks he is coming over as a spy for Dundas. Rather think he has been puffing his own weight among the Catholics, with Ministers in England, and finding himself suddenly dismissed by letter, he is come over, trusting to the powers of his effrontery, that the Catholics will not have the spirit to maintain their letter face to face. Fancy he will find himself in the wrong. They all seem exasperated against him, and he richly deserves it. His impudence is beyond all I have ever known. Sad dog! Edmund Burke has Gog's boys now on a visit at Beaconsfield, and writes him a letter in their praise. The scheme of this obvious enough. He wants to enlist Gog, on behalf of his son; but it won't do: Gog sees the thing clear enough. Sad! sad! Edmund wants to get another 2000 guineas for his son, if he can; dirty work! Edmund no fool in money matters. Flattering Gog to carry his point. Is that sublime or beautiful? The Catholics will not be had, as I judge, by the pitiful artifice of the father or the determined impudence of the son.

6. Gog has had his interview with Burke, and given him his *congé*. Burke as mad as the devil, but can't help himself. He deserves it all and more. Wait on Simon Butler with queries, for his opinion on the circular letter signed E. Byrne. Plump in our favour. Wait on Mr. Smith, who declines, and pleads privilege of Parliament. Not quite fair. Burston. He reads the queries; gives a general opinion in our favour, as to the principle; and promises to consider the question as to the mode: ten guineas to him and Butler.

7. Breakfast with the Vintner, and ride out with him to Burston, about the opinion, which he promises in less than a week. The Vintner a very sensible man. Sub-committee. Agree that Gog, M'Donnell, and T. Braughall, shall call on Conolly on Sunday next, and that Mr. Hutton shall go down to-morrow to county Kildare, to secure Wogan Browne to introduce them.

8. County Kildare. Find my little boy grown a fine fellow.* Dine at Rathcoffy; Wogan Browne; Archery; ride late, and sleep at Clain.

9. Sunday. Drive in Browne's carriage to Celbridge, and

* Myself.—Editor.

meet the Catholic Commissioners to the South; agree to call first on the Duke of Leinster; set off to Carton, and find Conolly there; much conversation; Gog very bad and diffuse; T. B. very well; M'Donnell excellent; says more in *three* words than all the other commissioners; Mr. Hutton almost silent, Gog seeming determined to shine; the Duke very friendly, and declares his approbation of the whole of the Catholic proceedings, and more especially of the plan. Conolly a strange rambling fool; talked for near an hour, without the least connexion, about a Union, the Regency, Mr. Fox, the Whig Club, the Catholics, a pension bill, a place bill, a Union, *Da capo*, &c. &c. &c. The Duke took much pains to set and keep him right; has ten times the understanding of Conolly; the result was, that we convinced the latter we intended nothing violent or hostile, and then he declared himself satisfied. He condemned the grand juries extremely, and particularly his own county Derry; told us, as a great discovery, that Government were at the bottom of all this. Lord help him! Shocking to think that such an ass should have influence any where; necessary to us, however; think we may count upon him next session. The Duke hollow with us; *Bon!* Conolly offers to go security his whole fortune on the good behaviour of the Catholics; all fair; the Duke asks us to dine, also Conolly; refuse both with many thanks, and go off to dine at Castle Browne with Rowan, &c. *Beau jour.* Rowan a fine fellow, and Wogan Browne just as good. Drink—"The spirit of the French mob to the people of Ireland."

12. Dublin in the boat; Captain Tone very ill (my uncle); fear he will not live through the winter; sorry for him; a gallant officer.

13. Ride out with the Vintner to Burston for his opinion; plump with us; all fair; well done, Burston! Sub-committee; agree to publish the opinions in the papers, and also as a circular letter. Simon Butler asks me to dine, and meet Burke; returns from Cork; see the Protestant ascendancy resolutions of the Common Council of Dublin; boobies! Please God we will try to pick a hole or two in them.

14. Write to Dr. Toole about Capt. Tone; write to Devereux, and advise him to have the opinions reprinted, either in the Wexford paper, or in handbills to distribute previous to the county meeting. Meet the Abbé; he tells me a friend of his (Lord Rawdon) is expected to-night; settle that he shall call on me to-morrow morning. The Abbé seems very eager to preoccupy that gentleman against false representations.

15. The Abbé calls to tell me that his friend has turned back; that his coming is fixed, but the time uncertain. D—n it! Write a letter to the Corporation of Dublin on their reso-

lutions against the Catholics, signed "A Protestant Freeman." Dull enough; very stupid all this day. Write a letter soliciting contributions from Irish Catholics resident in foreign parts.

16. Ride out with Tom Warren; wet to the skin; broach a proposal to him of a general emigration to America, in case we fail in our present schemes. He approves of it highly, and thinks we should get Catholics enough to join us, and a vast property. A choice plan! P. P. and his brother; Whitley Stokes Principal of a College to be founded, &c. Warren and Mr. Hutton got drunk talking of their plan. God bless every body!

17. Gog's man has been dunning me for 20*l.*, I believe without orders, Gog being out on his mission. Give the man a short rebuke, but do not pay him. The Devil to pay in Paris. The mob have broken open the prisons, and massacred all the prisoners (Montmorin, the Princess Lamballe, &c.) with circumstances of great barbarity, but robbed no one, and were stopped from breaking into the Temple by a blue ribbon stretched across the street, reminding them that their Magistrates were responsible for the King's safety. Strange mixture of cruelty and sentiment! An Irish mob would have plundered but shed no blood. A Parisian mob murders, but respects property; which is best? I lean to the Frenchman; more manly. Our mob, very shabby fellows. Never would have stood as the Parisians did on the 10th of August. A Sergeant's Guard would drive the mob of Dublin.

18. Pay Gog, and resolve to have no more to do with him in the money way. Receive a choice letter from the Colonel, (Barry,) in answer to one of mine written some time back. Hope to bring the Noble General (Lord Rawdon) round; of the very last importance to Ireland to get *him*. He may, if he chooses, as I think, be one of the greatest men in Europe. Dine in the country with M'Donnell: pleasant!

20. Write to Gog mysteriously on the subject of Lord Rawdon. God Almighty send we may be able to arrange that business.

21. Burston angry that his opinion was published, and confesses that it is because he does not wish to offend the Chancellor. Shabby! Agree to publish that it was inserted without his knowledge. The Vintner dreads any thing which may bring his name in question. Understand this apprehension arises from the consciousness of some peccadilloes in the way of trade, which he is apprehensive the Castle papers will lay hold on, and abuse him! Receive a letter from the Rev. Mr. Fleming, (Vicar to Dr. Plunket, Bishop of Meath,) whom I met at Drogheda, and admired so much. Plunket doing his business like a man. To send Fleming thirty sheets of parchment, thirty

declarations, sixty plans, and one hundred and eighty opinions, for the counties of Meath and Westmeath. Bravo! We began to be afraid of those Counties. *Ca ira.*

23. *Sunday.* Write a second "Protestant Freeman." The first has turned out better than I expected, or than in my own mind it deserved. I do not own them, nor will I, unless my vanity gets the better of me, own any newspaper thing hereafter. Read over a pamphlet which I wrote last winter, but which never was published. Very curious to see what pains I took to prove fifty things which are now received as axioms. Called at Moira House; apprehend I am out of favour there for holding democratic principles. Cannot be helped.

24. Send off the parchments, &c., to Mr. Fleming. Write sundry letters, one to P. P. Very fond of P. P. after dinner. *I had dined.* Staid at home all the evening like a virtuous man. This morning introduced to an aristocrat, the Earl of Granard. Seems a pleasant man. The Abbé a good fellow, *toujours gai!* Lord Moira afraid of the Papists. Fancy I am out there, though the Abbé will not tell me so. The "Protestant Freeman" in to-day's paper, but I hear nobody praise it. Cruel!

25. Write an account of the Wexford meeting in consequence of a letter from Devereux, and send it to the Hibernian Journal. Determined to set off to-morrow, and see the Translator. Sleep in my clothes at an inn near the canal, to be off early.

26, 27, 28. At Ballybrittas. The Translator in very bad spirits, and with great reason. Advise him to send his daughters to a boarding-school, and try his fortune for a few months in London as an author, for which I think him very well qualified. He seems to approve of the plan. His affairs in as bad a situation as possible, and his temper badly adapted to recover them. Wants resolution and energy; too much of the milk of human kindness. Poor fellow!

29. Dublin. Gog returned. Go to Mr. Jerome and breakfast. All well in Munster. Write resolutions for the Limerick Catholics. Pretty good; have brought on the Catholics to complain of being taxed without being represented, and bound by laws to which they do not consent; a great stride! Gog's mode of considering the question a good one.—His way of putting it is, that for want of the protection of the elective franchise, the poorer Catholics are turned out of their little farms, at the expiration of their leases, to make room for Protestant freeholders, who can assist their landlords by their votes. A good mode, but makes the question a mere matter of convenience. My mode puts it on the broad basis of right; lucky that both are very compatible, and strongly support each other. In high favour with Gog. Much conversation about an *expiration* to Dungannon. Gog's plan is as follows: That I should go to George

Knox, and suggest to him, that if Lord Abercorn would take up the cause of the Catholics, and assume the Lieutenancy of Ireland, he might make terms with Lord Shannon and his friends, and, if possible, with the Ponsonbys, keeping the negotiation a profound secret from the Beresford party. That the affairs of Ireland are in such a situation as must make them a considerable object of anxiety to the British Government; that our present administration, and particularly Fitzgibbon, are making things worse by their violence; that, therefore, the English Minister will naturally fall in with the men and measures which will keep this country quiet, and, consequently, we may reckon on his concurrence. That the Beresford party are very odious here, and have little weight personally, but are supported by the patronage of Government, which, if removed, they would fall at once with the unanimous consent of the nation. That Lord Abercorn should, having previously made his terms (by direct bribery) with Lord Shannon, and being also sure of the support of the whole of the Catholics, and at least a part of the Protestants, propose to the Beresford party to grant the elective franchise, &c. to the Catholics, which they would, to a moral certainty, refuse to do; that he should then at once turn out the whole party, which would sink directly, being odious to the nation and having little personal weight, and fill up their places with new men, Lord Shannon, the Knoxes, &c.: that this vast patronage falling into his hands at once would enable him to make such terms as would carry every thing easily: that, as to Lord Abercorn, it would make him the most popular Lord Lieutenant that ever was in Ireland, and secure him the strongest government: that, as to the Knoxes, it would make a short cut for them to arrive at powers and honours, which, on the present system, they will but slowly, if ever, arrive at: that the mode itself is an honourable one, being the granting, or rather restoring, their just rights to three millions of people, &c. Such is the outline of Gog's system, in which he seems very sanguine. What do I think of it? If I go to Dungannon, I will certainly put it as fairly and as strongly to George Knox as I can; but I confess I should be sorry to succeed. I feel myself bound in duty to do every thing in my power to procure liberty to the Catholics of Ireland; but this appears to me a bad scheme. In the first place, it is at once giving up the question of reform, or at least postponing it for an indefinite time; and is so far at once knocking up all that we have done, for this last twelvemonth, towards effecting a union between the Dissenters and the Catholics. Not that I think the former would have any right to complain, for they have not come forward in support of Catholic emancipation, *save only in Belfast;* and the Catholics are not to renounce all separate measures for the sake of that one town: I believe if they were properly supported by the body of the Dissenters, they would keep faith; but the fact is, they are not. In the next place, it would strengthen the hands of the English Government in this country, for a considerable time to come. At present (1792) England, except in commercial regulations, where she buys us with our own money, has not a great deal of influence here; on the contrary, administration rather holds them at defiance, and, in the present Catholic question, has actually, by bullying, prevented their interference; which, by the by, is a circumstance in favour of Gog's plan: whereas, with the example of the great change intended, future Irish administrations would be more shy of opposing, much less of attempting to bully, the English Minister. In the third place, it would naturally, from gratitude, throw the whole Catholic interest into the support of a Government to which they would owe so much, and, I am unalterably satisfied, that the crown, as it is improperly said, but more truly, the *oligarchy*, has already much too great a portion of power in our system; which power I have never hitherto known them to exercise for any good purpose, and which they would be less likely, at least for a considerable time, (if my judgment be right,) to use for that end, inasmuch as I conceive English influence would be considerably increased. These objections occur to me on the moment, but I must consider the question much more maturely. One conversation with Knox will do more than twenty soliloquies. Admitting all my objections, if the scheme be practicable, *quere*, is not the emancipating three millions of Catholics a great accession of strength and even of liberty to Ireland? and besides, though the immediate consequence would be an improper increase of strength to a vile government, yet this could not continue for any great length of time. The Catholics, having enjoyed a qualified degree of freedom for a few years, would come to think like other people, and especially from the information which would naturally accompany the prosperity consequent on their emancipation. Gratitude soon wears out; and when they were more advanced in prosperity, they would, besides being more capable of judging, actually feel the evils of a bad government much more; which looks like a paradox, but is very true. Mr. E. Byrne, besides being a better judge, *actually feels* the extended mischief of our vile system much more than one of his porters. Apply this idea. What is to be done on the whole? "6 times 12 is 72, 2 and carry 7; *how are we ruined?*" I believe if the Catholics were emancipated, no matter on what compact with Government, in a little time they would become like other people. At any rate, they cannot bind their children by such compact, (*vide* Thomas Paine). I abhor all capitulating with a bad government, if it could be helped. Natural enough, that the Catholics should seek for, and be glad to accept of, liberty from any quarter. Oh, why are not these fellows in the

North sufficiently enlightened to join heartily with us? Then, indeed, something might be done. Reform, liberty, and equality! The Catholics would, I think, join them; yet I remember when I thought they were incurable Tories, and that is not eighteen months since. Live and learn. What if the Duke of Leinster were included? He is a friend to the Catholics, and no enemy to a good place. Suppose Grattan and Forbes secured by stipulating for one or two of their popular bills? Reform seems a good way off, and all this would be gaining ground in the mean time. It would be making something like a people of which something might be made. If these men come in, we should have a tolerably honest, I believe, but certainly a very strong Government. What would become of Mr. Hutton in that case? and P. P.? "I am lost in sensations of troubled emotions." What will Knox say to all this? Is it castle-building or not? A fine fellow I am to-night, not worth a groat, and planning the subversion of ministers. Oh Lord! Oh Lord! I will go to bed.

October 1. This day eighteen counties have completed the return of their delegates to the General Committee, and nine more are in progress, besides all the great towns. Correct the resolutions of the Roscommon and and Leitrim Catholics. Middling enough. All that is good in them, borrowed from the Sligo resolutions, written by that able and steady friend to the interests of Ireland, Mr. John Hutton.

2. Dine with Gog. Talk over the plan of my Dungannon *expiration*. I fear, after all, Lord Rawdon will not have the sense to see what a great game he might play here. He would rather dangle at the tail of an English party, when, I think, he might be every thing but King of Ireland. Mug with Gog, and walk home elevated with liquor.

3. Call at Moira House, and see every body. Most graciously received. Introduced to Lady Granard, who takes charge of my letter to Col. Barry. Dinner, and a great deal of wine. Frivolous day. Generally drunk. Fine doings twice running. Hear that the Duke of Brunswick has defeated the French under Dumourier, and cut the whole army in pieces. Hope it is a lie. If Dumourier fights, he will infallibly be beaten. Never fight an invading enemy. Keep on his flanks, and harass his convoys, &c. &c.

4. Sick as a dog. Rode out to Gog. "Smoke the rhyme." Has had a letter from Myles Keon, requiring somebody of the committee to go to Ballinasloe to meet the Catholic gentry of Mayo and Galway. Dennis Browne playing tricks in the former county. Recommends a separate petition, and condemns the plan. Wishes, if he could, to act the patron to the Catholics, that he might make sale of 3,000,000 of clients at the Castle. A blockhead, without parts or principles! But

it won't do: the Catholics here smoke him. Last winter they used to stare at me for speaking contemptuously of him—a man who was brother to a Lord, and a Member of Parliament. They have got over all that now. Burke has disappeared these some days, and is gone no one knows whither.—To return to Mayo. Agreed that Tom Warren and I should go, and Randel M'Donnell, if we can get him, to Ballinasloe to-morrow, to convert the Catholic gentry of that county and of Galway. Gog is afraid of *wet sheets.* Is that the real truth? No matter, we will go without him. Call on M'Donnell, but do not find him. This jaunt knocks up one I had planned for Saturday to Rathcoffy, where there are to be great doings. Rowan has invited Mrs. Tone and me to meet Simon Butler and other *Sans Culottes.* Cannot be helped. Public business must take place of pleasure and vain delight. Settle with Warren to leave town to-morrow at twelve. "This is the first time that Mr. Hutton has been trusted on a separate negotiation." How will he acquit himself? Gog has had a letter from the Jacobin, praising Mr. Hutton to the skies. *Thereby hangs a tale.* A plot between the Jacobin and Mr. Hutton, to raise the latter gentlemen in the eyes of the Catholics. Poor Gog falls in the snare. *All fair.* Tea with Hamilton Rowan, who shows me a letter to Lord Abercorn, containing three-fourths of the plan as detailed in this *Gurnal.* Very odd that Gog and he should coincide so exactly without communication.

5. Tom Warren cannot go to Ballinasloe, being detained by his wife, who is just ready to lie in. Tom Braughall, all of a sudden, offers to go instead. Load my pistols, and pack up. N. B. For the miraculous events in that journey, see book—— wherein they are fully detailed, being "*moving accidents by flood and field; how we were taken by the insolent foe, and sold to slavery, and our redemption thence,*" *&c. &c.*

Journal of the proceedings of Mr. John Hutton, in his peregrination to convert the natives of Connaught, and more especially of Galway and Mayo, to the true political faith.

October 5, 1792. Left Dublin at eight in the evening in a post-chaise, with Mr. Braughall, commonly called in this journal T. B. Loaded with good advice by Gog in the morning, who has given me a broad hint to puff him in Connaught. An adventure! Stopped by three foot-pads near the park-gate, who threaten to exterminate the post-boy if he attempts to move; T. B. valiant, also Mr. Hutton. Mr. Hutton uses menacing language to the said foot-pads, and orders the post-boy, in an imperious tone of voice, to drive on. The *voleurs,* after about three minutes' consideration, give up the point, and the carriage proceeds. If they had persisted, we should have shot some of them, being well armed. Mr. Hutton in a fuss; his first emotion was to jump out and combat on foot; very odd! but his fear always comes on *after the danger*; much more embarrassed a quarter of an hour after, than during the dialogue; generally stout, and would have fought, but had rather let it alone; glad we did not kill any of the villains, who seemed to be soldiers. Drive on to Kinnegad—another adventure!! The chaise breaks down at three in the morning: obliged to get out in the mud, and hold up the chaise with my body, whilst the boy puts on the wheel; all grease and puddle! melancholy! arrive at Kinnegad at past four; bad hours!

6. Set off at eight; sick for want of sleep; meet Dr. French, Catholic Bishop of Elphin, at Athlone; seems a spirited fellow, and much the gentleman. T. B. no great things in a post-chaise; arrive late at Ballinasloe, and get beds with great difficulty. Meet Mr. Larking, the parish priest; a sad vulgar booby, but very civil to the best of his knowledge. Mr. Hutton falls asleep in company; victuals bad; wine poisonous; bed execrable; generally badly off; fall asleep in spite of ten thousand noises; wish the gentlemen over my head would leave off the bagpipes, and the gentlemen who are drinking in the next room would leave off singing, and the two gentlemen who are in bed together in the closet would leave off snoring: sad, sad! All quiet at last and be hanged!

7. *Sunday*. Find Mr. Larking has been so diligent that he has got nobody to meet us—dunce! Send out ourselves for one or two gentlemen, whom T. B. knows, and who engage to get us some of the Mayo people, after 12 o'clock prayers. Breakfast; the waiter brings us beef-steaks, fried with a great quantity of onions; nice feeding, but not to my taste. Asked to dine with sundry Catholics; how will it turn out? Meet Mr. Peter Lynch, and find him cool, or rather adverse; Dennis Browne has been tampering with him; he seems disinclined to give us a meeting. Meet Mr. Patrick Lynch, cool also; talk with him, and convert him. He engages to get a meeting of the Mayo gentry to-morrow at 3 o'clock. *Bon!* General O'Donnel; he knows nothing of politics. James Plunket; bravo! He engages to go among the Mayo people this evening, and bring them to-morrow; he also engages to convert Peter Lynch, who, it seems, is a great man amongst the Catholics. He says the parochial electors of Mayo are already chosen.

8. Breakfast, more beef-steak and onions. "Blow gentle gales." Fragrant and pretty. Go and see the fair; great show of bullocks; the greatest cattle-fair in Europe, except one in Hungary, as T. B. tells me. James Plunket seems to have found the Mayoman's slack; cannot be helped. Go at three to meet the gentlemen of Galway and Mayo; find a very respectable number assembled. Sir Thomas French takes the

chair; a fine young fellow, and of consequence among the Catholics *de son pays; Bon!* Braughall makes a very long, rambling, diffuse, bad statement of the proceedings of the General Committee, and of the objects of our mission. Followed by Mr. Hutton; not much better. That gentleman no great orator at a set speech, though he converses well enough. What is the reason? Because he is, in fact, not only modest, but sheepish, which is a shame. Mr. Hutton had probably better talents, and, to a moral certainty, better education, and, beyond all question, more knowledge of the subject than any of his hearers; yet, after all, he made but a poor exhibition. However, it passed, but by no means satisfied that truly able gentleman. No speaking without much study and continual practice; must try and mend, and get rid of that vicious modesty which obscures the great splendour and brilliancy of his natural talents. Gog, in his digressive, rambling style, would have beat Mr. Hutton all to nothing, which is a great shame to the latter gentleman. Sir Thomas French states two objections: one to that part of the circular letter which states that Lord Fingal approves the plan, inasmuch as he has been well assured, on good authority, (the Bellows, (*Rascals*) and Donellan of Bally Donellan, as we suppose), that such assertion arises from misconception, if not from wilful misstatement; the other, that the Committee had assumed to themselves, in the new system, a power of expelling such members as might prove refractory. These objections, stated by Sir Thomas French with great perspicuity and candour, we replied to satisfactorily to all the gentlemen, who fix upon Saturday the 20th next, and Glentane, for the time and place of choosing their delegates, of which Sir T. French will now be one; a great point gained. No Mayo men present, but Mr. James Lynch, of Cullen, who tells us the races at Castlebar begin on Saturday next, where all the Catholic gentry of Mayo will meet, and he has no doubt will elect delegates. He seems very indignant at the idea of Mr. Dennis Browne, or Mr. Peter Lynch, or any one man, directing the whole county: a good spirit which we endeavour to aggravate. The meeting breaks up, all parties well pleased. Galway is now finally settled, and Mayo in a fair way. They are the two great Catholic counties in Ireland, and the cream and flower of the Catholic gentry. They have been, hitherto, rather adverse to the General Committee, from the bad spirit of aristocracy, which has done the cause so much mischief by producing disunion; but we trust we have now fairly beat the Castle out of Galway, and are pretty confident we have done the same in Mayo. *Ca ira.* Dinner very bad. Retire early to my crib and read Chesterfield's Letters, which has been my great resource against ennui. His lordship, a great scoundred; he advises his son to attack Madame De Blot, because she has been married a year and loves her husband. D——n his blood, the rascal! I wish I was kicking him! I do not pretend to more virtue than other people, but I have no notion of such cold-blooded villany on deliberation. Till I read this infamous letter, I thought the character of Valmont, in *Les Liaisons Dangereuses*, was a monstrous fiction; but I see now that Lord Chesterfield had the inclination, though perhaps not the talent, to be as great a scoundrel. All this is for the edification of P. P., and perhaps of my son, if he ever lives to be old enough to read these memorandums. He is now above a twelvemonth old, and it is time for me to begin to think of forming his mind and his principles. I will never advise him to debauch his friend's wife, only because she is such a fool as to love her husband. Base! base! I lose my temper at it. It is the 30th of the Letters, 2d vol., wherein this precious paternal advice is communicated. I mention it particularly, because the fact is so unnatural that one would wish it could not be true. It is something like the case of Mrs. Parslow, and Sykes, another scoundrel. I have preached enough, and I will go to sleep. Indeed, I have preached more than enough; but what can I do better in this vile inn?

9. James Plunket will go to the meeting at Castlebar, and take Lord Dillon in his way, with a view of converting his Lordship, by exposing the game which Dennis Browne is playing, endeavouring to become the *padrone* of the Mayo Catholics, and establish thereby a strong interest in the county, which might enable him hereafter to hold Lord Dillon at defiance. T. B. writes a hundred letters to different people; Mr. Hutton not one, save an official to the Sub-committee. Our bill monstrous! A guinea for my crib (without window or fire-place) for two nights. Oh Lord! Oh Lord! what will this world come to? Oh Miss Culahaun, Miss Culahaun, where is your conscience? All will not do. *Il faut payer.* No letters from Galway. If this mail brings us none from Dublin, to change our present intentions, we shall set off for Athlone at five this evening. Mr. Hutton extremely sick of Ballinasloe in fair time. Dinner with James Plunket and eight Galway bucks. All civil, but intolerably dull. Handycapping; wagers; horseracing; swapping. Never saw such a scene before, and hope, sincerely, I never may again. No chaise for Dublin.

10. No chaise yet. Our conscientious landlady, Miss Culahaun, asks twelve shillings for a buggy to Athlone. Jew! skinflint! Fear we must take it after all; but determine to wait till twelve o'clock, and try for a place in the mail. Walk about the town as a crutch to poor T. B., who is lame. Strange curiosity of T. B., to read all manner of handbills. Mr. Hutton

something in the same way. The mail arrives empty. Take our places and set off. *No adventures*. Arrive in Dublin at nine in the morning.

Dublin.

October 11. The story of Dumourier a great lie. Huzza! Huzza! Brunswick and his army dying of the flux and running out of France, with Dumourier pursuing him. Huzza! If the French had been beaten, it was all over with us. All safe now for this campaign. Huzza!

14. Dine with Magog: a good fellow; much better than Gog. Gog a Papist. "Wine does wonders." Propose to revive volunteers in this city. Magog thinks we may have 1000 Catholics by the 17th March next. Agreed that he shall begin to canvass for recruits immediately, and continue through the winter. If he succeeds, he will resign his office of Secretary to the Catholic Committee, and commence a mere volunteer. Bravo! All this looks well. Satisfied that volunteering will be once more the salvation of Ireland. A good thing to have 1,500 men in Dublin. Green uniforms, &c.

15. Choice letters from Connaught. All well there. Galway and Mayo secure. A letter from P. P. He is envious of the laurels of Dumourier, and determined to go to France and outdo that illustrious democrat. Wants my advice, as he has made up his mind, and also to know if I can do any thing by way of letters of recommendation. P. P. a gallant fellow, and quite right. If Mr. Hutton were a single man, he would go and supersede Kellerman. To try Kirwan for a letter to Condorcet; also Wogan Browne, Hamilton Rowan, and Ed. Byrne the Vintner, for letters to Paris. Sorry for P. P., but entirely approve his plan and his spirit. Writes the best stuff of any man in the world.

Sub-Committee. Read the reply to the grand juries. Many alterations suggested. Agree to call an aggregate meeting of the Catholics of Dublin, proposed and pressed by Gog, who wants to shine. All fair! It will serve the cause. Gog's vanity sometimes, as in the present instance, of use. Emmett introduced to the Sub-committee. All say *Oh!* to him, and he richly deserves their admiration. Emmett, the best of all the friends to Catholic emancipation, always excepting Mr. Hutton.

16. Dr. Bellew, Catholic Bishop of Killala, wants subscriptions to found a Catholic seminary in Connaught. Mr. Hutton suggests that it would be advisable to extend the plan, and educate all the Catholic clergy at home,—an object which has long been a favourite with that gentleman. No doubt but many Protestants would subscribe for so wise and so benevolent a purpose. Agreed that T. Braughall and Mr. Hutton shall

wait on Kirwan, the philosopher, to talk over this plan. If a good system were devised, it would execute itself; that of the Catholic bishops a poor one, on a pitiful scale. Gog and Mr. Hutton had been talking over something of this kind already, in their last expedition to the North. Gog then afraid that the clergy would be adverse; has a sneaking kindness for Catholic priests. Mr. Hutton of opinion that the breaking up of the seminaries in France would oblige them to consent, and that in that light, as in ten thousand others, the Revolution was of infinite service to Ireland. *This education business appears to me of infinite importance, for a thousand reasons which I shall detail hereafter.* A strange letter from Burke, at Cork. He *will* be agent to the Catholics, whether they will or not, and absolutely commits a rape upon the Committee. His impudence is beyond what I could have imagined, and his vanity greater. He has the modesty to say, that the *existence* of Ireland depends on his enjoying the confidence of the Catholics, and many other sallies equally extraordinary. The Catholics, astonished and angry at all this persevering insolence, resolved that Gog shall write to him, and tell him he *is not* the agent of the Catholics, and that, if he desires it, the Committee will publish to that effect in the papers. I cannot help again expressing my admiration of his effrontery, which is consummate beyond all belief. He will not desist until he compels the Committee absolutely to advertise him, with a "warning that no one shall trust him, as," &c.

18. Spend the evening with Kirwan. Very pleasant, but no talk of our education plan. Hear that DD. Troy and Reilly, the Catholic Archbishop of Dublin and Catholic Primate, refuse to concur in a general system.—D—n them! ignorant bigots.

20. Introduced to Captain Sweetman, of Wexford. He reads his speech to the Sub-committee; it is one of the best popular harangues I ever heard, and filled with choice animosity against the English. Sweetman has been a Catholic, and served in the Irish brigade (Walsh's regiment), and is now a Protestant, and captain in the British service.

21. *Sunday.* Dine with the Vintner and a large company. Extremely pleasant. The Vintner hates this Government most cordially. His daughters pleasant women. Mrs. Atkinson there. Mr. Hutton a puppy! **** interesting, ***, &c.

22. Dine with M'Donnell. My son and heir come to town. Home early.

23. At work with Emmett, on the reply to the grand juries. Gog sick these three or four days, and no business done. Dine with Sweetman at the Green, and a long set. Nothing but dine with this Catholic, and that Catholic; very idle work. Mr. Hutton meditates leaving off the use of wine altogether.

24. See the Galway resolutions. Two of them very bad,

reflecting on the French. This Lynch's nonsense. Cannot he let the French alone? Breakfast with George Knox. Very long conversation on the subject of our proposal for a new ministry (*vide* this journal of September 29). Knox seems a good deal struck with the proposition. Enters into all the articles minutely. Dine with my father. Walk out in the evening in complete armour to Gog, and tell him the result of my conversation with Knox. Gog extravagantly delighted. Insists on my calling on Knox in the morning, and sending him to dispatch Lord Abercorn to Pitt. Foolish enough of Gog. Proposes to obtain an audience of Knox. Mr. Hutton shies the same, and desires it may be submitted entirely to his discretion; to which Gog submits. Gog has been disgusted with Dr. Bellew, Catholic Bishop of Killala, on the subject of a national college. The Bishop wants to get money from the laity to endow it, and to exclude them from all share in the management! Gog revolts like a fury, and tells Mr. Hutton he begins to see they (the Catholic Bishops) are all scoundrels. *All fair.* Two or three things like this may cure Gog of his sneaking kindness for "Bishops, Priests, and Deacons." Sleep at Gog's.

25. This is the King's (God bless him!) accession. *How many more accessions shall we have?* Breakfast with George Knox. Walk round the Green and talk over our scheme. Knox appears to think seriously of it, but says, as the truth is, that the success thereof is very uncertain, as depending on so many events, any one of which failing would destroy the whole. Mr. Hutton presses all the arguments again, and dwells particularly on the strength of the Government which would be formed in such an event, viz. Lord Shannon and the Ponsonbys, purchased by dint of money;—The Duke of Leinster, who would, it is presumed, be glad to come in, *cum suis*;—Grattan, and the two or three honest men who might be secured by agreeing to as many popular bills, as the place, pension bills, &c. which would give *eclat* to administration, without depriving them of any degree of essential power. (In this assertion Knox completely concurs.) This, added to their own family interest, and the natural influence of the Castle, would form a very powerful government. What would be the opposition? The Beresfords, &c. who, in losing their offices, would lose every thing; for they are most odious to the people, and have no natural weight;—and the bigoted Protestant squirearchy of Ireland. Ridiculous to talk of such an opposition! Who would listen to Mark Beresford, talking of the corruption of Government? Absurd! The new administration would be *tolerated*, if not supported, by the North, for the sake of Grattan, and as coming in on popular grounds, with two or three bills which are favorites, though, in fact, they signify nothing. This might be puffed so as to satisfy them;

and, as for the Catholics, we should have them to a man, on the ground of the elective franchise. Knox tells me he has written to the Marquis of Abercorn. That shows he has taken it up, for it was only broached to him yesterday. He refuses to see Gog, and asks, *Could Gog expect that he would open himself to him?* Knox ambitious and proud, but not interested, *as I judge.* What will all this come to? Mr. Hutton is decidedly of opinion that the Government of Ireland must either alter their whole system, or be subverted by force, of which God knows the event, the Catholics are so totally changed, and so thoroughly roused, &c. Knox and he agree that there is no *immediate* danger of violence on the part of the people, but that there is a gradual mass of discontent forming, which will, at no short day, break out, and especially if a war should arise; and that this discontent is inflamed and accelerated by the gross petulance and indiscretion of Government here. This may probably be dissipated without breaking, by such an arrangement as we meditate.

26. Dennis Browne has been playing the rascal in Mayo. Procured a meeting on the 16th, and knocked up our plan by securing the measure of a separate petition from that county. D—n him! Yet he talks of his love for the cause, &c. The Catholics here in a horrible rage. More and more losing their respect for the brothers of Lords and Members of Parliament.

27. Randel M'Donnell has had a letter from the Secretary of the Mayo Catholics at the late meeting, by which it appears possible that we may yet have delegates from that county. Write a letter from the Sub-committee, exhorting them to that measure. Good letter! Meet the parochial delegates in the evening, and settle every thing for the aggregate meeting of the Catholics of Dublin.

28. The town has been filled these three or four days with reports of some seditious paper said to be circulated among the soldiers of the garrison. I do not believe it. One officer (Colonel of the Royal Irish Artillery) is said to have been so wise as to draw up the regiment on the parade, and harangue them, exhorting them to obedience, and warning them against "The Rights of Man," &c. Dunce! Blockhead! Could not take a readier way to create the mischief against which he wished to guard. Another report is, that the artillery and all the cavalry are to be ordered to England and replaced by English troops. I hope this is a lie too. These reports, however, show the agitation of the public mind.

29. Advertisements are this day handed about, ordering a general illumination on account of the expulsion of the German armies from France. I don't know what to think. The illumination is good; but it may be made a handle for rioting, and if so, very mischievous, for Government would rejoice at any

thing which would give them an excuse to let the dragoons loose on the people. The illumination set on foot by Oliver Bond and James Tandy. Write a letter to the Draper, with resolutions for the Northern Whig Club, at their next meeting, in favour of the Catholics. Suppose he will not be able to carry them, but good to try.

30. The illumination has gone off quietly, notwithstanding the Lord Mayor issued a proclamation forbidding it, and threatening very hard, &c. The horse and foot were out in great force. It should seem, by their being called out so frequently, that Government are determined to accustom the people to see them in the streets. Emmet and I read over the Catholic address for the last time, and make corrections. N. B. The said Emmet henceforward to be called "The Pismire."—*Sub-Committee;* a very full meeting to settle the plan for to-morrow. Mr. Hutton reads the address. D. T. O'Brien objects to the resolution thanking the Volunteers of Ulster, because it may look like cultivating the friendship of *armed men.* Nobody seconds him. R. Macdonnel wishes we had 100,000 of them to thank. Divers Protestants summoned to the meeting tomorrow; Butler, Rowan, Tandy, the Pismire, Mr. Hutton, &c. Gog at home all day rehearsing. All fair. This meeting will do good. N. B. All the good publications on the Catholic side, almost, are written by Protestants. Mr. Hutton chooses, for reasons which he does not wish to explain, to insert here, the names of the present Sub-Committee of the Catholics of Ireland:—Thomas Fitzgerald; John Keogh; Thomas Braughall; Edward Byrne; Randal Macdonnel; Thomas Ryan, M. D.; Martin F. Lynch; Richard McCormick; Hugh Hamill; Dennis Thomas O'Brien; Thomas Warren; John Sweetman, Secretary.

31. The grand day. A full and respectable meeting. Six hundred and forty summonses taken at the door, besides many who came in without any. Dr. Ryan's speech the best. Gog mortified thereat; consults Mr. Hutton whether he shall venture to speak after the Doctor! Fishing! Mr. Hutton advises him to speak by all means, and throws in sundry compliments, whereat Gog rises. All fair! Gog's speech rambling and confused, but full of matter. Dine and crack nuts at my father's.

November 1. Dinner at Warren's. A long set of the chief United Irishmen. All very pleasant and good. Mr. Hutton endeavours, being *entre deux vins,* to delude the gentlemen present into forming a volunteer company on good principles, civil and military. A. H. Rowan rises thereat, also Magog. Mr. Hutton a little mad on the subject of volunteering; would be a great Martinet "Army, d—n me!" Talk a great deal of tactics and treason. Mr. Hutton grows warm with the subject; very much surprised, on looking down to the table, to see two glasses before him; finds, on looking at Hamilton Rowan, that he has got four eyes; various other phenomena in optics equally curious. Mr. Hutton, like the sun in the centre of the system, fixed, but every thing about him moving in rapid rotation; perfectly sober, but perceives that every one else is getting very drunk; essays to walk across the room, but finds it impossible to move rectilinearly, proceeding entirely from his having taken "a sprig of watercresses" with his bread at dinner. "God bless every body." Sundry excellent toasts. A round of *citizens*; that coming into fashion; trifling as it is, it is a symptom. All embrace and depart at 12. Fine doings! fine doings!

3. Go out to Gog to prepare his speech. Correct it abundantly. Dine with Gog, who fishes for compliments with the old bait—civilities to Mr. Hutton on his *excellent pamphlet*, &c. Mr. Hutton rises and throws a bucket full of flattery in Gog's face, who receives it with great affability. Mr. Hutton comes into town and writes twelve letters to different persons, enclosing copies of the proceedings of 31st; all well written, and done very speedily. Mr. Hutton would make a good private secretary. Apropos! On the 31st, Mr. Hutton being at breakfast with the Honourable George Knox, and talking with great asperity and vehemence, according to his custom, against the folly and wickedness of the Government, the following dialogue ensues:

Mr. Hutton. I wish to God, Knox, you were Secretary here.

Knox. I wish I was; will you be my private Secretary?

Mr. Hutton. That I will, most willingly.

Knox. Very well, remember.

Mr. Hutton. Remember.—*Exit Mr. Hutton.*

4. *Sunday.* Dine at Macdonnel's with United Irishmen. Tandy tells me the volunteers refused to parade round King William's statue, this being the birth-day of that monarch; they have also abolished orange cockades. Bravo! A few of them met to-day as at an ordinary parade, and wore national (green) cockades. This is a striking proof of the change of men's sentiments, when "Our Glorious Deliverer" is so neglected. This is the first time the day has passed uncommemorated since the institution of volunteers. Huzza! Union and the People for ever! Mr. Hutton exercised his franchise this week by voting for common councilmen among the Sadlers. Mr. Hutton a free Sadler, and invited to dine with the candidates, which he respectfully declines.

5. Gunpowder Treason!

> "This is the day, I speak it with sorrow,
> That we were all to 've been blown up to-morrow.—ROCHESTER.

Mr. Hutton, on his return from the post-office this evening, (where he had been to put in a letter to P. P.) is startled by a vision of Guy Vaux, which appears to him at Alderman Hart's door. Mr. Hutton speaks Latin to the said vision, on which it proves to be a police man. Mr. Hutton diligently inspects the pantry, lest the Catholics might have conveyed combustibles therein, to burn him and his innocent family in their beds. Wishes to have a fire-engine in his bed-chamber, for fear of accidents from these bloody, barbarous, and inhuman Papists.

9. At court. Wonderful to see the rapid change in the minds of the bar, on the Catholic question; almost every body favourable. Some for an immediate abolition of all penal laws: certainly the most magnanimous mode, and the wisest. All sorts of men, and especially Lawyer Plunkett, take a pleasure in girding at Mr. Hutton, "who takes at once all their seven points on his buckler, thus." Mr Hutton called *Marat*. Sundry barristers apply to him for protection in the approaching rebellion. Lawyer Plunkett applies for Carton, which Mr. Hutton refuses, inasmuch as the Duke of Leinster is his friend, but offers him Curraghmore, the seat of the Marquis of Waterford. This Mr. Hutton does to have a rise out of Marcus Beresford, who is at his elbow listening. Great laughter thereat.

10. Hear that Government is very much embarrassed to know what to do. My own conviction is, that they must *concede*. Gog, Magog, and Warren, three leading Catholics, had rather be refused this session, in order, thoroughly, to rouse the spirit of the people. Right! I rely very much on the folly and intemperance of Government for the complete emancipation of the country. Early and moderate concessions to the just demands of the nation may prevent mischief, but that is a degree of wisdom which Fitzgibbon never will be able to reach. My advice has been for the Catholics, at every refusal, to rise in their demands, like the ancient Sibyl; which they seem determined to do. *No want of spirit apparent yet.* The Committee, under the new organization, is called for the 3d December. We have this day returns from twenty-five counties and all the great cities of Ireland, with a strong confidence that we shall have the remainder before the day of meeting. Custine is said to have advanced so far in Flanders, that his retreat is cut off. A lie, I hope, like that about Dumourier. *Right or wrong, success to the French; they are fighting our battles; and if they fail, adieu to liberty in Ireland, for one century!* Apropos of fighting! Mr. Hutton has bought a fine sword, of which he is as vain the devil; intends to sleep on it to-night. *Quere,* May he not wear it in the court of chancery, with his wig and gown, to edify Lord Fitzgibbon? Mr. Hutton proposes to make it the pattern-sword for his regiment,—when he has one.

11. *Sunday.* George Knox shows me a memorandum or abstract of Lord Abercorn's answer to his letter on the subject of Gog's famous plan for turning out the Ministers here, Lord Abercorn quite wild; his idea is, that the Catholics

should renounce their present system, for the *chance* of what he would do for them. D—d kind! Mr. Hutton observes, coolly, that his lordship does not bid high enough, and so the negociation ends; Knox declaring himself of Mr. Hutton's opinion.

12. At Gog's to prepare papers, viz. petition to the King, petition to Parliament, address to the nation, &c. Hear a report that Foster is afraid of being assassinated. The rascal deserves it, if any thing can justify assassination. Hard at work.

13. Major and Secretary Hobart has sent for Dr. Troy, to pump him; talks a deal of stuff, that Government is determined to resist all violence; that Government in England will support them; that we have not the North, save only Belfast, &c. By laying such stress upon *the North*, he is exposing his own weak side, and, please God, the hint shall not be lost.

14. All the morning at work. Dine in town, at R. Dillon's. After dinner, turn the discourse to the probability of raising a new corps of volunteers. Resolve that the party shall meet on Saturday next, to devise a plan. All provoked at an unnecessary affront the Dublin corps received last Sunday; an officer of the regulars took away a drummer, belonging to his regiment, whom the volunteers had hired for the day, and the poor fellow has been sentenced to receive two hundred lashes. Strange policy of Government, in such a time as this, to choose to pick a quarrel with the volunteers!

15. Hear, to-day, that Ponsonby is come over. If it be so, a great point. Hard at work.

16. Hear that the Castle-men say, our address to the King, if we persist in that idea, will embarrass his Majesty.—The devil it will! And who doubts, or who cares? We will address him, please God, and let him refuse it, if he pleases. Better that his Sacred Majesty should be embarrassed, than a nation kept in slavery. More and more at work.

17. In town, at the Sub-committee. Read the intended address to the King. Very much liked, even by some of our timid people. Mr. Hutton very well pleased thereat. Gog also pleased. Compliments Mr. Hutton, and says that he (Mr. Hutton) has given the tone to all the Catholic politics; which Mr. Hutton, with that amiable modesty which eminently adorns him, and gives a beautiful gloss to all his splendid actions, denies, and says, with a becoming diffidence, that if he has any merit, it was only in seeing their true interest a little earlier than some of themselves; and that it is their own good understandings, and not his arguments, that have set them on the right scent. This is partly true; and, at any rate, it is pretty in Mr. Hutton. It would not be for that gentleman's advantage to be thought wiser than Gog. Much better to stand behind

the curtain and advise him. Mr. Hutton not anxious to appear on the canvass, provided the business be done, and if any thing serious should ensue, *he will find his own level.* If he deserves to rise, he will probably rise; if not, he cannot help it. Spend the evening at home, with my innocent family. After all, home is home. I had like to forget. Attended, as Secretary, a meeting for the purpose of raising a new volunteer corps; vote 1000 men in ten companies. If this takes, it will vex the Castle, and they may not like to come and take *our* drum from us.

18. *Sunday.* Mr. Jerome again. Dinner with J. Plunkett, of Roscommon, and J. Jos. M'Donnel, of Mayo. Conversation right good. The Country Catholics, I think, will *stand fire.* All seem stout. Mayo has returned, in spite of Dennis Browne, who is as vexed as the Devil, and cannot help himself. Huzza! Drink like a fish till past twelve. *God bless every body.* Embrace the Connaught men, and go to bed as drunk as a Lord. It is downright scandalous to see in this, and other journals, how often that occurrence takes place;—yet I call myself a sober man!

20. Mr. O'Beirne, of county Leitrim, a sensible man. Gog takes great pains to put him up to Catholic affairs, and does it extremely well. Gog lucky to-day; never lets an opportunity pass to convert a country delegate—which answers two ends; it informs them, and gives him an influence over the country gentlemen. O'Beirne says the common people are up in high spirits, and anxious for the event. Bravo! Better have the peasantry of one county than twenty members of Parliament. Gog seems to-day disposed for all manner of treason and mischief; separation of the countries, &c.; a republic, &c.; is of opinion this will not end without blows, and says he for one is ready. Is he? Mr. Hutton quite prepared, having nothing to lose. Come to town to meet the Committee for framing the new corps. The whole evening spent in settling the uniform, which is at last fixed to be that of the—*Garde Nationale.* Is that quite wise? Who cares? The parties do not seem quite hearty in the business, and it is likely, after all, the corps will come to nothing. This does not look very well. Mr. Hutton a little disgusted. No body universally and at all times right, except that truly spirited and patriotic character.

Hiatus for two months.

Fragments of the Journals of 1793.

January 21. I find it very hard to keep these Journals regularly. I wish I could bring myself to set apart some *certain* time for journalizing; but as that would be something approaching to *system,* I despair of ever reaching it.

In the Sub-committee, Sir T. French, Byrne, Keogh, and M.

Donnell despatched to Hobart, to apprise him that nothing short of *unlimited* emancipation will satisfy the Catholics. They return, in about an hour, extremely dissatisfied with each other, and, after divers mutual recriminations, it appears, by the confession of all parties, that, so far from discharging their commission, they had done directly the reverse; for the result of their conversation with the Secretary was, that he had declared explicitly against the *whole* measure, and they had given him reason, in consequence, to think that the Catholics would acquiesce contentedly in a *half* one. And so Gog's puffing is come to this! I always thought, when the crisis arrived, that he would be shy. Agreed by the S. C. that a letter should be written to Hobart to rectify this mistake, which is done accordingly, after many alterations. It is not well done after all; for, instead of putting the question on the true ground, it only says that his Majesty's gracious intentions towards the Catholics cannot be fulfilled, unless by the repeal of the penal laws. I wanted to express it a great deal stronger, and to hint at the danger of trifling, but was overpowered. Gog damped them by puffing his readiness, for one, to face any danger which might ensue from a strong representation. Owen O'Connor asserted that he was ready too, upon which Gog asked him, "Was he prepared to enter the tented field?" He answered "he was." Now the fact is, the question was put to frighten Ned Byrne; and another fact is, that O'Connor was ready and Gog was not. He is a sad fellow, after all. I see, if ever the business is done, it will be by the country gentlemen. In the evening wrote three official letters to Devereux, Chargé d'Affaires at the Court of London.—*Mauvais jour.*

22. Called on Sir Thomas French. A council of war. The Baronet, James Plunket, Edward Sweetman, P. P. and Mr. Hutton: agreed unanimously that the cause has gone back materially, from the conversation of yesterday; that a sneaking spirit of compromise seems creeping in, which, if not immediately checked, may be fatal. Agreed that Sweetman shall prepare a strong address to the nation, to show Ministers that we are as resolute as ever. Agreed that, if all be given except the two houses, the gentry of the Catholics will be the only disfranchised body in the Nation. All the country gentlemen present in a rage thereat, which Mr. Hutton and P. P. aggravate to an extreme degree.

23. Sweetman produces his paper at the Sub-committee, which is very strong and good. Mr. Hutton produces an amendment in the shape of a most virulent attack on the Lord Chancellor (Fitzgibbon). The Sub-committee staggered thereat. The whole referred to a Committee.

24. Sir T. French opens the business by a strong attack on the meeting, for the lukewarm spirit which they have manifested

for these last few days. I am very glad of this step, which indeed I put the Baronet upon. Sweetman's paper, with my amendments, brought in, read, and received coldly enough. This is hard! They have now a noble opportunity of punishing their old enemy Fitzgibbon, and I am afraid they will let it slip. It is objected to, on two grounds: 1st, as an attack on the privileges of Parliament; and, 2d, inasmuch as being below their dignity to enter into an altercation with the Chancellor. The last is most insisted upon, the first appearing to savour a little of timidity. The fact is, they *are* afraid, which is d——d bad. They were much stouter three months ago, when they were, beyond all comparison, weaker. Now they have, I may say, the whole North, the sanction of the King's name, and their own party in the highest spirits and most anxious expectations,—and all of a sudden they are gone unaccountably backward. *This is vile.* It will give our execrable Government time to recollect themselves. They are now rocking to their very foundation, and they are still more frightened than hurt. We are going to take them very kindly out of this panic, and, by the fluctuation and indecision of our councils, to show them that they have nothing to fear from us. The intended paper is at length got rid of, by referring it to those who are called our *Parliamentary friends.* I never knew good come through that channel.

25. Gog comes into town, and makes a most amazing flourish. He has found out that he is losing ground on the score of courage; and therefore he proposes to the Sub-committee to send proper persons to Dungannon, to propose to the Convention which is to meet there on the 15th of February, that the Catholics will accept of no relief unless a reform be granted, provided the Dissenters will accept of no reform which shall not include the Catholics on a footing of equality. All this a rhodomontade. Gog knows very well that the Sub-committee will not agree to such a proposal, which, in the present state of the business, would be foolish; and that, if they were disposed to do so, they have neither authority nor power.

26 to 31. The Sub-committee is infected more and more with Gog's timidity, which is now, to all intents, as ruinous as downright treachery. T. Fitzgerald, who behaved infamously in the Convention, and was odious to Gog, is in town, and they have formed a most unnatural coalition. They have poisoned T. Warren between them. The Vintner is cowardly, and, besides, is under Gog's influence; M'Donnell is perpetually wavering. The country delegates do not step out. Altogether, every thing looks ill. A deputation has been with Hobart again, as to presenting the petition. He objects to the prayer as being too specific. He is asked, if it be altered to the very words of that presented to the King, will he then present and

support it? This he declines, but says, if they choose to give it to any of their own friends, it will make no alteration in his conduct relative to the extent of the measures which he will support. This is a good opening, if the Catholics have the grace to avail themselves of it, for the Minister is bound by the King's recommendation, and Opposition will be bound, as bringing in the petition. The only use of Hobart's bringing it in, is, that it may pledge him to the whole measure.

Sub-committee. After sundry debates for two or three days, the prayer of the petition is altered. This is very bad; not that the alteration is very material, but that it betrays a sad decay in our spirit.

A scuffle between MM. Gog and Hutton. In the last debate on the alteration, Mr. Hutton mentioned some expressions which he had heard out of doors. Gog, in his reply, remarked, in a very pointed manner, "that the Sub-committee were not to be influenced in their decisions by reports of *conversations with persons whom they knew nothing about.*" And in another part, "that they were not to attend to conversations that were *held in corners.*" Mr. Hutton taketh fire thereat, as the insinuation is too strong and pointed to be overlooked. He riseth in great heat. T. Warren adviseth him not to speak, but he sweareth with vehemence that he will. In the mean time Edward Sweetman addresses the chair, and pronounces a handsome eulogium on Mr. Hutton, which a little abates the choler of that illustrious patriot, and also gives him a moment's time to recollect himself. He determines to make the apology as easy as possible to Gog, that he may have no reason to accuse himself. He therefore, fixing his eyes on Gog, says, with great *mildness,* "that he is sure that gentleman did not intend to cast any imputation on him; but as, unluckily, the words he had used might be construed so as to bear a bad sense, he thought it but right to give him an opportunity to explain them. That he (Mr. Hutton) had never had a conversation with any one on Catholic affairs that he would not hold before every man in the room; nor done any action, in a corner or elsewhere, which he would not repeat at the Royal Exchange at noonday. That he had no *secret,* and, consequently, no fear. That he mentioned this in justice to Gog, to induce him to give a proper explanation, *for he would not suffer himself to suppose that Gog could intend to convey the smallest imputation upon his conduct.*"

These last words brought up Gog in a fuss. He payeth Mr. Hutton sundry compliments, and appeals to the Sub-committee, whether he had not always expressed the obligations which the Catholic cause owed to his exertions and talents, and whether he had not always said that the Catholics were bound, in honour, not only to *reward him, but to raise his fortune.* That he thought his (Mr. Hutton's) measures for the last few days (alluding to the business of the petition,) had tended too much to commit the Catholics with Parliament, but was satisfied, at the same time, of the perfect purity of his intentions; that, as to the expressions himself had used, he never intended by them to convey the smallest imputation on Mr. Hutton, and, particularly as to what he had said about "corners," which he now saw was equivocal; and he was sorry it had escaped him.

Now the fact is, Gog knew very well what he was saying, and *did* intend to attach an oblique censure on Mr. Hutton, which would have stuck to that gentleman, if he had not immediately resented it. Another fact is, *that Gog is not a firm man,* which is so much the better for Mr. Hutton, who has, thereby, a claw upon the said Gog. If he had not apologized, Mr. Hutton would have sent a certain officer, of the name of Edward Sweetman, (who is indeed delegate for Wexford, and does not much love Gog,) with a message, which would, as is presumed, have speedily brought him to a proper sense of his duty. *The fellow will ruin me yet with the Catholics, if he can: let him! but I will do, at all risks, what I feel to be my duty.*

The paper, with the attack on the Chancellor, seems universally given up. No body mentions it.

The King of France was beheaded on the 21st;—*I am sorry it was necessary.* Another interview with Hobart; he agrees to present the petition as altered, but takes care to protest against his being thereby committed to the whole measure. He says he will go so far as he is supported by the House; and the Catholics give him the petition to present, saying they hope his conduct will be such as to entitle him to the gratitude, and his Majesty's Government to the support, of the Catholics. They are all wrong, in my judgment. They should give it to some independent man, for Hobart is bound already to do what he can by the speech from the throne, and this imposes no additional tie, whilst it cripples Opposition; besides, he did not appear any way anxious to present it, and they in a manner forced it upon him, which is very bad, as it betrays a want of confidence in themselves and their friends.

February 1. Debate on the late business with the Goldsmith's corps. A few days ago they paraded, when they were informed by Alderman Warren, that if they attempted to march, he would take the officers into custody; on which, after some consideration, it was agreed to disperse, the reason whereof was, that some individuals threatened to resist by force, and it was not thought advisable to commit the volunteers with Government just now. There are about 250 volunteers in Dublin, and the garrison is not less than 2,500, so that resistance is out of the question for the present. Do Government mean to carry the principle on with other corps? Will they go on and disarm us all? I hope not.

4. Hobart presented the petition, and moved for leave to bring in a bill, which is granted.*

5. Gog has exhibited a master-stroke! He moved this day, when only nine gentlemen were present, "that, in order to unite secrecy and despatch, the gentlemen who have been appointed to wait on the Minister be requested to continue their applications, in order to carry into effect the object of the petition." This seems innocent enough, but what does it mean? It is a delegation of the whole power of the Catholic body to seven men, who have no definite instructions, who are not bound to report their proceedings, and who have no responsibility. The Sub-committee is thus adjourned *sine die*, and the Catholic body is governed by a Septemvirate, Gog being Dictator. This is all d——d fine, but it won't do. What makes it more curious is, that, of the nine men who voted this wise measure, *five* were of the deputation. Magog, Mr. Hutton, and every body else, are thus fairly excluded from all knowledge of or interference in Catholic affairs, and that without the least bustle or noise. This scheme will never do. We must have a counter-revolution, or an open meeting. Gog is as deep as a draw-well. Mr. Hutton informs Magog of this unexpected change. Magog in a rage; swears he will take Gog off his stilts. Goes off to inflame the citizens against the *Septemviri*. Their reign, I see clearly, will be very brief.

6. A meeting of malcontents: present, Magog, Capt. Sweetman, P. P., and Mr. Hutton. Much railing against the new Dictator; a formal conspiracy against his authority. Magog has poisoned the whole city. Agree to call the Sub-committee, and rescind the vote appointing the *Septemviri*; if defeated in the Sub-committee, to call the General Committee. Gog's new authority tottering already. Mr. Hutton and P. P. walk together; much laughing at Mr. Hutton, who is indeed an ex-minister, and no longer possesses the confidence of the Catholics. All this will soon be rectified.

7. Magog is ready, and has summoned the Sub-committee for to-morrow.

8. A complete counter-revolution effected, and the *Septemviri* removed without tumult or disturbance. Magog moved that the order of the 5th be rescinded, which, after a feeble opposition from the Dictator, (who is once more, indeed, become plain Gog,) is carried *unâ voce*. Gog lays down the fasces, and walks forth a private citizen—Huzza! Huzza! Mr. Hutton re-

* For an enumeration of the provisions of this bill see Vol. I. p. 139, *et seq.*

stored, also Magog, also all good Catholics. Huzza! that business is over, and the Dictatorship at an end, after an existence of three days. May all unjust power have as speedy a termination! The deputation report, that they were sent for this morning by Hobart, to tell them, "That nothing could be done in the business of the bill for the relief of the Catholics, unless he should be enabled to say, that they would be satisfied with the measures at present intended; that, by being satisfied, is meant, that the public mind should not be irritated in the manner it has been for some time past; that it is not meant to say, that future applications may not be made, but that if they (the Catholics) will not for the present be satisfied, it is better to make a stand here, than to concede, and thereby to give them strength, by which they might be able farther to embarrass Administration, perhaps next session. This is pretty stout language of the Secretary. It is observable that, last night, 20,000 army and 16,000 militia were voted by the House of Commons, and that Opposition, and particularly Grattan, were as earnest in the measure as the Treasury bench. They are a fine set, to be sure, altogether. Grattan dreads the people as much as Monck Mason. A long conversation amongst the Catholics on the point of declaring themselves satisfied, or not, with Hobart's bill.* For satisfaction, Sir Thomas French, Bellew, Byrne, O'Connor, and Keogh; against it, O'Gorman, Sweetman, M'Cormick, and James Plunkett. This is as important a crisis as any which has occurred in Catholic affairs. After much altercation and repetition on both sides, the Sub-Committee broke up, without coming to any determination. *I see the whole measure is decidedly lost.*

TWO MEMORIALS

On the present state of Ireland, delivered to the French Government, in Feuuary 1796.

FIRST MEMORIAL.

The genius of the English nation, their manners, their prejudices, and their government, are so diametrically opposite to those of the French Republic, in all respects, that it is unnecessary to dwell upon this subject. I assume it as an axiom, that there is an irreconcilable opposition of interests between the two nations. Since the French Revolution, there is one still more irreconcilable between the Governments, so that neither can be said to be in security while the other is in existence.

The war, hitherto, however glorious to France, has not been unprofitable to England; her fleets were never more formidable, and, in the true spirit of trade, she will console herself for the

* For the debate which ensued on this subject see Vol. I. p. 132, *et seq.*

disgrace of her arms by land, in the acquisition of wealth, and commerce, and power, by sea; but these very acquisitions render it, if possible, incumbent, not merely on France, but on all Europe, to endeavour to reduce her within due limits, and to prevent that enormous accumulation of wealth which the undisturbed possession of the commerce of the whole world would give her; and this reduction of her power can be alone, as I presume, accomplished with certainty and effect by separating Ireland from Great Britain.

The French Government cannot but be well informed of the immense resources, especially in a military point of view, which England draws from Ireland. It is with the beef and the pork, the butter, the tallow, the hides, and various other articles of the first necessity, which Ireland supplies, that she victuals and equips her navy, and, in a great degree, supports her people and garrisons in the West Indies. It is with the poor and hardy natives of Ireland that she mans her fleets and fills the ranks of her army. From the commencement of the present war to the month of June, 1795, not less than 200,000 men were raised in Ireland, of whom 80,000 were for the navy alone. It is a fact undeniable, though carefully concealed in England, that TWO THIRDS of the British navy are manned by Irishmen; a circumstance which, if it stood alone, should be sufficient to determine the French Government to wrest, if possible, so powerful a weapon from the hands of her implacable enemy. I shall not dwell longer on the necessity of the measure which I shall propose, but will endeavour to show how it may best be executed, and on what grounds it is that I rest my confidence of success, if the attempt be but once made.

For the better elucidation of the plan, it is necessary to take a review of the actual state of Ireland. I shall condense the facts as much as possible, as I trust the French Government is already in possession of those which are most material.

The people of Ireland consist of about 4,500,000 persons, distributed under three different religious sects, of whom the Protestants, whose religion is the dominant one, and established by law, constitute 450,000, or one-tenth of the whole; the Dissenters, or Presbyterians, about 900,000, or one fifth; the Catholics form the remaining 3,150,000. They may also be considered with regard to property, which is necessary, in some degree, to explain the political situation of the country.

The Protestants, who are almost entirely the descendants of Englishmen, forming so very small a minority as they do of the whole people, have yet almost the whole landed property of the country in their hands; this property has been acquired by the most unjust means, by plunder and confiscation during repeated wars, and by the operation of laws framed to degrade and destroy the Catholics, the natives of the country. In 1650, the people of three entire provinces were driven by Cromwell into the fourth, and their property divided amongst his officers and soldiers, whose descendants enjoy it at this day. In 1688, when James II. was finally defeated in Ireland, the spirit of the Irish people was completely broken, and the last remnant of their property torn from them and divided amongst the conquerors. By these means, the proprietors of estates in Ireland, feeling the weakness of their titles to property thus acquired, and seeing themselves, as it were, a colony of strangers forming not above one-tenth part of the population, have always looked to England for protection and support; they have, therefore, been ever ready to sacrifice the interests of their country to her ambition and avarice, and to their own security. England, in return, has rewarded them for this sacrifice by distributing among them all the offices and appointments in the church, the army, the law, the revenue, and every department of the state, to the utter exclusion of the two other sects, and more especially of the Catholics. By these means, the Protestants, who constitute the aristocracy of Ireland, have in their hands all the force of the government; they have at least five-sixths of the landed property; they are devoted implicitly to the connexion with England, which they consider as essential to the secure possession of their estates; they dread and abhor the principles of the French Revolution;—and, in case of any attempt to emancipate Ireland, I should calculate on all the opposition which it might be in their power to give.

But it is very different with regard to the Dissenters, who occupy the province of Ulster, of which they form, at present, the majority. They have among them but few great landed proprietors; they are mostly engaged in trade and manufactures, especially of linen, which is the staple commodity of Ireland and is almost exclusively in their hands. From their first establishment, in 1620, until very lately, there existed a continual animosity between them and the Catholic natives of the country, grounded on the natural dislike between the old inhabitants and strangers, and fortified still more by the irreconcilable difference between the genius of the religions of Calvinism and Popery, and diligently cultivated and fomented by the Protestant aristocracy, the partizans of England, who saw in the feuds and dissensions of the other two great sects their own protection and security.

Among the innumerable blessings procured to mankind by the French Revolution, arose the circumstance which I am about to mention, and to which I do most earnestly entreat the particular attention of the French Government, as it is, in fact, the point on which the emancipation of Ireland may eventually turn.

The Dissenters are, from the genius of their religion and the spirit of inquiry which it produces, sincere and enlightened republicans; they have ever, in a degree, opposed the usurpations of England, whose protection, as well from their numbers and spirit as the nature of their property, they did not, like the Protestant aristocracy, feel necessary for their existence. Still, however, in all the civil wars of Ireland, they ranged themselves under the standard of England, and were the most formidable enemies to the Catholic natives, whom they detested as Papists and despised as slaves. These bad feelings were, for obvious reasons, diligently fomented by the Protestant and English party. At length, in the year 1790, the French Revolution produced a powerful revulsion in the minds of the most enlightened men amongst them. They saw that, whilst they thought they were the masters of the Catholics, they were, in fact, but their gaolers, and that, instead of enjoying liberty in their own country, they served but as a garrison to keep it in subjection to England: the establishment of unbounded liberty of conscience in France had mitigated their horror of Popery; one hundred and two years of peace had worn away very much of the old animosity which former wars had raised and fomented. Eager to emulate the glorious example of France, they saw at once that the only guide to liberty was justice, and that they neither deserved nor could obtain independence, whilst their Catholic brethren, (as they then, for the first time, called them,) remained in slavery and oppression. Impressed with these sentiments of liberality and wisdom, they sought out the leaders of the Catholics, whose cause and whose suffering were, in a manner, forgotten; the Catholics caught with eagerness at the slightest appearance of alliance and support from a quarter whose opposition they had ever experienced to be so formidable, and once more, after lying prostrate for above 100 years, appeared on the political theatre of their country. Nothing could exceed the alarm, the terror, and confusion, which this most unexpected coalition produced in the breasts of the English Government, and their partizans, the Protestant aristocracy of Ireland. Every art, every stratagem, was used to break the new alliance, and revive the ancient animosities and feuds between the Dissenters and Catholics. Happily such abominable attempts proved fruitless. The leaders on both sides saw, that as they had but one common country, they had but one common interest; that while they were mutually contending and ready to sacrifice each other, England profited of their folly, to enslave both; and that it was only by a cordial union and affectionate co-operation, they could assert their common liberty and establish the independence of Ireland. They, therefore, resisted and overcame every effort to disunite them, and, in this manner, has a spirit of union and regard succeeded to near two centuries of civil discord; a revolution in the political morality of the nation of the most extreme importance, and from which, under the powerful auspices of the

French Republic, I hope and trust her independence and liberty will arise.

"I beg leave again to call the attention of the French Government to this fact of the national union; which, from my knowledge of the situation of Ireland, I affirm to be of importance equal to all the rest. Catholics and Dissenters, the two great sects, whose mutual animosities have been the radical weakness of their country, are at length reconciled; and the arms which have been so often imbrued in the blood of each other are ready, for the first time, to be turned in concert against the common enemy.

I come now to the third party in Ireland, the Catholics, who are the Irish, properly so called, and who form almost the entire body of the peasantry of the country. The various confiscations produced by wars of the five centuries, and the silent operation of the laws for 150 years, have stripped the Catholics of almost all property in land; the great bulk of them are in the lowest degree of misery and want, hewers of wood and drawers of water; bread they seldom taste, meat never, save once in the year; they live in wretched hovels; they labour incessantly; and their landlords, the Protestant aristocracy, have so calculated, that the utmost they can gain, by this continual toil, will barely suffice to pay the rent at which these petty despots assess their wretched habitations; their food, the whole year round, is potatoes; their drink, sometimes milk, more frequently water; those of them who attempt to cultivate a spot of ground as farmers are forced, in addition to a heavy rent, to pay tythes to the Priests of the Protestant religion, which they neither profess nor believe; their own Priests fleece them. Such is the condition of the peasantry of Ireland, above 3,000,000 of people. But though there be little property in land, there is a considerable share of the commerce of Ireland in the hands of the Catholic body; their merchants are highly respectable, and well informed; they are perfectly sensible, as well of their own situation, as that of their country. It is of these men, with a few of the Catholic gentry, whose property escaped the fangs of the English invaders, that their General Committee, of which I shall have occasion to speak by-and-by, is composed, and it is with their leaders that the union with the Dissenters, so infinitely important to Ireland, and, if rightly understood, to France also, has been formed.

I have now stated the respective situation, strength and views, of the parties of Ireland;—that is to say: *First*, The Protestants, 450,000; comprising the great body of the aristocracy, which supports and is supported by England. Their strength is entirely artificial, composed of the power and influence which the patronage of Government gives them. They have in their hands all appointments in every Department, in the church, the army, the revenue, the navy, the law, and a great proportion of the landed property of the country, acquired and maintained as has been stated: but it cannot escape the penetration of the French Government that all their apparent power is purely fictitious; the strength they derive from Government results solely from opinion; the instant that prop is withdrawn, the edifice tumbles into ruin; the strength of property acquired, like theirs, by the sword, continues no longer than the sword can defend it; and, numerically, the Protestants are but one tenth of the people.

Second The Dissenters, 900,000, who form a large and respectable portion of the middle ranks of the community These are the class of men best informed in Ireland; they constituted the bulk of what we called the volunteer army in 1782, during the last war, which extorted large concessions from England, and would have completely established their liberty, had they been then, as they are now, united with their Catholic brethren. They are all, to a man, sincere Republicans, and devoted with enthusiasm to the cause of liberty and France; they would make perhaps the best soldiers in Ireland, and are already in a considerable degree trained to arms.

Third. The Catholics, 3,150,000. These are *the Irish*, properly so called, trained from their infancy in an hereditary hatred and abhorrence of the English name, which conveys to them no ideas but those of blood and pillage and persecution. This class is strong in numbers and in misery, which makes men bold; they are used to every species of hardship; they can live on little; they are easily clothed; they are bold and active; they are prepared for any change, for they feel that no change can make their situation worse. For these five years they have fixed their eyes most earnestly on France, whom they look upon, with great justice, as fighting their battles, as well as those of all mankind who are oppressed. Of this class, I will stake my head, there are five hundred thousand men who would fly to the standard of the Republic, if they saw it once displayed in the cause of liberty and their country.

From what I have said, it appears that all the artificial strength of Ireland is implicitly devoted to England, and decidedly adverse to France: that all the natural strength is equally devoted to France, and adverse to England; for this plain reason, that in the one they look for a deliverer, in the other they see a tyrant. It is now necessary to state the organization of the people of Ireland; and here I must be allowed to observe, that even if there were no previous organization, the measures which I shall submit would not be the less advisable and practicable. Organization, like machinery, may be necessary to enable a small force to raise a great weight; but a whole people can act by their natural strength. The Republic may rely with confidence to meet support from the Dissenters, actuated by reason and reflection—from the Catholics, impelled by misery and inflamed by detestation of the English name. These are the actual force of Ireland, and, in addition to their strength, they are organized also.

In the year 1791, the Dissenters of Belfast, which is the principal city in Ulster, and, as it were, the metropolis of that great body, formed the first club of United Irishmen—so called, because in that club, for the first time in Ireland, Dissenters and Catholics were seen together in harmony and union. A similar club was immediately formed in Dublin, which became speedily famous for its publications and the sufferings of its members, many of whom were thrown into prison by the Government, whose terror at this rising spirit of union amongst the people may be estimated from the severity with which they persecuted those who were most active in promoting it. This persecution, however, far from quelling the spirit, only served to make the people more cautious and guarded in their measures. Means have been adopted to spread similar clubs throughout Ulster, the seat of the dissenting power, the object of which is to subvert the tyranny of England, to establish the independence of Ireland, and to frame a free republic on the broad basis of liberty and equality. These clubs were rapidly filled, and extended, in June last, over about two-thirds of that province. I am satisfied that by this time they embrace the whole of it, and comprise the activity and energy of the Dissenters of Ireland, including, also, numbers of the most spirited and intelligent of the Catholic body. The members are all bound by an oath of secrecy, and could, on a proper occasion, I have not the smallest doubt, raise the entire force of the province of Ulster, the most populous, the most warlike, and the most informed quarter of the nation.

For the Catholics, from what has been said of their situation, it will appear that little previous arrangement would be necessary to ensure their unanimous support of any measure which held out to them a chance of bettering their condition; yet they also have an organization, commencing about the same time with the clubs last mentioned, but comprising Catholics only. Until within these few months, this organization baffled the most active vigilance of the Irish Government, unsuccessfully employed to discover its principles, and to this hour they are, I believe, unapprized of its extent. The fact is, that in June last it embraced the whole peasantry of the provinces of Ulster, Leinster, and Connaught, three-fourths of the nation; and I have little doubt but it has since extended into Munster, the remaining province. These men, who are called Defenders, are completely organized on a military plan, divided according to their respective districts, and officered by men chosen by themselves;

the principle of their union is implicit obedience to the orders of those whom they have elected for their Generals, and whose object is the emancipation of their country, the subversion of English usurpation, and the bettering the condition of the wretched peasantry of Ireland. The eyes of this whole body, which may be said, almost without a figure, to be *the people of Ireland*, are turned, with the most anxious expectation, to France, for assistance and support. The oath of their union recites, "That they will be faithful to the united nations of France and Ireland," and several of them have already sealed it with their blood. I suppose there is no instance of a conspiracy, if a whole people can be said to conspire, which has continued for so many years as this has done, where the secret has been so religiously kept, and where, in so vast a number, so few traitors have been found.

This organization of the Defenders embraces the whole peasantry of Ireland, being Catholics. There is also a farther organization of the Catholics, which is called the General Committee, and to which I have already alluded. This was a representative body, chosen by the Catholics at large, and consisting of the principal merchants and traders, the members of professions, and a few of the remaining Catholic gentry of Ireland. This body, which has sat repeatedly in the capital at the same time with the Parliament, and has twice within four years sent ambassadors to the King of England, possesses a very great influence on the minds of the Catholics throughout the nation, and especially decides the movements of the city of Dublin—a circumstance whose importance, when well directed, it is unnecessary to suggest to men so enlightened as those who compose the Government of France. It is true that, by a late act of the Irish Legislature, this body is prevented from meeting in a representative capacity; but the individuals who compose it still exist, and this act, without diminishing their power or influence, has still more alienated their minds from the British Government in Ireland, against which they were already sufficiently, and with great reason, exasperated. It is but justice to the General Committee, in whose service I had the honour to be during the whole of their activity, and whose confidence I had the good fortune to acquire and retain, to say, that there is no where to be found men of purer patriotism, more sincerely attached to the principles of liberty, or who would be more likely in an arduous crisis to conduct themselves with abilities and firmness. I can add, from my personal knowledge, that a great majority of those able and honest men who compose it are sincere republicans, warmly attached to the cause of France, and, as Irishmen and Catholics, doubly bound to detest the tyranny and domination of England, which has so often deluged their country with their best blood.

I have now stated the three modes of organization which exist in Ireland—

1. The Dissenters, with some of the most spirited and enlightened of the Catholics, under the name of *United Irishmen*, whose central point is Belfast, the capital of Ulster.

2. The Defenders, forming the great body of the Catholic peasantry, amounting to 3,000,000 of people, and who cover the entire face of the country.

3. The General Committee of the Catholics, representing the talents and property of that body, possessing a very great influence every where in Ireland, and especially deciding the movements of the capital.

I hazard nothing in asserting that these three bodies are alike animated with an ardent desire for the independence of Ireland, an abhorrence of British tyranny, and a sincere attachment to the cause of the French Republic; and, what is of very great consequence, they have a perfect good understanding and communication with each other, (that is to say, their leaders,) so that, on any great emergency, there would be no possible doubt of their mutual co-operation. Many of the most active members of the General Committee, for example, are also in the clubs of the United Irishmen; many of the officers of the Defenders, particularly those at the head of their affairs, are also either members of those clubs, or in unreserved confidence and communication with those who regulate and guide them. The central point of all this is undoubtedly Belfast, which influences, and which deserves to influence, the measures of all the others; and, what I consider as extremely singular, the leaders of the Defenders in Ulster, who are all Catholics, are in more regular habits of communication, and are more determined by the Dissenters of Belfast, than by their Catholic brethren of Dublin, with whom they hold much less intercourse.

I shall add a few words on the military force of Ireland, and on the navy, and then I shall conclude this memorial, which, in spite of all my efforts to condense it, I feel growing under my hands.

In the month of June, 1795, when I left Ireland, the army, as I believe, amounted to about 30,000 men, of which 12,000 were troops of the line, or fencibles, and 18,000 were militia; a great proportion of the former, viz. the cavalry and artillery, and all the latter, being Irish. I believe a considerable number have been since detached to the West Indies and elsewhere; if so, the relative proportion of Irish must be increased, as the militia cannot be ordered on foreign service. For the cavalry and artillery, which, taken together, may make 3,000 men, or upwards, I cannot speak with certainty; but my belief is, that if they saw any prospect of permanent support they would not act against their country. For the remaining 9,000 men of the troops of the line and fencibles, they are a wretched assemblage of old men and boys, incapable of the duties of active service; any resistance they could make, if they were inclined to resist, could be but trifling, and I have reason to believe they would not be so inclined, several of the fencible regiments being Scotch, and already more than half disaffected to the Government. For the militia, they consisted, at the time I mention, of about 18,000 men, as fine troops as any in Europe. Of these, at least 16,000 were Catholics, and a very great portion of them were actually sworn Defenders, who were compelled to enter the service to avoid persecution. I learn, that since my departure from Ireland, Defenderism has spread rapidly among them, and that numbers have been imprisoned on that account. I have not a shadow of doubt on my mind, but that the militia would, in case of emergency, to a man, join their countrymen in throwing off the yoke of England, provided proper measures were taken, and that they saw a reasonable prospect of success.

For the navy, I have already said that Ireland has furnished no less than 80,000 seamen, and that two-thirds of the English fleet are manned by Irishmen. I will here state the grounds of my assertion. First, I have myself heard several British officers, and among them, some of very distinguished reputation, say so. Secondly, I know that when the Catholic delegates, whom I had the honour to attend, were at St. James's, in January, 1793, in the course of the discussion with Henry Dundas, principal Secretary of State, they asserted the fact to be as I have mentioned, and Mr. Dundas admitted it, which he would most certainly not have done if he could have denied it. And, lastly, on my voyage to America, our vessel was boarded by a British frigate, whose crew consisted of 220 men, of whom no less than 210 were Irish, as I found by inquiry. I submit the importance of this fact to the particular notice of the French Government.

From all which has been said, I trust it will appear that it is the interest of France to separate Ireland from England; and that it is morally certain that the attempt, if made, would succeed, for the following reasons:—1st. That all the Dissenters are disaffected to England, attached to France, and sufficiently organized. 2d. That the whole Catholic peasantry of Ireland, above 3,000,000 of people, are, to a man, eager to throw off the English yoke; that they also are organized, and that part of the fundamental oath, by which they are bound as Defenders, is to be true as well to France as to Ireland. 3d. That there is a certainty of a perfect harmony and co-operation between these two great bodies, which constitute nine-tenths of the population of Ireland. 4th. That the British Government cannot reckon on any firm support from the army, above two-thirds of which are Irishmen, and, of that number, nearly 10,000 being, as I am informed and believe, actually sworn Defenders. 5th. That it is at least possible that, by proper measures to be adopted, relative to the Irishmen now serving in the navy of England, her power at sea might receive such a shock as it has never yet experienced: and 6th, and lastly, that if these facts be as I have here stated them, it would be impossible for the Protestant aristocracy in Ireland to make any stand whatsoever, even for an hour, in defence of the connexion with England.

Having now submitted the actual situation of Ireland to the notice of the French Government, I shall offer, in a second memorial, the plan which I conceive most likely to effectuate the separation of that country from Great Britain.

SECOND MEMORIAL.

Having stated, in a former memorial, the actual situation and circumstances of Ireland, I shall now submit those means which, in my judgment, will be most likely to effectuate the great object of separating that country from England, and establishing her as an independent Republic, in strict alliance with France. I shall first mention those measures whose execution depends on the French Republic, and next those which will be to be executed by the people of Ireland.

In the first place, I beg leave to lay it down as indispensable, that a body of French troops should be landed in Ireland, with a General at their head of established reputation, whose name should be known in that country,—a circumstance of considerable importance; and I must be permitted to observe here, that, if humbling the pride and reducing the power of England be an object with the French Republic, I know no place where the very best General in their service could be employed, either with more reputation to himself or benefit to the public cause.

With regard to the strength of this army, it is my duty to speak with candour to the Government. It ought, if possible, to be of 20,000 men, at least 15,000 of which should land as near the capital as circumstances would admit, and 5,000 in the North of Ireland, near Belfast. If an imposing force, such as I have mentioned, could be sent in the first instance, it would save a vast effusion of blood and treasure. By having possession of the capital, we should, in fact, have possession of the whole country. The Government in existence there would fall to pieces, without a possibility of effort. We should have in our hands at once the Treasury, the Post Office, the Banks, the Custom-House, the seat of the Legislature, and, particularly, (what is even of more consequence,) we should have the reputation which would result from such a commencement If we could begin by the capital, I should hope we should obtain possession of the entire country without striking a blow, as in fact there would, in that case, be no organized force to make resistance; but for this, 20,000 men would be necessary. If, however, the other indispensable arrangements of the French Republic would render it impossible to send such a force, I offer it as my opinion, and I entreat it may be remembered, that 5,000 is the very lowest number with which the attempt could be made with any thing like certainty of success; in which case, the landing should be effectuated in the North of Ireland, where the people are in the greatest forwardness as to military preparation. It is unnecessary to observe here, that, commencing our operations at 100 miles distance from the capital, of which the enemy would be in full possession, would give them very great advantages over us at first; they would still have, in a degree, the law of opinion in their favour, and they would, at least for some time, retain the Treasury, the Post Office, and all the other advantages which an established organization would naturally give them Nevertheless, with 5,000 men, an able General, and the measures which I shall hereafter mention, I should have no doubt of our ultimate success; but then we should have to fight hard for our liberties, and we should lose many great advantages which a sufficient force in the commencement would give us, particularly that of disorganizing at once the existing Government of Ireland.

Supposing the number to be 5,000, a large proportion should be artillerists, of which we are quite unprovided. They should be the very best troops that France could furnish, men who had actually seen hard service, and who would be capable of training and disciplining the Irish army. The necessity of this is too obvious to need any further comment. I do not go here into any military detail on the conduct of the war; if the measure be adopted, I shall hope to be admitted to a conference with the General who may be appointed to the command, and then, with the map of the country before us, I will submit, with great deference, my ideas on that head.

Before I quit the subject of the force necessary, I wish to observe that, in my first memorial, I have always said that the army, and especially the militia, would, I was satisfied, declare for their country "*if they saw a reasonable prospect of support*," by which I would be understood to mean an imposing force in the first instance. I cannot commit myself as to what might be their conduct in case 5,000 men only were landed. I hope, and I believe, but I cannot positively affirm, that they would join the standard of their country; but, even if they were, contrary to my expectations, to adhere to the British Government, the only difference would be that, in such event, we should have a civil war, which I would most earnestly wish, if possible, to avoid. As to the people at large, I am perfectly satisfied that, whether there were 20 or 10, or even 5,000 men landed, it would, as to them, make no manner of difference. I know they would flock to the Republican standard in such numbers as to embarrass the General-in-chief. It would be just as easy in a month's time to have an army in Ireland of 200,000 men as of 10,000, and therefore it is that, reckoning on this disposition of the people, I say, and repeat, that I would not have a shadow of doubt of our ultimate success, provided we had a body of even 5,000 disciplined troops to commence with; a smaller number would, I apprehend, be hardly able to maintain themselves until they could be joined by the people, as the Government of Ireland would be able instantly to turn against them such a body of troops (who, in that case, would, I fear, adhere to it,) as would swallow them up; the consequence of which would be, besides the loss to France of the men and money, the bringing Ireland, even more than she is at present, under the yoke of British tyranny; the breaking for ever the hopes and spirits of her people; and the rendering all prospect of her emancipation, at any future period, utterly impracticable and desperate.

As to arms and ammunition, I can only say, that the more there is of both, the better. If the Republic can send to Ireland 100,000 stand of arms, there are double the number of hands ready to put them in. A large train of artillery, that is to say, field-pieces, (as we have no fortified places,) is absolutely indispensable, together with a considerable proportion of experienced cannoniers; engineers, used to field practice, are also highly necessary. As to money, I am at a loss to determine the sum. If 20,000 men were sent, I should say that pay for 40,000 for three months would be amply sufficient, as, before that time was expired, we should have all the resources of Ireland in our hands If but 5,000 be sent, I submit the quantum necessary to the wisdom and liberality of the French Government, observing only that we could not, in that case, calculate at once on the immediate possession of the funds, which, in the other instance, we could seize directly.

Very much would depend upon the manifesto to be published on the first landing. I conceive the declaration of the object and intentions of the Republic should contain, among others, the following topics:—

1st. An absolute disavowal of all idea of conquest, and a statement that the French came as friends and brothers, with no other view than to assist the people in throwing off the yoke of England. 2d. A declaration of perfect security and protection to the free exercise of all religions, without distinction or preference; and the perpetual abolition of all ascendancy, or connexion, between church and state. 3d. A declaration of perfect security and protection of persons and property to all who should demean themselves as good citizens and friends to the liberty of their country; with strong denunciations against those who should support or countenance the cause of British tyranny and usurpation. 4th. An invitation to the people to join the Republican standard, and a promise to recommend to the future legislature of their country every individual who should distinguish himself by his courage, zeal, and ability. 5th. An invitation to the people immediately to organize themselves, and form a national convention, for the purpose of framing a government, and of administering the affairs of Ireland until such government could be framed and put in activity.

Other topics will naturally suggest themselves; but these seem to me, from my knowledge of Ireland, to be among the most likely, as well to raise the people, as to remove the fears and anxieties, (especially on the great heads of property and religion,) of many who might otherwise be neutral, or perhaps adverse, but who would gladly support the independence of their country, when satisfied as to these points. It is with the most sincere pleasure that I can assure the French Government, that their singular moderation with regard to Holland, when that country lay at their mercy, had an inconceivable effect on the mind of every independent man in Ireland, and removed, almost entirely, the reluctance which many felt to put themselves to the hazard and uncertainty of a revolution.

To recapitulate. What I conceive would be indispensably necessary to be furnished, on the part of the French Republic, would be: 1st. *An armed force*, not exceeding 20,000 men, nor less than 5,000. If 20,000, to be landed as near Dublin as possible; if a smaller number, in the North of Ireland, near Belfast. 2d. A general whose name and character should be well known in Ireland. 3d. Arms and ammunition, as much as could be spared: a train of artillery, with an adequate number of experienced cannoniers and engineers. 4th. Such a sum of money as the French Government might feel necessary, and could grant, consistently with their other arrangements.

On the part of the people of Ireland, the measures which I conceive would be most immediately necessary to ensure success and establish our independence, would be as follow:

First, of course, to raise as many soldiers as we had arms to put into their hands, which would be the only limitation as to numbers.

Secondly, To call a national convention, for which a basis is laid in the General Committee of the Catholics, mentioned in my first memorial, who, when joined by Delegates from the Dissenters, would be actually the representatives of nine-tenths of the people. The first act of the Convention thus constituted should be, to declare themselves the representatives of the Irish people, free and independent, and, in that capacity to form an alliance, offensive and defensive, with the French Republic—stipulating, that neither party should make peace with England without the other, and until the two Republic were acknowledged,—and also a treaty of commerce, on terms of mutual advantage. As the immediate formation of a national convention is of the last importance, I wish earnestly to press on the notice of the French Government the unspeakable advantage of having, if possible, an imposing force in the first instance, for this reason; that the men of a certain rank in life, and situation as to property, (for instance, the actual members of the Catholic Committee, who must be those who naturally would form the convention,) would, in that case, at once declare themselves, and begin to act, which I cannot venture to ensure that they would do, at least for some time, if they saw but a small force landed. For the great body of the people, whom I have mentioned as being organized under the name of Defenders, and a great proportion of theDissenters, the number to be landed is of little consequence as to them; for my firm belief is, that if but one thousand French were landed, it would be impossible to prevent the peasantry of Ireland from rising, as one man, to join them; but then, we should lose the inestimable advantages which would result from the immediate organization of a body which could call itself the Government of Ireland, and, as such, instantly assume the legislative and executive functions, raise money, grant commissions, and, especially, conclude the alliance with France, the eclat of which must naturally produce the most beneficial and important consequences. Without such an arrangement, our commencement would have more the air of an insurrection than a revolution; and though, I again repeat, I would have no doubt of the ultimate success of the attempt, yet the difficulties, at first, would be multiplied, in proportion to the smallness of the force which might be landed. The measures I am now about to mention, which can only be effectually executed by a body that might, with some appearance of justice, call itself the Irish Government, will show, at once, the indispensable necessity of a national convention being organized; that not an hour should be lost in framing it; and, of course, that every possible effort should be made to send such force as would ensure its formation in the first instance.

The convention, being once formed, should proceed to publish, among others, the following proclamations; from every one of which, I have no shadow of doubt, would result the most powerful effects;—

1st. One to the people at large: notifying their independence and their alliance with the French Republic; forbidding all adherence to the British Government, under the penalty of high treason; ordering all taxes and contributions to be paid only to such persons as should be appointed by the Convention to receive them; and, in the mean time, making all collectors and public officers responsible, with life and property, for all moneys in their hands. This would at once set the law of opinion on their side, and give a spirit to every individual embarked in the cause. It would then be a war, not an insurrection; and even that circumstance, as operating on the minds of the soldiery, I consider as of great importance.

2d. One to the militia of Ireland: recalling them to the standard of their country, paying the value of their arms, and granting an immediate discharge to all who should demand it; and ensuring a preference in all military promotion, and a provision in land, or otherwise, at the end of the war, (according to the rank and services of each,) to those who should enter into the service of their country. I am convinced, as I am of my existence, that this single proclamation would bring over the entire militia of Ireland, which is, in fact, the only formidable force in the country! but I must add, at the same time, that this proclamation can only be published, with effect, by a National Government.

3d. One addressed to all Irishmen now serving in the navy of England: recalling them directly from that service; reminding them that they are a majority, in the proportion of two to one, and, therefore, exhorting them to seize on the vessels, and bring them into the Irish ports,—engaging the faith of the nation to purchase the ships at their value, as prizes; to give, as in the case of the militia, an immediate discharge to all who should desire it, ensuring promotion, in preference, to all who should remain in the service; stating the hardships to which they are subject in the British service, into which they have been forced either by hunger or the press-gang; dwelling particularly on the unjust distribution of their prize-money, stating the enormous disproportion between the share of an admiral or a captain, and that of a common seaman; ensuring them an equitable rate in that respect, to be established in the future Irish navy; and reminding them of the immense wealth to be made by captures on the prodigious expanse of the British commerce, which now embraces that of the whole world. From such a proclamation, issuing from an Irish Government, I am sanguine enough to expect the most powerful effects. Let it never be forgotten, that two-thirds of the British seamen, as they are called, are, in fact, Irishmen. I will not say that this proclamation would bring one ship into the Irish harbours; but this I say—that if human nature be human nature, it would raise such a spirit of jealousy and distrust in the naval service of Great Britain, as must most materially serve the cause of the Republic. Will any English Admiral leave Portsmouth with confidence, with such a proclamation as that hanging over his head—against which, too, he has nothing to oppose but the mere force of discipline? How much will that discipline be necessarily relaxed from the fear, lest, by enforcing it strictly, the majority of the crew should instantly mutiny and carry the ship where they would meet with protection and support amongst their friends and connexions, their wives and children—in one word, in their native country? Will any English captain be found to tie up an Irish seaman for a trifling offence, and flog him before the face of the crew, two-thirds of whom are Irish, with the terror of such a proclamation before his eyes? And, especially, what weapon has the English Government to oppose in return? I supplicate the attention of the French Government to this point, which is, in my judgment, of the very highest importance. It would be in her navy that England would be, then, first found vulnerable. If there were no other object proposed but this single one, I affirm with confidence, it is of magnitude, by itself, sufficient to decide the French Government to make every effort to obtain it; which can only be effected through the medium of a national Government to be established in Ireland. It would be easy to add a thousand arguments on this topic: but I trust, knowing as I do the superior talents and information of those whom I address, that what I have said will be sufficient to open the subject; and I do again most earnestly entreat them to follow, in their own minds, the long chain of consequences which must flow, as to the naval power of England, from the measure which I have mentioned, supposing it to have that success which I cannot myself for a moment doubt but it must.

4. A proclamation recalling, in general terms, all Irishmen from the dominions of Great Britain, whether in the land or sea service, or otherwise, within a certain period, under pain of being treated as emigrants. The effect of this measure will be seen when I come to speak of the actual and casual resources of Ireland.

5. An address to the people of England and Scotland, as distinguished from the Government: stating the grounds of the conduct of the Irish nation, and declaring their earnest desire to avoid the effusion of blood; that they wish merely for the independence of their country, which, at all hazards, they are determined to maintain, warning the English people, by the examples of the American and French Revolutions, how impossible it is to conquer a whole people determined to be free; demonstrating, by calculation, the expense of the war, and applying to their interests, as a commercial people, contrasted and opposed to the personal views of their King and Government; showing them how little they could gain in the most prosperous event, how much blood and treasure they must necessarily expend, and, finally, pointing out the certain consequences to Eng-

land, if she should fail in the contest. If this proclamation were published, I apprehend, as its principles are just, it might embarrass the British Minister considerably in his operations, so as, perhaps, to render it impossible for him to continue the war. But, as I do not at all calculate on the good sense or spirit of the British people, who seem to me for some years to have totally renounced that share of both which they once possessed, I will submit that, if it totally failed in its object, and the English nation were so infatuated as to support the Minister in the war, this proclamation should be followed by the next.

6th. The immediate confiscation of every shilling of English property in Ireland, of every species, moveable or fixed, and appropriating it to the national service, which would then be an act of strict justice, as the English people would have made themselves parties in the war. In this manner, I submit, one of two things must happen; either the English people would decidedly oppose the war—and, if so, peace, and the establishment of the independence of Ireland, would directly follow—or they would support the war, in which case they lose, at once, an immense property in Ireland, which is instantly transferred, and becomes a weapon against them in the hands of their enemies—not to speak of the discontents which the loss of such a vast property in land, in money lent on mortgages, in goods, and in debts, must produce amongst all ranks, and more especially amongst the merchants and traders in England.

I will not trespass longer on the time of the French Government, but hasten to give a brief sketch of the actual and casual resources of Ireland, and then conclude. First, her population, 4,500,000. It is necessary to state on what grounds I assert this: in 1788 there existed a tax on hearths in Ireland, by which means the number of houses was known with sufficient accuracy to those who administered the revenue. The number of people in Ireland, allowing six to a family, was, in that year, calculated by one of the commissioners, who, of course, had perfect information, at 4,100,000, and it was allowed to be under the truth, as well because some houses must necessarily have been omitted, as that the proportion of six to a family was less than what was usually found in Ireland, where the people are naturally prolific. I speak here from memory, but the calculation is to be found in the transactions of the Royal Academy of Ireland, which may, perhaps, be in the National Library, and it will justify my assertion that the people of Ireland amount to 4,500,000. But, though Ireland is populous, she is poor! We are, thanks to the ruinous connexion with England, almost without trade or manufactures; and while that connexion holds, we shall continue so, for this, among other reasons,—that a wretched Irish peasant is tempted even by the scanty pay and subsistence of a foot-soldier, from which a well-fed and well-clothed English artizan turns with contempt. The army of England is supported by the misery of Ireland.

Ireland would, however, in case of a revolution, possess, amongst others, the following resources: 1st. Her actual revenues, amounting, at present, to about 2,000,000*l.* per annum, making 48,000,000 livres. 2d. The church, college, and chapter lands, whose exact value I do not know, but which are of vast amount. 3d. The property of absentees who never visit the country at all, amounting, at least, to 1,000,000*l.* sterling, or 24,000,000 livres. 4th. The casual property of emigrants, which would amount to a very great sum, but which, as depending on circumstances, cannot be reduced to calculation. 5th. The property of Englishmen in Ireland, whether vested in land, mortgages on land, trade, manufactures, bonds, bills, book debts, or otherwise, to be confiscated, and applied to the discharge of the obligations incurred in the acquisition of the independence of Ireland; I cannot say what the amount of this might be, but it must be immense. One English nobleman, Earl Mansfield, (formerly Ambassador to Paris, under the name of Lord Stormont, and an implacable enemy of France,) has 300,000*l.* sterling, or 7,200,000 livres, lent on mortgages in Ireland; another English gentleman, Mr. Taylor, has 150,000*l.* sterling, or 3,600,000 livres, lent in like manner. I mention these instances to point out to the French Government what unspeakable confusion the measure I propose would be likely to produce in England, and what a staggering blow the separation of Ireland would be, in a commercial point of view, not to speak of the military, or, which is of far more consequence, the naval part of the question.

I have now done. I submit to the wisdom of the French Government, that England is the implacable, inveterate, irreconcilable enemy of the Republic, which never can be in perfect security whilst that nation retains the dominion of the sea; that, in consequence, every possible effort should be made to humble her pride, and to reduce her power; that it is in Ireland, *and in Ireland only*, that she is vulnerable—a fact, of the truth of which the French Government cannot be too strongly impressed; that, by establishing a free Republic in Ireland, they attach to France a grateful ally, whose cordial assistance, in peace and war, she might command, and who, from situation and produce, could most essentially serve her; that, at the same time, they cut off from England her most firm support, in losing which she is laid under insuperable difficulties in recruiting her army, and, especially, in equipping, victualling, and manning her navy, which, unless for the resources she drew from Ireland, she would be absolutely unable to do; that, by these means, and suffer me to add, *by these means only*, her arrogance can be effectually humbled, and her enormous and increasing power at sea reduced within due bounds, an object essential not only to France, but to all Europe; that it is at least possible, by the measures mentioned, that not only her future resources, as to her navy, may be intercepted and cut off at the fountain-head, but that a part of her fleet may be actually transferred to the Republic of Ireland; that the Irish people are united and prepared, and want but the means to begin; that, not to speak of the policy or the pleasure of revenge, in humbling a haughty and implacable rival, it is, in itself, a great and splendid act of generosity and justice, worthy of the Republic in Europe, to rescue a whole nation from a slavery under which they have groaned for six hundred years; that it is for the glory of France, after emancipating Holland, and receiving Belgium into her bosom, to establish one more free Republic in Europe; that it is for her interest to cut off, for ever, as she now may do, one half of the resources of England, and lay her under extreme difficulties in the employment of the other. For all these reasons, in the name of justice, of humanity, of liberty, of my own country, and of France herself, I supplicate the Directory to take into consideration the state of Ireland; and by granting her the powerful aid and protection of the Republic, to enable her at once to vindicate her liberty, to humble her tyrant, and to assume that independent station, among the nations of the earth, for which her soil, her productions and her position, her population and her spirit, have designed her.

A LETTER

From General to Mrs. Tone, written on the point of his embarking in the Bantry Bay Expedition.

Head Quarters, at Brest, Nov. 30, 1796.

My dearest Love, I wrote to you on the 26th of May last, desiring you to remove with all our family to France by the first opportunity, but the ship which carried my letter was taken by the English, so I suppose you never received it. I wrote to you a second time, repeating my orders, and giving you very full directions for your conducting yourself, in case of my not being in France at the time of your arrival; this letter I gave to the American consul at Paris, who promised to forward it by a safe hand, on the 28th of July last, so I am in hopes it reached you; and by calculating the dates, and allowing for your lying-in and recovery, I presume you are by this on your passage to Havre, and I cannot express the unspeakable anxiety I feel for your safety, and that of our dear little babies, exposed to all the inconveniences and perils of a winter passage. I trust in God you will get safe and well, and that by the time you will receive this, we shall have finished our business; in which case, you and I will devote the remainder of our lives to each other, for I am truly weary of the perpetual separation that we have lived in, I may almost say, from the day of our marriage.

The Government here has at length seriously taken up the affair of Ireland, and, in consequence, shortly after my last letter to you, I received orders to join General Hoche, who commands the expedition, in chief, at Rennes, where he was quartered. After remaining at Rennes near two months, we set off for Brest, in order to proceed to our destination; but great bodies move slowly; it is only to-day that our preparations are completed, and the day after to-morrow I expect to embark on board the Indomptable, of 80 guns. Our force will be of fifteen ships-of-the-line, and ten frigates, and, I suppose, (for I do not exactly know,) of at least 10,000 of the best troops in France. If we arrive safe, with that force, I have not the least doubt of success, especially as Ireland is now wound up to the highest pitch of discontent. I have the rank of Adjutant General, and I am immediately in General Hoche's family. I offered to serve with the grenadiers, who will form the advanced guard of the army, as being the post of danger and of honour; but the General refused me, very handsomely, saying that it was necessary for his arrangements that I should be immediately about his person. You see by this, that, as a military man, I am infinitely better off than I had any reason to expect. There is the very best spirit in the troops, both officers and soldiers, and, in short, nothing can prevent our success, unless it is that we should be totally defeated by the British fleet on our passage. I have no doubt but they are cruising to intercept us; and if we fall in with them, the engagement will be, perhaps, the most desperate one that has ever been fought at sea between the two powers—for our orders are to submit (I mean the army on board) to the Captain's orders in every thing except to strike to the enemy; of course we must fight to the last extremity, and I have no doubt but we will do so; if we should even be defeated, they will not take us all, and, in that case, those who escape will, I hope, push on for Ireland; in short, now we are at sea, I think we will not turn back without finishing our business.

I would not write thus to terrify you needlessly, but long before you receive my letter the affair will be over, one way or the other; I hope happily for us, in which case I once more promise you never to quit you again for any temptation of fame, honour, or interest. After all we have suffered, a little tranquillity is now surely due to us.

The circumstances under which I write compel me to address you in the most serious style. On the eve of such an expedition as I am about to embark in, and with the prospect of such an action before me as that in which it is likely we may be engaged, I cannot conceal from you nor myself that I have to expect the greatest danger, and, it is possible, in short, that I may fall in the contest; should that event happen, I hope you will have the courage to support the loss as may become you, as well for your own sake as that of our dear children. I know, by what I feel at this moment, how severe will be the trial which, in that case, you will undergo; but the evil will be then inevitable, and the duty you owe to our darling babies must incite you to a great exertion of the firmness which I know you possess; and, in short, whatever the effort may cost you, you must not sink under it. I need not add any cold arguments on the folly of grieving for what is not to be retrieved. I entreat you, as you love me, for your own sake, and for that of our little ones, that you may collect all your courage, and should the very worst happen, remember, you will be then their only parent. I need not, indeed, I cannot say more.

In case of any thing happening to me, and that the expedition should succeed, you will, of course, remove by the first opportunity to Ireland. I do not think so ill of my country, or of my friends, as to doubt that, in that case, provision will be made for you and my children. In case of my death and the failure of the expedition, I confess I am at a loss to advise you. However, not to be wanting to yourself, you will address yourself, by petition, to the French Executive Directory, and particularly to Carnot, (with whom I am acquainted, and with whom I have done all my business since my arrival in France,) stating the circumstances, and praying relief; you will, also, address yourself to General Clarke, to whom you may write under cover to Carnot, to Colonel Shee, who is my particular friend, and embarked with me on this expedition; and, lastly, to General Hoche, who knows my services, and will, I am sure, in that case, be of use to you. God knows whether all this may produce any thing, for the Government here is, I know, in the last distress for money; however, you will at least try. If that fails, as Matt will, I trust in God, be with you, I leave it to your common judgment and prudence to determine what may be most advisable, whether to remain in France or to return to America; in which latter case, as the little you now have will be almost totally gone, you must go to Carolina or Georgia, where alone it will be possible for you to exist; and, in that case, I commit you to the goodness of that Supreme Power who has so often almost miraculously preserved us, entreating only of Matt, as he cherishes the memory of a brother who very sincerely and affectionately loved him, that he may not quit you for a moment, while he can be useful to you, but act as a faithful friend to you and a father to my darling babies.

I have now finished the most painful hour of my life; I have advised and prepared you for the very worst event, and be assured that the prospect of our separation cannot be more terrible to you than it is to me, but I hope we have, notwithstanding, both of us courage sufficient to contemplate it with steadiness. Let us now turn the picture, and see what the bright side of it offers to our view.

If we do not meet the English fleet, or, meeting them, if we force our way, and, in short, if I reach Ireland in safety, (*that is to say, with my ten thousand French lovers at my back,*) there is not a shadow of doubt of our success; and when the country is once emancipated, there will be, I think, no situation that I will, in reason, demand, which will be refused me, and, in that case, you will see whether or not the principal desire of my life be not to make you happy; indeed, my dearest love, you are the main-spring of every action of my life and every thought of my heart. Remember, I am now in the high road to fortune, and, I hope, to fame—for, if we succeed, I think I may say I have earned some reputation; but I can also say, that neither fame nor fortune are an object with me, farther than as they will enable me to manifest my sense of your goodness and virtues. As I shall arrive there with the rank of Adjutant-General, and with the favour of the Commander in Chief, and, I hope, the good-will of my countrymen,—and as an Irish army will be, of course, directly formed,—I shall, I presume, not be offered a lower rank than I now hold, and if I behave, as I hope I shall, in a manner becoming a good officer, I have, at least, as good a chance of promotion as another, so at last I shall be, as Miss Mary, to whom I beg my compliments, used to say, in my *etat militaire.* In that case, as I shall have at least a regiment, I shall be able to settle Matt to our satisfaction, and, I think, as the Citizen Arthur has made a voyage also in the cause, I will have a right to demand a place for him also; so Miss Mary will have a chance to see three of her brothers in very gaudy green coats, and with long sabres by their sides, and then I hope she will be easy. I wear at present a fine embroidered scarlet cape and cuffs on my uniform, and a laced hat, which is only permitted to the General officers, but I shall be happy on the first occasion (would to God it were to-morrow!) to change my blue coat for one as green as a leek, which I think will be *more becoming.* If I arrive in safety the other side, the first thing I shall do will be to appoint Matt my aid-de-camp, in his absence, and that will set him going advantageously; in short, I have a thousand fine things in my head for you all, if Messieurs, the English, allow me to pass clear, for, as the poet hath it—

> "If we meet with a privateer, or a lofty man of war,
> "We will not stay to wrangle, to chatter, nor to jar."

It is not our business to fight those gentlemen at sea, if we can possibly avoid it, and you may be sure we will do every thing in our power, and I hope yet we may get clear; in which case, as I have already said ten times, you shall see what you shall see.

I have now finished the best and the worst that can happen to us, but there remains a third way, which is, that it may happen that we should be beaten back, in spite of all our efforts, and that I should, so, return *in safety* to France. In that case, I think I shall be able to retain my pay as Adjutant General, which, as things go here, will be a vast addition to our little fortune; I will then buy or hire a small farm within a few miles of Paris, and devote the remainder of my life to making you happy and educating our children. This last way, though not so bad as my first supposition, is yet just now to me a very gloomy prospect, for the reasons I am about to mention.

Since my arrival in France I have had no communication whatsoever with Ireland, but I have seen the English papers pretty regularly, by favour of Madgett, who is in the Bureau of the Minister for Foreign Affairs; I had, in consequence, the mortification to read, in May last, that John Keogh was arrested, by order of Government, with Sir Edward Bellew, (a great aristocrat,) and several others; however, I watched the papers carefully for some months after, and as I saw no farther mention of the business, I am in very great hopes that they were immediately released, and that the affair blew over, but I have no certainty. Since that time (indeed, within these few days) while we were on our march to Brest, I found an English paper, wherein there was an article, copied from the Northern Star of September 16, by which I saw, to my most unspeakable distress and anxiety, that Harry Haslitt, and two persons of the name of Osborne and Shanaghan, had been arrested that day at Belfast, on a charge of high treason, and that Sam. Neilson and Russell had surrendered themselves voluntarily You will judge how I felt this blow! The instant I arrived, I ran to Hoche to communicate the news, and we agreed immediately to dispatch a proper person to Ireland, on board an American vessel, partly to obtain intelligence, but principally to give notice to my friends, through a channel which I pointed out, to avail themselves of every chicane and artifice of the law to put off their trials, in order to give us time, if possible, to arrive to their relief. This person left Brest the 7th of this month, and I trust he arrived safe, but, in the mean time, I am in the most extreme anxiety and distress of mind. If we reach Ireland, which we may now, as I hope, do, in ten days, (supposing no unlucky accident,) we shall, I trust, be in time to extricate them; but if unfortunately we should be too late for that, at least we shall be in time to revenge them, and, in that case, woe to their persecutors!

While I am on the subject of my friends, I am to acquaint you that our poor friend Major Sweetman was unfortunately killed in a duel near London, in January last. It was in the English papers I saw this intelligence, and I do not think I was ever more shocked in my life; I did not recover my spirits for a month after, and even yet I think of his death with the utmost regret, in which I am sure you will join me. Not to speak of my personal regret for him, I need not mention what a loss we have of him at this moment, when his courage, talents, and patriotism, would be of such essential service. I am most sincerely sorry for him on every account, public and private, and I did not think I could have been so affected as I was by his death.

To return to our own affairs. On your arrival at Havre, you will of course, agreeably to my former directions, have written to Madgett, who will forward you this, as I send it to him under cover. My first design was, that you should go on to Paris, but, on farther recollection, living there is so very expensive, as well as travelling also, that you had better fix yourselves, until you hear from me, at some of the villages within a few leagues of Havre, where you will hire lodgings and make your own kitchen, &c. There is a village called Yvetot, that I think would suit you. If any thing should happen to me, you will have no business on to Paris; and, in that case, if your determination be to settle in France, you can fix yourself in some little spot in that neighbourhood as well as any where else, and Matt must do his best for you all, in my place. If you should resolve to return to America, you will be near Havre, from whence you will have the most frequent opportunities; *and I confess, under the circumstances, I would recommend Carolina, and especially Georgia, where land is very cheap, before France, where you will labour, I fear, under insurmountable difficulties, from your ignorance of the language, customs, and manners.* If, as I hope and trust, I arrive safe in Ireland, and we succeed, as in that case I think we infallibly shall, still I wish you rather to be at *Yvetot*, for example, than at Paris, for the sake of economy, as well as a thousand other reasons. If you do not arrive soon, it is probable you may receive another letter with this, for the very first thing I shall do after our landing will be, you may be sure, to write to you, under cover, as before, to Madgett, and I will also take care to remit you money for your occasions, and the very first moment that my duty will permit, I will fly with the utmost eagerness to embrace you all; God only knows how I long for that moment.

This letter is dreadfully unconnected, but the fact is, I write in a state of the utmost anxiety and incertitude; if I remained in France, and you were, with my babies, on the ocean, it would be full sufficient to keep me in continual uneasiness; or, if you were here, safe arrived, and I was embarked, though my anxiety would be infinitely lessened, still I should have fully sufficient to occupy me; but situated as we are, I have both to encounter: uncertain of your fate and that of our children—uncertain of my own, in which you and they are so deeply interested—I think it is hardly possible to conceive a more painful and anxious situation; add to this, that I am obliged to devour my uneasiness, from the fear of appearing disheartened at the moment of embarkation. Well, the uncertainty of the affair, at least, will soon have an end. Ten days, I think now, must settle it, and I am sure no extremity, scarcely, can be so terrible as the state of suspense in which I now find myself. If we succeed in our enterprise, I never will again hazard my happiness and your's for any imaginable temptation of honour or interest; if we fail, at least it is in an honourable cause and on just principles; and, in either case, you shall not hear of my behaving in a manner to cause you, or my children, to blush for me.

I have this moment received orders to embark in half an hour. I have, of course, time to add no more. I recommend you all to the protection of Heaven. God Almighty for ever bless and preserve you! Adieu, my dearest life and soul? Kiss my darling babies for me ten thousand times, and love me ever as I love you.

Once more adieu!

T. W. TONE.

BREST, *December* 2, 1796.

THE END.

LONDON:
PRINTED BY S. AND R. BENTLEY, DORSET STREET.

CPSIA information can be obtained
at www.ICGtesting.com
Printed in the USA
LVHW080905241122
733912LV00011B/504

9 780530 533155